Memoir and Letters of Sara Coleridge, Ed. by Her Daughter [E. Coleridge]

MEMOIR AND LETTERS

OF

SARA COLERIDGE.

Sara Coleridge.

65 CORNHILL, AND 12 PATERNOSTER ROW, LONDON.

1875.

MEMOIR AND LETTERS

OF

SARA COLERIDGE.

EDITED BY

HER DAUGHTER.

"A Spirit, yet a Woman, too."
WORDSWORTH.

FOURTH EDITION, ABRIDGED.

HENRY S. KING & CO.,
65 CORNHILL, AND 12 PATERNOSTER ROW, LONDON.
1875.

PREFACE TO THE FIRST EDITION.

———◦◦◦———

"Poor is the portrait that one look pourtrays,
It mocks the face on which we loved to gaze." *

AND if this be true of such external resemblances as pictorial art is employed to produce, it is equally true of that unconscious self-portraiture, that revelation of the inner mind, which is contained in a greater or less degree in any collection of published letters. The interest which such works are intended to excite is, in the main, biographical, and their object is not merely to preserve and bring to light a number of writings of intrinsic merit and beauty, but still more, perhaps, to present to the reader a record, however imperfect, of the personal characteristics, both moral and intellectual, of the writer.

But how faint and inadequate, if not incorrect, is that image of the departed, which can alone be thus reproduced! Even the original correspondence, could it be given entire in all its details (which is, for obvious reasons, impossible),

* Lines in " Phantasmion."

would be but as a mirrored reflection—a selection from the
correspondence is but its scattered fragments.

The difficulty which must attend on all such under-
takings as that on which I have been engaged, in editing
the letters of my mother, is rather increased than diminished by that very quality which constitutes their peculiar
charm, I mean their perfect genuineness and life-like
reality.

Touching descriptions of personal feeling, acute remarks
and wise reflections occur here in abundance, which seem,
to the eye of affection, to be gems " of purest ray serene,"
the utterances of a heart full of sensibility, and an intellect
at once subtle and profound. Yet, severed as they must
often be from the context which justified and explained
them, these thoughtful comments on the life within and
around her may, it is to be feared, either lose their full
significance, or assume one that is exaggerated and untrue.

Even those portions of the following collection which
seem, at first sight, to be most abstract and elaborate (such
as the critical discussions on art and poetry, and those
which intimate the results of speculative thought and
religious inquiry), will be found, on consideration, to be
full of personal references, suggested by special occasions,
and connected at all points with the realities of life.

The letters of Sara Coleridge were not acts of authorship,
but of friendship; we feel, in reading them, that she is not
entertaining or instructing a crowd of listeners, but holding
quiet converse with some congenial mind. Her share of

that converse we are privileged in part to overhear, while the response is borne away by the winds in another direction.

A book composed of epistolary extracts can never be a wholly satisfactory one, because its contents are not only relative and fragmentary, but unauthorized and unrevised. To arrest the passing utterances of the hour, and reveal to the world that which was spoken either in the innermost circle of home affection, or in the outer (but still guarded) circle of social and friendly intercourse, seems almost like a betrayal of confidence, and is a step which cannot be taken by survivors without some feelings of hesitation and reluctance. That reluctance is only to be overcome by the sense that, however natural, it is partly founded on delusion —a delusion which leads us to personify "the world" to our imagination as an obtuse and somewhat hostile individual, who is certain to take things by the wrong handle, and cannot be trusted to make the needful allowances, and supply the inevitable omissions. Whereas it is a more reasonable as well as a more comfortable belief, that the only part of the world which is in the least likely to concern itself with such volumes as these, is composed of a number of enlightened and sympathetic persons, who, it is hoped, though strangers to all but the name of Sara Coleridge, may yet derive from her letters some portion of the gratification which they once afforded to those who knew and loved her. And if it be well for us to "think on whatsoever things are true, whatsoever things are pure, whatsoever things are lovely," and to rejoice in "any virtue and any praise," we ought surely to be willing that all who desire it should hear the music of the words in which these things are uttered, and see the light of the life in which they shone.

In conclusion, I have only to offer my respectful and grateful acknowledgments to those who have rendered this memorial possible, by their kindness in entrusting me with these treasured records of a friendship long past, yet never

PREFACE TO THE FOURTH EDITION.

A NEW edition of the "Memoir and Letters of Sara Coleridge" having been called for, I gladly avail myself of the opportunity to express my grateful appreciation of the favourable manner in which this book has been received by the public. It was my purpose and endeavour, in preparing it, to preserve a truthful, though necessarily incomplete, record of the chief characteristics of my mother's mind and life, in the confident hope that such a record would prove to be generally acceptable. This endeavour of mine has been met by the kind interest and warm sympathy of a wide circle of readers; and my anticipation of its results has been almost more than realized. The name of Sara Coleridge recalls now, I am happy to think, to many beside personal friends, an image which they would not willingly part with.

But while thus dwelling on what is so gratifying to me, it would not be candid to avoid all allusion to the adverse criticism that has appeared in certain quarters. According

to some of these notices, there is an excess of the intellectual and abstract element in the correspondence, over-
laying its personal interest; while according to others, it
contains too many passing references to trifling matters,
social or domestic, about which no one at the present day
can be expected to know or care anything. It is very
probable that both these opposite objections may have
some foundation in truth; but though I sincerely regret
that my judgment on several points has not been approved,
I am still glad to find it generally acknowledged that the
defects complained of are not in the letters themselves, but
in the selection made from them for publication.

It was not, indeed, my *principal* object, in this new
edition, to amend, so much as to abridge; to present the
main substance of my mother's written discourse in a more
convenient and compendious form, and by this means to
place it in the hands of a more numerous class of readers.
But this object could not be attained without a considerable
remodelling, amounting almost to a fresh selection from
the materials already in print; and in the execution of this
somewhat difficult task, I have been ready and willing to
adopt, from any remarks or criticisms that have come
before me, whatever seemed likely to aid me in offering to
the public not merely a shorter, but in some respects a
better book. To persons of a conservative turn of mind,
all changes are a grievance; to a filial editor, all omissions
are a loss; yet since omissions were inevitable, I can only
hope that they have been made in the right directions, and

that the book will be thought, upon the whole, to have rather gained than lost by compression.

It cannot be denied, however, that this process of compression, when exercised upon a collection of familiar letters, though the result may be to a certain extent an improvement, is not without a counter-balancing disadvantage. In every correspondence extending over many years, a change, if not a progress of opinion on many important topics, is sure to be perceptible; and it is feared that these signs of advancing thought and increased experience, which, in a biography of the ordinary length, are felt to be both natural and interesting, may have the appearance of inconsistency, when brought together within the narrower limits of a volume of epistolary extracts. It would have been easy indeed to secure an artificial uniformity by the simple expedient of suppressing the earlier, perhaps the less mature, utterances. But I have preferred to leave the reconciliation of these slight discrepancies to the consideration of the thoughtful reader, in the belief that such a course is most in conformity with that which was my mother's one standard—truth.

It will not, I trust, appear needlessly explanatory if I add that, in determining the contents of this volume, I have not proceeded in every instance solely on my own responsibility, but have enjoyed the advantage of consulting with persons on whose judgment I could thoroughly rely. The first of these is one who takes a deeper interest in the following memorials than can be felt by any one else

now living, except myself, and who is on all accounts best
fitted to decide on what ought to form a part of them—
I mean my mother's only surviving brother, the Rev.
Derwent Coleridge. The others are gentlemen to whose
care, zeal, and experience this work is already much
indebted, my publishers, Messrs. Henry S. King & Co.

E. C.

HANWELL RECTORY,
  October 3rd, 1874.

CONTENTS.

MEMOIR.

RECOLLECTIONS OF SARA COLERIDGE. WRITTEN BY HERSELF, IN A LETTER TO HER DAUGHTER.

CORRESPONDENCE.

CHAPTER I.—1833.

CHAPTER II.—1834.

CHAPTER III.—1834 (continued).

mother

CHAPTER XXIII.—*July—December,* 1850.

CHAPTER XXIV.—1851.

CHAPTER XXV.—*July—December*, 1851.

LETTERS TO MR. ELLIS YARNALL, PROFESSOR HENRY REED, AUBREY DE VERE, ESQ., THOMAS BLACKBURNE, ESQ., MISS FENWICK, 403-431.

Memoir.

RECOLLECTIONS

OF THE

EARLY LIFE OF SARA COLERIDGE.

WRITTEN BY HERSELF,

In a Letter addressed to her Daughter.

odd way
of dividing life,
based on age + time

I.

September 8th, 1851, *Chester Place.*

MY DEAREST E——,—I have long wished to give you a little sketch of my life. I once intended to have given it with much particularity, but now *time presses*[*]—my horizon has contracted of late. I must content myself with a brief compendium.

I shall divide my history into childhood, earlier and later, youth, earlier and later, wedded life, ditto, widowhood, ditto, and I shall endeavour to state the chief moral or reflection suggested by each—some maxim which it specially illustrated, or truth which it exemplified, or warning which it suggested.

My father has entered his marriage with my mother, and the births of my three brothers, with some particularity, in a Family Bible, given him, as he also notes, by Joseph Cottle on his marriage; the entry of my birth is in my dear mother's handwriting, and this seems like an omen of

---

[*] The fragment of autobiography was begun by my mother during her last illness, a few months before her death.—E. C.

B

starts with
father + illness → life
most imp part of life

seperation

BOO!

our lifelong separation, for I never lived with him for more than a few weeks at a time. He lived not much more, indeed, with his other children, but most of their infancy passed under his eye. Alas! more than any of them I inherited that uneasy health of his, which kept us apart. But I did not mean to begin with alas! so soon, or so early to advert to the great misfortune of both our lives—want of bodily vigour, adequate to the ordinary demands of life, even under favourable circumstances.

I was born at Greta Hall, near Keswick, December 22nd, 1802. My brother Hartley was then six years and three months, born September 19th, 1796, at Bristol; Derwent, born September 14th, 1800, at Keswick, two years and three months old. My father, married at Bristol, October 4th, 1795, was now twenty-nine years of age, my mother thirty-one. Their second child Berkeley, born at Nether Stowey, May 10th, 1798, died while my father was in Germany, February 10th, 1799, in consequence of a cold caught after inoculated small-pox, which brought on decline. Mama used to tell me mothers' tales, which, however, were confirmed by my Aunt Lovell, of this infant's noble and lovely style of beauty, his large, soft eyes, of a "London-smoke" colour, exquisite complexion, regular features, and goodly size. She said that my father was very proud of him, and one day, when he saw a neighbour approaching his little cottage at Stowey, snatched him away from the nurse half-dressed, and with a broad smile of pride and delight, presented him to be admired. In her lively way, she mimicked the tones of satisfaction with which he uttered, "this is my second son." Yet, when the answer was, "Well, this is something like a child," he felt affronted on behalf of his little darling Hartley.

During the November, and great part of December, previous to my birth, my father was travelling in Cornwall with Mr. Tom Wedgewood, as I learn by letters from him to my mother. The last of the set is dated December 16th, and in it my father speaks as if he expected to be at Ambleside, Thursday evening, December 23rd. He writes with great tenderness to my mother on the prospect of her confinement. I believe he reached home the day after my birth. Several of his letters, the last three, are from Crescelles, the house of Mr. Allan, father of Lady Mackintosh and of Mrs. Drew, the brother of Lady Alderson.

Mama used to tell me that, as a young infant, I was not so fine and flourishing as Berkeley, who was of a taller make than any of her other children, or Derwent, though not quite so small as her eldest born. In a few months, however, I became very presentable, and had my share of adoration. "Little grand-lamas," my father used to call babes in arms, feeling doubtless all the while what a blessed contrivance of the Supreme Benignity it is that man, in the very weakest stage of his existence, has power in that very weakness. Then babyhood, even where attended with no special grace, has a certain loveliness of its own, and seems to be surrounded, as by a spell, in its attractions for the female heart, and for all hearts which partake of woman's tenderness, and whose tenderness is drawn out by circumstances in that particular direction.

My father wrote thus of Hartley and of me in a letter to Mr. Poole of 1803:—"Hartley is what he always was, a strange, strange boy, 'exquisitely wild,' an utter visionary: like the moon among thin clouds, he moves in a circle of light of his own making. He alone is a light of his own. Of all human beings I never saw one so utterly naked of self. He has no vanity, no pride, no resentments; and, though very passionate, I never yet saw him angry with anybody. He is, though seven years old, the merest child you can conceive; and yet Southey says he keeps him in perpetual wonderment; his thoughts are so truly his own. His dispositions are very sweet, a great lover of truth, and of the finest moral nicety of feelings; and yet always dreaming. He said very prettily, about half a year ago, on my reproving him for some inattention, and asking him if he did not see something: 'My father,' quoth he with flute-like voice, 'I see it—I saw it, and to-morrow I shall see it again, when I shut my eyes, and when my eyes are open, and I am looking at other things; but, father, it is a sad pity, but it cannot be helped, you know; but I am always being a bad boy when I am thinking of my thoughts.' If God preserve his life for me, it will be interesting to know what he will become; for it is not only my opinion, or the opinion of two or of three, but all who have been with him talk of him as a thing that cannot be forgotten.

"My meek little Sara is a remarkably interesting baby, with the finest possible skin, and large blue eyes; and she smiles as if she were basking in a sunshine, as mild as moonlight, of her own quiet happiness."

In the same letter my father says: "Southey I like more and more. He is a good man, and his industry is stupendous; take him all in all, his regularity and domestic virtues, genius, talent, acquirements, and knowledge, and he stands by himself."

Of this first stage of my life, of course, I have no remembrance; but something happened to me when I was two years old, which was so striking as to leave an indelible trace on my memory. I fancy I can even now recall, though it may be but the echo or reflection of past remembrances, my coming dripping up the Forge Field, after having fallen into the river, between the rails of the high wooden bridge that crossed the Greta Hall hill. The maid had my baby-cousin Edith, sixteen months younger than I, in her arms; I was rushing away from Derwent, who was fond of playing the elder brother on the strength of his two years' seniority, when he was trying in some way to control me, and in my hurry slipped from the bridge into the current. Luckily for me young Richardson was still at work in his father's forge. He doffed his coat and rescued me from the water. I had fallen from a considerable height, but the strong current of the Greta received me safely. I remember nothing of this adventure but the walk home through the field. I was put between blankets on my return to the house; but my constitution had received a shock, and I became tender and delicate, having before been a thriving child. As an infant I had been nervous and insomnolent. My mother has often told me how seldom I would sleep in the cradle, how I required to be in her arms before I could settle into sound sleep. This weakness has accompanied me through life.

bodily weakness

One other glimpse of early childhood my mind retains. I can just remember sitting by my Aunt Lovell in her little downstairs wingroom, and exclaiming in a piteous tone, "I'se miseral!" A poor little, delicate, low-spirited child I doubtless was, with my original nervous tendencies, after that escape from the Greta. "Yes, and you will be miserable," Aunt Lovell compassionately broke out, as mama has told me, "if your mother doesn't put you on a cap." The hint was taken, and I wore a cap till I was eight years old. I appear in a cap, playing with a doll, in a little miniature taken of me at that age by the sister of Sir William Benthorn, who also made portraits in the same style of my Uncle and Aunt Southey, my mother, Aunt Lovell, and Cousins Edith and Herbert.

I cannot leave this period of my existence without some little allusion to my brother Derwent's sweet childhood. I often heard from mama what a fine, fair, broad-chested little fellow he was at two years old, and how he got the name of Stumpy Canary when he wore a yellow frock, which made him look like one of these feathery bundles in colour and form. I fancy I see him now, as my mother's description brought him before me, racing from kitchen to parlour, and from parlour to kitchen, just putting in his head at the door, with roguish smile, to catch notice, then off again, shaking his little sides with laughter. Mr. Lamb and his sister, who paid a visit of three weeks to my parents in the summer of 1802, were charmed with the little fellow, and much struck with the quickness of eye and of memory that he displayed in naming the subjects of prints in books which he was acquainted with. "Pi-pos, Pot-pos," were his names for the striped or spotted opossum, and these he would utter with a nonchalant air, as much as to say," Of course I know it all as pat as possible." "David Lesley, Deneral of the Cock Army," was another of his familiars. Mr. Lamb calls him "Pi-pos" in letters to Greta Hall, after his visit to the Lakes.

My parents came to Keswick in 1800. My father writes to my Uncle Southey, urging his joining him in the North, and describing Greta Hall, April 13th, 1801. See Southey's Life, vol. ii., p. 146.

I find in a letter of mama to Aunt Lovell, written but not sent, this record of early Greta Hall times :—

"Well, after poor Mrs. Southey's death you all removed to Bristol, where the first child, Margaret, was born and died. Soon after this period Southey, Edith, and you (Mrs. Lovell) came to Keswick. How well I recollect your chaise driving up the Forge Field! The driver could not find the right road to the house, so he came down Stable Lane, and in at the Forge Gate. My Sara was seven months old, *very sweet*, and her uncle called her 'Fat Sal.'

"My husband, I think, was then in Malta, where he remained three years, there and in Sicily and Rome. Soon after his return in the autumn of 1806, Coleridge went away with Hartley to the Wordsworths at Coleorton; thence he went to London, and wrote to me to bring the other two children to Bristol, and wait there in College Street at Martha's with mother till he should join us to go to Stowey and Ottery together. Accordingly, I set off to Penrith, stayed a night at old Miss Monkhouse's, and next day proceeded towards Liverpool, where we were met by Dr. Crompton's carriage, and taken to Eton Hall, four miles out of Liverpool, where we stayed a fortnight, to the great happiness of Derwent and Sara. Thence we got to Birmingham, stayed a few days with the Misses Lawrence, saw Joseph Lovell and wife and children, and then proceeded to Bristol, to Martha's in College Street.

"After some time Samuel Taylor Coleridge brought Hartley from London to join us, and we five all proceeded to Stowey, to Mr. Poole's most hospitable abode, remaining most pleasantly with him for more than two months, and did not go to Ottery at all. (I believe they had illness there.) We made visits to Ashhall (Mr. Brice's), to Bridgewater, at the Chubbs'. Then I, with my children, returned to Bristol, hoping to be rejoined by father. At length he came, but was not for returning with us to Keswick. We set forward with Mr. De Quincey to Liverpool, where we (*i.e.*, myself and children) remained a few days with the Coster family, and were again joined by Mr. De Quincey, and reached Grasmere, where we were joyfully received by the Wordsworths at their cottage, and the next day took a chaise to Keswick, on which occasion poor Hartley was so afraid that he should not again be a pet of dear friend Wilsy,* that he screamed out of a window of the chaise, ' O Wilsy, Wilsy, let me sleep with you ! ' "

* Mrs. Wilson, the landlord's housekeeper.—See Memoir of Hartley Coleridge, p. xxix.—E. C.

memory)

I was in my fifth year during this visit to the South, and my remembrances are partial and indistinct glimpses of memory, islanded amid the sea of non-remembrance. I recollect more of Derwent than of Hartley, and have an image of his stout build, and of his resolute, managing way, as we played together at Bristol. I remember Mrs. Perkins, with her gentle Madonna countenance, and walking round the Square with her daughter, who gave me currants when we came round to a certain point. I have faint recollections too, of Stowey, and of staying at the Costers' at Liverpool. At this time I was fond of reading the original poems of the Miss Taylors, and used to repeat some of them by heart to friends of mama's. Aunt Martha I thought a fine lady on our first arrival at College Street. She wore a white veil— so it seems to my remembrance—when I first saw her. I can but just remember Aunt Eliza, then at Mrs. Watson's, and that there was an old lady, very invalidish, at College Street, Mrs. Fricker, my mother's mother.

My brothers were allowed to amuse themselves with the noble art of painting, which they practised in the way of daubing with one or two colours, I think chiefly scarlet, over any bit of a print or engraving in vol., or out of it, that was abandoned to their clutches. It was said of Derwent, that upon one of these pictorial occasions, after diligently plying his brush for some time, he exclaimed, with a slow, solemn, half-pitying, half-self-complacent air, " Thethe little minute thingth are *very* difficult; but they *mutht be done!* ethpethially *thaithes!* " * This " *mutht be done!*" conveyed an awful impression of resistless necessity, the mighty force of a principled submission to duty, with a hint of the exhausting struggles and trials of life.

Talking of struggles and trials of life, my mother's two unmarried sisters were maintaining themselves at this time

* *i.e.*, chaises.—E. C.

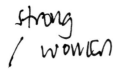
strong
/ women

by their own labours. Aunt Martha, the elder, a plain, but lively, pleasing woman, about five feet high, or little more, was earning her bread as a dressmaker. She had lived a good deal with a farmer, in the country, Uncle Hendry, who married Edith Fricker, her father's sister; but not liking a female-farmer mode of life, came to Bristol, and fitted herself for the business. Uncle Hendry left her a small sum of money, some hundreds, and would have done more, doubtless, had she remained with him. Burnet offered marriage to my Aunt Martha, during the agitation of the Pantisocracy scheme. She refused him scornfully, seeing that he only wanted a *wife in a hurry*, not her individually of all the world.

Aunt Eliza, a year or twenty months younger, about the same height, or but a barleycorn above it, was thought pretty in youth, from her innocent blue eyes, ingenuous florid countenance, fine light-brown hair, and easy light motions. She was not nearly so handsome in face, however, as my mother and Aunt Lovell, and had not my Aunt Southey's fine figure and quietly commanding air. Yet, on the whole, she was very feminine, pleasing, and attractive. Both sisters sang, but had never learned music artistically.

Such were my Aunts Martha and Elizabeth Fricker in youth; but they had sterling qualities, which gave their characters a high respectability. Without talent, except of an ordinary kind, without powerful connections, by lifelong perseverance, fortitude, and determination, by prudence, patience, and punctuality, they not only maintained themselves, but, with a little aid from kind friends, whom their merits won, they laid by a comfortable competency for their old age. They asked few favours, accepted few obligations, and were most scrupulous in returning such as they did accept, as soon as possible. They united caution and discretion with perfect honesty and truth, strict frugality and self-control, with the disposition to be kind and charitable, and even liberal, as soon as ever it was in their power. Their chief faults were pride and irritability of temper. Upon the whole, they were admirable women. I say were; but one, Aunt Eliza Fricker, still survives, in the Isle of Man. Aunt Martha died of paralysis, at the Isle of Man, September 26, 1850, at the age of seventy-three. Aunt Eliza is ailing; she must be seventy-three, I believe now, or seventy-two.*

Our return to Greta Hall has left an image on my mind, and a pleasant one. I can just remember entering the parlour, seeing the urn on the table, and tea things laid out, and a little girl, very fair, with thick yellow hair, and round, rosy cheeks, seated, I think, on a stool near the fire. This was my Cousin Edith, and I thought her quite a beauty. She looked very shy at first, but ere long we were sociably travelling round the room together on one stool, our joint vessel, and our childish noise soon required to be moderated. I was five years old, the Christmas after this return, which, I believe, was latish in autumn. I remember how Mr. De Quincey jested with me on the journey, and declared I was to be his wife, which I partly believed. I thought he behaved faithlessly in not claiming my hand.

I will now describe the home of my youth, dear Greta Hall, where I was born, and where I resided till my marriage, at twenty-six years of age, in September 1829. It was built on a hill, on one side of the town of Keswick, having a large nursery-garden in front. The gate at the end of this garden opened upon the end of the town. A few steps further was the bridge over the Greta. At the back of Greta Hall was an orchard of not very productive apple-trees and plum-trees. Below this a wood stretched down to

* Miss Fricker died at Ramsay, in the Isle of Man, in September 1868.—E. C.

the river side. A rough path ran along the bottom of the wood, and led, on the one hand (the Skiddaw side of the vale), to the Cardingmill Field, which the river nearly surrounded; on the other hand, the path led below the Forge Field, on to the Forge. Oh, that rough path beside the Greta! How much of my childhood, of my girlhood, of my youth, was spent there!

But to return to the house. Two houses inter-connected under one roof, the larger part of which my parents and my Uncle and Aunt Southey occupied, while the smaller was the abode of Mr. Jackson, the landlord. On the ground floor was the kitchen, a cheerful, stone-flagged apartment, looking into the back-place, which was skirted by poultry and other out-houses, and had trees on the side of the orchard, from whence it was separated by a gooseberry hedge. There was a drooping laburnum-tree outside our back-kitchen, just in the way as you passed to the Forge Field portion of the kitchen-garden.

A passage ran from the kitchen to the front-door, and to the left of this passage was the parlour, which was the dining-room and general sitting-room. This apartment had a large window, looking upon the green, which stretched out in front, in the form of a long horse-shoe, with a flower-bed running round it, and fenced off from the great nursery-garden by pales and high shrubs and hedges. There was another smaller window, which looked out upon another grass-plot. The room was comfortably but plainly furnished, and contained many pictures, two oil landscapes, by a friend, and several water-colour landscapes. One recess was occupied by a frightful portrait of mama, by a young lady.

The passage ran round the kitchen, and opened into two small rooms in one wing of the rambling tenement, one which Aunt Lovell sat in by day, and another which held the mangle, had cupboards as a pantry, but was called the mangling-room. Here were kept the lanterns and all the array of clogs and pattens for out-of-door roamings. The clog shoes were ranged in a row, from the biggest to the least, and curiously emblemed the various stages of life.

The staircase, to the right of the kitchen, which you ascended from the passage, led to a landing-place filled with bookcases. A few steps more led to a little bedroom which mama and I occupied; that dear bedroom where I lay down, in joy or in sorrow, nightly for so many years of comparative health and happiness, whence I used to hear the river flowing, and sometimes the forge hammer in the distance, at the end of the field; but seldom other sounds in the night, save of stray animals. A few steps further was a little wing bedroom,—then the study where my uncle sat all day occupied with literary labours and researches, but which was used as a drawing-room for company. Here all the tea-visiting guests were received. The room had three windows, a large one looking down upon the green with the wide flower-border, and over to Keswick Lake and mountains beyond. There were two smaller windows looking toward the lower part of the town seen beyond the nursery-garden. The room was lined with books in fine bindings; there were books also in brackets, elegantly lettered vellum-covered volumes lying on their sides in a heap. The walls were hung with pictures, mostly portraits, miniatures of the family and some friends by Miss Bentham; of Uncle and Aunt Southey by Down-man, now engraved for the Life of Southey; of my Cousin Edith and me by Mr. Nash; and the three children, Bertha, Kate, and Isabel, by the same hand. At the back of the room was a comfortable sofa, and there were sundry tables, beside my uncle's library table, his screen, desk, etc. Altogether, with its internal fittings up, its noble outlook, and something pleasing in its proportions, this was a charming room. I never have seen its like, I think, though it would look mean enough in my eyes, as a mere room, could I see it now, as to size, furnishing, etc. The curtains were of French grey merino, the furniture-covers, at one time, buff; I cannot tell what they were latterly. My uncle had some fine volumes of engravings, which were sometimes shown to visitors; especially, I remember, Duppa's sketches from Raffaelle and Michael Angelo from the Vatican.

On the same floor with the study and wing bedrooms was a larger bedroom above the kitchen, looking into the back-yard. This was my uncle and aunt's sleeping apartment. A passage, one side of which was filled with bookshelves, led to the Jackson part of the house, the whole of which after his decease (and some rooms before) belonged to our party. There was a room which used to be my father's study, called the organ room, from an old organ which Mr. Jackson placed there; a bedroom generally occupied by Aunt Lovell looking into the back-place; this was a comfortable but gloomyish room. At the end was a wing bedroom. Thence stairs led down to Wilsy's bedroom, Hartley's parlour, Wilsy's kitchen and back-kitchen.

In the highest storey of the house were six rooms, a nursery, nursery bedroom, maid's bedroom, another occupied by Kate and Isabel at one time, a sort of lumber-room, and a dark apple-room, which used to be supposed the abode of a bogle. Then there was a way out upon the roof, and a way out upon the leads over one wing of the house, whence we could look far out to the Penrith Road, Brow Top, and the Saddleback side of the region.

My young life is almost a blank in memory from that well-remembered evening of my return from our series of southern visits, till the time of my visit to Allan Bank,

memory

when I was six years old. That journey to Grasmere gleams before me as the shadow of a shade. Some goings on of my stay there I remember more clearly. Allan Bank is a large house on a hill overlooking Easedale on one side, and Grasmere on the other. Dorothy, Mr. Wordsworth's only daughter, was at this time very picturesque in her appearance, with her long, thick, yellow locks, which were never cut, but curled with papers, a thing which seems much out of keeping with the poetic simplicity of the household. I remember being asked by my father and Miss Wordsworth, the poet's sister, if I did not think her very pretty. "No," said I, bluntly; for which I met a rebuff which made me feel as if I was a culprit.

My father's wish it was to have me for a month with him at Grasmere, where he was domesticated with the Wordsworths. He insisted upon it that I became rosier and hardier during my absence from mama. She did not much like to part with me, and I think my father's motive, at bottom, must have been a wish to fasten my affections on him. I slept with him, and he would tell me fairy stories when he came to bed at twelve and one o'clock. I remember his telling me a wild tale, too, in his study, and my trying to repeat it to the maids afterwards.

I have no doubt there was much enjoyment in my young life at that time, but some of my recollections are tinged with pain. I think my dear father was anxious that I should learn to love him and the Wordsworths and their children, and not cling so exclusively to my mother and all around me at home. He was therefore much annoyed when, on my mother's coming to Allan Bank, I flew to her, and wished not to be separated from her any more. I remember his showing displeasure to me, and accusing me of want of affection. I could not understand why. The young Wordsworths came in and caressed him. I sate benumbed; for truly nothing does so freeze affection as the breath of jealousy. The sense that you have done very wrong, or at least given great offence, you know not how or why—that you are dunned for some payment of love or feeling which you know not how to produce or to demonstrate on a sudden, chills the heart, and fills it with perplexity and bitterness. My father reproached me, and contrasted my coldness with the childish caresses of the little Wordsworths. I slunk away, and hid myself in the wood behind the house, and there my friend John, whom at that time I called my future husband, came to seek me.

It was during this stay at Allan Bank that I used to see my father and Mr. De Quincey pace up and down the room in conversation. I understood not, nor listened to a word they said, but used to note the handkerchief hanging out of the pocket behind, and long to clutch it. Mr. Wordsworth, too, must have been one of the room walkers. How gravely and earnestly used Samuel Taylor Coleridge and William Wordsworth and my Uncle Southey also to discuss the affairs of the nation, as if it all came home to their business and bosoms, as if it were their private concern! Men do not canvass these matters now-a-days, I think, quite in the same tone. Domestic concerns absorb their deeper feelings, national ones are treated more as things aloof, the speculative rather than the practical.

My father used to talk to me with much admiration and affection of Sarah Hutchinson, Mrs. Wordsworth's sister, who resided partly with the Wordsworth's partly with her own brothers. At this time she used to act as my father's amanuensis. She wrote out great part of the " Friend " to his dictation. She had fine, long, light brown hair, I think her only beauty, except a fair skin, for her features were plain and contracted, her figure dumpy, and devoid of grace and dignity. She was a plump woman, of little more than five feet. I remember my father talking to me admiringly of her long light locks, and saying how mildly she bore it when the baby pulled them hard in play.

Miss Wordsworth, Mr. Wordsworth's sister, of most poetic eye and temper, took a great part with the children. She told us once a pretty story of a primrose, I think, which she spied by the wayside when she went to see me soon after my birth, though that was at Christmas, and how this same primrose was still blooming when she went back to Grasmere.   .

My father had particular feelings and fancies about dress, as had my Uncle Southey and Mr. Wordsworth also. He could not abide the scarlet socks which Edith and I wore at one time. I remember going to him when mama had just dressed me in a new stuff frock. He took me up and set me down again without a caress. I thought he disliked the dress; perhaps he was in an uneasy mood. He much liked everything feminine and domestic, pretty and becoming, but not fine-ladyish. My Uncle Southey was all for gay, bright, cheerful colours, and even declared he had a taste for the *grand*, in half jest.

Mr. Wordsworth loved all that was rich and picturesque, light and free in clothing. A deep Prussian blue or purple was one of his favourite colours for a silk dress. He wished that white dresses were banished, and that our peasantry wore blue and scarlet and other warm colours, instead of sombre, dingy black, which converts a crowd that might be ornamental in the landscape into a swarm of magnified ants. I remember his saying how much better young girls looked of an evening in bare arms, even if the arms themselves were not very lovely, it gave such a lightness to their general air. I think he was looking at Dora when he said this. White dresses he thought cold, a blot and disharmony in any picture, in door or out of door.

My father admired white clothing, because he looked at it in reference to woman, as expressive of her delicacy and purity, not merely as a component part of a general picture.

My father liked my wearing a cap. He thought it looked girlish and domestic. Dora and I must have been a curious contrast,—she with her wild eyes, impetuous movements, and fine, long floating yellow hair,—I with my timid, large blue eyes, slender form, a little fair delicate face, muffled up in lace border and muslin. But I thought little of looks then; only I fancied Edith Southey, on first seeing her, most beautiful.

I attained my sixth year on the Christmas after this my first Grasmere visit. It must have been the next summer that I made my first appearance at the dancing school, of which more hereafter. All I can remember of this first entrance into public is, that our good-humoured, able, but rustical dancing-master, Mr. Yewdale, tried to make me dance a minuet with Charlie Denton, the youngest of our worthy pastor's home flock, a very pretty, rosy-cheeked, large-black-eyed, compact little laddikin. But I was not quite up to the business. I think my beau was a year older. At all events, it was I who broke down, and Mr. Yewdale, after a little impatience, gave the matter up. All teaching is wearisome; but to teach dancing of all teaching the wearisomest.

The last event of my earlier childhood which abides with me, is a visit to Allonby, when I was nine years old, with Mrs. Calvert. I remember the ugliness and meanness of Allonby (the town, a cluster of red-looking houses, as far as I recollect,) and being laughed at at home for describing it as " a pretty place," which I did conventionally, according to the usual practice, as I conceived, of elegant letter writers. The sands are really fine in their way, so un-

c

broken and extensive, capital for galloping over on pony-back. I recollect the pleasures of these sands, and of the seaside animation and vegetation; the little close, white Scotch roses; the shells, the crabs of every size, from Lilliputian to Brobdignagian, crawling in the pools; the sea-anemones with their flower-like appendages, which we kept in jugs of salt water, delighted to see them draw in their petals, or expand them by a sudden blossoming; the sea-weed with its ugly berries, of which we made hideous necklaces. All these things I recollect, but not what I should most regard now, the fine forms of the Scotch hills on the opposite coast, sublime in the distance, and the splendid sunsets which give to this sort of landscape a gorgeous filling up.

Of the party, beside J. and R. Calvert and M., their sister, were Tom and William M——, two sons of Mrs. Calvert's sister, Mrs. M——. We used to gallop up and down the wide sands on two little ponies, a dark one called Sancho, and a light one called Airey, behind the boys. M. and I sometimes quarrelled with the boys, and, of course, in a trial of strength got the worst of it. I remember R. and the rest bursting angrily into our bedroom, and flinging a pebble at M., enraged at our having dared to put crumbs into their porridge; not content with which inroad and onslaught, they put mustard into ours the next morning, the sun having gone down upon their boyish wrath without quenching it. One of them said, it was all that little vixen, Sara Coleridge; M. was quiet enough by herself.

I had a leaven of malice, I suppose, in me, for I remember being on hostile terms with some little old woman, who lived by herself in a hut, and who took offence at something I did, as it struck me, unnecessarily. She repaired to Mrs. Calvert to complain, and the head and front of her accusation was, that "un (meaning me) ran up and down the mound before her door." Mrs. C. thought this no heinous offence; but it was done by me, no doubt, with an air of derision. The crone was one of those morose, ugly, withered, ill-conditioned, ignorant creatures who in earlier times were persecuted as witches, and tried to be such. Still, I ought to have been gently corrected for my behaviour, and told the duty of bearing with the ill-temper of the poor and ignorant and afflicted.

At this time, on coming to Allonby, I was rather delicate. Oh me, how rough these young Calverts and M——s were! and yet they had a certain respect for me, mingled with a contrary feeling. I was honoured among them for my extreme agility,—my power of running and leaping. They called me "Cheshire cat" because I "grinned," said they. Almost as pretty as Miss Cheshire, said Tom M. to me one day, of some admired little girl.

Such are the chief *historical* events of my little life up to nine years of age. But can I in any degree retrace what being I was then, what relation my then being held to my maturer self? Can I draw any useful reflection from my childish experience, or found any useful maxim upon it? What *was* I? In person very slender and delicate, not habitually colourless, but often enough pallid and feeble looking. Strangers used to exclaim about my eyes, and I remember remarks made upon their large size, both by my Uncle Southey and Mr. Wordsworth. I suppose the thinness of my face, and the smallness of the other features, with the muffling close cap, increased the apparent size of the eye, for only artists, since I have grown up, speak of my eyes as large and full. They were bluer, too, in my early years than now. My health alternated, as it has done all my life, till the last ten or twelve years, when it has been unchangeably depressed, between delicacy and a very easy, comfortable condition. I remember well that

nightmares

nervous sensitiveness and morbid imaginativeness had set in with me very early. During my Grasmere visit I used to feel frightened at night on account of the darkness. I then was a stranger to the whole host of night-agitators, ghosts, goblins, demons, burglars, elves, and witches. Horrid ghastly tales and ballads, of which crowds afterwards came in my way, had not yet cast their shadows over my mind. And yet I was terrified in the dark, and used to think of lions, the only form of terror which my dark-engendered agitation would take. My next bugbear was the Ghost in Hamlet. Then the picture of Death at Hell Gate in an old edition of Paradise Lost, the delight of my girlhood. Last and worst came my Uncle Southey's ballad horrors, above all the Old Woman of Berkeley. Oh, the agonies I have endured between nine and twelve at night, before mama joined me in bed, in presence of that hideous assemblage of horrors, the horse with eyes of flame! I dare not, even now, rehearse these particulars, for fear of calling up some of the old feeling, which, indeed, I have never in my life been quite free from. What made the matter worse was that, like all other nervous sufferings, it could not be understood by the inexperienced, and consequently subjected the sufferer to ridicule and censure. My Uncle Southey laughed heartily at my agonies. I mean at the cause. He did not enter into the agonies. Even mama scolded me for creeping out of bed after an hour's torture, and stealing down to her in the parlour, saying I could bear the loneliness and the night-fears no longer. But my father understood the case better. He insisted that a lighted candle should be left in my room, in the interval between my retiring to bed and mama's joining me. From that time forth my sufferings ceased. I believe they would have destroyed my health had they continued.

Yet I was a most fearless child by daylight, ever ready to

how childhood has affected her

take the difficult mountain-path and outgo my companions'
daring in tree-climbing. In those early days we used to
spend much of our summer-time in trees, greatly to the
horror of some of our London visitors.

On reviewing my earlier childhood, I find the predomi-
nant reflection

. . . .
. . . .
. . . .

II.

Thus abruptly terminates, in the very middle of a sentence,
the narrative of Sara Coleridge's childhood. The history of
her wedded life and widowhood, which would have been of
such deep interest as told by herself, had time and strength
been granted, is, fortunately, to a great extent contained
in her correspondence. In order, however, to combine the
scattered notices of the letters, and put readers at once in
possession of the main facts; and still more, in order to
provide some partial substitute for that chapter of her
youth, which would otherwise remain a blank, it has seemed
desirable to preface the correspondence by a slight biographical sketch. In doing this I shall gratefully avail
myself of the valuable reminiscences most kindly imparted
to me by friends, both of earlier and later date, as well as
of an interesting memoir of my mother which appeared
shortly after her death in an American journal,* composed
by one who, though personally unknown to her, was yet a
highly esteemed correspondent, the lamented Professor
Henry Reed of Philadelphia.

In that dear home of her childhood, remembered with

* "The Daughter of Coleridge," written for the *Literary World*, July,
1852.

such loving minuteness after more than twenty years of absence, Sara Coleridge grew up as fair and sweet as one of the exquisite wild flowers of her native vale. The childish prettiness which had excited the admiration of her young playfellows at Allonby, changed first into the maidenly bloom of fifteen; at which age she is mentioned by the painter William Collins, as " Coleridge's elegant daughter Sara, a most interesting creature," of whom he made a sketch, which was greatly admired by her father for its simplicity and native refinement. It represents her in the character of the Highland Girl, seated in rustic fashion under a tree. Five years later these girlish graces had matured into a perfection of womanly beauty, which is thus described by Sir Henry Taylor :—

" I first saw your mother," he writes in a letter which I have lately had the pleasure of receiving from him, " when in 1823 I paid my first visit to Mr. Southey at Greta Hall, where she and her mother were staying. I suppose she was then about twenty years of age. I saw but little of her, for I think she was occupied in translating some mediæval book from the Latin, and she was seen only at meals, or for a very short time in the evening; and as she was almost invariably silent, I saw nothing and knew nothing of her ¦mind, till I renewed my acquaintance with her many years after. But I have always been glad that I did see her in her girlhood, because I then saw her beauty untouched by time, and it was a beauty which could not but remain in one's memory for life, and which is now distinctly before me as I write. The features were perfectly shaped, and almost minutely delicate, and the complexion delicate also, but not wanting in colour, and the general effect was that of gentleness, indeed I may say of composure, even to stillness. Her eyes were large, and they had the sort of serene lustre which I remember in her father's.

"After her marriage, I think, I did not see her till the days of her widowhood, in young middle life, when she was living in Chester Place, Regent's Park. Her beauty, though not lost, was impaired, and with the same stillness and absolute simplicity which belonged to her nature, there was some sadness which I had not seen before in the expression of her face, and some shyness of manner. I think I was myself shy, and this perhaps made her so, and the effect was to shut me out from the knowledge, *by conversation*, of almost any part of her mind and nature, except her intellect. For whenever she was shy, if she could not be silent, which was impossible when we were alone together, she fled into the region where she was most at home and at ease, which was that of psychology and abstract thought; and this was the region where I was by no means at ease and at home. Had we met more frequently (and I never cease to wish that we had) no doubt these little difficulties would soon have been surmounted; and we should have got into the fields of thought and sentiment which had an interest common to us both. But I was a busy man in these years, and not equal in health and strength to what I had to do, and it was in vain for me to seek her society, when I was too tired to enjoy it; and then came her illness and her early death, and she had passed away before I had attained to know her in her inner mind and life. I only know that the admirable strength and subtlety of her reasoning faculty, shown in her writings and conversation, were less to me than the beauty and simplicity and feminine tenderness of her face; and that one or two casual and transitory expressions of her nature in her countenance, delightful in their poetic power, have come back to me from time to time, and that they are present with me now, when much of what was most to be admired in her intellectual achievements or discourse, have passed into somewhat of a dim distance."

Of all the personal influences which had to do with the formation of my mother's mind and character in early life, by far the most important were those exercised by the two eminent men with whom she was so intimately connected, by ties of kindred or affection, her Uncle Southey, and her father's friend Mr. Wordsworth. In attempting to estimate the value of these various impressions, and trace them to their respective source, I am but repeating her own remark when I say, that in matters of the intellect and imagination, she owed most to Mr. Wordsworth. In his noble poetry she took an ever-increasing delight, and his impressive discourse, often listened to on summer rambles over the mountains, or in the winter parlours of Greta Hall and Rydal Mount, served to guide her taste and cultivate her understanding. But in matters of the heart and conscience, for right views of duty and practical lessons of industry, truthfulness, and benevolence, she was " more, and more importantly, indebted to the daily life and example of her admirable Uncle Southey," whom she long afterwards emphatically declared to have been " upon the whole,.the best man she had ever known."

There is a third province of human nature beside those of the intellect and the moral sense,—that of the spiritual, where the pure spirit of Sara Coleridge breathed freely, as in an "ampler ether, a diviner air." In these serene and lofty regions she wandered hand in hand with her father, whose guidance she willingly followed, with a just confidence in his superior wisdom, yet with no blind or undiscriminating submission. He, like herself, was but a traveller through the heavenly country, whose marvels they explored together; and the sun of Reason was above them both to light them on their way. In September, 1825, when not quite three-and-twenty, she was reading the " Aids to Reflection," " and delighted with all that she could clearly understand," as she says in a letter of that date to Sir John Taylor Coleridge. "Do you not think," she adds, with modest deference to the opinion of a highly respected elder cousin, "that in speaking of free will, and the other mysteries of religion, my father, though he does not attempt to explain what I suppose is inexplicable, puts the subject in a new and comfortable point of view for sincere Christians?" The "new and comfortable point of view," thus early perceived and adopted, was still more deeply appreciated, when years of experience and reflection had increased her sense of its importance. Led by circumstances, as well as by natural congeniality of mind, to a study of her father's philosophy, she then devoted herself, with all the fulness of matured conviction, to the task of illustrating those great principles of Christian truth which it was the main object of his life to defend. If, in following this path, she approached the dusty arena of controversy (though without actually entering it), and watched the combatants with approving or disapproving eye, it will yet, I believe, be acknowledged, even by those who differ most widely from her conclusions, that in her mode of reaching them she combined charity with candour. Possessing, as she did, a knowledge of theology, both as a history and a science, rare in any woman (perhaps in any layman), she had received from heaven a still more excellent gift, "even the ornament of a meek and quiet spirit."

These solemn investigations were, however, the appropriate employment of a more advanced stage of life than that of which I am now speaking. In youthful days my mother's favourite pursuits were chiefly literary and linguistic. Before she was five-and-twenty she had made herself acquainted with the leading Greek and Latin classics, and was well skilled in French, Italian, German, and Spanish. These acquirements were mainly the result of her own efforts; though it is needless to point out the advantages she derived in her studies from the advice and direction of a man like Mr. Southey, and from the use which she was kindly encouraged to make of his valuable library.

Natural History, too, in all its branches, especially those of botany and zoology, was a subject in which she found endless attractions. The beauty of nature manifested in bird or insect, flower or tree, delighted her poetical imagination; while the signs of Divine Wisdom and Goodness, revealed in all the works of creation, furnished a constant theme for the contemplations of a thoughtful piety. Other advantages accompanied these studies, so healthful both to mind and body. The out-door interests which they provided, the habits of careful observation which they rendered necessary, aided in the harmonious development of her faculties, and served to counterbalance the subjective tendencies of her intellect. She could turn at any time from the most abstruse metaphysical speculations, to inspect the domestic architecture of a spider, or describe the corolla of a rose.

The work referred to by Sir Henry Taylor in his interesting letter, as that upon which my mother was engaged at the time of his first visit to Greta Hall, was probably her translation of the "Memoirs of the Chevalier Bayard, by the Loyal Servant;" which was published by Mr. Murray, in 1825. The trouble of rendering the accounts of battles and sieges, from the French of the sixteenth century, into appropriate English, was considerable; but was lightened by the interest inspired by the romantic character and adventures of Bayard, the Knight "sans peur et sans reproche."

This was not, however, her earliest appearance in print. Her first literary production was one concerning which `Professor Reed gives the following particulars, in the notice above referred to. After observing that it "manifestly had its origin in connection with some of Southey's labours," * he proceeds thus :—" In 1822 there issued from the London press a work in three octavo volumes, entitled, 'An Account of the Abipones, an Equestrian people of Paraguay. From the Latin of Martin Dobrizhoffer, eighteen years a Missionary in that country.' No name of translator appears, and a brief and modest preface gives not the least clue to it ; even now in catalogues the work is frequently ascribed to Southey. At the time of the publication Miss Coleridge was just twenty years of age, and therefore this elaborate toil of translation must have been achieved before she had reached the years of womanhood. The stout-hearted perseverance needed for such a task is quite as remarkable as the scholarship in a young person. Coleridge himself spoke of it with fond and just admiration, when, in 1832, he said :—

" 'My dear daughter's translation of this book is, in my judgment, unsurpassed for pure mother-English, by any-thing I have read for a long time.'

" Southey in his 'Tale of Paraguay,' which was suggested by the missionary's narrative, paid to the translator a tribute so delicate, and so controlled, perhaps, by a sense of his young kinswoman's modesty, that one need be in the secret to know for whom it is meant. It is in the stanza which mentions Dobrizhoffer's forgetfulness of his native speech, during his long missionary expatriation, and alludes to the favour shown him by the Empress Maria Theresa.

" ' But of his native speech because well-nigh
Disuse in him forgetfulness had wrought,
In Latin he composed his history,
A garrulous but a lively tale, and fraught

---

* The work was undertaken, in the first instance, for the purpose of as-sisting one of her brothers in his college expenses. The necessary means were, however, supplied by his own exertions ; and the proceeds of the translation (£125) were funded in Sara Coleridge's name, for her own use.—E. C.

With matter of delight and food for thought,
And if he could in Merlin's glass have seen
By whom his tomes to speak our tongue were taught,
The old man would have felt as pleased, I ween,
As when he won the ear of that great Empress Queen.'
Canto III., stanza 16.

"Charles Lamb, in an epistolary strain, eminently characteristic, echoes the praise bestowed upon his friend's child, and her rare achievement. Writing to Southey, in 1825, in acknowledgment of a presentation copy of the 'Tale of Paraguay,' he says:

"'The compliment to the translatress is daintily conceived. Nothing is choicer in that sort of writing than to bring in some remote impossible parallel—as between the great empress and the unobtrusive quiet soul, who digged her noiseless way so perseveringly through that rugged Paraguay mine. How she Dobrizhoffered it all out puzzles my slender latinity to conjecture.*'"

There is a graceful allusion to my mother's classical attainments in that lovely strain composed in her honour by the great poet whose genius, especially in its *earlier* manifestations, she so highly admired and reverenced:—

" Last of the Three, though eldest born,
Reveal thyself, like pensive morn,
Touched by the skylark's earliest note,
Ere humbler gladness be afloat ;
But whether in the semblance drest
Of dawn, or eve, fair vision of the west,
    Come with each anxious hope subdued
By woman's gentle fortitude,
Each grief, through meekness, settling into rest.
Or I would hail thee when some high-wrought page
Of a closed volume lingering in thy hand,
Has raised thy spirit to a peaceful stand
Among the glories of a happier age.
Her brow hath opened on me, see it there
Brightening the umbrage of her hair,

---

* "Talfourd's Letters of Charles Lamb," vol. ii. p. 189.

So gleams the crescent moon, that loves
To be descried through shady groves.
Tenderest bloom is on her cheek,
Wish not for a richer streak,
Nor dread the depth of meditative eye,
But let thy love upon that azure field
Of thoughtfulness and beauty, yield
Its homage, offered up in purity.
What wouldst thou more ?   In sunny glade,
Or under leaves of thickest shade,
Was such a stillness e'er diffused
Since earth grew calm, while angels mused !
Softly she treads, as if her foot were loth
To crush the mountain dewdrops, soon to melt
On the flower's breast ; as if she felt
That flowers themselves, whate'er their hue,
With all their fragrance, all their glistening,
Call to the heart for inward listening ;
And though for bridal wreaths and tokens true
Welcomed wisely ; though a growth
Which the careless shepherd sleeps on,
As fitly spring from turf the mourner weeps on,
And without wrong are cropped the marble tomb to strew."

My mother was once told by a poetical friend that, till he knew the original, he had always taken this passage in the Triad for a personification of the Christian grace of Faith. She used to smile at her involuntary exaltation, and maintain that there must be something exaggerated and unreal in a description which was liable to such a misinterpretation. Yet the conjecture may have been a right one in the spirit, though not in the letter. Certainly no one who knew my mother intimately, and was privileged to see " the very pulse of the machine "—

" A being breathing thoughtful breath,
A traveller betwixt life and death,
The reason firm, the temperate will,
Endurance, foresight, strength, and skill "—

could doubt that such a life as hers could only be lived " by faith."

That light of faith, which shone so brightly in declining years, had been early sought and found between the troubled clouds of life's opening day. In 1828, when the "Triad" was written, Sara Coleridge was no stranger to the most powerful emotion which can agitate a woman's heart, either for joy or sorrow. The "anxious hope" alluded to by the poet, with almost parental tenderness, was for the joyful time when she might be enabled peacefully to enjoy the "dear and improving society" of him to whom she had given her affections; the "grief" that settled into the "rest" which is promised to the meek and lowly, arose not so much from the postponement of her own happiness as from the sympathy with his disappointment, and sorrow for its cause, which was principally the uncertainty of health and means on both sides.

In 1822, while on a visit to her father at Highgate, she had first met her cousin, Henry Nelson Coleridge, a younger son of James Coleridge, Esq., of Heath's Court, Ottery St. Mary, who was educated at Eton College, and at King's College, Cambridge, where his course was not unmarked by academical honours. He was then practising as a Chancery barrister in London, and made frequent pilgrimages to Highgate, one result of which was that series of notes to which the world is indebted for the "Table Talk of S. T. Coleridge."

The attachment thus formed between the two youthful cousins, under the roof of Mr. Gillman, was never for a single moment regretted by my mother, in spite of the solicitudes to which it exposed her, and the sorrows which, in after years, cast a shade of sadness over the stillness which characterized her gentle face.

"She was a maid," thus writes Hartley Coleridge of his only sister :—

> "Not easily beguiled by loving words,
> Nor apt to love; but when she loved, the fate
> Of her affections was a stern religion,
> Admitting nought less holy than itself."

These "seven years of patience" did not pass without bringing forth precious fruits of piety and goodness in a heart already enriched with the dews of heavenly blessing. "Your virtues," writes my father to his betrothed in a letter of 1827, "never shone so brilliantly in my eyes as they do now; and it is a spring of deep and sacred joy in my heart to think that, however weak and wavering my steps may be in the ways of religion, you are already a firm traveller in them, and indeed a young saint upon earth. The trials to which our engagement has exposed you have been fatiguing and painful; but you have borne them all, not only without impatience or murmuring, but with a holy cheerfulness and energetic resignation, than which no two states of the heart are more difficult to man, or more acceptable to God.

"I made a true remark to you once, which I feel every day justified by our own correspondence, that spiritual things differ from mere things of sense in this amongst other points, that sensual objects, capacities, and enjoyments are all naturally bounded, short, and fugitive, whilst pure love and pure intellectual communion are essentially without limits, and that to the pure-hearted a boundless ascent towards identity of moral being lies open, and that every day fresh depths of love and thought might open to the tender and assiduous sympathies of two mutually adoring persons. I have always loved you as much as my heart could feel at the time; but my respect, my veneration for you has gone on increasing as I knew you more intimately. I hope I shall always have the sense to submit myself to your guiding influence in all cases of moral election. The more closely I imitate your habits, thoughts, and actions, the better and happier man shall I become."

The noble affection thus generously expressed was as fully returned by her on whom it was bestowed. In a letter written on the eve of her marriage she thus addresses the expected bridegroom, "You will not, I know, grudge a few tears to my dearest mother, to dear Keswick, dear Greta Hall, and its dear and interesting inmates. These changes, these farewells, are types of the great change, the long farewell, that awaits us all hereafter. We cannot but be thoughtful upon them. Yet I know and feel that *this* change is to be infinitely for the better; and in your dear and improving society I trust I shall learn to look upon that other change as a blessed one too. The sadness of my present farewell will be tempered by the prospect of meeting all here frequently again upon earth, as, I hope, all dear friends will be reunited in heaven. But that speculation would lead me too far. Fear not, Henry, that such speculations, or rather, such a tendency in my nature to speculation and dreaminess, will render me an unfit wife for you. Does not Wordsworth point out to us how the most excursive bird can brood as long and as fondly on the nest as any of the feathered race?* This taste for the spiritual I consider a great blessing, crowned by that other inexpressibly great one, the having found a partner who will tolerate, approve, sympathize in all I think and feel, and will allow me to sympathize with him."

On the 3rd of September, 1829, Henry Nelson Coleridge and Sara Coleridge were married at Crosthwaite Church, Keswick. After a few months spent in a London lodging, they began their frugal housekeeping in a tiny cottage on Downshire Hill, Hampstead, where their four elder children were born, of whom the twins, Berkeley and Florence, died in infancy. In 1837 my parents removed to a more commodious dwelling in Chester Place, Regent's Park, where a third daughter, Bertha Fanny, was born in 1840, who survived her birth but a few days.

My mother's married life was, as Professor Reed has

* "True to the kindred points of heaven and home."—*The Skylark.*

truly observed, "rich in the best elements of conjugal
happiness,—wedded to a gentleman of high moral worth,
and of fine mind and scholarship, one who blended literature with his professional pursuits,—she was not exposed
to the perils of intellectual superiority."

The compositions (chiefly on classical subjects) which
occupied his leisure, while his health lasted, and which
displayed the varied powers of an acute and polished
intellect, and the elegant taste of an accomplished scholar,
formed a topic of common interest, and one which is
frequently referred to, in the letters of that period, with
visible pride and pleasure. With respect to moral and
personal qualities, too, my father was, as she afterwards
said to a friend when describing her grief at his loss, "of
all men whom she had ever known, best suited to her;"
and this quite as much by force of contrast as of resem-
blance. Of sensitive temperament, reserved though deeply
earnest feelings, and manners which illness and suffering
rendered serious, though not usually sad, she was especially
likely to feel the charm of the wit, gaiety, and conversa-
tional brilliancy, which, on social occasions, made her
husband the "life and soul of the company," as well as of
the joyous frankness and overflowing affectionateness which
made him the delight of his home.

In that genial atmosphere of loving appreciation, free
from the cares and depressing circumstances of her girlhood, she was encouraged and enabled to put forth all her
best powers—

"A thousand happy things that seek the light,
Till now in darkest shadow forced to lie," *

began to "show their forms and hues in the all-revealing
sun." The poetical genuis which she inherited from her
father (together with his turn for philosophical reflection,
developed in her at a later date) found its most perfect

* From a song in "Phantasmion."—E. C.

D

expression in her romance of Phantasmion, published in 1837. The wild and beautiful scenery of her birthplace, vividly remembered and fondly dwelt on in the enforced seclusion of sickness (for she was now unhappily an invalid), reappears here, idealized by imagination, to form the main subject of the picture; while groups of graceful and dignified figures give animation to the landscape, and fairy forms flitting above or around them, spirits of the wind, the woods, or the waters, serve as a connecting link between humanity and nature.

"Nothing has appeared in this species of writing," says a friendly American critic, "to be for one moment compared with 'Phantasmion,' since Fouquè produced his inimitable 'Undine.' There is one characteristic feature in this book that will render it peculiarly acceptable to all lovers of nature. We do not allude to its accuracy in the delineating of the infinite phases of earth and air, sea and sky, though nothing can be more perfect in this respect; but what we mean, is its remarkable freedom from the conventional forms and usages of life. It has the patriarchal simplicity, the beautiful truthfulness of primitive ages; while it is at the same time enriched and ennobled by the refinement of a more advanced period. . . . Do you ask what is its grand characteristic? It is beauty,—beauty truly feminine, beauty of conception, character, and expression. It is indeed a wilderness of sweets illumined by the richest hues of earth and heavens, and through which a stream of magic melody is for ever flowing. . . . The 'Songs of Phantasmion!' what sweetness of verse! what breathings of a tender spirit! whose voice—who but the writer's own Spirit of the Flowers—could do them justice?"

This beautiful fairy tale was at first intended (though it soon outgrew its original limits) as a mere child's story for the amusement of her little boy, whose beauty, vivacity, and early intelligence are described with maternal love

and pride, in one of the letters of that period, in reply to
the questions of her brother Hartley, about his unseen
nephew. The education of her children was now their
mother's principal object, an object on which she deemed
it no waste to lavish the charms of her genius, and the
resources of her cultivated understanding. Latin grammar,
natural history, geography, and the " Kings of England,"
were all made easy and attractive to the little learners by
simple and appropriate verses, written on cards, in clear
print-like characters. Even a set of wooden bricks, which
was a favourite source of amusement, was thus agreeably
decorated, in the hope that those tough morsels, *hic, hæc,
hoc*, and their congeners, might glide gently over the youthful palate, sweetened with play and pleasure. From these
Sibylline leaves of the nursery a selection of juvenile poetry
was published in 1834, by my father's desire, who wished
that other children might have some share in the advantages enjoyed by his own. The little volume, entitled
" Pretty Lessons for Good Children," proved a popular
work, and passed through five editions.

> " Learning, Herbert, hath the features
> Almost of an angel's face ;
> Contemplate them steadfastly,
> Learn by heart each speaking grace.
> Truth and wisdom, high-wrought fancy,
> In those lineaments we trace ;
> Never be your eyes averted
> Long from that resplendent face ! " *

Happy the boy who is permitted to see those glorious
lineaments reflected in the "angel-face" of a wise and tender
mother ! It may not be uninteresting to the sympathizing
reader to learn that he who enjoyed the blessing of such
rare guardianship lived to appreciate and reward it, and to
attest its value by those public honours that are won by

* Fifth stanza of a poem on the Latin declensions in " Pretty Lessons,"
—*Facies, a Face.*

industry and talent.*   And that, when disease came to
blight the hopes of his manhood, and cut short a promising
career, Learning was, to him as to her, a shield from the
monotony of the sick-room and an exceeding great reward;
and that as long as anything earthly could claim his attention, it was seldom "averted from that resplendent face."

But it is time to return to an earlier stage of the
narrative, when that domestic happiness so patiently
waited for, and thankfully enjoyed, was smitten by the
hand of death.   All that was earthly of it fell to the earth,
and was no more; but there remained to the desolate
widow the Christian's hope of a heavenly re-union, which
proved an anchor of the soul sure and steadfast, when the
waves of affliction rose high.   In 1841 my father's health
began to give way; and in January, 1843, he died of spinal
paralysis, after a trying illness of nine months.

In her deep distress my mother again endeavoured to act
upon that principle of "energetic resignation" (so different
from the aimless broodings of mere submission), which had
been early noticed in her by the discriminating eye of
affection.   "I feel it such a duty, such a necessity," she
writes to a friend three months after her bereavement, "to
cling fast to every source of comfort, to be, for my
children's sake, as happy, as willing to live on in this heart-
breaking world, as possible, that I dwell on all the blessings
which God continues to me, and has raised up to me out of
the depths of affliction, with an earnestness of endeavour
which is its own reward;—for so long as the heart and
mind are full of movement, employed continually in not
unworthy objects, there may be sorrow, but there cannot
be despair.   The stagnation of the spirit, the dull, motion-

* My brother was the Newcastle and Balliol scholar in 1847 and 1848,
and took a double first class at Oxford in 1852, which latter honour his
mother did not live to witness.   He was a fine Icelandic scholar; and at
the time of his death, which took place in 1861, he was engaged in preparations for the new English dictionary projected by the Philological
Society, of which he was a member.—E. C.

less brooding over one miserable set of thoughts, is that against which, in such cases as mine, we must both strive and pray."

There is another, an equally interesting, though less personal, point of view, in which this great bereavement was an important turning-point in the life of Sara Coleridge. Her husband was Mr. Coleridge's literary executor, and the editorial task, first undertaken by my father, now devolved upon his widow. It has been beautifully remarked by Professor Reed, as a peculiarity of my mother's truly feminine authorship, that it was in no case prompted by mere literary ambition, but that there was ever some "moral motive,"—usually some call of the affections, that set her to work, and overcame her natural preference for retirement. This helpful, loving, and unselfish spirit, which had actuated her hitherto, now took a more commanding form, and led her to dedicate the whole of her intellectual existence to the great object of carrying out a husband's wishes, of doing justice to a father's name. In the fulfilment of this sacred trust, she found occasion to illustrate and adorn the works which fell under her editorship with several compositions of no inconsiderable extent, and displaying powers of critical analysis, and of doctrinal, political, and historical research and discussion, of no common order. The most important of these are the "Essay on Rationalism, with a special application to the Doctrine of Baptismal Regeneration," appended to Vol. II. of the "Aids to Reflection," the "Introduction" to the Biographia Literaria; and a Preface to the collection of her father's political writings, entitled, "Essays on his Own Times, by S. T. Coleridge," which contains, in Professor Reed's opinion, the most judicious and impartial comparison between British and American civilization, and the social and intellectual conditions of the two countries, that has yet been written. "And thus."

continues her accomplished friend and biographer, "there have been expended in the desultory form of notes, and appendices, and prefaces, an amount of original thought and an affluence of learning, which, differently and more prominently presented, would have made her famous. There is not one woman in a thousand, not one man in ten thousand, who would have been thus prodigal of the means of celebrity."

> " Father ! no amaranths e'er shall wreath my brow ;
> Enough that round thy grave they flourish now !
> But Love his roses 'mid my young locks braided,
> And what cared I for flowers of richer bloom ?
> Those too seemed deathless—here they never faded,
> But, drenched and shattered, dropt into the tomb." *

This blended expression of the wife's and the daughter's affection was recorded when she was in the midst of her pious duties. Ere long she too was called upon to resign the work, still unfinished, into another, but a dear and well-skilled hand.† Seven years of waiting for the happiness so long expected—again seven years—not always of mourning, but of faithful memories and tender regrets for that which had past away for ever; and then came preparations for the "great change, the long farewell," to which she had learned to look forward when on the very eve of bridal joys and earthly blessedness. She who had once called marriage the type of death, now heard the summons to the heavenly Marriage Feast with no startled or reluctant ear. Solemn indeed is the darkness of the Death Valley, and awful are the forms that guard its entrance—

> " Fear, and trembling Hope,
> Silence, and Foresight,"

but beyond all these, and revealed to the heart (though not

---

* From an unpublished poem by Sara Coleridge.—E. C.
† Her brother, the Rev. Derwent Coleridge, the present Editor.—E. C.

to the eye) of the humble and believing Christian, are the
blissful realities of Light and Love.

After a lingering and painful illness of about a year and
a half, Sara Coleridge was released from much suffering,
borne with unfailing patience, on the 3rd of May, 1852, in
the forty-ninth year of her age. In the old churchyard of
Highgate (now enclosed in a crypt under the school chapel)
her remains lie, beside those of her parents, her husband,
and her son.

The following letter will be read with pleasure, not only
for its own sake, but as a tribute to my mother's memory,
from one whose friendship, correspondence, and society
helped to brighten her latter years, and to whom this work
owes some of the most interesting portions of its contents.

"I rejoice to hear," Mr. de Vere writes to me, on the
subject of the present publication, "that a portion of your
mother's letters will be published so soon. To those who
knew her she remains an image of grace and intellectual
beauty that time can never tarnish. A larger circle will
now know, in part at least, what she was. Her correspondence will, to thoughtful readers, convey a clearer impression than aught beside could convey of one who of course
could only be fully understood by those who had known her
personally and known her long.

"In their memories she will ever possess a place apart
from all others. With all her high literary powers she was
utterly unlike the mass of those who are called 'literary
persons.' Few have possessed such learning; and when
one calls to mind the arduous character of those studies,
which seemed but a refreshment to her clear intellect, like
a walk in mountain air, it seems a marvel how a woman's
faculties could have grappled with those Greek philosophers
and Greek fathers, just as no doubt it seemed a marvel

when her father, at the age of fourteen, woke the echoes of that famous old cloister with declamations from Plato and Plotinus. But in the daughter, as in the father, the real marvel was neither the accumulated knowledge nor the literary power. It was the spiritual mind.

> ' The rapt one of the Godlike forehead,
> The heaven-eyed creature,'

was Wordsworth's description of Coleridge, the most spiritual perhaps of England's poets, certainly of her modern poets. Of her some one said, 'Her father had looked down into her eyes, and left in them the light of his own.' Her great characteristic was the radiant spirituality of her intellectual and imaginative being. This it was that looked forth from her countenance.

"Great and various as were your mother's talents, it was not from them that she derived what was special to her. It was from the degree in which she had inherited the feminine portion of genius. She had a keener appreciation of what was highest and most original in thought than of subjects nearer the range of ordinary intellects. She moved with the lightest step when she moved over the loftiest ground. Her 'feet were beautiful on the mountaintops' of ideal thought. They were her native land; for her they were not barren; honey came up from the stony rock. In this respect I should suppose she must have differed from almost all women whom we associate with literature. I remember hearing her say that she hardly considered herself to be a woman 'of letters.' She felt herself more at ease when musing on the mysteries of the soul, or discussing the most arduous speculations of philosophy and theology, than when dealing with the humbler topics of literature.

"As might have been expected, the department of literature which interested her most was that of poetry—that is, poetry of the loftiest and most spiritual order, for to much of what is now popular she would have refused the name. How well I remember our discussions about Wordsworth! She was jealous of my admiration for his poems, because it extended to *too many* of them. No one could be a true Wordsworthian, she maintained, who admired so much some of his late poems, his poems of accomplishment, such as the 'Triad.' It implied a disparagement of his earlier poems, such as 'Resolution and Independence,' in which the genuine Wordsworthian inspiration, and that alone, uttered itself! I suspect, however, that she must have taken a yet more vivid delight in some of her father's poems. Beside their music and their spirituality, they have another quality, in which they stand almost without a rival,—their subtle sweetness. I remember Leigh Hunt once remarking to me on this characteristic of them, and observing that in this respect they were unapproached. It is like distant music, when the tone comes to you pure, without any coarser sound of wood or of wire; or like odour on the air, when you smell the flower, without detecting in it the stalk or the earth. As regards this characteristic of her father's genius, as well as its spirituality, there was something in hers that resembled it. One is reminded of it by the fairylike music of the songs in 'Phantasmion.'

"There is a certain gentleness and a modesty which belong to real genius, and which are in striking contrast with the self-confidence and self-assertion, so often found in persons possesssed of vigorous talents, but to whom literature is but a rough sport or a coarse profession. It was these qualities that gave to her manners their charm of feminine grace, self-possession, and sweetness. She was one of those whose thoughts are growing while they speak, and who never speak to surprise. Her intellectual fervour was not that which runs over in excitement; a quietude belonged to it, and it was ever modulated by a womanly instinct of reserve and dignity. She never 'thought for *acts 'as' women ' should' so not given 'propts' due*

effect,' or cared to have the last word in discussion, or
found it difficult to conceive how others should differ from
her conclusions. She was more a woman than those who
had not a tenth part of her intellectual energy. The
seriousness and the softness of her nature raised her above
vanity and its contortions. Her mind could move at once
and be at rest.

"I fear that the type of character and intellect to which
your mother belonged must be expected to grow rarer in
these days of 'fast' intellect. Talents rush to the market,
the theatre, or the arena, and genius itself becomes
vulgarized for want of that 'hermit heart' which ought to
belong to it, whether it be genius of the creative or the
susceptive order. There will always, however, be those
whose discernment can trace in your mother's correspondence and in her works the impress of what once was so
fair. But, alas! how little will be known of her even by
such. Something they will guess of her mind, but it is
only a more fortunate few who can know her yet higher
gifts, those that belong to the heart and moral being. If
they have a loss which is theirs only, they too have remembrances which none can share with them. They
remember the wide sympathies and the high aspirations,
the courageous love of knowledge, and the devout submission to Revealed Truth; the domestic affections so tender,
so dutiful, and so self-sacrificing, the friendships so faithful
and so unexacting. For her great things and little lived on
together through the fidelity of a heart that seemed never
to forget. I never walk beside the Greta or the Derwent
without hearing her describe the flowers she had gathered
on their margin in her early girlhood. For her they
seemed to preserve their fragrance, amid the din and the
smoke of the great metropolis."

To these high and discerning praises, any addition from
me would be indeed superfluous. Yet one word of con-

firmation may here find a place; it is this, that such as
Sara Coleridge appeared to sympathizing friends and
admiring strangers, such she was known to be, by those
who, as her children, lived with her in habits of daily
intimacy, and depended on her wholly for guidance, affection, and support. To such an one her memory is almost
a religion ; or, to speak more soberly as well as more
Christianly, it is prized not only out of love for herself, but
as a practical evidence of the truth of that Religion which
made her what she was.

CHAPTER I.

LETTERS TO HER ELDEST BROTHER, HARTLEY
COLERIDGE, AND TO MISS TREVENEN: 1833.

I.

Importance of indirect Influences in Education—Description of her Son at three years old—A Child's first effort at Recollection.

To HARTLEY COLERIDGE, Esq., Grasmere.

Hampstead 1833.—I THINK the present hard-working, over-busy, striving age, somewhat over-does the *positive* part of education, and forgets the efficacy of the negative. *Not* to make children irreligious by dosing them with religion unskilfully administered—*not* to make them self-important by charging them on no account to be conceited (which you used to complain of so bitterly)—*not* to make them busy-bodies and uncharitable by discussing the misdemeanours of all belonging to them, whom they ought to hold in reverence, in their hearing, giving them the fruit of the tree of ill knowledge (a fruit which both puffs up and imparts bitterness) before their stomachs have acquired firmness enough to receive it without injury (before the secretions of the mind are all settled, and such knowledge can subsist without disturbing the sweet juices of charity and humanity)—*not* to create disgust, or excite hypocrisy, by attempting to pour sensibility, generosity, and such other good qualities, which cannot be supplied from without, but must well up from within, by buckets full into their hearts, —*not* to cram them with knowledge which their minds are not mature enough to digest (such as Political Economy), the only result of which will be to make them little superficial coxcombs,—in short, to give nature elbow room, and not to put swathes on their minds, now we have left off lacing them upon their infant bodies, to trust more to happy influences, and less to direct tuition, not to defeat our own purpose by over-anxiety, and to recollect that the powers of education are even more limited than those of circumstances, that nature and God's blessing are above all things, and to arm ourselves against the disappointment that may attend our best directed and most earnest endeavours; all these considerations, I think, are treated too slightingly in the present day. Folks are all too busy to think; churches are built in a fortnight—but not quite such as our ancestors built. The only wonder is that there is so much childish innocence and nature left in the world. But, as an old nurse said, "O Lord, ma'am, it's not very easy to *kill a baby*," so I think it not very easy to spoil a child. Nature has a wonderful power of rejecting what does not suit her; and the harangue which is unfitted for juvenile hearts and understandings, often makes no impression upon either. How often does a child that was certainly to be ruined by mismanagement disappoint all the wise Jeremiahs, and turn out an amiable member of society!

You say you cannot bring before your mind's eye our little Herby. A mother is qualified to draw a child's portrait, if close study of the original be a qualification. High colouring may be allowed for. I will try to give you some notion of our child. He is too even a mixture of both father and mother to be strikingly like either; and this is the more natural as Henry and I have features less definite than our expressions. This may, perhaps, account for that flowing softness and more than childlike indefiniteness of outline which our boy's face presents: it is all colour and expression—such varying expression as consists with the sort of corporeal moulding which I have described; in which the vehicle is lost sight of, and the material of the

veil is obscured by the brightness of what shines through it—
not that pointed sort of fixed expression which seems more
mechanically formed by strong lines and angular features.
To be more particular, he has round eyes, and a round
nose, and round lips and cheeks; and he has deep blue
eyes, which vary from stone grey to skiey azure, according
to influences of light and shade; and yellowish light-brown
hair, and cheeks and lips rosy up to the very deepest,
brightest, tint of childish rosyhood.   He will not be a
handsome man, but he is a pretty representative of three
years old, as Derwent was a "representative baby," and
folks who put the glossy side of their opinions outermost
for the gratified eyes of mothers and nurses, and all that
large class with whom rosy cheeks are the beginning,
middle, and end of beauty, say enough to make me—as
vain as I am.   I don't pretend to any exemption from the
general lot of parental delusion; I mean that, like most
other parents, I see my child through an atmosphere which
illuminates, magnifies, and at the same time refines the
object to a degree that amounts to a delusion; at least,
unless we are aware that to other eyes it appears by the
light of common day only.   My father says that those who
love intensely see more clearly than indifferent persons;
they see minutenesses which escape other eyes; they see
"the very pulse of the machine."   Doubtless, but then,
don't they magnify by looking through the medium of their
partiality?   Don't they raise into undue relative importance by exclusive gazing—don't wishes and hopes, indulged
and   cherished long, turn into realities, as the rapt
astronomer gazed upon the stars, and mused on human
knowledge, and longed for magic power, till he believed
that he directed the sun's course and the sweet influences
of the Pleiades?

   To return to our son and heir; he is an impetuous,
vivacious child, and the softer moments of such are

particularly touching (so thinks the mother of a vehement urchin). I lately asked him the meaning of a word; he turned his rosy face to the window, and cast up the full blue eyes, which looked liquid in the light, in the short hush of childish contemplation. The innocent thoughtfulness, contrasted with his usual noisy mirth and rapidity, struck my fancy. I had never before seen him condescend to make an effort at recollection. The word usually passed from his lips like an arrow from a bow; and if not forthcoming instantly there was an absolute unconcern as to its fate in the region of memory. The necessity of brainracking is not among the number of his discoveries in the (to him) *new* world. All wears the freshness and the glory of a dream; and the stale, flat and unprofitable, and the *improbus labor*, and the sadness and despondency, are all behind that visionary haze which hides the dull reality, the mournful future of man's life. You may well suppose that I look on our darling boy with many fears—but "fortitude and patient cheer" must recall me from such "industrious folly;" and faith and piety must tell me that this is not to be his home for ever, and that the glories of this world are lent but to spiritualize us, to incite us to look upward; and that the trials which I dread for my darling are but part of his Maker's general scheme of goodness and wisdom.

II.

Mrs. Joanna Baillie—"An Old Age Serene and Bright"—Miss Martineau's Characters of Children—"A Little Knowledge" of Political Economy "a Dangerous Thing"—Comparison of Tasso, Dante, and Milton.

To Miss EMILY TREVENEN, Helston, Cornwall.

Hampstead, 1833.—Our great poetess, or rather the sensible, amiable old lady that *was* a great poetess thirty years ago, is still in full preservation as to health. Never did the flame of genius more thoroughly expire than in her

case; for though, as Lamb says, "Ancient Mariners,"
"Lyrical Ballads," and "Kehamas," are not written in the
grand climacteric, the authors of such flights of imagination generally give out sparkles of their ancient fires in
conversation; but Mrs. Joanna Baillie is, as Mr. Wordsworth observes, when quoting her non-feeling for Lycidas,
"dry and Scotchy:" learning she never possessed, and
some of her poetry, which I think was far above that of any
other woman, is the worse for a few specks of bad English;
but then her criticisms are so surprisingly narrow and
jejune, and show so slight an acquaintance with fine
literature in general. Yet if the authoress of "Plays on
the Passion" does not now write or talk like a poetess, she
looks like one, and is a piece of poetry in herself. Never
was old age more lovely and interesting; the face, the
dress, the quiet, subdued motions, the silver hair, the calm
in-looking eye, the pale, yet not unhealthy skin, all are in
harmony; this is winter with its own peculiar loveliness of
snows and paler sunshine; no forced flowers or fruits to
form an unnatural contrast with the general air of the
prospect.

I never could relish those wonderfully young-looking old
ladies that are frequently pointed out to our admiration,
and who look like girls at a little distance; so much the
greater your disappointment when you come close. Why
should an old person *look* young? ought such an one to *feel*
and *think* young? if not, how can the mind and person be
in harmony; how can there be the real grace and comeli-
ness which old age, as old age, may possess, though not
round cheeks and auburn ringlets?

Do you read Miss Martineau? How well she always
succeeds in her portraits of children, their simplicity and
partially developed feelings and actions; and what a pity
it is that, with all her knowledge of child nature, she should
try to persuade herself and others that political economy is

a fit and useful study for growing minds, and limited capabilities, a subject of all others requiring matured intellect and general information as its basis! This same political economy, which quickens the sale of her works now, will, I think, prove heavy ballast for a vessel that is to sail down the stream of time, as all agree that it is a dead weight upon the progress of her narratives, introducing the most absurd incongruities and improbabilities in regard to the dramatic propriety of character, and setting in arms against the interest of the story the political opinions of a great class of her readers. And she might have rivalled Miss Edgeworth! What a pity that she would stretch her genius on such a Procrustes bed! And then what practical benefit can such studies have for the mass of the people, for whom it seems that Miss Martineau intends her expositions? they are not like religion, which may and must mould the thoughts and acts of everyday life, the true spirit of which, therefore, cannot be too much studied and explained; but how can poor people help the corn-laws, except by sedition, and what pauper will refuse to marry, because his descendants may, hundreds of years hence (if hundreds of things don't happen to prevent it), help among millions of others to choke up the world? Who, in short, will listen to dry and doubtful themes, when passion calls? A smattering of Greek or Latin is, in my opinion, a harmless thing; nay, I think it useful and agreeable, just according to its extent; a little is good, more is better, if people are aware how short a way they have proceeded, and what length of road is before them, which they have more opportunity of seeing than those who have never set out. But a little learning is, indeed, a dangerous thing, when no part can be seen clearly without a view of the whole, and when knowledge, or fancied knowledge, is sure to incite to practice. . . .

I admire the elegant and classical Tasso, but cannot

E

agree with those who call him the great poet of Italy. He
borrowed from the ancients, not, as Milton did, to melt down
the foreign with the original ore of his own mind, and to
form out of the mass a new creation wholly his own in
shape and substance, and in its effect on the minds of
others. It appears to me that he only produced a vigorous
and highly-wrought imitation of former copies, into which
he combined many new materials, but the frame and body
of which was not original. Dante's was the master-mind
that wrought, like Homer and Milton, for itself from the
beginning, and which influenced the poetry of Italy for
ages.

III.

Characteristics of English Scenery—Somerset, Yorkshire, Devon,
Derbyshire, and the Lakes—Visit of H. N. Coleridge to Mr.
Poole at Nether Stowey.

To Miss E. TREVENEN, Helston, Cornwall.

Hampstead, October, 1833.—Henry agrees with me in
thinking the Somerset landscape the ideal of *rurality,* where
nature is attired in amenity rather than in grandeur. The
North of England is more picturesque; you are there
ever thinking of what might be represented on canvas;
parts of Yorkshire are far more romantic, especially in the
mellowing lights and hues of autumn, when its old ruins
and red and yellow trees and foaming streams bring you
into communion with the genius of Scott; Derbyshire is
lovely and picturesque, but to me it is unsatisfactory, as
mimicking, on too small a scale, a finer thing of the
same sort. Dovedale may have a character of its own;
I understand it is more pastoral than the English Lake-
land, yet with a portion of its wilder beauty, but Matlock
struck me as a fragrant of Borodale, without the fine
imaginative distance. Devon is a noble county, but less
distinctly charactered, I think, than the sister one; it

displays specimens of variously-featured landscapes, here
the river-scenery of Scotland, there a smiling meadow-land;
in one place reminding you of the North of England, in
another a wild desolate moor, or fine sea-view peculiar to
itself; still, in the general face of the country I have felt
that there was the want of individuality and a due proportion of the various features of the scene;—in many
parts the trees, though superb specimens in themselves,
domineer, in their giant multitude, too exclusively over
the land, and prevent the eye from taking in a prospect
where the perfection of parts is subservient to the soul-
entrancing effect of the whole. Devonshire has sometimes
struck me as the workshop of nature, where materials of
the noblest kind and magnitude are heaped together. The
only defect, Henry says, in Somersetshire, is the fewness
and unclearness of the streams. With Nether Stowey he
was especially delighted; it is indeed an epitome of the
beauties of the county; he was much interested with the
marked original character, and gratified by the attentions of
his host, our old friend Mr. Poole; he visited my father's
tiny cottage, where my brother Hartley trotted and
prattled, and where my unknown baby brother Berkeley, a
beautiful infant, was born; the pleasant reminiscences of
my father's abode in the village gave Henry much pleasure.

CHAPTER II.

LETTERS TO HER HUSBAND AND MISS TREVENEN :
1834.

I.

Mrs. Hannah More—Girlish view of her literary pretensions confirmed by maturer judgment—A group of Authoresses—Remarks
on Jane Austen's novels by the Lake Poets—Hannah More's
celebrity accounted for—Letters of Walpole and Mrs. Barbauld—
Love of gossip in the reading Public.

To Miss E. TREVENEN, Helston, Cornwall.

Hampstead, August, 1834.—You speak of Mrs. Hannah
More. I have seen abundant extracts from her " Remains,"
and I think I could not read them through if I were to meet
with them. I fear you will think I want a duly disciplined
mind, when I confess that her writings are not to my taste.
I remember once disputing on this subject with a young
chaplain, who affirmed that Mrs. Hannah More was the
greatest female writer of the age. "Whom," he asked, " did
I think superior ? " I mentioned a score of authoresses
whose names my opponent had never even heard before.
I should not now dispute doggedly with a divine in a stage
coach, but years of discretion have not made me alter the
opinion I then not very discreetly expressed, of the dispro-
portion between Mrs. More's celebrity and her literary
genius, as compared with that of many other female writers
whose fame has not extended to the Asiatic Islands. I
cannot see in her productions aught comparable to the
imaginative vigour of Mrs. J. Baillie, the eloquence and
(for a woman) the profundity of Madame de Stael, the
brilliancy of Mrs. Hemans (though I think *her* over-rated),

the pleasant broad comedy of Miss Burney and Miss Ferrier, the melancholy tenderness of Miss Bowles, the pathos of Inchbald and Opie, the masterly sketching of Miss Edgeworth (who, like Hogarth, paints manners as they grow out of morals, and not merely as they are modified and tinctured by fashion) ; the strong and touching, but sometimes coarse pictures of Miss Martineau, who has some highly interesting sketches of childhood in humble life ; and last not least, the delicate mirth, the gently-hinted satire, the feminine decorous humour of Jane Austen, who, if not the greatest, is surely the most faultless of female novelists. My Uncle Southey and my father had an equally high opinion of her merits, but Mr. Wordsworth used to say that though he admitted that her novels were an admirable copy of life, he could not be interested in productions of that kind ; unless the truth of nature were presented to him clarified, as it were, by the pervading light of imagination, it had scarce any attractions in his eyes ; and for this reason, he took little pleasure in the writings of Crabbe. My Uncle Southey often spoke in high terms of " Castle Rackrent ; " he thought it a work of true genius. Miss Austen's works are essentially feminine, but the best part of Miss Edgeworth's seem as if they had been written by a man. " Castle Rackrent " contains genuine humour, a thing very rare in the writings of women, and not much relished by our sex in general. "Belinda " contains much that is powerful, interspersed, like the fine parts of Scotland, with tracts of dreary insipidity; and what is good in this work I cannot think of so high an order as the good things in " Castle Rackrent" and "Emma." I have been led to think that the exhibition of disease and bodily torture is ﹝but a coarse art to " freeze the blood." Indeed, you will acquit me of any affected pretence to originality of criticism, when you recollect how early my mind was biassed by the strong talkers I was in the habit of listening to. The spirit of what I sport on critical matters, though not always the application, is generally derived from the sources that you wot of. Yet I know well that we should not go by authority without finding out a reason for our faith; and unless we test the opinions learned from others with those of the world in general, we are apt to hold them in an incorrect, and, at the same time, a more strong and unqualified way than those do from whom we have derived them.

Though I think with the *Spectator*, etc., that Mrs. More's very great notoriety was more the work of circumstances, and the popular turn of her mind, than owing to a strong original genius, I am far from thinking her an *ordinary* woman. She must have had great energy of character and a sprightly versatile mind, which did not originate much, but which readily caught the spirit of the day, and reflected all the phases of opinion in the pious and well-disposed portion of society, in a clear and lively manner. To read Mrs. More's new book was a sort of good work, which made the reader feel satisfied with him or her self when performed; and it is agreeable to have one's very own opinions presented to one in handsome language, and placed in a highly respectable point of view. Then Mrs. More entered the field when there were few to make a figure there beside, and she was set agoing by Garrick and Johnson. Garrick, who pleased all the world, said that the world ought to be pleased with her: and Johnson, the Great Mogul of literature, was gracious to a pretender whose highest ambition was to follow him at a humble distance. He would have sneered to death a writer of far subtler intellect, and more excursive imagination, who dared to deviate from the track to which he pronounced good sense to be confined. He even sneered a little at his dear pet, Fanny Burney; *she* had set up shop for herself, to use a vulgarism; she had ventured to be original. I must add that Mrs. More's steady devotion to the cause of piety and good morals added the stamp of respectability to her works, which was a deserved passport to their reception; though such a passport cannot enable any production to keep its hold on the general mind if it is not characterized by power as well as good intention.

I admired some of Walpole's Letters in this publication, and I read a flattering one from Mrs. Barbauld, who was a very acute-minded woman herself. Some of her Essays are very clever indeed. I like Mrs. More's style,—so neat and sprightly. The Letters seem to contain a great deal of anecdote, the rage of the reading public, but that is an article which I am not particularly fond of.

II.

Dryden and Chaucer.

To her Husband.

Hampstead, September, 1834.—Dryden's fables are certainly an ideal of the rapid, compressed manner. Each line packs as much meaning as possible. But Dryden's imagination was fertile and energetic rather than grand or subtle; and he is more deficient in tenderness than any poet of his capacity that I am acquainted with. His English style is animated and decorous, full of picture-words, but too progressive for elaborate metaphors.

In " Palamon and Arcite " there is all Dryden's energy and richness; but you feel in such a subject his want of tenderness and romance. He seems ever playing with his subject, and almost ready to turn the lover's devotion, and the conquering Emily herself, into a jest. The sly satire of Chaucer suited his genius; but there is a simple pathos at times in the old writer which is alien to Dryden's mind. Chaucer jested upon women like a laughing philosopher; Dryden like a disappointed husband.

III.

Cruelty.

To the Same.

Hampstead, September, 1834.—Man is lord of the creation, yet his is not an absolute monarchy. There are limitations which the demands of his own heart, rather than their rights, insist upon; but they are not very easily defined, and the line between use and abuse has never yet been strictly drawn. To take an abstract pleasure in sorrow of the meanest thing that feels is the mark of a degraded nature—to indulge in such a pleasure is to degrade it wilfully; but how far may we justifiably consult our pleasure or our pride, regardless of such suffering? Falconry and hare-hunting have their apologists among the refined and reflective, as well as angling and shooting, which indeed occasion less protracted misery. Bird-nesting has not been defended, because peasant boys care not to defend themselves from imputations on their sensibility. All perceive that it is unworthy of a reasonable creature to inflict pain by way of venting irritated feelings; but how far we may make it matter of amusement, or at least connect amusement with it, the conscience does not so readily determine. The contemplation of suffering for itself alone is, in very rare instances, I believe, the source of gratification. Cruelty is said to be natural, because children tease and kill living creatures, but in the same breath you are told that they do it out of ignorance, which no doubt is united with a pleasing sense of power. No; I believe that positive cruelty is a mark of the utmost corruption of our sin-prone nature, and, as in Nero and Domitian, the result of sophistication. Even boys that torture a mouse or a hedgehog are not delighted, I should think, with the pain of the animal—they do not image that very distinctly, but are amused with observing its conduct under those trying circumstances. In this case the sensibilities are dormant, or, put it at the worst, they are naturally torpid or obtuse, not excited and demonized, as in some extraordinary cases, where a hard and turbulent nature has been stimulated and trained by very peculiar circumstances. I think we may say that the more the excitement of any sport with animals proceeds from the exhibition of suffering, and the more inconsiderable are the benefit and pleasure arising collaterally in proportion to the suffering occasioned, the more it may be reprobated as cruel and degrading.

IV.

The Drama and the Epic.

To the Same.

Hampstead, September, 1834.—In a Drama the event is to display character; in an Epic the characters are to carry on the event. Drama is biography, the Epic history. Lear, Othello, are the subjects of those dramas, the Loss of Eden, the destruction of Priam's power and domestic blessing by the anger of Achilles, those of Milton's and Homer's poems. In an Epic, only such a diversity of characters as the event would naturally assemble, and such qualities in the hero as would bring about the event, are essential to the conception of this sort of poem. In the Drama characters are chosen for the subject, because their qualities are interesting and remarkable; and the proof of this is their bringing about particular events, or showing a certain line of conduct in peculiar circumstances. The Epic would be retarded by the exhibition of passion in all its stages, such as we have in Othello; it would be out of proportion, and would engross the whole attention from the general narrative.

V.

Miss Herschel.

To the Same.

Mrs. J—— says that Caroline Herschel, sister of the late Dr. Herschel, is a person of uncommon attainments and abilities, and is a Fellow of the Royal Society. She is now eighty-four; her letters from Berlin, where she resides, are full of vigour and spirit. She says:—" My brother and I have sometimes stood out star-gazing till two o'clock, and have been told next day that, the night before, our neighbour's pigs had died of the frost."

———

Hard Words in the Latin Grammar useful to young Learners.

Those odd words, *Genitive, Vocative, Præterpluperfect,* etc., are helps to the memory. They have a quaint uniform of their own, and are something like one another, but unlike all other things.

———

Geography made Easy.

How much knowledge may be put into a child, by good economy of instruction, without employing his mind more than is perfectly wholesome! To Herby the map is a sort of game, and one that contains far more variety than any play that could be devised. To find out Sumatra or Owhyhee, to trace the Ganges, and follow the Equator in every different map, is a supreme amusement; and the notions of hot and cold, wet and dry, icy seas and towering palm-trees, with water dashing, and tigers roaming, and butterflies flitting, and his going and seeing them, and getting into tossing boats, and climbing by slow degrees up the steep mountain, are occupying his little mind, and give a zest to the whole affair. And then there is the pleasure of preaching it all over again to Nurse!

Right Opinions must be held in the right Spirit.

It is a fortunate thing to be induced by any circumstances to adopt the most edifying opinions, whichever they may be ; but of still more consequence is the manner in which we hold and maintain them. Indeed, even in the most vital considerations, the *manner of holding it* is almost more than the speculative, abstract creed. I never can forget that the most (apparently) Christian-spirited creature I ever knew was a Unitarian.

CHAPTER III.

LETTERS TO HER HUSBAND AND TO MRS. PLUMMER :
1834.

I.

Note on Enthusiasm—Mischievous effect of wrong Names given to
Moral Qualities.

To her Husband.

1834.—My mind misgives me about some notelets that I
have pencilled in J——'s " Journal of Art." Most of them
are about facts in Natural History ; but one is on the use of
the word "Enthusiasm." Knapp says, "he must disclaim
the epithet *Enthusiastic.* His is not an ecstasy that glows,
fades, and expires, but a calm, deep-rooted conviction, etc."
I have said—"Must Enthusiasm expire? That of Linnæus
survived through pain and weakness. Neither can I
think that enthusiasm precludes calmness and rationality.
That ardour which does so is fanaticism. But the enthusiasm of great minds is a steady heat, and though
opposite, not contrary, to sobriety, as generosity is opposed
to prudence, not exclusive of it. Enthusiasm with some
persons is a synonym for extravagance. But how otherwise can we designate that habit of mind which impels to
the most arduous and persistent efforts in pursuit of what
must be its own reward, and the object of an abstract
devotion? and was not this the primary meaning of enthusiasm?" I do think that words from being used
in a half wrong, or wholly wrong sense, reflect upon the
things originally signified a portion of that misappre-
hension. The word enthusiasm is taken for extravagance,
and thus *genuine* enthusiasm is looked upon as in some

sort extravagant. Over-strict religionists are called *serious*, till undistinguishing worldlings connect superstition or spiritual self-deception with staid reflective piety. Persons of warm fancy and weak judgment are called *romantic*, through which an elevated spiritual temper, and imaginative mode of viewing subjects and objects is deemed inseparable from a certain degree of self-delusion and want of skill in the executive government of daily life; and people will not perceive that true poetry is truth, and that fiction conveys reality, because both have been falsified and made false to their proper aim; the vehicle itself, and the thing to be conveyed, being both corrupted.

romantic: wang?

II.

Cowper's "Iliad and Odyssey"—Requisites for a successful Translation of Homer.

To the Same.

1834.—I hate Cowper's slow, dry, blank verse, so utterly alien to the spirit of the poem, and the minstrel mode of delivery. How could it have suited any kind of recitative or melody, or the accompaniment of any music? It is like a pursy, pompous, but unpolished man moving laboriously in a stiff dress of office. Those boar and lion-hunting similes, describing swift motion, are dreadfully dragging in this sort of verse. In Milton there is little of this rapidity and flash to be conveyed. How meditative are the speeches of the fallen host! We feel conscious of the scope of the poem—that they have ages of time before them to work in, that they are not planning a scheme to be executed in days, or weeks, or months. In Homer the time of action seems to be the life of individual men, and all is measured according to this scale. In Milton we are reading of superhuman agencies, of times with which day, month, or year had nothing to do.

The only sort of translation of Homer, I think, which

would be thoroughly gratifying, should be on Pope's plan, but better executed. There should be his brilliance and rapidity,—or rather that of Dryden's in the Fables,—with that thorough understanding of the spirit and properties of the whole poem which would enable the translator (he being a person of some poetical genius) to give substitutes for the exact physical meaning of certain passages, yet to preserve the spirit and to maintain the rich flow of verse, and keep the genius of the language unviolated, at the same time that he transported us to ancient times and distant places. Cowper's poetry is like a Camera Lucida portrait,—far more unlike in expression and general result than one less closely copied as to lines and features. In a different material there must be a different form to give a similar effect.

III.

Quiet Conclusion of " Paradise Lost," and of the Part of Shylock in the " Merchant of Venice "—Silence of Revenge ; Eloquence of Love and Grief and Indignation.

To the Same.

Hampstead, October, 1834.—I think the concluding verses of " Paradise Lost " are truly sublime. There is an awful beauty about them :

> The cherubim descended ; on the ground,
> Gliding meteorous, as evening mist
> Risen from a river o'er the marish glides,
> And *gathers ground* fast at the labourer's heel,
> Homeward returning."

How skilfully are the points of likeness here just pointed at, and then the image is abandoned, just when it has done its work, and attention is drawn off to a new one ; the flaming sword of God, the comet, the Libyan sands. Then the pathetic gentle-heartedness of the angel, hastening, yet leading them away ; and they looking back once more saw their " once happy seat " waved over by that threat-

ening hand; and then the few sad, subdued lines, so like
human life and its submission, with a sort of sad effort
after reparation, to an inevitable calamity. Just so quietly
does Shylock go off the scene: "I am not very well,
I would go home." It is remarkable how devoid all
Shylock's language is of exaggeration. There is no am-
plifying, no playing with the subject, and waving it up
and down like a streamer to catch different lights and display itself in various fantastic attitudes, as Shakespeare's
lovers expatiate and add stroke after stroke to the picture
of their possessed fancy. Shylock's passion of revenge is
expressed, according to the view in my father's preface,
by a bare, keen reiteration of certain matters of fact; he
seems to shrink and double himself up like a crouching
tiger, in order to shoot out all his energies when let loose
upon their prey; when the moment patiently waited for
arrives, he thrusts forth his cutting blade in the face of
his enemy—you did thus and thus—see, you fool, what
you imagined of me, and what I have made you. It is
these sharp contrasts of neither more nor less than the
actual facts, which constitute all his oratory, and all his
feelings of hatred are shown by hugging the reality with
a fierce intensity, saying the very thing which was in every
part of his heart over and over again. Indignation that
breathes scorn, and believes deeply in the wrongfulness of
the offender, but is not transfigured into malice; strong
grief that has not collapsed into despair, are almost as
expatiative as love; "O that I were a mockery-king of
snow, to melt before the sun of Bolingbroke," is the language of a wandering fancy. And the Scriptures are full
of such illustrations of sorrowfulness; for grief rushes out
eager for a vent, and roams forth, seeking for employment,
for a change from the intolerable misery of passiveness.
Anger will talk much and strongly, but not so fancifully
as love and grief; it stems the fancy by its violence, and

those passions which, like revenge, impel to action, employ
the energies in another way. As a watery mirror shaken
by the wind presents only the confused fragments of a
picture, the mind agitated by vehement anger reflects no
continuous imagery, like sorrow, which is still and meditative. Yet there is a sort of sullen resentment, which
seems to stupify the soul, and a scorn which is unutterable;
it fears to be dissipated in words, and imparts an energy
which facilitates restraint. Scorn argues self-possession;
a man in a passion cannot scorn.

IV.

On the Death of Samuel Taylor Coleridge *—Details of his last
Illness—His Will, Letters, and Literary Remains—Respect and
Affection felt for him by those with whom he lived—Probable
Influence of his Writings on the Course of Religious Thought—
Remarks on his Genius and Character by different Critics—His
last Readings and Notes.

To Mrs. PLUMMER.

Hampstead, Oct. 1834.—My dearest L., Your affectionate
and interesting letter gave me great pleasure, and gratified
my feelings in regard to my dear father, whose memory
still occupies the chief place in my thoughts. Your appreciation of his character and genius, my dear friend, would
endear you to me were there no other ties between us. In
his death we mourn not only the removal of one closely
united to us by nature and intimacy, but the extinction of a
light which made earth more spiritual, and heaven in some
sort more visible to our apprehension. You know how long
and severely he suffered in his health; yet, to the last, he
appeared to have such high intellectual gratifications that
we felt little impulse to pray for his immediate release;
and though his infirmities had been grievously increasing of
late years, the life and vigour of his mind were so great

* At Mr. Gillman's house, the Grove, Highgate, on the 25th of July, 1834.
—E. C.

body vs. mind

that they hardly led those around him to think of his dissolution. His frail house of clay was so illumined that its decaying condition was the less perceptible. His departure after all seemed to come suddenly upon us. We were first informed of his danger on Sunday, the 20th of July, and on Friday, the 25th, he was taken from us. For several days after fatal symptoms appeared, his pains were very great; they were chiefly in the region of the bowels, but were at last subdued by means of laudanum, administered in different ways; and for the last thirty-six hours of his existence he did not suffer severely. When he knew that his time was come, he said that he hoped by the manner of his death to testify the sincerity of his faith; and hoped that all who had heard of his name would know that he died in that of the English Church. Henry saw him for the last time on Sunday, and conveyed his blessing to my mother and myself; but we made no attempt to see him, and my brothers were not sent for, because the medical men apprehended that the agitation of such interviews would be more than he ought to encounter. Not many hours before his death he was raised in his bed and wrote a precious faintly-scrawled scrap, which we shall ever preserve, recommending his faithful nurse, Harriet, to the care of his family. Mr. Green, who had so long been the partner of his literary labours, was with him at the last, and to him, on the last evening of his life, he repeated a certain part of his religious philosophy, which he was especially anxious to have accurately recorded. He articulated with the utmost difficulty, but his mind was clear and powerful, and so continued till he fell into a state of coma, which lasted till he ceased to breathe, about six o'clock in the morning. His body was opened, according to his own earnest request—the causes of his death were sufficiently manifest in the state of the vital parts; but that internal pain from which he suffered more or less during his whole

body

life was not to be explained, or only by that which medical men call nervous sympathy. A few out of his many deeply attached and revering friends attended his remains to the grave, together with my husband and Edward;* and that body which did him such " grievous wrong " was laid in its final resting-place in Highgate churchyard. His executor, Mr. Green, after the ceremony, read aloud his will, and was greatly overcome in performing his task. It is indeed a most affecting document. What little he had to bequeath (a policy of assurance worth about £2560) is my mother's for life, of course, and will come to her children equally after her time. Mr. Green has the sole power over my father's literary remains, and the philosophical part he will himself prepare for publication; some theological treatises he has placed in the hands of Mr. Julius Hare, of Cambridge, and his curate, Mr. Sterling (both men of great ability). Henry will arrange literary and critical pieces— notes on the margins of books, or any miscellaneous pro- ductions of that kind that may be met with among his MSS., and probably some letters will appear if they can be collected. I fear there will be some difficulty in this; but I have understood that many written by him at different times exhibit his peculiar power of thought and expression, and ought not to be lost to the world if they could be recovered. No man has been more deeply beloved than my dear father; the servants at the Grove wept for him as for a father, and Mr. and Mrs. Gillman speak of their loss as the heaviest trial that has ever befallen them, though they have had their full share of sorrow and suffering. Mrs. Gillman's notes, written since his death, are precious testimonies to me of his worth and attaching qualities. In one of them she speaks of " the influence of his beautiful nature on our domestics, so often set down by friends or neighbours to my good management, his forgiving nature,

---

* The Rev. Edward Coleridge, his nephew.—E. C.

his heavenly-mindedness, his care not to give offence unless
duty called on him to tell home truth; his sweet and cheerful temper, and so many moral qualities of more or less
value, and all adorned by his Christian principles. His
was indeed Christianity. To do good was his anxious
desire, his constant prayer — and all with such *real*
humility—never any kind of worldly accommodating the
truth to any one—yet not harsh or severe—never pretending to faults or failings he had not, nor denying those he
thought he had! But, as he himself said of a dear friend's
death, ' it is recovery, and *not death*. Blessed are they that
sleep in the Lord—his life is hidden in Christ. In his
Redeemer's life it is hidden, and in His glory will it be
disclosed. Physiologists hold that it is during sleep chiefly
that we grow; what may we not hope of such a sleep in
such a Bosom?'" Much more have I had from her, and
formerly heard from her lips, all in the same strain; and
during my poor dear father's last sufferings she sent a note
to his room, expressing with fervency the blessings that he
had conferred upon her and hers, and what a happiness
and a benefit his residence under her roof had been to all
his fellow-inmates. The letters which I have seen of
many of his friends respecting his lamented departure have
been most ardent; but these testimonies from those who
had him daily, hourly, in their sight, and the deep love and
reverence expressed by Mr. Green, who knew him so
intimately, are especially dear to my heart. My dear
Henry, too, was deeply sensible of his good as well as his
great qualities; it was not for his genius only that he
reverenced him, and it has been one of many blessings
attendant on my marriage, that by it we were both drawn
into closer communion with that gifted spirit than could
otherwise have been the case. There was everything in the
circumstances of his death to soothe our grief, and valuable
testimonies (such as I have mentioned, with many, many

others) from valued persons have mingled their sweetness in the cup.

We feel happy, too, in the conviction that his writings will be widely influential for good purposes. All his views may not be adopted, and the effect of his posthumous works must be impaired by their fragmentary condition; but I think there is reason to believe that what he has left behind him will introduce a new and more improving mode of thinking, and teach men to consider some subjects on principles more accordant to reason, and to place them on a surer and wider basis than has been done hitherto. It is not to be expected that speculations which demand so much effort of mind and such continuous attention, to be fully understood, can ever be *immediately* popular,—the written works of master spirits are not perused by the bulk of society whose feelings they tincture, and whose belief they contribute to form and modify,—it is through intervening channels that " sublime truths, and the maxims of a pure morality," are diffused among persons of various age, station, and capacity, so that they become " the hereditary property of poverty and childhood, of the workshop and the hovel." Heraud, in his brilliant oration on the death of my father, delivered at the Russell Institution, observes that religion and philosophy were first reconciled—first brought into permanent and indissoluble union in the divine works of Coleridge; and I believe the opinion expressed by this gentleman, that my father's metaphysical theology will prove a benefit to the world, is shared by many persons of refined and searching intellect both in this country and in America, where he has some enthusiastic admirers; and it is confidently predicted by numbers that this will be more and more felt and acknowledged in course of time. My dear L——, I will not apologize to you for this filial strain; I write unreservedly to you, knowing that you are alive to my father's merits as a philosopher and a poet, and believing that you will be pleased to find that he who was misunderstood and misrepresented by many, and grossly calumniated by some, was and is held in high honour as to moral as well as intellectual qualities by good and intelligent persons. "Hereafter," says a writer in *Blackwood*, "it will be made appear that he who was so admirable a poet was also one of the most amiable of men." The periodicals have been putting out a great many attempts at accounts of his life—meagre enough for the most part, and all more or less incorrect as to facts. We have been very much hurt with our former friend, Mr. De Quincey, the Opium Eater as he chooses to be styled, for publishing so many personal details respecting my parents in *Tait's Magazine*. As Henry says, "the little finger of retaliation would bruise his head;" but I would not have so good a Christian as my father defended by any measure so unchristianlike as retaliation, nor would I have those belonging to me condescend to bandy personalities. This, however, was never intended by my spouse; but I believe he has some intention of reckoning with the scandal-monger for the honour of those near and dear to us. Some of our other friends will be as much offended with this paper of his as we are. He has characterized my father's genius and peculiar mode of discourse with great eloquence and discrimination. He speaks of him as possessing "the most spacious intellect, the subtlest and most comprehensive" (in his judgment) that ever existed amongst men. Whatever may be decided by the world in general upon this point, it is one which, from learning and ability, he is well qualified to discuss. I cannot believe that he had any enmity to my father, indeed he often speaks of his kindness of heart; but "the dismal degradation of pecuniary embarrassments," as he himself expresses it, has induced him to supply the depraved craving of the public for personality, which his talents would have enabled him in some measure to correct.

My next letter, my dear L., shall be of a more lightsome and general nature, but this is dedicated to my dear father's memory; and I could say much more on that subject if I had more strength and more paper, and were not afraid of wearying even you, who are a reader and lover of his works. When Mr. Poole, of Nether Stowey, received his copy of the will, in which his name was affectionately mentioned, he read it aloud to his niece, Mrs. Sandford, who expressed her admiration with tears in her eyes. One of the last books that my dear father ever perused is the " Memoir and Diary of Bishop Sandford," which he greatly approved; some notes pencilled on the margin are among the last sentences he wrote.

V.

Attachment of Mr. Wordsworth to the Church of England.

To the Same.

Hampstead, 1834.—I am always hoping, my dear L——, that the chances of life—happy ones, I trust, in your case —will bring you to reside in the south. Of livings—of anything connected with our dear, excellent, venerable Church Establishment, I hardly dare to speak. I really shudder as I turn over the menacing pages of the *Spectator*, and that organ of destructiveness, *Tait's Magazine*. How well do I remember Mr. Wordsworth, with one leg upon the stair, delaying his ascent till he had uttered, with an emphasis which seemed to proceed from the very profoundest recesses of his soul—" I would lay down my LIFE for the Church !" This was the conclusion of a long and eloquent harangue upon that interesting subject.

CHAPTER IV.

LETTERS TO HER HUSBAND, MRS. PLUMMER, AND MRS. HENRY M. JONES : 1835.

I.

Education—Cramming—Deaths of Charles Lamb and Edward Irving.

To Mrs. PLUMMER.

Hampstead, 1835.—We have been much grieved lately by the death of our old friend Mr. Charles Lamb, of the India House. He was a man of amiable manners, and kind and liberal heart, and a rare genius. His writings exhibit a rare union of pathos and humour, which to me is truly delightful. Very interesting short memoirs of him have already appeared, and I see new editions of his works advertised. So soon after my father, whom, humanly speaking, he worshipped! Irving is also gone. He was one whose good and great parts my father saw in a strong light, and deeply did he lament the want of due balance in his mind, which ended in what may be almost called madness. Irving acknowledged that to my father, more than to any one, he owed his knowledge of " the truth as it is in Jesus."

II.

Union of Thought and Feeling in the Poetry of Wordsworth—The White Doe of Rylstone : lofty Moral of the Poem, and beauty of particular passages.

To Mrs. HENRY M. JONES, Heathlands, Hampstead.

Downshire Place, Hampstead, July, 1835.—We are expecting a new set of Mr. Wordsworth's poems, including the " Excursion ; " and I really think the murmuring river

Wharfe, the grey rocks, the dusky trees, and verdant sod, the ancient abbey, and the solitary Doe, " white as lily of June," will be pleasant subjects of contemplation in this hot, languid weather. The poetry of Wordsworth will give you at least as much fervour and tenderness as you will find in Byron or Hemans; and then, in addition, you will find in it a high philosophy, a strengthening and elevating spirit, which must have a salutary tendency for the mind.

Mr. Wordsworth opens to us a world of suffering, and no writer of the present day, in my opinion, has dealt more largely or more nobly with the deepest pathos and the most exquisite sentiment; but for every sorrow he presents an antidote; he shows us how man may endure, as well as what he is doomed to suffer. The poem of the " White Doe of Rylstone " is meant to exhibit the power of faith in upholding the most anguish-stricken soul through the severest trials, and the ultimate triumph of the spirit, even while the frail mortal body is giving way.

> " From fair to fairer, day by day
> A more divine and loftier way,
> Even such this blessed pilgrim trod,
> By sorrow lifted towards her God,
> Uplifted to the purest sky
> Of undisturbed mortality."
> —*White Doe*, Canto vii.

The first and last cantos are much superior in point of imaginative power to the others upon the whole; but the speech of Francis to his sisters in the second is beautiful. I remember that it was greatly admired by dear Hartley.

> " Hope nothing, if I thus may speak
> To thee, a woman, and thence weak :
> Hope nothing, I repeat, for we
> Are doomed to perish utterly.

> Forbear all wishes, all debate,
> All prayers for this cause, or for that,
>
> . . . . .
>
> Espouse thy fate at once, and cleave
> To fortitude without reprieve."
> —Canto ii.

The address of the father to Francis in the fifth canto is a favourite of mine.

> "Might this our enterprise * have sped,
> Change wide and deep the land had seen,
> A renovation from the dead,
> A spring-tide of immortal green.
> The darksome altars would have blazed
> Like stars when clouds are rolled away ;
> Salvation to all eyes that gazed,
> Once more the Rood had been upraised
> To spread its arms, and stand for aye ! "
> —Canto v.

III.

Charles Lamb, his Shyness and Tenderness—A lifelong Friendship.

To Mrs. H. M. JONES, Heathlands, Hampstead.

Hampstead, 1835.—I agree to your criticism on Lamb, and sympathize most entirely in your preference of field, and grove, and rivulet, to square, garden, street, and gutter. I always feel so particularly *in*secure in a street. Nevertheless I can quite understand Lamb's feeling. A man is more especially alone, very often, in a crowd. Nowhere can an individual be so isolated, so independent as in London. Nowhere else can he see so much and be himself so little observed. This I think is the " sweet security of streets " † which the eccentric old bachelor delighted in.

---

* The " enterprise " referred to was the " Rising of the North," in the 12th year of Elizabeth, 1569, under the Earls of Northumberland and Westmoreland, " to restore the ancient religion."—E. C.

† I care not to be carried with the tide that smoothly bears human life to eternity, and reluct at the inevitable course of destiny. I am in love with

And then he had been educated at Christ's Hospital, all
his boyish recreations, when life was new and *lifesome*, had
passed in streets, and we all know that the circumstances
of our childhood give the prevailing hue to our involuntary
tastes and feelings for the rest of our lives.   I cannot
picture to myself a Paradise without lakes and mountains.
Our poor friend was much affected by my father's death,*
and had a fanciful presentiment that he should not remain
long behind.   He must have remembered some interesting
remarks † connected with this subject in an old preface of
my father's, the preface to a volume containing united
poems of Coleridge and Lamb.

IV.

Spiders—their Webs and Ways.

To her Husband.

This day, 5th of October, I saw a large primrose-coloured
butterfly, which looked the very emblem of April or May.
Also I examined three or four spiders, and saw quite plainly
the spinnerets in their tails, and once I clearly perceived
the thread issuing from the apertures.   The thread of a

this green earth, the face of town and country, the unspeakable rural soli-
tudes, and the sweet security of streets. I would set up my tabernacle
here.—*Lamb's Essays.   New Year's Eve.*—E. C.

* Mr. Lamb's visit to Highgate, shortly after my grandfather's death, is
thus described by Judge Talfourd:—"There he asked leave to see the
nurse who had attended upon Coleridge ; and being struck and affected
by the feeling she manifested towards his friend, insisted on her receiving
five guineas from him—a gratuity which seemed almost incomprehensible
to the poor woman, but which Lamb could not help giving as an immediate expression of his own gratitude.   From her he learned the effort by
which Coleridge had suppressed the expression of his sufferings, and the
discovery affected him even more than the news of his death.   He would
startle his friends sometimes by suddenly exclaiming 'Coleridge is dead,'
and then pass on to common themes, having obtained the momentary
relief of oppressed spirits."—*Letters of Charles Lamb*, vol. ii. p. 304.—
E. C.

† The reference is probably to the Latin motto printed on the title-page
of the second edition of " Poems by Coleridge, Lamb, and Lloyd," which
appeared in May, 1797 :—*Duplex nobis vinculum, et amicitiæ, junctarumque
Camænarum ; quod utinam neque mors solvat ; neque temporis longinquitas.*
Charles Lamb died on the 27th of December, 1834, five months and two
days after the friend whom he loved so well.—E. C.

spider's net is composed of such a multitude of threadlets that it gives one a good notion of the infinite divisibility of matter. A spider, when examined, feigns death, and lies back with all his arms and legs closely pinioned to his sides, so that he shrinks up into as small a space as possible. In this condition he is a good symbol of some wretched slave, stupified and collapsed into stillness in the presence of a mighty one. I have often marvelled at the strength of a spider's web, which offers far more resistance to my finger, as I push and bend it, than a net made of silken threads of the same apparent substance would do. This firmness is procured by the multiplicity of threadlets of which every thread is composed, which circumstance also hastens the drying of the fluid gum, so great a surface being exposed to the air. While we compare natural objects or operations with artificial ones, we are so taken up with the likeness that we forget the difference. There is no other thing in art or nature similar to the spinning of spiders. Evelyn would watch spiders for five hours together.

spiders = extraordinary.

original spider   masc

vs.

dream spider.   fem

CHAPTER V.

LETTERS TO HER HUSBAND, MISS TREVENEN, AND MISS ARABELLA BROOKE: 1836.

I.

"The Boy and the Birds," and the "Story without an End"—
Defects of the latter as a Book for Children—A Critic's Foible.

To Miss EMILY TREVENEN.

Hampstead, August, 1836.—Both the children enjoy "The Boy and the Birds." As to the "Story without an End,"* I admire it, but think it quite unfit for juvenile readers. None but mature minds, well versed in the artificialities of sentimental literature, can understand the inner meanings of it; and I do not think it has that *body* of visual imagery and adventure which renders many a tale and allegory delightful to those who cannot follow the author's main drift. Bees, and flies, and leaves, and flowers are talked about, but not described, so as to give the child any clearer notion of them and their properties than he originally had, and all that is ascribed to them, all the sentiments put into their mouths, as one may say, are such as can breed naught but confusion in the juvenile brain. "*That child* is always asleep, or else dreaming," I overheard Herby say to himself, as he looked at the picture with an air of contempt. . . .

O reviews! if you yourselves were reviewed, how you might be cut up and exposed. A common fault of reviewers, and one which makes them desert good sense, is that they are so desirous to take a spick-and-span new view of any

* Translated by Mrs. Austin from the German of Carové.

debated point. They smell down two roads, and if both have been trodden before, they rush at once down the third, though it may lead to nothing, like a blind alley. So it is with the Edinburgh Reviewer; he perks up his nose, and tries to say some third thing, which never has been said before, and which is the worst thing of the three.

II.

"The *shaping* Spirit of Imagination"—Mrs. Hemans.

To her Husband.

Ilchester, Somerset, October 25, 1836.—Chemists say that the elementary principles of a diamond and of charcoal are the same; it is the action of the sun or some other power upon each that makes it what it is. Analogous to this are the products of the poet's mind: he does not *create* out of nothing, but his mind so acts on the things of the universe, material and immaterial, that each composition is in effect a new creation. Many of Mrs. Hemans' poems are not even in this sense creations; she takes a theme, and this she illustrates in fifty different ways, the verses being like so many wafers, the same thing in blue, green, red, yellow. She takes descriptions from books of natural history or travel, puts them into verse, and appends a sentiment or a moral, like the large red bead of a rosary at the end of several white ones. But all these materials have undergone no fusion in the crucible of imagination. We may recognize the author's hand by a certain style of selection and arrangement, as we might know a room furnished by Gillow or Jackson, according to the same rule; but there is no stamp of an individual mind on each separate article.

III.

"The Remains" *—Metaphysics like Alum.

To the Same.

Ilchester, November, 1836.—How delightful are the "Remains!" I quite grieve to find the pages on my left hand such a thick handful. One wants to have such a book to dip into constantly, and to go on reading such discussions on such principles and in such a spirit, on a thousand subjects·

It does not seem as if the writer was especially conversant with this or that, as Babbage with mechanics, and Mill with political economy ; but as if there was a subtle imaginative spirit to search and illustrate all subjects that interest humanity. Sir J. Mackintosh said that " S. T. C. trusted to his ingenuity to atone for his ignorance." But in such subjects as my father treats of, ingenuity is the best knowledge.

Like all my father's works, the "Remains" will be more sold at last than at first. Like alum, these metaphysical productions melt slowly into the medium of the public mind ; but when time has been given for the operation, they impregnate more strongly than a less dense and solid substance, which dissolves sooner, has power to do. Why ? Because the closely compacted particles are more numerous, and have more energy in themselves. By the public mind I mean persons capable of entertaining metaphysical discussions.

IV.

Abbott's "Corner-Stone," and other Religious Works—Comparison of Archbishop Whately with Dr. Arnold, in their mode of setting forth the Evidences of Christianity—Dr. Chalmers—The Greek Language.

To Miss Arabella Brooke.

Ilchester, November, 1836.— My dear Miss Brooke—

* Published now under the following titles :—Lectures on Shakespeare, etc. ; Notes on English Divines ; and Notes Theological, Political, etc.—E. C.

Though I am under orders to write to no one except my
husband and mother, or sister, I must thank you with
my own hand for thinking so affectionately of me in my
trouble,* as you evidently have done, and as I felt sure you
would do.

. . . .

Since I saw you, I have read with great attention, and
I humbly hope, not without profit, Abbott's "Young
Christian," "Corner-Stone," and "Way to do Good." In
a literary point of view these works are open to much
criticism, though their merits in that way may be considerable; and certainly, in several points, the author is
far from being what a sincere member of our Church can
call orthodox. For instance, his view of the Atonement
seems to me below the right standard; he dwells solely
on the effect produced in man, entirely leaving out of sight
the mysterious propitiation towards God; and his illustration of the "Lost Hat" strikes me as inadequate and presumptuous. But notwithstanding these exceptionable
points, and several others,—his very diffuse style, and a
frequent want of harmony between his expressions and the
deep reverential feelings which he aims to excite,—I think
very highly of Abbott, as an energetic, original, and fresh-
minded writer; and I think his works calculated to do
great good, by leading those who peruse them to scrutinize
their own spiritual state, and the momentous themes of
which he treats with zeal and fervour, if not always with
perfect judgment.

I wish I could put into your hand a book from which
I have derived great pleasure, Whately's "Essays on some
Difficulties in the Writings of St. Paul." The Archbishop
does not seem to be a profound, subtle, metaphysical writer,
neither does he aim at anything of the kind. What he

---

* A serious illness, which detained my mother for several weeks at
Ilchester on her way home from a visit in Devonshire.—E. C.

does aim at he seems to me to have well accomplished. He reasons clearly to particular points from a general view of Revelation, not from the nature of things in themselves ; and his style is vigorous, simple, and perspicuous. In this respect it resembles that of Dr. Arnold, but the latter does not so exclusively address the understanding ; he does more in the way of touching the heart, at the same time that (when party spirit is out of the question) he reasons forcibly and clearly, as far as I can judge, I mean.

The substance of what pleases you in Abercrombie,* I have lately read in Chalmers's Bridgewater Treatise ;† and, oh ! when the wordy Doctor does get hold of an argument, what a splutter does he make with it for dozens of pages. He is like a child with a new wax doll, he hugs it, kisses it, holds it up to be admired, makes its eyes open and shut, puts it on a pink gown, puts it on a blue gown, ties it on a yellow sash ; then pretends to take it to task, chatters at it, shakes it, and whips it ; tells it not to be so proud of its fine false ringlets, which can all be cut off in a minute, then takes it into favour again ; and at last, to the relief of all the company, puts it to bed.

I wish very much that some day or other you may have time to learn Greek, because that language is an *idea*. Even a little of it is like manure to the soil of the mind, and makes it bear finer flowers.—My dear A——, your truly affectionate friend,

SARA COLERIDGE.

---

* Inquiries concerning the Intellectual Powers and the Investigation of Truth.   By Dr. Abercrombie.—E. C.
† On the Adaptation of External Nature to the Moral and Intellectual Constitution of Man.   By the Rev. Dr. Thomas Chalmers.—E. C.

CHAPTER VI.

LETTERS TO HER HUSBAND, MISS TREVENEN,
MISS A. BROOKE : 1837.

I.

The English Beppoists.

To Miss E. TREVENEN.

10, *Chester Place*, 1837.—I cannot think that the English Beppoists have any authority among the Italians for their style. Ariosto conceived his subject to a certain degree lightly and sportively; and Pulci has a vein of satire; but these ingredients in them are interfused so as to form a *tertium aliquid*—not grape-juice and water, but *wine*. Their satire and their sentiment, their joke and their earnest, do not intersect each other in distinct streaks, like the stripes of red and blue in the Union Flag.

II.

"Phantasmion, a Romance of Fairyland "—Defence of Fairy Tales by Five Poets—" Mary and Florence," by Miss Tytler—" Newman's Sermons "—" Maurice's Letters to the Quakers."

To Miss ARABELLA BROOKE.

10, *Chester Place, Regent's Park, July* 29, 1837.—This little book* was chiefly written the winter before I last saw you, when I was more confined to my couch than I am now; and whether any friends agree with my husband (the most partial of them all) in thinking it worth publishing or no, they will attach some interest to the volume as a record of some of my recumbent amusements, and be glad to perceive that I often had out-of-door scenes before me in a lightsome, agreeable shape, at a time when I was almost

* Phantasmion.—E. C.

G

wholly confined to the house, and could view the face of nature only by very short glimpses.* It requires no great *face* to publish now-a-days; it is not stepping upon a stage where the eyes of an audience are upon you, but entering a crowd, where you must be very tall, strong, and striking indeed, to obtain the slightest attention. In these days, too, to print a Fairy Tale is the very way to be *not read*, but shoved aside with contempt. I wish, however, I were only as sure that *my* fairy tale is worth printing as I am that works of this class are wholesome food, by way of variety, for the childish mind. It is curious that on this point Sir Walter Scott, and Charles Lamb, my father, my Uncle Southey, and Mr. Wordsworth, were all agreed. Those names are not so great an authority to all people as they are to me; yet I think they might be set against that of Miss Edgeworth, powerfully as she was able to follow up her own view. Sir W. Scott made an exception in her favour, when he protested against the whole generation of moral tales, stories of naughty and good boys and girls, and how their parents, pastors, and masters did or ought to have managed them. It is not to be denied that such stories are exciting to children, and indeed spoil their taste utterly for works which have less of everyday life, though not less of truth, in them. But the grand secret of their sale seems to be that they interest the *buyers* of the books,

---

* L'ENVOY OF PHANTASMION.

Go, little book, and sing of love and beauty,
To tempt the worldling into fairy land;
Tell him that airy dreams are sacred duty,
Bring better wealth than aught his toils command,
    Toils fraught with mickle harm.

But if thou meet some spirit high and tender,
On blessed works and noblest love intent,
    Tell him that airy dreams of nature's splendour,
With graver thoughts and hallowed musings blent,
    Prove no too earthly charm.—S. C.

Written in a copy of Phantasmion about the year 1845.—E. C.

mamas and governesses, who see in such productions the history of their own experience, and the reflection of minds occupied with the same educational cares as their own. In this way, "Grave and Gay," by Miss Tytler, sister of the historian, was very interesting to me; but I would not put it into the hands of my children, excellent manual of divinity as it is thought by some. It is not in such scraps, nor with such a context, however pretty in its way, that I should like to present the sublime truths of Christianity to the youthful mind: "Florence put the cherry in her mouth, and was going to eat it all up," etc.,—just before or after extracts from the Sermon on the Mount or allusions to the third chapter of St. John's Gospel. The Bible itself, that is, the five Books of Moses, and the four Gospels, with a mother's living commentary, together with the Catechism and Liturgy, appear to me the best instruments for teaching the Christian religion to young children.

I have lately been reading, certainly with great interest, the sermons of John Henry Newman; and I trust they are likely to do great good, by placing in so strong a light as they do the indispensableness of an orthodox belief, the importance of sacraments as the main channels of Christian privileges, and the powers, gifts, and offices of Christian ministers derived by apostolical succession;—the insufficiency of personal piety without Catholic brotherhood—the sense that we are all members of one body, and subjects of one kingdom of Christ;—the danger of a constant craving for religious excitement, and the fatal mistake of trusting in any devotional thoughts and feelings, which are not immediately put into act, and do not shine through the goings on of our daily life. But then these exalted views are often supported, as I think, by unfair reasonings; and are connected with other notions which appear to me superstitious, unwarranted by any fair interpretation of Scripture, and containing the germs of Popish errors.

The letters of Maurice to the Quakers should be taken in conjunction with these discourses, to qualify them and keep the mind balanced. Maurice is a profound thinker, a vigorous though rough writer; and I trust you would not like him the worse for sharing my father's spirit. His divinity seems based on the Aids to Reflection, and though no servile imitator, he has certainly borrowed his mode of writing and turn of thought very much from S. T. C.

III.

Definition of "Force" and "Liveliness" in Poetry—The Homeric Mythology not Allegorical—Symbolical Character of the Imagery of Milton and Wordsworth—Originality of Virgil.

To her Husband.

Sept. 13*th*, 1837.—In regard to *force* and *liveliness*, may we not call the latter one mode of the former, rather than a separate property? Scott's poems afford samples of lively force, but they contain little of that force which seizes the imagination and obliges it to contemplate fixedly something spiritual, which has nothing in it of a corporeal life. The "Leech Gatherer" is a poem which is forcible but solemn; it arrests and fixes the mind, instead of hurrying or leading it on. Yet the illustrations of this poem are as lively as the main design is far removed from bodily attributes. The stone is absolutely endued with motion by the comparison with a sea-monster that had crept out upon the shore to sun himself. Liveliness expresses the motion, the action of life, that by which life is manifested. When the lively is also sublime, as the "Battle of the Gods," we do not apply to the mixed effect the term of a quality which so generally describes the less exalted movements and acts of life; but Homer's force, as you have observed, always consists of liveliness. In him there is no force like that of Dante, Milton, Wordsworth, Schiller, Coleridge, where lively metaphors and life-

like images are but to adorn or partly represent the various
realities of abstract being. Their force results from the
thing signified, together with the outward symbol, from the
union and mutual fitness of the two. Philosophers may
fancy that the Grecian mythology was allegorical, but the
force of Homer is not derived at all from those inner signi-
fications. His divine and human battling is sublime, from
being vast, fearful, and indistinct. It is *animated*, full of
animal motion; it is a picture that strikes and pleases in
and for itself alone; it is conceived and executed with all
the power of mature genius, inspired by the circumstances,
the wants, desires, hopes, lives of a peculiar state of human
life, a state which precluded contemplation, and demanded
action. Compare Homer's poetry with Milton's first books
of " Paradise Lost." With what does the latter possess
our minds ? "With greatness fallen, and the excess of
glory obscured." It is the *force* with which this subject is
made to engross our contemplations, to tinge the whole of
that dark fiery region and those prostrate angel warriors
with an awful sadness, the aptness of that region so
described to shadow out eternal bale, of those vast and
dimly lustrous images to represent the warring evils of our
spiritual part, this it is which constitutes the peculiar perfection of that grand product of imagination. In this it is
essentially different from Homer, life and progression are
not its characterizing spirit. They are represented by the
older poet with the greatest conceivable truth and power,
and Milton availed himself of that prototype in the embodying of his conceptions. He imitated Homer in as far
as he trode the same ground with him, but the main scope
of his poem was an aboriginal of his own intellect. In
regard to Virgil, whom Dryden rather unfairly, as I think,
contrasts with Homer, it appears to me that he has been
rather misappreciated by being constantly looked at in his
aspect of an imitator, and that his having cast his poem

in a ready-made mould, has prevented most critics from
observing the peculiarities of his own genius in the substance of thought, and in the external ornaments of diction.
A finer and more true criticism might be exerted by discovering and expressing that which was his own, rather
than that which he borrowed.

IV.

"Parochial Sermons" by John Henry Newman—Power and Beauty
of his Style—Tendency of his Teaching to exalt the Passive
rather than the Active Qualities of Humanity—The Ordinance
of Preaching.

To the Same.

Chester Place, September 23rd, 1837.—I think your expressions about Newman quite well chosen. Decidedly I
should say he is a writer, first, of *great talent;* secondly, of
beauty. The *beauty* of his writing is shown for the most
part in the tasteful simplicity, purity, and lucid propriety
of his style; but now and then it is exhibited in well chosen
and brief metaphors, which are always according to the
spirit of the subject. Speaking of children, in allusion to
our Saviour's remark, that of such is the kingdom of
heaven, he observes that this is only meant of little ones in
their passive nature; that, like water, they reflect heaven
best when they are still. However, it seems to be a point
with the Oxford writers, either for good or evil, very much
to represent, not children only, but men, as the *passive*
un-co-operating subject (or rather, in one sense, *object*) of
divine operation. They are jealous of holding up, or
dwelling much upon, grace as an *influence* on the conscious
spirit, a stimulator and co-agent of the human will, or
enlightener of the human intellect. That view, they think,
is insufficient, leads to an inadequate notion of Christian
ordinances, and of our Christian condition, and causes a
confusion between God's general dealings with the human

race, or His subordinate workings with Christians and His special communications to the members of the New Covenant. "Salvation" is to be considered (exclusively) "as God's work in the soul." But whether it be not just as much God's work if carried on with the instrumentality of those faculties which He originally conferred, may be a question. Again, the Oxford writers dwell much on the necessity of a belief in mysteries not level to our understanding (of which my father says that they cannot run counter to our reason, because they do not move on any line that can come in contact with it, being beyond the horizon of our earthly faculties). But the question is whether our Saviour ever spoke of any operations on men, the effects of which they were not enabled plainly and clearly (if their hearts be well disposed) to judge of. The *operations* themselves are not our concern, any more than the way in which God created the earth, and all that is therein. The operations themselves belong to that heaven which none can understand but He that is in heaven, and which consequently I cannot believe that God ever meant us to understand, the symbols which the inspired writers employ on this subject being more probably intended to convey a notion of the desirability and accessibility of heaven than of heaven itself. Whately truly says, in relation to subjects of this kind, that a blind man may be made to understand a great deal *about* objects of sight, though sight alone could reveal to him *what they are.*

To return to my theme. It is an undoubted truth that the manner in which God operates upon man is and must be as unintelligible to man as the way in which God created him at first; but does it flow from this truth, or does it appear from the tenor of Scripture, that Christ, who constantly appealed to the reason and the will of His hearers (as Newman himself urges against the Predestinarians), ever spoke of divine operations on man, the effects of which he might not judge of by intelligible signs? The Syrian was commanded to bathe in a certain river, and how it was that bathing in that river could heal his leprosy, it was not given him to know. But was he commanded to believe that he had been healed of leprosy, while to all outward appearance, and by all the signs which such a thing can be judged of, the leprosy remained just as before? Surely it is not from the expressions of Scripture, but from the supposed necessary consequences of certain true doctrines, according to a certain mode of reasoning, that the non-intelligibility of the *effects* of God's working is contended for. Newman himself urges that Baptism is scarcely ever named in Scripture without the mention of spiritual grace; that Baptism is constantly connected with regeneration. And then I would ask, is not spiritual grace generally mentioned in Scripture, either with an implication or a full and particular description of those good dispositions and actions which are to proceed from it, and which men may judge of, as a tree from its fruits? And is regeneration ever mentioned in Scripture in such a way as to preclude the notion that it is identical with newness of life? and is not newness of life, according to our Saviour and St. Paul, identical with doing justice and judgment for Christ's sake, doing righteously because of feeling righteously? Are we ever led by the language of Scripture to suppose that regeneration is a mystical something, which, though it may, and in certain circumstances must, produce goodness and holiness, yet of its own nature need not absolutely do so; which may exist in unconscious subjects, as in infants, acknowledged incapable of faith and repentance, which might, as to its own essence (though the contrary actually is the case), exist even in the worst of men? In short, that regeneration is the receiving of a new nature, a more divine, and yet not better or more powerful nature. Surely here are words without thoughts. What notion have we of a *divine* nature which does not include or consist of the notions of goodness and power ? Newman illustrates the subject by the case of devils, who, he says, have a divine but not a good nature. To elucidate the obscure doctrine of regeneration by reference to evil spirits is like attempting to brighten twilight by the shades of night, and is a perfect contrast to the proceeding of our Saviour, who was accustomed to explain "the kingdom of heaven" by parables and stories about things which His listeners daily saw with their eyes, and handled with their hands.

In the same spirit of being mysterious above what is written, Newman and his fellow-labourers in the Oxonian vineyard are wont to contend that preachers are bound to preach the gospel, as a blind servant is bound to deliver a message about things which he can never see, as a carrier-pigeon to convey a letter, the contents of which it cannot understand. They are not to preach for the sake of saving souls, nor to select and compose from the gospel in order to produce a good effect, nor to grieve if the gospel is the savour of death to those who will not hear. In short, it would be presumption and rationalism in them to suppose that their intellect or zeal was even to be the medium through which God's purposes were to be effected. What God's purposes *are* in commanding the gospel to be preached, and sending His only Son into the world, they maintain that we cannot guess (as if God had not plainly revealed it Himself throughout the Bible). They are merely to execute a trust, to repeat all the truths of the gospel, one as much and as often as the other. For what practical result of such a principle can there be, unless it be this, that a clergyman is to preach as many sermons on the Trinity and the Incarnation as on faith and hope and charity, and the necessity of a good life, along with its details. Yet Newman is the very man who would accuse such a proceeding of irreverence, and too great an exercise of intellect.

V.

Graphic Style of the Old Testament Narratives.

To the Same.

September 30th, 1837.—I think Herby is more struck with Exodus than with Genesis, for the former is even more strikingly objective than the latter, and the account of the various plagues arrests the attention even of the youngest mind. The most objective passages in Roman and Grecian history unfortunately are not the really important ones and the hinges of great events; they are biographical episodes or anecdotes, for the most part ; as the striking off the heads of the poppies, the death of Regulus, and much of what relates to Alexander, the Roman emperors and their private follies. But in the Old Testament a great battle is won by the Israelites because Moses sits upon a *stone* on a *hill,* and has his *arms held up* on either side by Aaron and Hur. The whole history is a series of pictures. If you make pictures of Roman history, you must imagine the postures, the accessory parts, all the detail of surrounding objects ; but in the Bible they are made out for you. Thus you can call to mind the main course of events in Jewish history by means of such pictures impressed upon the memory ; but Roman history could not correctly be represented in any such manner. A series of its most picturable scenes would not recall the march of the principal events.

Married Happiness.

Marriage, indeed, is like the Christian course—it must either advance or go backwards. If you love and esteem thoroughly, the more you see, and do, and feel, and talk together, the more channels are opened out for affection to run in ; and the more room it has to expand, the larger it grows. Then the little differences and uncongenialities that at first seemed relatively important, dwindle into nothing amid the mass of concord and tenderness ; or if their flavour still survives, being thus subordinate, like mustard or other condiments which would be intolerable in large proportions, it adds a zest to the whole dish.

VI.

Conservative Replies to some Arguments of the Radical Party—The British Constitution not originally Popular but Paternal— An appeal to Universal Suffrage not an appeal to the Collective Wisdom of the Age, but to its Collective Ignorance—" The Majority *will* be always in the right ; " but not till it has adopted the views of the Minority—Despotism of the Mob in America regretted by many Americans—English Government not a mere machine for registering Votes—How are the People to be trained to a right Exercise of their Liberties?

To Mrs. H. M. JONES, in reply to a Political Essay by Dr. PARK.

" The British Constitution is *founded* on public opinion." The institutions and forms of government in which this idea is more or less adequately manifested have been wrought out by public opinion, yet surely the idea itself is not the result and product, but rather the secret guide and groundwork of public opinion on the point in question, as embodied in definite words and conceptions. But what public opinion was that which moulded our admired policy, and fashioned the curious and complicated mechanism of our state machine? Did it reflect the minds and intellects of the majority? Or was it not rather the opinions of the best and wisest, to which our aristocratic forms of government gave both publicity and prevalence?

Surely we have little reason to say that public opinion, taken *at large*, is necessarily just and wise by virtue of its being public,—necessarily that to which the interests of the nation may be safely entrusted. If we identify it with the opinions of the majority at all times and on all subjects, it cannot be identified with the collective wisdom of the age. Like foam on the surface of the ocean, pure if the waters below are pure, soiled and brown if they are muddy and turbid, it can but represent the character of that from which it proceeds, the average understandings and morals of the community. How are the masses to be purified and tranquillized? How rendered capable of judging soundly on affairs of state as far as that is possible to men of humble station? Surely not by the introduction of a vote-by-ballot system, which virtually silences the gifted few, and reduces to inaction the highest wisdom of the day. Truth, it is said, must ever prevail; but unless utterance is given her,—nay, more, unless her voice is heard, not drowned by the clamours of the crowd, what means has she of prevailing? Public opinion is consonant to reason and goodness only inasmuch as it is influenced by the wise and good. It is often grossly absurd, and the public opinion of one year or month is condemned by that of the next. There is some truth in the notion of Miss Martineau, to which, by stress of arguments she has been driven, "that the majority *will be* in the right." The only rational inter-pretation of which seems to me to be this, that, *on given points*, the majority *ultimately* decide in favour of the truth, because, in course of time, the opinions of the wisest on those particular subjects are proved, by experience and successive accessions of suffrages from competent judges, to be just; they are stamped before the public eye and in characters which those who run may read (or as Habakkuk really has it, "he may run that readeth"), and in such points public opinion is in fact the adoption of *private* opinion by the public; the judgment approved by the majority is anything rather than that which the majority would have formed by aid of their own amount of sense and talent, for "nel mondo non è se non volgo." In time the whole lump is leavened with that which emanated from a few; but what practical application should be made of this axiom, "the majority will be in the right?" Ought it to be such as would lead us to throw political power, without stop or stay, directly into their hands, and abide all the consequences of their blundering apprenticeship, while in particulars in which the public interests are concerned, in which immediate action is required, they are *learning* to be right? Will it console us under the calamities which their ignorance may inflict, that they will know better in the end? And when the Commonwealth is in ruins, will this after-wisdom restore the shattered fabric, or indemnify those who have suffered during its disorganization? · This notion of a ruined Commonwealth appears no visionary bugbear to those who believe the continuance of a Christian and Catholic government essential to the well-being of the state.

Before we argue about public opinion, before we decide what this great power has already done, or what it ought to do, it would be as well to settle what we mean by the term. The public opinion of this country, on *particular points*, in *this* age of the world, is perfectly just and enlightened. On the Newtonian or Copernican system, for instance, public opinion now is identical with that of the philosopher in his closet. But what was public opinion on this same system in the age of Kelper and Galileo? (for Newton was anticipated in some measure by those great men). If, however, by public opinion be meant the opinions of the multitude taken collectively, the general body·of their opinions concerning all matters of which man can take cognizance,— this can no more be the best possible, than the mass of mankind are as able, moral, and enlightened as a certain number of individuals in every age. But ought not a state to be guided by the best possible opinions? Ought it to be swayed by the uncorrected thoughts of the multitude?

It is not high Tories and Churchmen alone who feel that in America public opinion is a tyrant,—because it is a public opinion not sufficiently acted on by the wisest and best individuals ;—their voice has utterance, and in time is heard, but by the forms of society and of government established there,—especially the want of a landed gentry and influential endowed Church,—they do not enough prevail over the voices of the crowd; and the will of the majority is too much felt for the welfare of the majority themselves. Many Americans are now admitting this, and it appears either implicitly or explicitly in the pages of every American traveller. Miss Martineau would have helped us to find it out had we needed her information.

With us, goverment hitherto has not been degraded in its character to that of a machine, the functions of those who are engaged in it being simply this, to ascertain and obey a popular will, like the index of a clock worked by a pendulum. Our laws and institutions have been moulded by the suggestions of a wise minority, which the mechanism of our state machinery enabled to come gradually into play ; so that the interests of the people have been consulted rather than their blind wishes. , Thus, our constitution, considered as an outward thing, has been formed according to an idea of perfection (never in this world to be more than partially realized)—an idea existing equally in the minds of all our countrymen, but most distinctly and effectively developed in those which are aided by an acute and powerful intellect, improved to the highest point by education, study, and reflective leisure.

Is it not obvious from Dr. Park's own abstract that our government has never been popular in the sense in which my father denies it to have been such ? Has it not ever been a "a monarchy at once buttressed and limited by the aristocracy ? " Was it ever popular as the American government is so ? If not, still less has it been popular after such a sort as our modern Liberals—our separators of Church and State—will leave no stone unturned to make it. On the other hand, is it not clear as noon-day—nay, gloried

in by numbers—that, notwithstanding the prolonged dura-
tion of Parliament, the remnant of lordly influence in the
popular elections and House of Commons, the standing
army, and national debt, the British State is more democratic in this nineteenth century than at any former
period.* Ought it to be still more democratic, still more
the mere representative of the multitude, and exponent of
their will? Are we likely to fare better under the dominion
of the people than this country did in former times, when
"government had not renounced its right to consult for the
benefit of the community, even independently of its inclination?" On the answer to this question depends the
answer to that of Dr. Park, were the acts above named
constitutional?

The sage Whig Hallam is of opinion that the Reform Bill
went too far in establishing democratic principles; and as
to such politicians as Hume, Warburton, Roebuck, and
their allies, I should imagine they sympathized but little in
the anxiety of reasoners like Dr. Park and S. T. C., for the
balance of powers, and so that they could but succeed in
overthrowing the Church and the aristocracy, would care
much less than a straw for the old and venerable idea of
the British Constitution.

A noble national character belongs to the people of
England, and grieved indeed should I be to suppose that
they wanted a "foundation of moderation and good sense."
But how are those good qualities to be most efficiently
improved, confirmed, elicited? How does a wise mother
act in regard to the children under her care,—those children
in whom she perceives with delight the germs and first
shoots of a thousand amiable affections and excellent dispositions? I need hardly say that she does not trust to

* We cannot surely imagine that more power and liberty were really
enjoyed by the people under the sway of the strong-headed, strong-handed
Cromwell, or that their interests were more attended to during the corrupt
reign of Charles II.—S. C.

them solely; that she remembers of what jarring elements man is a compound; and that she takes care to keep the passions and infirm tempers of her charge in due restraint, in order that their good feelings and reasoning habits may be strengthened and increased. Just so should a paternal government act towards the national family which it has to govern.

These are some of the thoughts which have been suggested to me by the perusal of Dr. Park's instructive abstract. I am aware that they are quite imperfect and inconclusive; but they give a notion of the way in which I have been led to look on the subject of government.

CHAPTER VII.

LETTERS TO HER HUSBAND, MRS. PLUMMER, MISS TREVENEN, MISS A. BROOKE: 1838.

I.

Seaside Occupations—Bathing : Childish Timidity not to be cured by Compulsion—Letter-writing.

To Mrs. PLUMMER, Gateshead.

Herne Bay, Aug. 30*th*, 1838.—You ask for a letter from Herne Bay, and I take the opportunity to comply with your request, now that papa and the children and Ann have just set off on the rumble of the coach for Canterbury. I have been strolling on the beach, rejoicing that the Canterbury visitors have so softly brilliant a day for their excursion, yet partly regretting that they have turned their backs on the bathing-place. This is quite a day to make Herby in love with the ocean waters. At first he suffered much from fear when he had to enter them, and he has not yet achieved the feat of going thoroughly overhead; but I think you will agree with us that no good would be done by forcing him. Troy town, as he long ago observed him-self in reference to the treatment of children, after all was *not* taken by force. Bathing is not like a surgical operation, which does good however unwillingly submitted to; and we cannot make children fearless by compelling them to undergo the subject of their fears. This process, indeed, has sometimes made cowards for life. There is much in habit, doubtless, but persons who act upon this truth, without seeing its practical limitations, often commit great errors.*

* It may be worth while to mention, in proof of the practical success of my mother's indulgent system, that the early nervousness here alluded to

H

I must not, however, proceed to state these limitations, and see whether or no they agree with your speculations on child-management, seeing that my paper and my time have their limitations too. *Apropos* to this last point, however, I must digress again, to say how few people have what I consider just and clear notions on the subject of letter-writing! * You are one of my few cordial, genial correspondents, who do not fill the first page of their epistles with asseverations of how much they have to do, or how little news they have to tell, and how sure you are, as soon as it is at all necessary to your well-being, to hear it from some other quarter. Why do these people waste time in visiting their friends of an evening, or calling on them of a morning? Why do they not pickle and preserve, and stitch and house-keep all day long, since those and such-like are the only earthly things needful? The answer doubtless would be, " Friendships must be kept up ; out of sight out of mind ; and as man is a social creature, he must attend to the calls of society." Now, it is exactly on this ground, and not, in nine cases out of ten, for the sake of communicating news, that letter-writing is to be advocated. It is a method of visiting our friends in their absence, and one which has some advantages peculiar to itself ; for persons who have any seriousness of character at all, endeavour to put the better part of their mind upon paper ; and letter-writing is one of the many calls which life affords to put our minds in order, the salutary effect of which is obvious.

completely passed away. My brother learned to swim as easily as most boys as soon as he went to school at Eton, where bathing and boating became his favourite amusements.—E. C.

* The lady whose letter-writing style is thus pleasantly described is the wife of the Rev. Matthew Plummer, and author of several useful works on Church matters.—E. C.

II.

The History of Rome, by Dr. Arnold—The Study of Divinity,
Poetry, and Physiology, preferred to that of History or Politics
—Christian Theology and Metaphysics.

To Miss ARABELLA BROOKE.

Herne Bay, September 8th, 1838.—We are reading Dr.
Arnold's "Rome," and feel that we now for the first time
see the old Romans off the stage, with their buskins laid
aside, and talking like other men and women. They do
not lose by this: the force of the Roman character is as
clearly brought out in Dr. Arnold's easy, matter-of-fact,
modern narrative, as it could have been in the stilted
though eloquent language of their own historians. People
say how Whiggish it is, in spite of the disclaimers in the
preface. There is certainly a great deal of anti-aristocracy
in it; but then, I imagine, if ever aristocracy showed itself
in odious colours, it must have been during the early times
of Rome; and no faithful historian could have concealed
this, though he might have manifested less zeal and
alacrity in the task of exposing it. However, I speak in
ignorance: politics and history are subjects in which I have
less of my desultory feminine sort of information than some
others which seem rather more within my compass. Divinity
may be as wide a field as politics; but it is not so far out
of a woman's way, and you derive more benefit from partial
and short excursions into it. I should say the same in
regard to poetry, natural history in all its branches, and
even metaphysics—the study of which, when judiciously
pursued, I cannot but think highly interesting and useful,
and in no respect injurious.

The truth is, those who undervalue this branch of philosophy, or rather this root and stem of it, seem scarce aware
how impossible it is for any reflective Christian to be without metaphysics of one kind or other. Without being

aware of it, we all receive a metaphysical scheme, either partially or wholly, from those who have gone before us; and by its aid we interpret the Bible. It is but few perhaps who have time to acquire any clear or systematic knowledge of divinity. When the heart is right, individuals may be in some respects first-rate Christians without any specu- lative insight, because the little time for study is caused by active exertion; and this active exertion, pursued in a religious spirit, and converted into the service of God by the way of performing it, is perhaps the most effective school of Christianity. But when there *is* time to read, then I do think that, both for the sake of others and of ourselves, the cultivation of the intellect, with a view to religious know- ledge, is a positive duty; and I believe it to be clearly established, though not cordially and generally admitted, that the study of metaphysics is the best preparatory exercise for a true understanding of the Bible. False metaphysics can be counteracted by true metaphysics alone; and divines who have not the one can hardly fail, I think, to have the other.

III.

Miracle of the Raising of Lazarus passed over by the Synoptical Gospels.

To her Husband.

Chester Place, September, 1838.—The more one thinks of it the more puzzling it seems that the raising of Lazarus is only recorded in St. John's Gospel. The common way of accounting for the matter cannot easily be set down, but yet it does not satisfy. We feel there may be something yet in the case which we do not fathom, and knowing as we do, from constant experience, how much there is in most things which transcend our knowledge,—what unsuspected facts and truths have come to light, and explained pheno- mena of which we had given quite different explanations previously,—we cannot but feel that the true way of accounting for this discrepancy has never yet come to light.

IV.

Connection between the Senses and the Mind—Early Greatness of great
Poets—Poetic Imagination of Plato.

To the Same.

Herne Bay, September 21*st*, 1838.—Herbert is a most sensitive child, as alive to every kind of sensation, as quick in faculties. Indeed I believe that this sensitiveness does itself tend to quicken and stimulate the intellect. He will have especial *need* of self-control, and I trust in time that he will have it; but at his age the sun of true reason has but sent up its rays above the horizon; its orb is not yet visible. If we are fearfully and wonderfully made in body, how much more so in mind, and how much less can we fathom the constitution of the latter than of the former! But considered in a *large sense* they are *one;* else how could the mind act on the body, the body on the mind? Where the senses are active and rapid ministers to the mind, supplying it abundantly and promptly with thought-materials, no wonder that the intellect makes speedy advances; and such sensitiveness is doubtless one constituent of a poet. Still, whether or not true greatness and high genius shall be discovered, must depend upon the constitution and properties of the intellect in itself; and this is the reason that so many fine buds prove but indifferent flowers, rather than the popular account of the matter, that the sooner the plant blossoms the sooner it will fade and fall. Never tell me that Milton and Shakespeare were not as wonderful children as the young Rosciuses, or any other modern prodigy, and hollow puff-ball! How exquisitely does Plato illustrate his subject out of his own actual history, out of things moving, sensuous and present, filling with life-blood the dry, though clear and symmetrical vein-work of his metaphysic anatomy!

V.

Description of the Falls of Niagara in Miss Martineau's
"Retrospect of Western Travel."

To Miss E. TREVENEN, Helston.

October, 1838.—Miss Martineau's " Retrospect of Western
Travel" I have read and enjoyed. It takes you through
out-door scenes, and though the politics are overpowering
now and then, it freshens you up by wanderings amid
woods and rivers, and over mountain brows, and among
tumbling waterfalls. I think Miss Martineau made one
more at home with Niagara than any of the other American
travellers. She gives one a most lively *waterfallish* feeling,
introduces one not only to the huge mass of rushing water,
but to the details of the environs, the wood in which the
stream runs away, etc. She takes you over it and under it,
before it and behind it, and seems as if she were performing
a duty she owed to the genius of the cataract, by making it
thoroughly well-known to those at a distance, rather than
desirous to display her own talent by writing a well-rounded
period or a terse paragraph about it.

VI.

Lukewarm Christians.

To the Same.

Chester Place, December, 1838.—I have no doubt that
—— disapproves of the Catholic party just as much as of
the Evangelicals, and on very similar grounds. It is not
the peculiar doctrines which offend thinkers of this description. About them they neither know nor care. It is the
high tone, the insisting upon *principles*, to ascertain the truth
or unsoundness of which requires more thought than they
are disposed to bestow on such a subject. It is the zeal
and warmth and eagerness by which tempers of this turn
are offended. The blunders and weaknesses of warm religionists are not the sources of their distaste, but the pretexts by

which they justify to themselves an aversion which has a very different origin. Be kind to the poor, nurse the sick, perform all duties of charity and generosity, be not religious over-much—above all, keep in the background all the peculiar cardinal doctrines of Christianity—avoid all vices and gross sins—believe the Bible to be true, without troubling yourself about particulars—behave as resignedly as you can when misfortunes happen—feel grateful to God for His benefits—think at times of your latter end, and try "to dread your grave as little as your bed," if possible. Such will ever be—more or less pronounced and professed —the sum of religion in many very amiable and popular persons. Anything more than this they will throw cold water upon by bucketsful.

CHAPTER VIII.

LETTERS TO HER HUSBAND, MRS. PLUMMER, MISS TREVENEN, MISS A. BROOKE: 1839.

I.

Characteristics of the Oxford School of Divines—Combinations, even for the best Purposes, not favourable to Truth—Superior Confidence inspired by an Independent Thinker—Are Presbyterians Excluded from the Visible Church?—Authority of Hooker cited against such a Decision—Defence of the Title of Protestant—Luther: Injustice commonly done to his Character and Work.

To Mrs. PLUMMER, Heworth Vicarage, Gateshead.

10, *Chester Place, Regent's Park, January* 17th, 1839.
—The "Letter of a Reformed Catholic," * and that on the "Origin of Popery," I think remarkably well done, clear, able, and popular. Such judgment as I have on such a matter I give unto you, and this need not imply any presumption on my part. But though I can sincerely express my approbation of the way in which these performances are *executed*, I must candidly confess that I do not follow your husband on the Oxford road, so far as he seems to have proceeded. On some subjects, specially handled by Newman and his school, my judgment is suspended. On some points I think the apostolicals quite right, on others clearly unscriptural and unreasonable, wilfully and ostentatiously maintaining positions which, if carried out to their full length, would overthrow the foundations of all religion. I consider the party as having done great service in the religious world, and that in various ways; sometimes by bringing forward what is wholly and absolutely true; sometimes by promoting

* A controversial pamphlet, by the Rev. Matthew Plummer.—E. C.

discussion on points in which I believe their own views to be partly erroneous; sometimes by exposing gross deficiencies in doctrine in the religion of the day; sometimes by keenly detecting the self-flatteries and practical mistakes of religionists. But the worst of them, in my opinion, is that they are, one and all, *party men;* and just so far as we become absorbed in a party, just so far are we in danger of parting with honesty and good sense. This is why I honour Frederic Maurice, and feel inclined to put trust in his writings, antecedently to an express knowledge of their contents, because he stands alone, and looks only to God and his own conscience. Such is human nature, that as soon as ever men league together, even for the purest and most exalted objects, their carnal leaven begins to ferment. Insensibly their aims take a less spiritual character, and their means are proportionately vulgarized and debased. Now, when I speak of *leaguing together,* of course I do not mean that Mr. Newman and his brother divines exact pledges from one another like men on the hustings, but I do believe that there is a tacit but efficient general compact among them all. Like the Evangelicals whom they so often condemn on this very point, they use a characteristic phraseology; they have their badges and party marks; they lay great stress on trifling external matters; they have a stock of arguments and topics in common. No sooner has Newman blown the Gospel blast, than it is repeated by Pusey, and Pusey is re-echoed from Leeds: Keble privately persuades Froude, Froude spouts the doctrines of Keble to Newman, and Newman publishes them as "Froude's Remains." Now, it seems to me that, under these circumstances, truth has not quite a fair chance. A man has hardly time to reflect on his own reflections, and ask himself, in the stillness of his heart, whether the views he has put forth are strictly the truth, and nothing more or less than the truth, if, the moment they have parted from him, they are eagerly embraced by a set of prepossessed partisans, who assure him and all the rest of the world that they are thoroughly excellent. (How many truly great men have modified their views after publication, and in subsequent works have written in a somewhat altered strain.)

These writers, too, hold the dangerous doctrine of the "economy of truth." Consistently with these views, if one of them wrote ever so extravagantly, the others would refrain from exposing him, for fear they should injure the cause, at least so long as he remained with them on principal points. God, of course, can bring good out of evil, and in this way I do believe that the errors of the party will serve His cause in the end as well as their sound tenets. Yet I cannot think that what I have described is the truest method of promoting pure religion; and it seems to me that the most effective workmen in the Lord's vineyard, those whose work tells most *in the end*, are they who do not agree beforehand to co-operate, but who pursue their own task without regard to the way in which others execute theirs.

.   .   .   .

Well, I have looked at the "Reformed Catholic" again, and think it as well done as I did at first; but still there are some points on which I am not quite of the writer's mind.

I cannot yet bring myself to believe that the Kirk of Scotland in no sense belongs to the Body of Christ—in no sense makes a part of the visible Christian Church. Would Hooker have said so?* One Lord, one Faith, one

---

* But we speak now of the visible Church, whose children are signed with this mark, "One Lord, one faith, one baptism." In whomsoever these things are, the Church doth acknowledge them for her children; them only she holdeth for aliens and strangers in whom these things are not found.—Hooker, Eccl. Pol. book iii. ch. 1.—E. C.

Baptism; these are the only essentials, I think, which he names. A man may even be a heretic, yet not altogether —nay, not at all—excluded from this communion, though he can never belong to the mystical invisible Church of the elect till he becomes a Christian in heart and mind, as well as in outward profession. The Kirk may have deprived herself of a privilege by losing the episcopal succession, may have thrown away a benefit by rejecting the government of bishops (if we only put the matter in the outward light), yet she may still make an erring part of that Church to which Christ's Spirit is promised.

This, however, is a difficult subject. I do not pretend to have very decided convictions upon it. Of one thing, however, I feel pretty sure, that I shall call myself a *Protestant* to the end of my days. Yes! a Catholic Christian, as I humbly hope,—and, *moreover*, a Protestant of the Church of England. I profess that "Reformed Protestant Religion" which our monarch swears to defend on his coronation; the Protestantism of Cranmer and Hooker, of Taylor, of Jackson, and of Leighton. These are great names, and dear and venerable are the associations with the title of Protestant in my mind. To call myself such does not make me a whit the less Christian and Catholic, nor imply that I am so; it does not mix me up with sectarians any more than the latter term connects me with the gross errors and grievous practices of Romanists, who, whether they are entitled to the name or not, will always assume it. As for its being a *modern* designation,—that which rendered a distinctive appellation necessary is an event of modern times; and that, I think, is a sufficient defence of it on this score. "Reformed Catholic" savours altogether of Newman and the nineteenth century.

In regard to Luther, I do not jumble him up with our reformers as to the whole of his theology;—on some points

he was less orthodox than they.   But I cannot think it
altogether just to say that he "left, rather than reformed
the Church."   It is the Oxford fashion to dwell upon what
he omitted, to throw into shade the mighty works which
he did; to hold him forth as a corrupter, to forget that he
was a great and wonderful reformer.   If there were
"giants in those days," the mightiest of them all was the
invincible German.   And how any man who thinks deeply
on religious subjects can bring himself to speak scorn of
this brave Christian warrior, or how he can divest his
spirit of gratitude towards so great a benefactor, to whose
magnanimity, more than to any other single instrument in
God's hand, it is owing that we are not blind buyers of
indulgences at this hour, I confess is past my comprehen-
sion.

> "In our halls is hung
> Armoury of the invincible Knights of old."

Blighting breaths may tarnish the lustre of those trophies
for a passing moment; but it is too late in the day to teach
us that Milton is *not a poet*, and that Luther, and Wycliffe,
and Ridley, and Latimer were not worthy champions of the
faith.

II.

A Little Lecturer—Stammering.

To her Husband.

Chester Place, Sept. 4th, 1839.—Herby preached last
night about chemical matters like a regular lecturer; I
thought he looked quite a little Correggiesque Mercury,—or
something between Hermes and Cupid,—as he stood on
the little chair *lecturing* volubly, and throwing out one leg
and arm, with his round face glowing with childish
animation, and a mixture of intelligence and puerility.
The conclusion was after a list of names a league long,
"and the last is something like so and so; but the
chemist's man had a pen in his mouth when he answered

my question about it, and I could not hear distinctly how he pronounced the name." It is wonderful how clearly he speaks when there is an impulse from within which over-bears and makes him forget the difficulty of articulation.* For it certainly is the pre-imagination of the difficulty of pronouncing a word that ties the tongue in those who stammer. F. M. could pronounce a studied oration with-out stuttering; I account for the fact in this way: it was the hurry of mind, excited by the anticipation of an *indefinite* field of words to be uttered, which paralyzed his articulating powers. With a paper before him, or a set speech on the tablet of his memory, he said to himself: thus much have I to pronounce and no more; whereas in extemporary speech there is an uncertainty, an unlimited-ness, the sense of which leads most talkers to inject a *plus quam sufficit* of *you knows* into their discourse, and which causes others to hesitate. The imagination is certainly the seat of the affection, or rather the source of it. The disorder may be defined as a specific weakness of the nerves in connection with a particular imagination, or it may arise and be generated during the inexplicable reciprocal action, *wechsel-wirkung*, of one upon the other, in which, as S. T. C. says, the cause is at the same time the effect, and *vice versa*. The curious thing is, that there is an idiosyncrasy in this, as perhaps to some degree in all other complaints, and every different stammerer stammers in his own way, and under different circumstances.

III.

Philosophy of the " Excursion."
To the Same.

Chester Place, Sept. 17*th*, 1839.—I am deep in the " Excursion," and am interested at finding how much of

* The slight impediment in his speech to which my brother was subject as a child, was never entirely outgrown, though it diminished considerably in after years.—E. C.

Kant and Coleridge is embodied in its philosophy, especially
in "Despondency Corrected." I should not say that the
"Excursion" was as intensely poetical, as pure poetry, as
ecstatic, as many of the minor pieces; it holds more of a
middle place between poetry, philosophy, and the thoughtful,
sentimental story. But it is exquisite, be it what it may.

IV.
Lord Byron on the Lake Poets.

To the Same.

Chester Place, October 4th, 1889.—"The Lake Poets are
never vulgar." I often think of this remark of Lord
Byron. Genius is an antiseptic against vulgarity; but still
no men that I ever met, except downright patricians, were
so absolutely unvulgar as Coleridge, Southey, and Wordsworth.

V.
Writing to Order—Sunday Stories and Spanish Romances.

To Miss E. TREVENEN, Helston.

Chester Place, 1889.—Miss ——'s stories are, as you
observe, "remarkably fit for their purpose." How she can
contrive to write so exactly as a story-composer for a
Society ought to write; how she can manage to be so
wholly and solely under the dictation of the *proper sort* of
spirit, I cannot imagine. I, for my part, am neither *goody*
enough nor good enough (and I humbly admit that to
submit on proper occasions to *goodiness* of a certain kind is
a part of goodness) for anything of the sort. I should feel
like a dog hunting in a clog, or a cat in gloves, or a
gentleman's carriage forced to go upon a railroad; or, to
ascend a little higher, as Christian and his fellow-pilgrim
did when they left the narrow path and got into the fields
by the side of it. I should always be grudging at the
Society's quickset hedge on the right hand and the left.
As for Herbert, he is deep in "Amadis de Gaul;" and the

boy that is full of the Endriago and Andandana, and Don Galaor, and the Flower of Chivalry himself, and his peerless Oriana, is not quite in the right mood to relish good charity-schoolgirls, and the conversion of cottagers that don't go to church, which Nurse, however, think worth all the Endriagos in the world.

VI.

Pain more bearable when its Cause is Known—Musings on Eternity —Descriptions of Heaven, Symbolical, Material, and Spiritual— Conjectures of Various Writers respecting the Condition of Departed Souls.

To Miss ARABELLA BROOKE, Gamstone Rectory, East Retford.

Chester Place, 1839.—It is painful to be unable to understand one's suffering, to translate it into an intelligible language, and bring it distinctly before the mind's eye. But it is already a sign that we are no longer wholly subdued by its power, when we can analyze it and make this very indefiniteness an object of contemplation. This evinces a degree of mastery over that which has of late been a tyrant. And if "to be weak is miserable" (oh! how often have I thanked Milton for that line!), to exercise any kind of power, or have any kind of strength, is so far an abatement of misery. To be sure, the explanation which my father gives of this mental fact, the uneasiness felt at the *unintelligibility* of an affection, when we cannot tell whence it arises nor whither it tends, is not a little abstruse, and what is popularly called transcendental. "There is always a consolatory feeling that accompanies the sense of a proportion between antecedents and consequents. It is eternity revealing itself in the form of time."

Dear Miss Brooke, there are not many persons to whom I should quote a metaphysical passage of S. T. C. in a letter; but I see you are one who like to be what the world calls idle—that is, outwardly still from the inward activity of thought—to pause and look down into the deep stream, instead of hastening on in view of the shallow, sparkling runnel. Dear me! some people *think* more over the first page of an essay than others do while they write a volume. Thinking too much, and trying to dive deeper and deeper into every subject that presents itself, is rather an obstacle to much writing. It drags the wheels of composition; for before a book can be written, there is a great deal to be *done*: contemplation is not the whole business. I am convinced that the Cherubim do not write books, much less publish them, or make bargains with booksellers, or submit to the ordeal of disgusting puffery and silly censure. I am convinced they do nothing but think; while the Seraphim are equally given up to the business of loving.

But I must consider the limits of this letter, and the observations which it ought to contain, and my letter-writing strength, which is at present but small. I am truly grieved that I cannot give a proper answer to your last, or its interesting predecessor, which came with Abercrombie's Essay. If I could but put on paper, without too much bodily fatigue, half the thoughts which your reflective epistles suggest to me, little as they might be worth your reading, you would see that your letters had done their work, and were not like winds passing across the Vale of Stones, but like those gales which put a whole forest in motion. That reminds me of another advantage enjoyed by the Cherubim and Seraphim. I am sure they do not write letters with pen, ink, or paper, nor put them into the post, nor stop to consider whether they are worth postage, nor look about for franks and private conveyances. They have a quintessence of our earthly enjoyments and privileges: the husk for them drops off, and all is pure spirit and intelligence.

All this nonsense is excusable in me, because I am poorly, out of humour with those activities in which I

illness causing
non sense

cannot share, and quite cross and splenetic because I am not as free from fleshly ills and earthly fetters as the angels in heaven. *Apropos* to which, I have not read Mr. Taylor's book, and from your account of it am afraid I should not be such a reader as he would wish to have, unless, indeed, he confines himself to the statement of a few principles which may guide our views respecting the life to come, instead of attempting to describe it particularly, like Dr. Watts and others. It seems to me so obvious, both from the reason of the thing and the manner in which Scripture deals with it, that " if one came from the dead " to tell us all about it, he would leave us as wise as he found us. In what language could he express himself? In a language of symbols? But that we have already in the Bible; and we want to translate it literally, or at least into literal expressions. We know that they who have pleased God shall be eternally blessed; that they who have sinned against the light will suffer from a worm that never dies: and what more can we know while we are roofed over by our house of clay? A true account of the other world would surely be to the inhabitants of earth as a theory of music to the deaf, or the geometry of light to the blind.

Inquirers into the future state are all either Irvingites or Swedenborgians, horrified as most of them might be to be compared either with Irving or Swedenborg. They either give us earth newly done up and furnished by way of our final inheritance, observing that man is essentially finite, and must therefore have a material dwelling-place; or they talk of a *spiritual* heaven, while the description they give of it is only a refined edition of the things and goings-on of this world. What else *can* it be? All conjecturers may not talk of " wax-candles in Heaven," but the spirit which dictated the thought is in every one of them.

I think I shall never read another sermon on the Intermediate State. Newman has no Catholic consent to show for his views on that subject, though doubtless they come in great measure from the Fathers. The supposition that blessedness and misery hereafter may both arise from increased powers, reminds me of an oft-quoted passage in a work of S. T. C., in which he conjectures that an infinite memory may be the Book of Judgment in which all our past life is written, and every idle word recorded in characters from which our eyes can never be averted. It was a fine thought in Swedenborg to represent the unblest spirits in the other world as *mad*. His visions are founded on many deep truths of religion. Had he given them as an allegorical fiction, like the "Pilgrim's Progress," it would have been well.

CHAPTER IX.

LETTERS TO HER HUSBAND, HER ELDEST BROTHER, MRS. J. STANGER, MRS. H. M. JONES: 1840.

I.

Love of Books and Classical Studies.

To her Eldest Brother.

January, 1840.—I have a strong opinion that a *genuine* love of books is one of the greatest blessings of life for man and woman, and I cannot help thinking that by persons in our middle station it may be enjoyed (more at one time, less at another, but certainly during the course of life to a great extent enjoyed) without neglect of any duty. A woman *may* house-keep, if she chooses, from morning to night, or she may be constantly at her needle, or she may be always either receiving or preparing for company, but whatever those who practise these things may say, it is not necessary in most cases for a woman to spend her *whole* time in this manner. Now, I cannot but think that the knowledge of the ancient languages very greatly enhances the pleasure taken in literature—that it gives depth and variety to reading, and makes almost every book, in whatever language, more thoroughly understood. I observe that music and drawing are seldom pursued after marriage. In many cases of weak health they cannot be pursued, and they do not tell in the intercourse of society and in conversation as this sort of information does, even when not a word of Greek or Latin is either uttered or alluded to.

II.

Lord Byron's Mazeppa and Manfred—His success in Satire and in
Sensational Writing.

To Mrs. H. M. JONES.

January 14*th*, 1840.—I have had great pleasure in refreshing my girlish recollections of the "Lament of Tasso"
and "Mazeppa." The latter is the only poem of Byron's
which reminds me of Scott. I think it most spirited and
impressive in its line. Byron is excellent in painting
intense emotion and strong sensation of body or mind; he
is also good in satire and sarcasm, though not very amiable;
but I do not like him when he attempts the philosophic,
invading the province of Goethe and Wordsworth; or when
he tries his hand at the wild and supernatural, in which
line I think him a mere imitator, and far outdone by Scott,
Shelley, and many others. "Manfred," I think, has been
greatly overrated, as indeed the public seems now beginning
to see—the poetical public at least. Still there are fine
things in it; but the graphic descriptions in the journal
are better, I think, than the corresponding passages in
verse.

III.

On the Death of an Infant Daughter.

To Mrs. JOSHUA STANGER, Wandsworth.

10, *Chester Place, Regent's Park, August* 10*th*, 1840.—My
dear Friend,—Your last kind note was written in a strain
which harmonized well with my feelings. Would that
those feelings which a trial such as we have lately sustained
must needs bring with it, to all who have learned, in any
degree however insufficient, to trust in Heaven, whether for
temporary consolation or for eternal happiness,—would
that those feelings could be more lasting than they are;
that they could leave strong and permanent traces; that
they could become " the *very habit* of our souls," not a mere
mood or passing state without any settled foundation. My

greif + motherhood

thoughts had turned the same way as yours, where all mourners and friends of those that mourn will naturally go for sure and certain hope and ground of rejoicing, to that most divine chapter of the raising of Lazarus. "Thy brother shall rise again." This indeed is spoken plainly, this is "no parable," no metaphor or figure of speech. But in the next chapter we see the same blessed promise illustrated by a very plain metaphor. "Except a corn of wheat fall into the ground and *die*, it abideth alone; but if it die, it beareth much fruit."

Our loss indeed has been a great disappointment, and even a sorrow; for, strange as it may seem, these little speechless creatures, with their wandering, unspeaking eyes, do twine themselves around a parent's heart from the hour of their birth. Henry suffered more than I could have imagined, and I was sorry to see him watch the poor babe so closely, when it was plain that the little darling was not for this world, and that all our visions of a "dark-eyed Bertha," a third joy and comfort of the remainder of our own pilgrimage, must be exchanged for better hopes, and thoughts more entirely accordant with such a religious frame of mind as it is our best interest to attain. I had great pleasure in anticipating the added interest that you would take in her as your godchild. But this is among the dreams to be relinquished. Her remains rest at Hampstead, beside those of my little frail and delicate twins.— God bless you, my dear Mary, and your truly attached friend,

                                        SARA COLERIDGE.

Note.—Bertha Fanny Coleridge was born on the 13th of July, 1840, and died eleven days afterwards.—E. C.

IV.

"They sin who tell us love can die."

To her Husband.

The Green, Hampstead, September 18*th*, 1840.—Will death at one blow crush into endless ruin all our mental growths, as an autumnal tempest prostrates the frail summer house, along with its whole complexity of interwoven boughs and tendrils, which had gradually grown up during a long season of quiet and serenity? Surely there will be a second spring when these firm and profuse growths shall flourish again, but with Elysian verdure, and all around them the celestial mead shall bloom with plants of various sizes, down to the tenderest and smallest shrublet that ever pushed up its infant leaves in this earthly soil. Surely every one who has a heart must feel how easily he could part with earth, water, and skies, and all the outward glories of nature; but how utterly impossible it is to reconcile the mind to the prospect of the extinction of our earthly affections, that such a heart-annihilation has all the gloom of a eternal ceasing to be.

V.

A Sunset Landscape.

To the Same

October 14*th*, 1840.—I was thinking lately of my days spent in the prime of childhood at Greta Hall. How differently all things then looked from what they now do! This world more substantial, more bright, and clothed in seemingly *fast colours*, and yet though these colours have waxed cold and watery, and have a flitting evanescent hue upon them, to change my present mind-scene for that one, rich as it was, would be a sinking into a lower stage of existence; for now, while that which was so bright is dimmer, wholly new features have come forth in the landscape, features that connect this earth "with the quiet of the sky," and are invested in a solid splendour which more evidently joins in with the glories of the heavens. The softened and subdued appearance of earth, with its pensive evening sadness, harmonizes well with the richer part of the prospect, and though in itself less joyous and radiant that it once was, now forms a fitting and lovely portion of the whole view, and throws the rest into relief as it steals more and more into shadow.

VI.
The true Art of Life.
To the Same.

10, *Chester Place, October* 20*th*, 1840.—We ought indeed, my beloved husband, to be conscious of our blessings, for we are better off than all below us, perhaps than almost all above us. The great art in life, especially for persons of our age, who are leaving the vale of youth behind us, just lingering still perhaps in the latter stage of it, and seeing the bright golden fields at the entrance of it more distinctly than those nearer to our present station, is to cultivate the love of doing good and promoting the interests of others, avoiding at the same time the error of those who make a worldly business and a matter of pride of pursuits which originated in pure intentions, and bustle away in this secular religious path, with as little real thought of the high prize at which they should aim, and as little growth in heavenliness and change from glory to glory, as if they served mammon more directly. Anything rather than undergo the mental labour of real self-examination, of the study, not of individual self, but of the characters of our higher being which we share with all men. For one man that *thinks* with a view to practical excellence, we may find fifty who are ready to *act* on what they call their own thoughts, but which they have unconsciously received from others.

CHAPTER X.

LETTERS TO HER HUSBAND, MRS. PLUMMER, MRS. THOMAS FARRER, MISS TREVENEN, MRS. H. M. JONES, THE REV. HENRY MOORE, THE HON. MR. JUSTICE COLERIDGE: 1841—1842.

I.
Necessity of Patience and Hope in Education.

To Mrs. PLUMMER.

April, 1841.—Patience is the most important of all qualifications for a teacher ; and the longer one has to do with managing young persons, or indeed persons of any sort or kind, the more one feels its value and indispensability.   It is that resource which we constantly have to fall back upon when all else seems to fail, and our various devices, and ways, and means, and ingenuities give way one after another, and seem almost good for nothing but to preach about.   By patience I do not mean that worthless substitute for it which hirelings (in *temper*, for a paid governess is often a much better instructor than a mama) sometimes make use of, a compound of oil and white-lead, as like putty as possible.   With patience, hope too must keep company, and the most effective of teachers are those who possess most of the arts of encouraging and inspiriting —spurring onward and sustaining at the same time—both lightening the load as much as may be, and stimulating the youngsters to trot on with it gallantly.

II.
The Lake Poets on Sport—The Life of Wesley.

To her Husband.

Chester Place, October 13th, 1841.—Southey and Wordsworth loved scenery, and took an interest in animals of all

sorts ; but not one could they have borne to kill ; and
S. T. C. was much of the same mind, though *he* would have
made more allowance for the spirit of the chase than the
other two. Wordsworth's " Hartleap Well " displays feelings of high refinement. Doubtless there is a sort of bar-
barism in this love of massacre which still keeps a corner
even in cultivated minds, but which the progress of cultivation must *tend* to dissipate, and perhaps with it some habits
that for some persons are more good than evil. Notwithstanding " Hartleap Well," Wordsworth always defended
angling, and so did Dora; but the Southeys, from the
greatest to the least, gave no quarter to any slaughterous
amusement.

What a biography the Life of Wesley is ! What wonders
of the human mind does it reveal, more especially in the
mental histories of Wesley's friends and coadjutors !

III.

Inflexibility of the French Language—The Second Part of Faust : its
Beauties and Defects—Visionary Hopes.

To the Same.

Chester Place, October 19*th*, 1841.—I feel more than ever
the inflexibility and fixedness of the French language,
which will not *give* like English and German. It has few
words for sounds,—such as clattering, clanking, jangling,
etc.,—whereas the Germans are still richer than we in such.
Derwent wanted, when here, to point out to me some of the
beauties of the fifth act of the second part of Faust, which,
in point of vocabulary, and metrical variety and power, is,
I do suppose, a most wonderful phenomenon. Goethe, with
the German language, is like a first-rate musician with a
musical instrument, which, under his hand, reveals a
treasure of sound such as an ordinary person might play for
ever without discovering. Derwent has a most keen sense
of this sort of power and merit in a poet, and his remarks

were interesting, and would have been more so if the book
had been at hand. He gives up the general *intention* of the
piece, which he considers a failure,—the philosophy confused, unsound, and not truly profound. The execution of
parts he thinks marvellous ; and as the pouring forth of an
old man of eighty-four, a psychological curiosity. . . .

Your delightful letter and the after-written note both
arrived at once. Your account of yourself is not worse,
and that is the best that can be said of it. The lane is
long indeed ; we could little have thought of all its turnings
and windings when we first entered it ; but I still trust that
it will issue out into Beautiful Meadows at last.

IV.

Reminiscences of a Tour in Belgium—Hemling's "Marriage of St.
Catherine" at Bruges ; and Van Eyck's "Adoration of the
Lamb" at Ghent—Devotional gravity of the early Flemish
Painters—Pathos of Rubens—Works of that Master at Antwerp
and Mechlin.

To Miss E. Trevenen, Helston.

Chester Place, October 27th, 1841.—Ostend is interesting
merely from old recollections, especially military ones, and
because it is foreign ; not so Bruges, which I think the
most perfect jewel of a town I ever saw, and how completely
is the spirit of the place transfused into my Uncle Southey's
interesting poem, "The Pilgrimage to Waterloo." Here
we visited the Hospital of St. John, saw the sisters tending
the sick, and studied the beautiful and curious works of
Hemling in the adjoining parlour. Do you remember the
"Marriage of St. Catherine," with its beautiful background
of vivid light green, and that exquisitely delicate and
youthful neck of the bride Saint, shaded with such transparent gauze. Mr. Milnes (whom we met at Ghent on our
return) specially admired Herodias' Daughter in the shutter
of this picture. He said she looked at the bloody head in
the charger so expressively, just as if she could not turn

her fascinated eyes from it, and yet shuddered at it. The cathedral is large and impressive, and contains a noble statue of Moses,—more like a Jupiter Tonans, however, than the Hebrew Legislator. At Ghent I visited St. Bavon's; what a superb cathedral it is, with its numerous chapels clustered round the nave! I do indeed remember that paradisiacal picture of the "Adoration of the Lamb," with its velvety green lawn, and hillocks, and luxuriant rose-bushes. It is said that these old masters first opened the way to the Italian school of landscape-painting, by the backgrounds of their pictures. There is a very peculiar air about them, an imaginativeness combined with lifelike everyday reality, and a minuteness of detail which interferes with anything like *intense* passion, but not with a sober, musing sort of emotion. A deeply religious character is impressed upon these pictures, and there is a mild and chastened wildness about them (if the seeming contradiction may be ventured on) which is very interesting, and specially suits some moods of the devotional mind. I think it is well, however, that the traveller for the most part sees these old paintings before he is introduced to those of Rubens ; the fire, life, movement, and *abandon* of his pictures quite unfit one, for a time, for the sedater excellencies of Hemling and Van Eyck. The "Descent from the Cross" is, perhaps, the finest and most *beautiful* of all that great master's performances; but no picture that I have ever seen (except in another line, the Sebastiano in our National Gallery) ever affected me so strongly as Rubens "Christ Crucified betwixt the Thieves," in the Antwerp Museum. That is really a *tremendous* picture; in the expression of vehement emotion, in passion, life, and movement, I think it exceeds any other piece I ever beheld. How tame and over-fine Vandyck shows beside Rubens! I cannot greatly admire him as an historical painter, especially on sacred subjects. He should always have been employed on delicate fine gentlemen and ladies, and folks about court. Some of his Maries and Magdalens are most graceful and elegant creatures ; but Rubens' youthful Magdalen at the foot of the Cross, imploring the soldier not to pierce the Saviour's side, moves one a thousand times more than all his lady-like beauties. However, I do not maintain, deep as is my admiration of Rubens, that his pictures thoroughly satisfy a religious mood of mind. They are somewhat over-bold; they almost unhallow the subject by bringing it so home, and exciting such strong earthly passion in connection with it. No sacred picture ever thoroughly satisfied me except the " Raising of Lazarus," by Sebastian del Piombo and Michael Angelo. The pictures at the Antwerp museum, I believe, you did not see; but were you not charmed with those at Mechlin? What a delicately brilliant piece is the " Adoration of the Magi," at· St. John's Church, with its beautiful shutters especially! and " St. John at Patmos," with that noblest of eagles over his head. Rubens ranked this among his finest productions. " The Miraculous Draught," too, in the Church of Notre Dame, painted for the Fishermen's Company, how splendid it is! And that *volet à droite* " Tobias and the Angel," is the loveliest of all Rubens' shutter-pictures. What " colours of the showery arch " are there! What delicate aerial lilacs and yellows, softening off the scarlet and crimson glow of the centrepiece.

V.

Prayer for the Dead.

To Mrs. J. STANGER.

Chester Place, January 12th, 1842.—Some long to pray for their departed friends. How far better is it to feel that they need not our prayers ; that we had best pray for ourselves and our surviving dear ones, that we may be where we humbly trust they are!

VI.

A Visit to Oxford.

To Mrs. THOMAS FARRER, 3 Gloucester Terrace, Regent's Park.

Chester Place, Easter, 1842.—Yesterday Mr. Coleridge and I returned from a very interesting excursion to Oxford. When I was in the midst of those venerable structures, I longed for strength to enter every chapel and explore the whole assemblage of antique buildings thoroughly. As it is, I have filled up the indistinct outline of imagined, but unseen Oxford, most richly. Magdalen Chapel, as a single object, is what pleased me the most, but the merit of Oxford, and its power over the feelings, lies in what it presents to the visitor collectively, the vast number of antique buildings which it presents to the eye, and of interesting associations which it brings into the mind.

VII.

Illness of her Husband, and Death of his only Sister.

10, *Chester Place, Dec. 7th,* 1842.—My dearest Louisa,— Little did I think, when I received your last but one letter, that I should be thus long ere I communicated with the writer, and little did I think (and this was in mercy) what trials were to come upon me before I renewed my inter- course with you. I well remember beginning a letter to you soon after I received yours—explaining some of my theological views, about Romish saints, or something of the sort—(you may remember our old theological discussions). Something prevented me from finishing it and sending it off ; week after week went on and the begun letter remained a beginning. Then commenced a new era with me of sorrow, and I humbly trust of purification. When these troubles began, I became reserved in writing to my friends, not from closeness of heart, but because I could not afford to expend my mental strength and spirits in giving accounts to them of my anxieties and troubles ; it was a prime

necessity to keep all my stock within me. It is a bad
plan, however, to put off writing to a friend from month to
month, till we feel that only a very long and excellent letter
can be fit to make up for such a silence. You must excuse
a very poor one from me now, dear friend, not proportioned, I assure you, to my interest in you, and wish that
you should continue to feel an interest in me and mine; but
to my present epistolary powers. I heard with great
pleasure from dear E. that you had been thinking much
of my husband's prostration, and with friendly sympathy;
on the whole he has throughout this trying dispensation
been wonderfully supported in mind. He has ever been as
hopeful as any one under the circumstances could be, and
he is quiet and resigned, and derives great comfort from
devotional reading, from prayer, and religious ministra-
tions. Our eldest brother has been a great soother and
supporter to him during the most alarming and suffering
part of his illness. J.'s company and conversation have
been a constant blessing, and, indeed, all his family have
shown him the tenderest affection during his illness. The
bonds that unite us have been drawn closer by this trial of
ours, than ever before. Alas! one of our circle, who has
for years been the centre of it, to which all our hearts were
most strongly drawn, is removed. O Louisa! hers was the
death-bed of a Christian indeed. No one could die as she
did, who had not made long and ample preparation beforehand. She foresaw the present termination of her illness,
when the rest of us were flattering ourselves with vain
hopes that she would live down her wasting malady, and
see a green old age. Keenly sensible as she was of the
blessings of her lot in this world, and no one could *enjoy*
more than she did those temporal blessings—a good
husband, honoured among men, very promising, affectionate children, easy circumstances, and if least, yet to
her not little, a charming country residence in her beloved

native county—she yet cast not one longing, lingering look behind, when called to quit all and go to the Saviour. So strong was her wish to depart and *be with Christ*, that she even was not diverted from it by her tender love for, her husband and children—which to me, who know her heart toward them, is really marvellous. Great must have been her faith to realize, as she did, the unseen world.* Her death-bed reminds me of the last days of one—a very different person from her in many respects—my dear father. He had just the same strong, steadfast faith— the same longing to leave this world for a better, the same collectedness of mind during his last illness. *He* retained his intellectual powers to the last moment of his waking existence, but was in a coma for some hours before life was extinct. She was unconscious during the last two hours, and, for some time previously, it was only conjectured that she heard and joined in the prayers offered at her bed- side.

VIII.

Religious Bigotry.

To the Rev. HENRY MOORE,† Eccleshall Vicarage, Staffordshire.

10, *Chester Place, Dec.* 1842.—We were amused by your account of the Puritanical Archdeacon. Religious bigotry is a dull fire—*hot* enough to roast an ox, but with no lambent, luminous flame shooting up from it. The bigots of one school condemn and, what is far worse, mutilate Shakespeare; those of another would, if they could, extin- guish Milton. Thus the twin-tops of our Parnassus would be hidden in clouds for ever, had these men their way.

---

* This lamented relative, both cousin and sister-in-law, between whom and my mother there always existed a most tender affection, was the daughter of James Coleridge, Esq., of Heath's Court, Ottery St. Mary, and wife of the Hon. Mr. Justice Patteson. She died in November, 1842, at Feniton Court, near Honiton.—E. C.

† At present Archdeacon of Stafford.—E. C.

IX.

"Hope deferred."

To Mrs. HENRY M. JONES, Hampstead.

December, 1842.—I try to think of that better abode in which we may meet each other, free from those ills which flesh is heir to. *We* have a special need to look and long for the time when we may be clothed upon "with our house which is from heaven;" for in this tabernacle we do indeed groan, "being burdened." Bodily weakness and disorder have been the great (and only) drawbacks, ever since we met twenty years ago, to our happiness in each other. It will seem chimerical to you that I have not yet abandoned *all* hope. But this faint hope, which perhaps, however, is stronger than I imagine, does not render me unprepared for what all around me expect. The Lord has given; and when He takes away, I can resign him to his Father in heaven; and looking in that direction in which he will have gone, I shall be able to have that peace and comfort which in no shape then will the world be able to give me.

To-day I attended the Holy Communion. To be away so long from my beloved husband was a great trial to me (of course I did not attend the morning service); but I knew he greatly wished it, and I made an effort to satisfy him. It requires no great preparation for one who leaves the room of severe sickness where all things point to a spiritual world—partly here around us, partly to come.

X.

Resignation.

To the Hon. Mr. JUSTICE COLERIDGE,* 4 Montague Place, London.

January, 1843.—I now feel quite happy, or, at least, satisfied. Could I arrest his progress to a better sphere of existence by a prayer, I would not utter it. When I once

---

* My father's elder brother, now Right Honble. Sir John T. Coleridge, Member of the Privy Council.—E. C.

know that it *is* God's will, I can feel that it is right, even if there were no such definite assurances of rest and felicity beyond this world. I cannot be too thankful to God, so far as my own best interests are concerned, that He is thus removing from earth to heaven my greatest treasure, while I have strength and probably time to benefit by the measure, and learn to look habitually above; which now will not be the spirit against the flesh, but both pulling one way, for the heart will follow the treasure. Thus graciously does the Blessed Jesus condescend to our infirmities, by earthly things leading us to heavenly ones.

CHAPTER XI.

LETTERS TO HER SON, HER ELDEST BROTHER, MRS. J. STANGER, HON. MR. JUSTICE COLERIDGE, REV. HENRY MOORE, EDWARD QUILLINAN, ESQ., MRS. THOMAS FARRER, MRS. H. M. JONES: 1843 (continued).

I.

Widowhood.

To her Son.*

January 26th, 1843.—My dear Boy,—My most beloved and honoured husband, your excellent father, is no more in this world, but I humbly trust in a far better. May we all go where he is, prepared to meet him as he would have us! God bless you! Live as your beloved father would have you live. Put your trust in God, and think of heaven, as he would wish you.

May we all meet above! May we all join with him the Communion of Saints, and be for ever with the Blessed Jesus! Your good Uncle James was with me at the last.

I make an effort to write to you, my dear boy, from beside the remains of the dear, blessed, departed one. For you alone could I do this; but it is due to his son, our child.—Your loving mother,

SARA COLERIDGE.

II.

Her Husband's Death—First meeting with him at Highgate.

To Mrs. GILLMAN.

February, 1843.—My dearest Mrs. Gillman,—You have ere now, I trust, received an announcement of my loss, of

---

* Written by my mother to my brother at Eton, on the day of my father's death.—E. C.

sorrow, loss

which I cannot now speak. My sorrow is not greater than I can bear, for God has mercifully fitted it to my strength. While I was losing my great earthly happiness, I was gradually enabled to see heaven more and more clearly, to be content to part with earthly happiness, and to receive, as a more than substitute, a stronger sense of that which is permanent. I should have deferred writing thus to you, dear friend, till I was stronger; but I think it right to tell you that, at my strong desire, the remains of my beloved husband are to be deposited in Highgate Churchyard, in the same precinct with those of my revered father.

It was at Highgate, at your house, that I first saw my beloved Henry.* Since then, now twenty years ago, no two beings could be more intimately united in heart and thoughts than we have been, or could have been more intermingled with each other in daily and hourly life. He concerned himself in all my feminine domestic occupations, and admitted me into close intercourse with him in all his higher spiritual and intellectual life. It has pleased God to dissolve this close tie, to cut it gradually and painfully asunder, and yet, till the last fatal stroke, to draw it even closer in some respects than before.—God bless you, my dear friend. I am ever your truly affectionate and respectful

SARA COLERIDGE.

---

* My father, who was then living in London, used to walk up to Highgate two or three times a week, attracted thither by the fascination of that wonderful discourse of which he has left so valuable a record in the "Table Talk." It was on one of these occasions, during the winter of 1822–23, that he was first introduced to his "Cousin Sara," who was on a visit to her father at Mr. Gillman's; and his impressions on seeing the fair girl, "dressed all in white, and reclining upon a sofa" (for she was just recovering from an illness), were afterwards confided to his sister, Lady Patteson.—E. C.

III.

On the same Subject—Trial of a Mourner's Faith, and how it was
met.

To the Rev. H. MOORE.

February 13*th*, 1843, *Chester Place.*—My dear Friend,—
Letter-writing is improper for me now, but I must pen two
or three lines to thank you for your last letter, and to tell
you that I accept, from my heart, all your offers of friendship to me and mine.   When I call your letter "most
brotherly," with *such brothers* as I have, it is the strongest
epithet I can use.   You loved, you still love and understand
and value my departed Henry; this would for ever make
me a friend to you, even if you had not expressed yourself
so kindly, as you have ever done, to me, and if we had not
another thought, or interest, or sympathy in common.

I must add but a line or two more, for I am suffering
very sadly from a nervous cough, which scarcely leaves me
a minute's peace night or day, except for a few hours in
the middle of the twenty-four, when I am least weak.   I
caught a violent cold in attending on my husband on the
Sunday and Wednesday nights of his final trial; but the
weak and relaxed state into which I immediately sank as
soon as the last call for exertion was over, has more to do
with my present suffering (the medical man thinks) than
this exposure.   Had I strength I could tell you much that
would interest you deeply of Henry's last days and months.
His energy, while his poor, dear, outward man was half
dead, was one of the most striking instances of the mind's
independence of the body that can well be imagined.   But
oh! dear Mr. Moore, when I backward cast my eye, or
rather when it reverts of itself to the various scenes of his
last illness, I feel that I have an ocean of natural tears yet
to shed.   At the time (except during the last fortnight), I
but half felt the deep sadness, because I looked upon all his
bitter sufferings as painful steps in the way to compara-

tively easy health, and felt as if every one of them was so much misery out of the way. Now that delirium, stupor, death are at the end of them, they have a different aspect. There is a comfort (I am speaking now of *mere* human feelings) in thinking that the anguish I have gone through, which will be merged, I humbly trust, before I go hence, in that peace which the world cannot give, is probably the heaviest part of my earthly portion, or that it must have seasoned me to bear well what remains behind.

But in this mingled cup there are other sorrows of a still deeper kind; for physical evil is not *evil* in the most real sense. The separation is a fearful wrench from one for whom, and in expectation of whose smile, I might almost say, I have done all things, even to the choice of the least articles of my outward apparel, for twenty years. But even that is not the heaviest side of the dispensation. It is to feel, not merely that he is taken from *me*, but that, as *appears*, though it is but appearance, he is not. That the sun rises in the morning, and he does not see it. The higher and better and enduring mind within us has no concern with these *sensations*, but they *will* arise, and have a certain force. While we remain in the tabernacle of the flesh they are the miserable, cloggy vapours that from time to time keep steaming up from the floor and the walls, and obscure the prospect of the clear empyrean which may be seen from the windows. The most effective relief from them which I have found, is the reminding myself that he who is past from my sight is gone whither I myself look to go in a few years (not to mention all those of whom the world was not worthy, before the publication of the Gospel, and since), and that if I can contemplate my own removal, not with mere calmness, but with a cheerfulness which no other thought bestows, why should I feel sad that he is there before me? But these of which I have spoken are only the sensations of the natural man and woman. I well know

in my heart of hearts and better mind, that if he is not
now in the Bosom of God, who is not the God of the dead,
but of the living, or if all these hopes are but dreams, I
can have but little wish to bring him back to earth again,
or to care about anything either in earth or heaven. In
my weakest moments, indeed, I have *never* wished that it
were possible to recall him, or to prevent his departure
hence. I thank God and the power of His grace, there has
been no agony in my grief, there has been no struggle of
my soul with Him. I have always had such a strong sense
and conviction that if this sorrow *was to be*, and was
appointed by God, it was entirely right, and that it was
mere senselessness to wish anything otherwise than as
infinite goodness and infinite wisdom had ordained it.
Forgive so much about my own feelings. Give my very
kind regards to Mrs. M., and respects to Miss H., and
believe me ever your affectionate friend,

SARA COLERIDGE.

IV.

Affectionate Kindness of Relatives and Friends—Special Gifts of a
  Christian Minister, in his Attendance upon the Sick and Dying.

To HARTLEY COLERIDGE, Esq., Grasmere.

10, *Chester Place, March 9th*, 1843.—My dear Brother,—I
have long been wishing to renew my suspended intercourse
with you. To do this requires some resolution, after all
that has passed since I last wrote to you. When I have
thought of taking up my pen to address you, a crowd of
strong emotions and deeply concerning thoughts and remembrances have rushed upon me, pressing for utterance,
and my spirits have sunk under the eagerness and intense-
ness of their requisitions. It is not because I anticipated
an inadequate sympathy from you that I have felt thus,
but from the very contrary. I have been answering kind
and tender letters from persons less near and dear to me,

who could not and *ought* not to feel for me as I am sure you have done, with comparative—I will not say calmness—(for since all uncertainty was removed, and my loss presented itself to me as fixed and inevitable, I have been more deeply calm in spirit than ever I was before in my life)—but with comparative lightness of feeling. Now, however, I take the first step of renewing a correspondence with you, which I hope will be cheerfully continued with pleasure and benefit to us both (if I may so far assume and presume) to the end of our lives. It is better to write little and often, than much at a time, and in this way, without formally asking your *advice*, which in a woman of my years is for the most part a mere form, I shall learn your views and feelings on many interesting subjects, and be, I humbly trust, improved and strengthened thereby. The great moulder of my mind, who was, perhaps, more especially fitted to strengthen my weak points and supply my deficiencies, and altogether to keep my mind straight and even, than any other man or woman living, is gone where I cannot come,—removed out of the sphere of my human understanding,—though not, I trust, out of spiritual communion both with me and all who are, or seek to be, in any vital sense Christians. On this account I have the more need to make much of the friendship of my brothers,—and no widow, I think, when withdrawn from the arms of a husband, can ever have been more affectionately sustained by those of brothers than I have been. The sadder my prospect grew, the more closely they circled round me; but a thousand times dearer to my heart than their kindness to me were the proofs they gave of affection, respect, and admiration for him who was soon to be taken away from our mortal sight. The expressions of dear John and of Frank were especially affecting. Of James * you have doubtless heard what he was to me

* Dr. Coleridge, Vicar of Thorverton, near Exeter, was my father's eldest brother.—E. C.

through all the last scenes of my trial.   Upon this so
important occasion, I found a brother—I may say an individual man—in him, whom before I knew not.   I now saw
for the first time what was the secret of his influence and
popularity in his own pastoral sphere.   He appears by the
bed of sickness and coming death (and he could not *so*
appear unless his heart were interested) entirely forgetful of
self, absorbed in what is before him.   His own opinions,
habits of mind, private interests, seem gone to a degree
which strikes a bystander like myself as unusual.   Then,
in performing his professional part, he is the more effective
from the absence of the intellectual in his mode of thought.
There is nothing theological about James.   From him you
have the pure spirit of Gospel consolation and assurance—
conditionally expressed—as it is in the Bible itself, with as
little mixture of foreign matter as possible.   This is not art
in him, or knowledge.   It is the result of the simple,
though not weak, character of his intellect.   He does not
reason on one side or the other, but lets the moral and
spiritual content of the inspired book produce its own effect
upon his mind, and find its own suitable utterance.   His
countenance and tone of voice are highly affecting and impressive, when he is thus seen in his best attitude of mind.
Frank seemed gratified by my evident appreciation of his
brother.   But I cannot thus speak of them without men-
tioning dear Edward * and Derwent too.   Both in their
several ways have been most soothing and helpful to me.
. . . My children are both going on well.   Herbert is very
well reported of from school, where his character for general
cleverness continues ; though he fails in verse composition,
and in other more essential points, I feel hopeful and
happy about him.   His letters to his sister are an amusing
mixture of pure childishness, childish pedantry, and affec-

* Rev. Edward Coleridge, Rector of Mapledurham, my father's younger
brother.—E. C.

tionate ruffianism. . . .—Believe me, my dear Hartley,
your much attached sister,   SARA COLERIDGE.

V.
Memoir of Nicholas Ferrer.
To the Hon. Mr. Justice COLERIDGE.

March 11*th*, 1843.—I am reading a very interesting
Memoir of Nicholas Ferrer,* who lived in the times of
James I. and Charles I. Were it not for certain expressions on the subject of grace, which clearly show that the
writer is no disciple of Pusey, one might suppose it a publication of the Oxford School,—the sentiments, and some of
the principles which it illustrates, being just such as Paget
seeks to recommend by his amusing Tales. Without intended disparagement to Paget, how great is the superiority
of the narrative to the fiction as a vehicle of truth!—
the one bears something the same relation to the other,
when carefully criticised, as the piece of linen or lace,
viewed through a microscope, to the natural leaf or slip of
wood examined in the same way.

VI.
A Quiet Heart.
To the Hon. Mr. Justice COLERIDGE.

March 22*nd*, 1843.— . . . I chat away thus to you,
my dear brother, as if I had a light gay heart, but I have
only a quiet one. When I go out of doors from the incessant occupation of mind and hands, the full sense of my
widowhood comes upon me, and the sunshine only seems to
draw it out into vividness. Hampstead is a sadder place
to me than Highgate. Yet sadness is not quite the word

* The friend of George Herbert, and editor of his Poems. Izaak Walton,
in his Life of Herbert, gives a striking account of this remarkable man,
who founded a Christian Society at Gidding Hall, Huntingdon, for purposes
of devotion and charity, in accordance with the principles of the Church.—
E. C.

for my feelings,—that seems too near to unhappiness. When I hear of happy marriages now, I do not feel that wretched sense of contrast with my own solitary state which I should once have felt. I rather feel a sort of compassionate tenderness for those who are entering on a career of earthly enjoyment, the transitoriness of which they must sooner or later be brought to a sense of. But for them, as for myself, there is a better communion beyond this present world, which, if begun here, will in the end supersede all other blessedness arising from union with objects of love.

VII.

Monument of Robert Southey—Recumbent Statues.

To the Hon. Mr. Justice COLERIDGE.

March 28th, 1843.—I scarce know what is finally settled about my uncle's monument. A modification of Lough's design seems most approved. The recumbent figure is all right in theory, but awkward in practice. Do what you will it looks deathy, with too real and actual a deathiness. This is one of the instances, I think, of the difficulty of reviving old fashions; if you alter them at all, or even take them from amid the circumstances and states of feeling among which they were originated, you have a spectre of the past rather than the living past itself, a kind of resurrection. The recumbent figures on the old tombs are rather death idealized than death itself. The armour veiled from view the lifelessness of the limbs, and brought the body, as by a medium, into harmony with the sepulchral stone. The full robe of the dame by the warrior's side did the same thing in another way, and contrasted well with the male attire; and that one attitude of the hands crossed upon the breast, or pressed together in prayer, alone perfectly agrees with the whole design. The brasses are not open to these remarks, because they are much further removed from life, and therefore cannot offend by the semblance of death.

VIII.

On her Loss—Injury done to the Mind by brooding over Grief.

To Mrs. PLUMMER, Gateshead.

10, *Chester Place, April* 27*th*, 1843.—Your letter was very welcome to me, and I will thank you for it at once, though I cannot now write at all as I wish, either as to matter or manner, so much am I occupied, and so unequal am I to getting much done in a short time, from bodily weakness and sensitiveness of nerves.

What you say, dearest, of your own particular grief in the loss that bears so heavily upon me, that but for very special mercy it must have crushed me to the earth, is extremely gratifying to me. Nothing soothes me so much as to hear *his* deserved praises, and to have assurances from his friends of the esteem and affection he excited. Few men have ever been more generally liked, or more dearly *loved* in a narrower sphere. Never before his illness did I fully know what a holy, what a blessed thing is the love of brothers and sisters to each other. By my bereavement all my relations seem to be brought closer to me than before, for pity excites affection, and gratitude for kindness and sympathy has the same effect. But my beloved Henry's brothers are twice as much to me as in his precious lifetime. John is such a friend and supporter as few widows, I think, are blest with. You will not, I am sure, dear friend, think me boastful, but grateful for saying all this. I feel it now such a duty, such a necessity, to cling fast to every source of comfort—to be for my children's sake as happy, as willing to live on in this heart-breaking world as possible, that I dwell on all the blessings which God continues to me, and has raised up to me out of the depths of affliction, with an earnestness of endeavour which is its own reward; for so long as the heart and mind are full of movement, employed continually on not unworthy objects, there may

be sorrow, but there cannot be despair. The stagnation of
the spirit, the dull, motionless brooding on one miserable
set of thoughts, is that against which in such cases as
mine we must both strive and pray. After all, it would be
impossible for one bereaved like me to care for the goings
on of this world, but for the blessed prospect of another ;
and it is a most thankworthy circumstance that the more
agitating our trials become, the brighter that prospect, after
a little while, beams forth, through the reaction of the mind
when strongly excited. The heaviest hours come on after
the subsidence of that excitement, when we come out again
from the chamber of death and mourning into all the
common ways of life. All the social intellectual enjoyments,
new books, the sight of sculpture, painting, the conversation of pleasant friends, are full of trial to me.   I turn
away from what excites any lively emotion of admiration or
pleasure, now that I can no longer share it with him who
for twenty years shared all my happiest thoughts.

IX.

Dryness of Controversial Sermons.

To the Hon. Mr. Justice COLERIDGE, Heath's Court, Ottery St. Mary.

June 27th, 1843.—Dr. Arnold's sermon is all you described
it. Would that of this sort, so practical, and appealing to ·
the heart and religious mind, were at least the *majority* of
preached sermons !   Some doctrinizing from the pulpit
may be necessary. But surely it ought to be subservient
and subordinate to the practical ; whereas, nine times out
of ten, the practical point merely serves as an introduction
or a pretext for a setting up the opinions of one school of
thinkers, and a pulling down the opinion of another, with
charges against the latter almost always one-sided and
unfair.   This sermon of Dr. Arnold's, and one which I
heard from Dr. Hodgson at Broadstairs on death and judgment, are quite oases in the hot sandy wilderness of

sermons which my mind's reverted eye beholds. I do not mean that many of them were not good; but when they are viewed altogether, a character of heat and barrenness seems to pervade them.

X.

A Visit to Margate—Domestic Economy in its Right Place—An Eton Schoolboy—Reading under Difficulties—High Moral Aim of Carlyle's "Hero-worship"—Joy of a True Christian—The Logic of the Heart and the Logic of the Head.

To Mrs. FARRER.

12, *Cliff Terrace, Margate, Sept. 5th*, 1843.—My dear Friend—Here we are, my children and Nurse and self, on the East Cliff at Margate, a few miles from the spot where I sojourned with you in June. That fortnight is marked among the fortnights of this my first year of widowhood with a comparative whiteness, in the midst of such deep (though never, I must thankfully acknowledge, never, even at the earliest period of my loss, quite unrelieved) blackness. I fixed upon this place, instead of Broadstairs or Ramsgate, on account of its greater cheapness, and because it could be reached with rather less exertion. Lodgings certainly are cheaper than I could have got them in an equally good situation at more genteel sea-bathing places ; but provisions are dear enough—lamb 8½d., and beef 9d.! I am so often twitted with my devotion to intellectual things, that I am always glad of an opportunity of sporting a little beef-and-mutton erudition, though I cannot help thinking that, as society is now constituted in the professional middle rank of life—still more in a higher one—women may get on and make their families comfortable, and manage with tolerable economy—by which I mean economy that does not cost more than it is worth of time and devotion of spirit—with less knowledge of details respecting what we are to eat, and what to put on, than used to be thought essential to the wise and worthy

matron. I dare say your dear C. will make her loved and
honoured S. as comfortable as if she had been studying
butchers' and bakers' bills, and mantua-making, and
upholstery in a little way, for the last seven years, instead
of reading Dante, and Goethe, and Richter, and Wordsworth, and Tennyson. But to return to this place, it is a
contrast to Broadstairs as looked out upon from the White
Hart, where we took up our abode the first night ; but the
East Cliff, where, by medical recommendation, we have
settled ourselves for a fortnight or three weeks, is neither
more nor less than the Broadstairs Cliffery continued ; and
as we return from the gully leading down to the sands (the
very brother to that which I so often went down and up
with you), Edy and I might almost fancy that we were
returning to the Albion Street lodgings, if it were not for
the tower of the handsome new church, where we attended
morning service last Sunday, which reminds us that we are
at Margate.

We were delayed in coming hither for some days by
Herbert's prolonged stay at Rickmansworth, where he
spent nearly three weeks in a sort of boys' paradise,
bathing two or three times a day.   Both Baron and
Lady A—— wrote about him to me in very gratifying
terms.   It is perhaps not right to repeat things honourable
to our children without being equally communicative about
their faults and ill-successes. But you have been so
specially friendly with me, and shown such kind interest
about all that concerns me, that I think I should withhold
a pleasure from you in not telling you what has very much
pleased me. Herbert thinks this place very *seedy*, and de-
spises the bathing. The tide seems never in a state to please
him ; but the truth is, he wants companions, and does not
like to be a solitary Triton among the minnows, or rather,
as those are fresh-water fish, among the crabs and seaweed.
However, he has got " Japhet in Search of a Father " from

the circulating library, reads a portion daily of Euripides, and has begun learning French ; and it is quite right that a little *seediness* should come in its turn after "jollity," and quietness and plain fare after "splendid lark," with "sock" of all sorts, that he may learn to cut out interests and amusements for himself out of home materials.

I must tell tales of the vessel that brought us hither, in order to deter you, dear friend, from ever trusting yourself to it in future. The "Prince of Wales" does certainly make its way fast over the water, but the vibration of its disproportionately small frame under the energy of its strong steam-engine is such that it fatigued me much more than a slower voyage would have done, and gave both Nurse and me a headache. The motion almost prevented me too from reading. Carlyle's "Hero-worship" trembled in my hand like a culprit before a judge ; and as the book *is* very full of paradoxes, and has some questionable matter in it, this shaking seemed rather symbolical. But oh! it is a book fit rather to shake (take it all in all) than to be shaken. It is very full of noble sentiments and wise reflections, and throws out many a suggestion which will not waste itself like a blast blown in a wilderness, but will surely rouse many a heart and mind to a right, Christian-like way of acting and of dealing with the gifted and god-like in man and of men. Miss Farrer lent me the work, and many others. Very pleasant to me was her stay at Gloucester Terrace, if *pleasant* is a fit word for an inter-course which awakened thoughts and feelings of "higher gladness" than are commonly so described. She is one who loves to reveal her mind, with all its "open secrets," to those who care at all for the one thing which is, and which she happily has found to be, needful ; and few indeed are the minds which will so well bear such inspection as she invites ; few can display such a pure depth of sunny blue without a cloud, such love for all men, and Christ above all—ascending from them whom she has seen to God whom she has not seen, and again honouring them and doing good to them, on principle, for His sake.   My doctrinal differences from her (and *some* doctrine we all must have in this world) are considerable ; but I could almost say, that were all men like her, no Christian *doctrine* would be needed.   She has much knowledge, too, of men and things—has read and seen much ; and pray tell your T. H. that I learned to thread the at first bewildering labyrinth of her discourse, after a while, much better than at first.   Even to the last her rapid transitions confounded me very often, and some of her replies to objections are rather appeals to the imagination and affections than properly answers.   But she has a logic of her own ; and though I do maintain that Christendom would fall abroad if it were not knit together by a logic of another sort, the want of which would be felt sorely, if it were possible that it could ever be wholly wanting, which the nature of man prevents,—yet this logic of the heart and spiritual nature is more than sufficient to guide every individual aright that possesses it in such high measure as she does.

XI.

Tunbridge Wells—Congenial Society.

To Mrs. JOSHUA STANGER, Fieldside, Keswick, Cumberland.

Tunbridge Wells, September 26th, 1843.—I am having every advantage here which a most agreeable family circle and daily drives in an easy carriage, in the most inspiriting air, through a lovely country, can give me; and I do fully believe that I shall be better in the end for having made the effort to come hither, and to mix myself up with my neighbour's concerns.   I seek to take an interest in all their little belongings, and cultivate cheerfulness as much as possible.   Enough of melancholy remembrance and

deep, irremovable regret is sure to remain, let me do what
I may to enter thankfully and genially into the present.

The landscape here, which I believe you are well
acquainted with, continually puts me in mind of Milton's
description of Paradise, the slopes are so emerald-velvety,
and the clumps and clusters of trees so varied and beautiful.
But there is an imperfection in the prospect from the want
of water. I long to introduce dancing rills, and fairy
waterfalls, and lucid pools, into the midst of these basin-
like valleys, and to people the glades with deer, and the
villages with a freer, finer peasantry. There is a great
want of water generally in the South of England. Devonshire has plenty of it; but the climate of Devon is to me a
drawback for which nothing can compensate.

The family party here consists of Judge Erskine, his wife,
two daughters, and eldest son: the youngest is at Eton.
The visitors are Miss M——, a charming young woman,
most animated and intelligent, a niece of Judge Erskine,
and myself. Judge E—— is one of the most agreeable
men in the family circle that I have ever known. He has
the indescribable air and way of a man of high birth about
him; and there is in his conversation that happy mixture
of seriousness, with light sportiveness and arch remark,
which everybody likes, and which is never jarring or
oppressive, whatever mood one may be in.

XII.

On her Loss—Cheerfulness instead of Happiness—Visits to Eton and
Tunbridge Wells.

To Mrs. HENRY M. JONES, Hampstead.

Eton, October 13*th*, 1843.—Of course I am not up to the
mark of easy, quiet enjoyment; yet I feel that, for a time,
it is good for me to be here. I cannot withdraw myself
from the world; I must live on in this outward scene
(though it continually seems most strange to my feelings

L

... . up in it and Her
.. .. I have been doomed
. ... for my children's sake as v
... . with as much spirit as
... . and movements of the sphere to wl
... that I should yet belong. Ever since 1
have cultivated cheerfulness as I never did b
my time of union I possessed *happiness* : no
I looked upon as a weed, the natural wild
soil, which must spring up of itself. Now I c
works of art, or the still more mind-occupyii
nature. I try to take an interest in the c
friends, to enter into the controversies of
become intimate with the mood of mind and
various persons, who are nothing to me (*I* h
to them), except as *studies*; just as a lichen
moss may be, only in a higher manner and
this with an earnestness unfelt in former t
certain extent I find my account in this: my n
loss, and rather full of desultory activity than,
better, concentrated energy; but it does not
do not brood miserably over my loss, or sink i
loss, inert despondency; I have even an upper
cheerfulness in my mind, more fixed than in
married days, but then it is only an upper stratum
it, unmoved and unmodified, is the sense of my

I have been interrupted, to see Dr. Hawtre
such an intimate friend of my beloved Henry
always, on this account, feel a special interest in
he is in himself much to be liked and appe
amiable in his domestic character, as son and bro
full of intellectual refinement; a good scholar,
accomplished modern linguist. .

I came hither for a holiday, but I assure you c
complete one. Herbert *makes* me read " Euripid.

..y. Reflection
..e enabled the
a new world
its lustre,
ar earthly
tive health
youth is
gh at my
ou do not
which we
-room, the
ate which
plained so
trouble."
are not all

of Early

.tophanes,
.rs of his
and me.
boy dis-
next line
only read
play that
se, from
the first
.gour of
, when
A and
is,
.

before my children, now in their
can enjoy it. I feel sadly for them
me. But they appear as glad as
l the great change to me bears
parison.

. . . .

g heartily at the " Frogs " again.
ad Homer with Herby ; but I feel
ough some of the harder, more
classical task that lies before him.
nderful so much as noticeable,—
ssics are in general for the youth-
indeed, the youthful mind of our
tract and subjective than modern

that I should yet be mixed up in it and Henry gone from it for ever). But since I have been doomed to outlive my husband, I must, for my children's sake as well as my own, endeavour to enter, with as much spirit as I can, into the interests and movements of the sphere to which it is God's will that I should yet belong. Ever since my widowhood I have cultivated cheerfulness as I never did before. During my time of union I possessed *happiness;* mere *cheerfulness* I looked upon as a weed, the natural wild produce of the soil, which must spring up of itself. Now I crave to see fine works of art, or the still more mind-occupying displays of nature. I try to take an interest in the concerns of my friends, to enter into the controversies of the day, to become intimate with the mood of mind and character of various persons, who are nothing to me (*I* being nothing to them), except as *studies;* just as a lichen or a curious moss may be, only in a higher manner and degree. All this with an earnestness unfelt in former times. To a certain extent I find my account in this; my mind is rest-less, and rather full of desultory activity than, what is far better, concentrated energy; but it does not stagnate. I do not brood miserably over my loss, or sink into an aim-less, inert despondency; I have even an upper stratum of cheerfulness in my mind, more fixed than in my happy married days, but then it is only an upper stratum; beneath it, unmoved and unmodified, is the sense of my loss.

I have been interrupted, to see Dr. Hawtrey. He was such an intimate friend of my beloved Henry. I shall . always, on this account, feel a special interest in him. And he is in himself much to be liked and approved, most amiable in his domestic character, as son and brother, and full of intellectual refinement; a good scholar, and an accomplished modern linguist. .

I came hither for a holiday, but I assure you I have no complete one. Herbert *makes* me read "Euripides" with him, and hear his Latin theme, I being as good a judge of Latin composition as a Great Cham of Tartary is of English.

My visit at Tunbridge Wells was a very agreeable one. I was quite astonished at the picturesque beauty and great variety of the country there, and found the family of Judge Erskine quite charming in everyday familiar life. Miss M——, who was my fellow visitant, I found more than an agreeable companion, though she is that in a high degree; her brilliancy and amusing humour is the mere sparkling, polished surface of a genuine jewel, in which the ground is invaluable. I cannot but add her to my list of *friends* made since marriage, in which list you, dear friend, are so prominent. Mama is looking anxiously for a sight of you. Your affectionate conduct towards her, dear Mrs. Jones, gives me more comfort than I can well express. I do not think she fails at all in mind, and in body her declension is very gentle and gradual.

I must get ready to drive out and see the oak forests of Windsor, in all the charming drapery of autumnal gleam and shadow.—I remain your truly attached friend,

SARA COLERIDGE.

Excuse the egotism of this letter. Sorrow makes one egotistical.

XIII.

Sympathy inspired by the Sorrows of Childhood and Youth.

To EDWARD QUILLINAN, Esq.*

Eton, October 24th, 1843.—I scarce know why it is that I feel far more moved by the griefs of childhood and of youth than those of middle age. One has a sense, I suppose, that the young have a sort of *right* to happiness, or rather to gladsomeness and enjoyment; that if they ever are to be gay and pretty then is the time. Sorrow and sallow cheeks

* The son-in-law of Mr. Wordsworth.—E. C.

Childhood

come to me at my time of life not unnaturally. Reflection
has preceded them, and ought at least to have enabled the
fading mourner to look beyond them, to see a new world
wherein dwelleth righteousness, and to drown in its lustre,
superinduced over the worsening remnant of our earthly
life, all its own melancholy hues. The comparative health
and beauty of those who have fairly parted with youth is
but a poor thing at the best. But you will laugh at my
moralizing on the subject of beauty, at least if you do not
bear in mind that I am not thinking of that which we
ascribe to *a beauty*, the admired of the ball-room, the
celebrated toast, but rather of that general attribute which
the Psalmist must have referred to, when he complained so
heavily that his " beauty was wasted for very trouble."
We all have, or have had *beauty*, though we are not all
" beauties."

XIV.

Readings in Aristophanes—Cheerfulness and Simplicity of Early
Poetry.

To the Hon. Mr. Justice COLERIDGE.

Chester Place, December 26th, 1843.—As to Aristophanes,
I quite accede to the justice of your representations of his
not altogether fitness for the joint perusal of Herby and me.
I had clean forgotten the uncleanness, till my boy discreetly observed that there was a word in the next line
which would not do to be voiced aloud. We shall only read
the " Frogs," but Herby is so delighted with this play that
it would be a pity for him not to finish it, as I believe, from
what Frere says, that there is but little, after the first
scene, to object to in it. The *spirit* of the humour of
Aristophanes a boy like Herbert may well enter into, when
the *material* is once cleared out of its concealing husk and
set before him. The temptation to read Aristophanes is,
that his plays are mirthful, and " as there's nought but
care on every hand," I am glad of every scrap of cheerful-

ness which I can lay before my children, now in their spring season when they can enjoy it. I feel sadly for them that this is a widowed home. But they appear as glad as others of their age, and the great change to me bears lightly upon them in comparison.

.   .   .   .

We have been laughing heartily at the " Frogs " again. It would be a lounge to read Homer with Herby; but I feel a wish to get him through some of the harder, more troublesome parts of the classical task that lies before him. It is wonderful,—*not* wonderful so much as noticeable,— how fitted the ancient classics are in general for the youthful mind. They contain, indeed, the youthful mind of our human race, are less abstract and subjective than modern compositions.

CHAPTER XII.

LETTERS TO HER ELDEST BROTHER, MISS MORRIS, JOHN KENYON, ESQ., MRS. EDWARD COLERIDGE, MRS. FARRER: 1844.

I.

" Travelling Onwards "—Differences of Mental Perspective in the Contemplation of Truth—Doctrine of the Millennium—Symbolism in the Bible—" Messiah's Kingdom " and the " Reign of the Saints "—Literal Explanation of the latter Prophecy by some of the Fathers.

To Miss MORRIS, Mecklenburg Square.

Chester Place, January, 1844.—" Geneva! " and "Rome! " My hope and trust is that we are *travelling onwards,* and shall in time leave these names, these badges of division, behind us. So far I understand and sympathize with Mr. Maurice, that I think there has been much of " notionalism " among all parties ; by which I take him to mean, in general, a losing sight, or at least a steady view, of spiritual *substance,* through the perplexing and deluding atmospheric medium of the mere understanding, its refractions and distorting reflections ; so that differences have arisen, not from pure perversity of heart, as believers are so apt to say of those who disagree with them, nor from an absolute blindness to truth, but from difference of position and a variableness and uncertainty in the medium itself. I sympathize with him, too, in this, that from being very strongly possessed with the thought which I have just mentioned, I am a good deal isolated from all the conflicting parties now on the arena, and cannot agree wholly either with Tractarians or Anti-Tractarians. For Maurice is at bottom quite as unlike any *party* in

his views as I have been led to be, though his language
would put him into the class of High Churchmen, somewhere between the old section and the new, with those who
read him but cursorily, without asking him and themselves
very strictly what that language, in *his* mouth, means.

If you will soon be addressing Mr. Bickersteth, pray
convey my best thanks to him for his last gift. I think
I have read all that he says on the Promised Glory, and
know the texts which he brings to the service of his
view. Certainly, looked at in one way, they serve it
effectively. I cannot, however, help seeing them in another.
The more we look back to the development and expression
of thought in past ages, the more, I think, we find that
great spiritual and moral truths were in the earlier times
continually presented in the form of the fable or myth.
Instead of sermons and scientific treatises, they had allegories and symbolical representations: all doctrines—moral,
religious, or metaphysical—were embodied and clad in sensuous forms. To speak of this, and draw inferences from
it in the interpretation of that *old book*, the Bible, is
considered a modern refinement, a piece of rationalism.
But rationalism did not invent the mythical mood of
writing: it does but point it out, and compare what it
presumes to be instances of it in Scripture with countless
others out of Scripture. I seem to myself to see plainly
that the descriptions of the Messiah's kingdom in the
Prophets are descriptions of Christianity itself, in all the
glory, and gladness, and purity of the idea, under the guise
of actual history, and with all the pomp of sensuous
imagery to render the symbol significant. In the same
way I read the Revelation; and it seems to me that on
this plan an interpretation may be given, which, though
at first it seems bold, yet is in truth more consistent with
itself, and more accordant with the language of Scripture,
when that is tried by the proper rules, than any other. I

cannot but think that the whole theory of the earthly millennial kingdom stands on an insecure foundation, because I always find from writers on the subject, that at bottom it rests with every one of them on Rev. xx. 4, as it did from the· first; and I do verily believe that the language of that text will not admit of the interpretation which their theory gives to it. The early Fathers, some of them, understood it so; but such symbolical texts they made sad work with, I believe, for the most part. We should not, any of us, like to accept their Biblical criticism all through; and criticism it was plainly enough, not traditional knowledge of any clear description.

II.

Critique on the Early Poems of Elizabeth Barrett (Mrs. Browning) —Favourite Pieces—Exuberance of her Style inappropriate to Solemn Themes—Hasty Objections made by Miss B—— to the Ideal Philosophy of Berkeley, and to the Wolfian Theory of Homer.

To JOHN KENYON, Esq.*

Regent's Park, 1844.—My dear Mr. Kenyon,—At last I return with thanks the Poems of Miss Barrett, which I now always mention in high terms to any of my acquaintances, when the conversation affords an opportunity. I think my favourites are the " Poet's Vow," " A Romance of the Ganges, " " Isobel's Child" (so like "Christabel" in manner, as Mama and I both thought), " The Island," " The

---

* A friend of Mr. Southey's, and relative of the gifted lady whose earlier works form the subject of this letter. It is proper to add that the two concluding paragraphs are only inserted here for the sake of the interesting remarks which they contain on Berkeley's system and the Homeric question, since the notes which originally called them forth were withdrawn in subsequent editions. In Mrs. Browning's later publication, my mother particularly admired the "Drama of Exile," the subject of which she thought "more within the sphere of poetic art" than that of the "Seraphim," "Lady Geraldine's Courtship," "The Cry of the Children," the "Rhyme of the Duchess May," and the " lovely sonnet " called "Irreparableness."—E. C.

Deserted Garden," and " Cowper's Grave." But my conception of Miss B——'s poetical merit is formed from lines
and stanzas occurring here and there in most of the poems
—from the general impression produced by the whole
collection, rather than from any number of entire pieces.
" The Seraphim " contains *very* fine passages ; and perhaps
no other single poem in the volume has impressed me so
strongly with the writer's power; and yet, taken as a
whole, with reference not to what others could produce, but
with what it ought to be, I confess it does not altogether
please me. If there be a subject throughout the range of
human thought which demands to be treated (if treated at
all as the prominent theme of any metrical composition)
with a sober Miltonic majesty of style, rather than with a
wild modernism and fantastic rapture, surely that subject
is the Crucifixion of a Saviour and the Redemption of a
fallen world. Even in that clever translation of the " Prometheus Bound " (for very clever it is), there occur some
phrases which want the Hebraic simplicity of the original.
" The faded white flower of the Titanic brow,"—do you
think that quite comes up to the manly broadness and
boldness of the Greek Dramatist, or suits the awful circumstances of the Titan fixed upon his rock ? There is a *flower*
in both cases, to be sure ; but Æschylus meant that *the
whole outward man* of Prometheus would be parched and
discoloured by the sun's heat ; and this he expressed by
a plain but untranslatable Græcism. I think that your
cousin should study a noble simplicity, especially as her
poetical aims are so high, lest she should be obliged to
finish the lofty temples of imagination with brass instead
of gold. You see how easy it is to *preach* even for those
who cannot practise ; but Miss Barrett *can* practise, and
will benefit, I trust, by preaching of more authority than
mine, the presumption of which will never reach her ears.

I cannot make an end of my preaching, however, without

venturing a remark or two on her summary manner of
dealing with the Homeric question, and with the opinions
of Berkeley. Surely no one, who understands what Berkeley's scheme of Idealism really was, would suppose that the
poor bishop was bound, in consistency with his metaphysical
principles, to let a cart run over him ! He tells us plainly,
that if by material *substance* he meant only that which is
seen and *felt*, then is he "more sensible of matter's existence
than any other philosopher." I question whether Miss
Barrett did not confound idealism with unreality, as persons
new to the subject invariably do. Few metaphysicians
would ratify her sentence that Berkeley was " out of his
senses ; " though none now perhaps believe his system true
in fact, or look upon it as other than a platform on which
a certain number of pregnant truths were exhibited in a
strong point of view. Channing observes how it has influenced the modes of thinking among metaphysicians.

Then, again, Miss Barrett's censure of all who believe in
the " Homeric speculation " is sweeping indeed. It sweeps
away, like chaff before the wind, not only almost all the
great scholars and fine critics of learned Germany, not only
" the eloquent Villemain," and numbers of French savans,
—not only men of genius and learning, such as Wolf and
Heyne, and the Italian Vico—but those of the highest *poetic*
feeling, who, both in this and other countries, are converts
to the system.

Before I conclude, however, let me add that I do not
quarrel with any one for sticking resolutely to the "blind old
man of Scio's rocky isle," nor pretend to have formed a
decided opinion on this puzzling point upon which great
doctors have agreed to differ ; though I *incline* to the belief,
that if Homer ever existed, he no more wrote *all* the books
of the Iliad, than one Hercules performed the twelve labours
ascribed to him. The books, to be sure, are extant, the
labours fabulous ; but I mean that the one, as the other,

may have been a nucleus around whose works those of others were collected, but whose name remained to the whole.

P.S.—Since writing the above, I have again read the "Seraphim," and am more impressed with its merit than at first. It is *full* of beauty.

III.

Gladsomeness of Childhood—Severe Discipline not suited to the Period of Early Youth.

To her Eldest Brother.

Chester Place, 1844.—There is a gladsomeness generally found in children happily circumstanced and managed by those who understand and will to act upon the simple rules, by observance of which these little ones are made and kept as happy as they can be ;—keeping black care quite out of their sight, addressing them with cheerful looks and tones, never keeping them long at any one task, yet enforcing a certain amount of work, with occasional half and some whole holidays, regularly,—never letting any trouble remain as a weight and grinding pressure upon their minds,—but inflicting at once whatever is absolutely necessary,—and then diverting their minds to what is easy and pleasant. A child must also have a certain amount of health and of intellectual activity, imaginativeness, and so forth, to be perpetually *gladsome*,—but with the positives and negatives that I have named, we shall find any child in a country or town cottage not only cheerful, but joyous.

Of course, I am not implying that to produce and maintain this gladness is the great work of education—but I feel assured that it is a true part of education, and that amid this ease from without, and consequent happiness from within, the affections, temper, and understanding expand and grow more favourably, and take a better and more

generous form than under other circumstances. What I
am now saying, however, applies to children as such ; this I
think the best *preparatory* state, because it best enables the
native powers to develop themselves ; but trial and hardship
are proper to exercise and consolidate them from time to
time as soon as they have gained a certain measure of
strength ; and to put the matter practically, I think that
parents should make their children as easy and happy as
ever they can without indulging them in what is wrong,
leaving *discipline* to be supplied by the ordinary and inevitable course of events, the sorrow, difficulty, and suffering
which life in this world brings to every individual. The
young people that are spoiled by an indulgent home are
spoiled, I think, not by over-happiness, but from having
been encouraged in selfishness, never made to understand
and led to practise Christian duty.

IV.

The Temple Church—Colour in Architecture.

To Mrs. EDWARD COLERIDGE, Eton.

June, 1844.—Yesterday, I saw with delight for the first
time the restored Temple Church. The restoration seems
to me to be in excellent taste, with the exception of the altar.
No doubt the great beauty of this interior consists in what
it always had, its general form, with the clustered pillars,
and exquisite interlacing of arches. But the decorative
part brings out and illuminates this original and essential
beauty, as I have so often seen the rich colours of sunset
illuminate the fine forms of my native hills.

V.

Use of Metrical Rules in Poetry—Versification of "Christabel" and "The Ancient Mariner"—Artificial Character of some of the Greek Metres.

To Miss MORRIS.

June 10*th*, 1844.—Have you been poetizing of late? Mind, I do not tie you down to these longs and shorts; but, depend upon it, there is much use in them. The more our ear can direct us the better, but rules help and educate the ear. Poetry is more of an *art* than people in general think. They know that Music and Painting are arts; but they imagine that Poetry must flow forth spontaneously, like the breath which we breathe, without volition or consciousness. All our finest metrists knew these rules: how far they went by them I cannot say; but I know that my father, whose versification has been greatly admired by critics, was fond of talking about anapæsts and iambuses; and if people admired "Christabel," as it were, by nature, he was never easy till he had put them in the way of admiring it more scientifically. Dr. Carlyle says he never succeeded in making him admire "The Ancient Mariner" properly. He was obliged, after all,.to go back to his own first rude impressions, and rely upon them.

The manner in which the ancient verse was constructed is a curious problem. It seems as if those very artificial metres, dependent on syllabic quantity, could never in any degree have been written by ear, or otherwise than as such verse is written now. All critics, however, agree that the best and seemingly most *easy* and *natural* styles, both in prose and verse, are those that have been most artfully written and carefully elaborated. Art alone will do nothing, but it improves and educes the natural gift. Cobbett taught wrong doctrine on this head; and so, I believe, did my Uncle Southey.

VI.

The "Life of Arnold" a Book to be "gloried in"—The Visible Church not to be Identified with any Single System—Dr. Arnold's View.

To THE HON. MR. Justice COLERIDGE.

July, 1844.—I cannot tell you in one short day, or the longest summer day that ever shone, what I feel and think about the " Life of Arnold,"—how I rejoice over it, how I glory in it, what good I augur from it. Not that I can see my way through the *whole* of Arnold's view, or perceive the justice of all his practical conclusions. I cannot but think with him that the *visible* Church is a human institution, sanctioned and blessed by God, and rendered the vehicle of His grace, just so far as it is really an efficient instrument of the preservation and propagation of true Christianity. I can see no sufficient reason to believe that it was supernaturally ordained by Him in detail—that it is not in this respect essentially different from its Jewish predecessor. I cannot doubt that it was full of error from the first, the Apostles during their life repressing, but not radically removing, wrong notions of the faith. I imagine that the Church, ʿas a spiritual power co-ordinate with the Word and the Spirit, is certainly realized through *a* visible machinery and system of outward ordinances, but by no means confined to one alone, and that one prescribed by Christ Himself: so far as any one answers its great end better than another, so far it is a more divine and a fuller organ of the Spirit. But putting the question on the grounds upon which Arnold himself would have placed it— moral evidence, reason, and the plain-speaking of Scripture —I cannot but infer that religion and affairs of policy ought to have distinct functionaries; and certainly the general judgment of mankind, and not a mere sect and party of Christians, has inclined to this view rather than the other.

VII.

" Nothing to do "—Isaac Taylor's Suggestion that there will be Work
    as well as Rest in Heaven—Seaside Views and Walks—Fellow-
    Lodgers—Idleness and Extravagance of London Shopkeepers—
    Two Sorts of Diffuseness—Lord Eldon—Reflections on his Char-
    acter and Portrait.

To Mrs. FARRER.

5, *Nelson Place, Broadstairs, August* 27*th,* 1844.—Dearest
Mrs. Farrer,—I will not defer writing to you till I have
" nothing else to do ; " for I hope that time will never come.
Mr. Taylor of Ongar, in his " History of Enthusiasm,"
takes pains to show that we shall have a great deal *to do* in
heaven, and even have to work hard there. My remark,
however, is quite limited to the time of this mortal life ; for
I think we are scarcely qualified as yet to cut out our work
in the world to come, or determine upon the manner in
which we shall spend eternity. Probably our present ideas
of labour and rest will not be among the things which we
shall carry along with us into the other state ; and I cannot
think Mr. Taylor is justified in accusing other Christians of
having *indolent notions* of heaven, because they have not
exactly his view of the *exertions* that are to be made there.
Be that as it may, however, the main part of my business
here at Broadstairs is to scribble on scraps of paper, sometimes on sheets ; and I am sure that after all your great
kindness to me, and concern shown for my comfort, I ought
to fill one of these little sheets, as well as I can, to you,
little indeed as I have to put into it.

I know you will be pleased to hear how very satisfactory
I find these lodgings. I never before had a *bedroom* with
an interesting prospect, and I undervalued to you what I
had scarce learned to prize. But nothing can be more
charming than the view which I have before me now. The
cornfield betwixt me and the sea takes off the sense of
dreariness, and occasional bleak chilliness, which a full

view of the "unfruitful ocean," and *that alone*, relieved only
by the not more fruitful or lifesome shore, has always
inspired me with. The sea thus viewed has something of
a lake-like aspect; but that soft green hue was never seen
upon any of my native lakes, although their calm bosoms
used to exhibit a great quantity of hues. I take short
walks, sometimes two or three times a day; yesterday I
walked out between seven and eight in the evening, in hopes
to see the moonlight shining on the sea. But the moon,
which had bathed the landscape in tender light the night
before, was hidden in clouds; but still I had a pleasant
walk towards Dampton Stairs, and saw the *earth*-stars,—
the lights on Goodwin sands and others, to advantage.
For a day and a half after your departure I felt low and
unequal to walking; but since then my mercury has risen
a little, and I feel as if the sea was (or "*were*"? no, *was* in
this case, I think) doing me that kind and degree of good
which it generally has done, whenever I have tried it under
tolerably favourable circumstances. The only drawback
has been the noisiness of the children. Yesterday afternoon I began to think it went beyond bounds, and all my
self-remindings that I had loud-voiced chatterers of my
own, did not bring me to feel complacently on the subject
of so much rattling up and down stairs, incessant slamming
of doors, and squeaking and squabbling. They say there
is no lane so long but it comes to an end at last. I find,
however, that *my* lane is a very short one, for the noise-
makers depart in a day or two; indeed, they have been
very bearable ever since yesterday. Their "pa" and
"ma" keep a shop in Oxford Street; and now that I am
able to make some calm, disinterested philosophic reflections on all that I have observed in this family, I am
confirmed in my old opinion that the inferior London shopkeepers are an ill-managing class. I *suspect*, at least,
(I will not venture to say more), that they have more

luxury with less in proportion of real respectability, that they partake more of the *civilization* of their times with less of the *cultivation*, than almost any other portion of the community. These children live on the stairs or in the kitchen, and never take a book or needle in their hands, and yet their parents are overburdening Mrs. Smith with cooking attendance, dressing well, and living for many weeks by the sea in commodious lodgings. The extravagance and recklessness that go on in the families of tradesmen in London is beyond what the rank above them even dream of. No wonder they hate the Church and band against her. The farmers may be still worse in grudging their money; but shopkeepers turn against the Church, I think, because they are better fed than taught, and because they hate regularity, and all that is stern and strict. Methodism and Quakerism have their own strictness; but *they*, many of them, stick to no sect, but go after this or that preacher. They represent the *bad* spirit of this age more completely than almost any other large class amongst us; but I believe they are to be pitied more than blamed, having great temptations to all they do amiss.

I heard Dr. H—— again last Sunday, and continued to like his manner of preaching, for its earnestness and practicability, and aiming at the one thing needful. The fault of his style is a verbosity and diffuseness; he gives you five branches of illustration, where one good solid bough would be quite enough. It is well to be reminded that we are better than the beasts that perish, and can give greater glory to God; but the various particulars of our superiority, beginning with our erect posture, etc., etc., might be left to our own minds to suggest. This is very different from such diffuseness as that of Lord Eldon, who had not, I conjecture, *more words than matter*, but more matter of various kinds than he could arrange to perfection; the minor matters overlaid the major, as the

M

muffling ivy prevents the fine figure of a noble oak, with its well proportioned trunk and branches, from being clearly discerned.   He was perspicuous in thought, but not equally perspicuous in expression.   I read to the end of this last volume of his life with very great interest of various kinds. The concluding portion, containing the vindication of his professional character, appeared to me very ably written, and upon the whole, more than triumphant, and the remarks on Chancery business, and the legal anecdotes interspersed, are very good also.   The perusal brought home to me, what I have long felt, how impossible it is that any eminently good and great and useful man should go through life without being perseveringly and violently misrepresented and ill-used.   That review of Justice W. is such a specimen of able, but untruthful and unfair writing! The portrait of Lord Eldon, the more I look at it, the more it seems to be the very man ; mild sensibility and weight of intellect, and moral firmness and sound judgment, are all marked in that countenance.

CHAPTER XIII.

LETTERS TO HER ELDEST BROTHER, THE HON. MR. JUSTICE COLERIDGE, AUBREY DE VERE, ESQ., MISS MORRIS, MISS ERSKINE, MRS. FARRER, THE HON. MRS. HENRY TAYLOR : 1845.

I.

Memories of her Native Vale—The *Quarterley Review* a greater Authority on Practical than on Poetical Matters—Dr. Arnold as a Man and a Writer—His peculiar Theory of Church and State—Definition of Humility and Modesty, suggested by a Note in the " Northern Worthies."

To HARTLEY COLERIDGE, Esq., Grasmere.

Chester Place, January 20th, 1845.—Your communications and comments are ever most interesting to me, partly because they are upon persons and things in my native land, to which I have turned since my loss with renewed love and longing—to thoughts of the hills and the lakes, and still more of the rivers and streamlets, my dearly-beloved Greta rushing over the stones by the Cardingmill Field, or sweeping past, swollen with rains ; and all the lovely flowers, especially the yellow globe flower, which fringe the banks, or lurk in the woods, or crowd and cluster in the open glades. But then my remembrance of all these things is inseparably associated with the feelings of early youth, which lends a glow to them. *Now,* if I were at the Blue-bell Bog, or on the slope of Goosey Green, I should be sinking with fatigue, not knowing how I should get back again. Even an easy saunter by Greta's side would be a very different thing, now that life, or the best part of it, is all behind me, from what it was when this same life was *before* me—a vision often broken and obscured indeed by fear and anxiety, but yet with the sun of Hope burning in its centre. This thought prevents me from lamenting, as I otherwise might, that I cannot look to spend my latter years in the lovely country of my youth. Yet I never take a solitary walk in the Park without longing that I could turn my steps towards dear old Friar's Crag. I think, in spite of middle age, and sickness and sorrow, I should still have much enjoyment in looking on the Lake, every day differently complexioned from the last, in gazing on the hills lit up by sunset, and all the manifold shows of nature among my native hills. Herbert H—— seems to miss the richness and variety of the lake-land exceedingly. In his last letter he observed how flat countries lose all their attractions in winter, which does but interestingly vary those of a mountainous district. Do not think, how-ever, from my speaking of having left the best part of life behind me, that I am unhappy. I do not in the least wish to be happier, in the sense of having more satisfaction and animated enjoyment in the things of this world. It is best for me as it is. . . .

It is remarkable how strong the *Quarterly Review* is in dealing with *matters of fact :* various as the writers in it must be, they always shine in that department. In abstract reasonings this " Review " is not great, and in æsthetics it is generally poor enough. Its poetical criticism is arbitrarily vague, without the slightest attempt at prin-ciple, and in a sneering, contemptuous spirit. Its treat-ment of Keats and Tennyson was ultra-zoilian. I admire Keats excessively. Mr. Wordsworth used to say of Shelley and Keats that they would ever be great favourites with the young, but would not satisfy men of all ages. There is a truth in this saying, though I should say that it is not *literally* true, for I myself and many other *mediævals* can read their productions with unabated pleasure. But yet I feel that there is in those writers a want of solidity; they do not embody in their poems much of that with which the deeper and the universal heart and mind of man can sympathize. To be always reading Shelley and Keats would be like living on quince-marmalade. Milton and Wordsworth are substantial diet for all times and seasons.

Your admiration of Arnold I fully share. I admire, and, what is more, deeply honour him as a man, and as a writer so far as the man appears in his writings. As a reasoner and speculator I surmise that he was not *great*, though what he does see clearly he expresses with great energy and lifesomeness. It seems to me that he arrived at much truth which subtler men miss, through sheer honesty and single-ness of heart and mind, through sheer impatience and imprudence, not through philosophy. His views of Church and State I cannot well understand (I have not seen his fragment on the Church): so far as I *can* understand them, I imagine (it seems presumptuous for such as I to *opine* positively on such a subject) that they are incorrect and inadequate. He was a great historian; yet I would fain see how he reconciled them with history, let alone philoso-phy. By unifying the State with the Church, does he not nullify and destroy the latter as a spiritual power, the anta-gonist of the world, and confer privileges and functions on the former incompatible with its proper and peculiar ones? I should say, in my ignorance, that this is after all but Romanism in disguise, at least practically. But perhaps I do not apprehend his scheme. He was and is a burning and a shining light in this country. His "Life and Letters" seem to have made a greater impression on the public mind than any book that has been published for many a day. . . .

Reading your "Life of Mason" lately (during the height of my illness I read the "Doctor" and your "Worthies:" I did not want *new* books, but soothing ones in which I took a special interest), I noticed that you said in a note, "Modesty and vanity are only different phenomena of one and the same disposition, viz., an extreme consciousness and apprehensiveness of being observed." * But this degrades modesty, methinks, into mere bashfulness, which belongs to the physical temperament, and is but modesty's shadow. Many a youth has both modesty and vanity; for modesty is directly opposed, not to vanity, but to impudence. Still, modesty is surely something more than the *fear of being observed*, which is, indeed, but a phase or mood of vanity, when it is not mere nervous bashfulness.

How shall we define Modesty? Surely it is an important virtue, and a grace to boot. Is it not *moderation*, viewed in its moral rather than its prudential aspect—ingenuous shame, and keen sensibility to all that is unseemly, unfitting, disproportionate in reference to self? It is closely allied to Justice, for he who does not overrate himself is the less likely to arrogate to himself more than is his due : it borders upon Humility and Piety, for he who is not disposed to exalt his own merits in his own eyes or in those of others, though not necessarily humble on that account, is yet far more in the way of being so than if he had a high notion of his relative excellence, and a desire to parade and proclaim it. Humility is not the mere consciousness of our low estate, but the disposition to act and suffer as if we had no high claims ; and this is different from modesty, yet, I think, akin to it. Humility, perhaps, is the being *content* with the low place and scant portion ; Modesty, a sense of the impropriety of claiming a higher and a better.

II.

The Royal Academy of 1845—Turner's Painting.

To Miss ERSKINE.

May 18th, 1845.—It is commonly said that this is not a striking Exhibition, simply, I think, because there is in it

* " Lives of Northern Worthies," by Hartley Coleridge, vol. ii. p. 256.— E. C.

no great glaring Maclise, nor the usual number of fine animal pieces, with fur which one longs to stroke, by Landseer. I should say, as some others say too, that it is upon the whole a very interesting collection of specimens of our modern English school of painting : it contains so many sweet landscapes by Stanfield (no Callcotts, alas !), by Collins, Creswick, Lee (one of whose pictures is almost a Gainsborough), Leitch, Harding, and Roberts, though about the productions of this last there is rather a tiring sameness.

In this list I have not included Turner, because I can find but few persons who agree with me that he *is* to be admired ; but I had the comfort of an accordant voice with mine in dear Lady Palgrave's. I do not like Turner's Venetian views, of which he has four in the present Exhibition, so much as two pictures called "Whalers," in which sea and sky are mixed up together in most (by me) *admired* confusion. No other man gives me any notion of that infinity of hues and tints and gradations of light and shade which Nature displays to those who have eyes for such sights, except Turner : no one else gives me such a sense of the power of the elements, no one else lifts up the veil and discloses the *penetralia* of Nature, as this painter does. The liquid look of his ocean and its lifesomeness, and that wonderful steam that is rising up and hovering over the agitated vessel, are what one might look for in vain in any but the Turnerian quarter.

On the other hand, I cannot admire Landseer's "Shepherd in Prayer" so much as it is the fashion to do. In this picture he aims at something in a higher line than he has attempted before ; and, to my mind, in this higher line he wants power. There is doubtless a sweet feeling about the picture : the shepherd is good, and he kneels before a most picturesquely rural crucifix, but the sheep are *de trop* ; such a quantity of dead fleece scattered around, and continued on the very horizon, I cannot away with, or rather, I wish it away. Neither can I satisfy Derwent in the amount of admiration which he demands for Eastlake's " Comus." It is very pure and harmonious, and finely coloured, but it wants intensity, and meaning, and spirit. The " Heiress " by Leslie is a most lovely girl ; and Clater's " Bride " as fair and vernal as the hawthorn wreath with which she is encircling her head, in contempt of Fashion with her orange-flowers. Etty has seven or eight pictures, all of which have his usual merits, more or less, and some of them are beautiful. His *flesh* is first-rate ; but one may look in vain in him for the spirit—that is, the spiritual and refined.

III.

Visitors before Luncheon.

To Miss MORRIS.

Chester Place, 1845.—First, I must reply to your proposal of coming to see me between twelve and one o'clock. My *rule* is, not to let my friends visit me at that early hour when they can with no great difficulty come at a later one ; because the two hours before my mid-day meal are with me the most uneasy in the whole twenty-four. Still, I do not wish to be more subjected to my bodily weakness than is unavoidable, and every now and then I am called down to some old friend whom I do not like to send away unseen. Old gentlemen especially *will* take their own way in such matters, and look in when it suits them rather than when it suits me. At first I feel faint and cross ; but when they begin laying down the law about this and that,—the Church and the Tract doctrines, and other such subjects,—as if there was but one opinion in the world that was really worth a straw, and that their own,—all other rea-soners and thinkers dancing about after vain shadows and will-o'-the-wisps,—I am provoked into a sort of enraged strength,—my controversial muscles begin to plump up,—

I lose sight of luncheon (a vision of which had been floating before my dull eyes before), and as soon as a pause
occurs, I fill it up with my voice, and, whether listened to
or not, improve by exercise my small powers of expressing
opinion.

IV.

Interpretations of Scripture Prophecies by Writers of the Evangelical
School—Contents of the Sixth Vial—Shelley's Atheism—Not
Papal but Pagan Rome the real Object of the Apocalyptic
Denunciations.

To Miss MORRIS.

10, *Chester Place, June 21st,* 1845.—I have felt that I
ought to have been conversing with you of late on a subject
upon which I have been venturing to write (I mean a *letter*
only)—the subject of prophecy.

I told Mr. B—— the impression which the different
passages in Scripture, most important in the Antichrist
controvery, and most dwelt upon by each party, as proving
their own particular views, make upon me, when I read
them without the medium of note or comment, and with no
theory intervening betwixt my mind's eye and the text. The
" little horn " of Daniel presents to me a staring likeness of
the Pope. That it was intended for him, and for none other
than he, I will not venture to say. I do not feel sure or
that, all things considered, so far as I can consider them.
But I say it is *awfully like* him,—that he *is* a little horn
that speaks great things, and has eyes, *such eyes* as no
other power in this world possesses, that he changes times
and laws presumptuously and iniquitously, and has worn
out a great many saints of God with persecutions. But
when I read the language of the New Testament on the
Man of Sin and Antichrist, instead of seeing this picture
enlarged and rendered more distinct,—on the contrary,
I see only a generalization. The mystery of iniquity is in
the Papacy ;—but that popery, and popery alone, is the

mystery of iniquity, I cannot persuade myself. Here, I think, Horsley, Palmer, and a hundred others, who oppose the theory which identifies Antichrist with the Pope or popery, are strong. That "wicked that is 'to be consumed' by the spirit of the Lord's mouth, and destroyed by the brightness of His coming," is certainly no popery that has existed yet. But it is said there is to be another manifestation of popery and its corruption, and this it is which is to be destroyed. Now, it is just this way of interpreting Scripture, this putting into the sacred text *ad libitum*, and filling up ever so great a gulf and gap with supposition, which seems to me so unwarrantable, and a method too which never leads to any conclusion, because every different theorist can resort to the same expedient to justify his opinions. See the tracts on Antichrist, and the use *they* make of this argument. If all the abominations, persecutions, presumptions, and impious pretensions of the Papacy, which history records, are the characters of the Man of Sin, then surely he has been already revealed, as he was not revealed in St. Paul's own day. To say that we have already witnessed these things, and that they constitute the wickedness of the wicked one, and yet that he is *still to be revealed* close before the advent of the Lord, and His reign upon earth, is not, in my opinion, to submit our minds to the text of Scripture, but make it say what we like. The "powers, and signs, and lying wonders" of Romanism, have been manifested at full. It is highly improbable that they can ever deceive the world again as they have done. What a crafty priesthood can contrive in one part of the civilized world, an active press and an irrepressible spirit of inquiry and opposition to superstitious falsity exposes and counteracts in another part. The passage in Timothy, on forbidding to marry, does not to my mind describe Romanistic errors, but religious notions of a somewhat different kind.

If such are my impressions from the Epistles, still more strongly do I feel on going on to the Apocalypse, that popery was not the object of the apostolic predictions and denunciations, except so far as *all* falsehood and corruption is so. I cannot pretend to assign the meaning of all the various symbols,—I *never* have seen them to my mind satisfactorily explained. The "vials" are filled, to every man's fancy, with just those exhibitions of evil which most strongly have excited his aversion, and alarmed his fears. Mr. B—— notices Shelley's "Revolt of Islam," under the sixth vial. Alas! poor Shelley! "I'se wae to think of him," as Burns was to think of old Nick and his gloomy fate. He had a religious element in his nature; but it was sadly overborne by a impetuous temper, and a certain presumption, which made him cast aside all the teaching of other men that did not approve itself at once to his judgment. But to mention him under the sixth vial is to give him an infamous sort of fame which he scarcely, I think, deserved. As an unbeliever, he was utterly insignificant,—made no proselytes, had no school, nor belonged to any school. He had ceased to be an atheist before he died, and never had any power, or excited any great attention, I think, except as a poet. In that line he has a station from which he cannot be moved while any genuine taste for poetry as such exists.

To conclude my impressions of prophecy, not from commentaries, but from the text, I own I can see nothing but Imperial and Pagan Rome in the Revelation, as the great object of the prophet's denunciations, from beginning to end. It should be borne in mind, I think, that the persecutions under the Roman Empire were the only warfare that ever has been carried on against Christianity as such, —against the *religion* itself under any form. The martyrs during that warfare were the only sufferers who could *properly* be said to have died for the faith for the testimony of Jesus. There have been anti-Papal martyrs enough for the purity of the faith ; but is it not putting the less before the greater to imagine that these, and not the thousands that were put to death and tortured for professing Christianity at all, are those of whom the Apocalypt wrote with such a pen of fire ? But the whole description of this Babylon the Great, and her downfall, this city on seven hills, to my mind, is expressive of the great Roman *Empire*, of which Rome itself was the representative, and not Papal Rome, which never sat upon seven hills ; and to convert those seven hills into seven electors of Germany, seems to me a more incredible transformation than any in Ovid's metamorphoses. Nothing can exceed the boldness of Scriptural metaphor ; but this boldness has its own laws, and the same figure which fits one sentence fits not another.

V.

Occasional Recurrence of Millennial Preachings—Bearing of the Parable of the Ten Virgins on this Subject—Various Styles of Contemporary Divines.

To Miss MORRIS.

1845.—I find that there has been a very general preaching of the Millennium in various parts of the country of late years. So it will continue to be, I think, ever and anon, till some victorious arm shall arise, or some victorious pen shall write some book in which a real advance shall be made in the elucidation of the subject. Hitherto there has been nothing more than a repeated eddying round a certain number of arguments, which contain a certain quantity of force, and are especially striking when first presented to the unprepared mind, but which, as I have been led to think, are not strong enough to bring the matter to a conclusion with the majority of the reflective and judicious. Hence the subject is often brought forward, eagerly enforced, makes a number of converts—some few permanent ones, others only for a season; but then it dies away again, without taking any deep hold of the Church at large. I know how your brother disposes of this fact in that judicious sermon of his on the " Actual Neglect," etc., which shows a clearer insight into the difficulties of the question, I think, than most Millennial discourses do. He observes that the *wise* virgins slumbered as well as the foolish, while the Bridegroom tarried. But if the *wise* as well as the foolish neglect this doctrine, what are they that attend to it? Our Lord leaves no room for them in His parable at all. Looking at the structure of it, I can hardly persuade myself that He meant by this slumber to indicate a blameable inattention to His coming again; for what could the wise virgins have done, had they kept awake the whole night, than provide oil for their lamps? what would they have gained more than admission to the marriage-feast? . . .

I agree with you quite about Mr. B——'s sermon and its " dry brilliancy." It reminds me of those bright, burnished insects whose juiceless bodies clink and rattle as they whisk glittering along. His style wants oiling.

Newman's sermon, " Faith against Sight," one of those addressed to the University, is an admirable specimen of his mind and manner. I think he is the finest writer, upon the whole, that we have at present; but, with all his power, he will never be able, as I believe, to establish more than one half of his body of opinion in this land.

VI.
Dr. Pusey's Preaching.

To Miss MORRIS, Mecklenburg Square.

Chester Place, July 7th, 1845.—We have had Pusey and Manning preaching here lately, the former three times. Pusey's middle sermon, preached in the evening, was the perfection of his style. But it is wrong to talk of *style* in respect of a preacher whose very merit consists in his aiming at no *style* at all. He is certainly, to my feelings, more impressive than any one else in the pulpit, though he has not one of the graces of oratory. His discourse is generally a rhapsody, describing, with infinite repetition and accumulativeness, the wickedness of sin, the worthlessness of earth, and the blessedness of heaven. He is as still as a statue all the time he is uttering it, looks as white as a sheet, and is as monotonous in delivery as possible. While listening to him, you do not seem to see and hear a *preacher*, but to have visible before you a most earnest and devout spirit, striving to carry out in this world a high religious theory.

VII.
Sunset over the Sea.

To Mrs. FARRER.

Herne Bay, August 9th, 1845.—Yesterday evening the soft blue of sea and sky, illumined with windows of bright rose-colour, which seemed like windows of heaven indeed, with the Apocalyptical city stretched out in gemmy splendour on the other side, as fancy suggested, was most lovely and tranquillizing.

VIII.

Canterbury Cathedral, and St. Augustine's College.

To the Hon. Mr. Justice COLERIDGE, Heath's Court, Ottery St. Mary.

Herne Bay, August 10th, 1845.—Last Wednesday we went to Canterbury to see the Cathedral and St. Augustine's. The former I admired more than ever; and Derwent's architectural lore made our excursion all round the outside, and through the inside of this more beautiful than sublime structure, all the more rememberable and interesting. Some of the old painted glass is the very ideal of that sort of thing, rich and gemmy with minute designs, and far removed from the modern *picture* style of painted window. We visited the precincts of St. Augustine's with very great interest, and were pleased to see with our own eyes, how considerable a part of the ancient structure will be woven into the view, and what a *physical continuity*, as Derwent says, there will be of the one with the other. The new dining-hall takes in the woodwork, to a great extent, of the old refectory for strangers; and the antique architectural forms (in the middle-pointed style) will be carefully reproduced. The old gateway will form a very imposing entrance to the modern college.

IX.

Re-union of Christendom—The Romish Clergy, and the Roman Church.

To the Hon. Mr. Justice COLERIDGE.

Chester Place, August 26*th,* 1845.—As for desire for re-union with the Church of Rome—I verily think that no one can exceed me in desire for the union of all Christendom, that all who call upon the name of the Lord, and acknowledge the moral law of the New Testament, and the necessity of obeying it, should be in communion with each other,— the millions of Methodists, Baptists, Congregationalists in America, as well as the Romanists of Italy and Spain. But such a union cannot be without concessions to a great extent on one side or the other, if not on both, unless the parties were to change their minds to a great extent, in which case the debate and the difficulty would be at an end; and I for one could never give up or adopt what would satisfy either body. I suppose, however, that you have a desire for a re-union with *Rome,* of a very different kind from any you may entertain for union with all Christians; you look upon Rome as a branch of the true Church, and the others above-named as out of the pale of the true Church. With this feeling I cannot pretend to have much sympathy, though it may be my error and misfortune not to have it. I think that the Congregationalists belong to the Church of Christ, as well as the others. The Church of

Rome I am accustomed to regard, not as the aggregate of
Christians professing Romish doctrine, but as the body of
the Romish clergy, together with the system of religious
administration upon which they proceed.   For the former,
the multitude of Romish individuals, I have no feelings of
dislike or disrespect whatever,—I believe that numbers of
them are full of true religion and virtue, and worship God
in spirit and in truth.   The Romish clergy, considered in
their corporate capacity, I cannot but look upon as full of
worldly wisdom and worldly iniquity, and I think, as you
do of the Reformation, that old Nick contemplates it—*i.e.*,
this body—with great satisfaction, the cockles of his heart
leaping up with delight at the view.   My Uncle Southey
was abused for calling the system of the Romish Church
" a monstrous structure of imposture and wickedness ;"—
yet I think he did a good deal to substantiate the charge;
he certainly had far more *information* on the subject than
our young inamoratos of the modern Romish Church can
any of them boast, and he had no sort of sympathy with
Dissenters and Low Churchmen to inspire him with enmity
against the opposite quarter of Christendom.   Still I am
endeavouring to get rid of Protestant prejudice; of all
feelings and views merely founded on habit, apart from
reflection and genuine spiritual perception,—and to consider
quietly whether or no there be not some good even in the
Romish ecclesiastical system ;—and some good I do believe
there is, *especially for the lower orders*, as I also think there
is some good in the Methodist system, with which, as well
as with the religious practices of the strict Evangelicals,
Blanco White is always comparing the system in which he,
to his misery, was brought up.   But I own it seems to me
that the good, whatever it may be, is inextricable from the
evil, both from the nature of the thing, and also because
the Romish body have never been known to make any *real*
concession of any kind or sort—none that was not meant

as a mere temporary expedient, to be withdrawn on the earliest opportunity : and looking upon them, as I do, as *a power of this world*, aiming at political domination and not inspired, as a body, with any pure zeal for the furtherance of the *truth*, be it what it may, I cannot believe they ever will.

X.

"New Heavens and a New Earth."

The following lines may fitly be inserted here, as a poetical expression of the writer's sentiments on these high subjects.—E. C.

To a Fair Friend arguing in Support of the Renovation, in a Literal Sense, of the Material System.

PHILONOUS TO HYLASIA.

I.

Keep, oh ! keep those eyes on me,
   If thou wouldst my soul persuade,
Soul of reasoner, bold and free,
   Who with pinions undismayed
Soars to realms of higher worth
Than aught like these poor heavens and earth.

II.

Talk no more of Scripture text,
   Tract and note of deep divine :
These but leave the mind perplexed—
   More effectual means are thine :
Through that face, so fair and dear,
The doctrine shines as noonday clear.

III.

Who that sees the radiant smile
   Dawn upon thy features bright,
And thy soft, full eyes the while
   Spreading beams of tender light,
But must long those looks to greet,
When perfect souls in joyance meet ?

IV.

Who that round some verdant home
   Day by day with thee hath strayed,
Through its pathways loved to roam,
   Sat beneath its pleasant shade,
But must hope that heavenly bowers
May wear such hues as these of ours ?

N

v.

O ye fair and pleasant places,
  Where the eye delighted ranges ;
O ye dear and friendly faces,
  Loved through all your mortal changes ;
Are ye but stars, to shine through this life's night,
Destined, in Heaven's great Day, to vanish from our sight?
                                        S. C., 1845.

To Miss MORRIS.

Eton, September 8th, 1845.—I have often spoken of you
to Mr. de Vere; and yesterday I told him that the views
which he was setting forth, in regard to the future world,
the glorified body, and the new heavens and earth, were in
spirit, and to a great degree in form, extremely similar to
those I had heard you express and warmly enlarge upon.
I am much more *dry*, alas! on these subjects ; at least I
am aware that my belief must appear very dry and cold to
all but those who entertain it. *We* somehow fancy that we
are to have a quintessence of all that is exalted, and glowing, and beautiful, in your new-world creed hereafter, only
not in the same way. Mr. de Vere cannot bear to part
with our human body altogether, nor with this beautiful
earth with its glorious canopy. He wants to keep these
things, but to have them unimaginably raised, and purified,
and glorified ! *I* think that *they* must go, but that all the
loveliness, and majesty, and exquisiteness, are to be unimaginably extracted and enshrined in a new, unimaginable
form, in another, and to us now, inconceivable state of
existence. He said (so like you), "But I want *this earth* to
have a fair trial, to have it show what it can be at the best,
in the highest perfection of which it is capable, which never
has been yet manifested."

XI.

Poetry of Keats : its Beauties and Defects—" The Grecian Urn " and " Endymion."

To AUBREY DE VERE, Esq., Curragh Chase, Ireland.

Eton, September, 1845.—I admire Keats extremely, but I think that he wants solidity. His path is all flowers, and leads to nothing but flowers. The end of the Endymion is no point : when we arrive there, it is looking down a land of flowers, stretching on *ad infinitum,* the separate parts indistinguishable. I admire all the minor poems which you have marked, three of them especially. In the " Grecian Urn " I dislike the third stanza : it drags out the substance of the preceding stanzas—which, after all, is stuff of *fancy,* not of the higher *imagination*—to weariness ; and it ends with an unpleasant image, expressed in no very good English. " High sorrowful " is Keats' English, if English at all.

I must say that, spite of the beautiful poetry, as far as words and images go, I've no patience with that Adonis lying asleep on a couch with his " white arm " and " faint damask mouth," like a "dew-dipped rose," with lilies above him, and Cupids all around him. If Venus was in love with such a girl-man as that, she was a greater fool than the world has ever known yet, and didn't know what a handsome man is, or what sort of a gentleman is " worthy a lady's eye," even as far as the mere outward man is concerned. I do think it rather effeminate in a young man to have even dreamed such a dream, or presented his own sex to himself in such a *pretty-girl* form. And where is the sense or the beauty of setting one woman opposite another, for a pair of lovers, instead of an Apollo or a Venus ? This effeminacy is the weak part of Keats. Shelley has none of it. There is no greater stickler than I am for the rights of woman—not the right of speaking in Parliament and voting at elections, but of having her own sex to herself, and all the homage due to its attractions. There

is one merit in Byron : he is always manly. The weaknesses he has are weaknesses of an imperfect man, not a
want of manliness.

You will perhaps tell me that the Greek poets have
sometimes ascribed a delicate beauty to Adonis. But I say
these poets must have been thinking of their own lady-loves
all the while, and that Venus herself would have admired a
very different swain. It is not the possession of any beauty
of form or hue that will make a man effeminate ; but it is
the presence of such beauty apart from something else to
which it is subordinated. It is the absence of this *something else*, and the presentation of that which in woman is
characteristic and prominent, without it, which makes this
picture of Keats so disagreeably feminine, at least to my
taste. I think I have a right to preach on *this* theme, just
because I am a woman myself. Men in general are frights,
especially before and after five-and-twenty. Nothing pro-
vokes ladies more than to hear men admiring one another's
beauty. It is less affronting for each man to admire his
own ; they fancy *that* is for their sakes !

I must take another half sheet to quarrel with you about
the "Endymion." How could you possibly, after making
so many marks, pass over that powerful description of
Circe torturing the metamorphosed wretches in the forest,
one of the most striking passages in the whole poem. I
am afraid you like nothing that is *horrid*, that you are too
fond of the "roses and the thistle-down," and find such
things "too flinty hard for your nice touch." To me it is
refreshing, after the sugar upon honey and butter upon
cream of much that precedes. It is fine, too, as an allegory. And is not that an energetic expression ?—

> "Disgust and hate,
> And terrors manifold, *divided me*
> *A spoil amongst them.*"

Especially powerful is that part beginning—

> " Avenging, slow,
> Anon she took a branch of mistletoe.".

The deliberate way in which she does the thing is so fine, and their anticipation of agony, and the poor elephant's pathetic prayer! One feels the cumbrous weight of flesh weighing one down in reading it.

Again, you take no notice of Cynthia's speech to her lover, so Beaumont-and-Fletchery—

> " O that the dreadful smiles
> Had waned from Olympus' solemn height,
> And from all serious gods!"

Brimful of love-sick silliness, no doubt, but so is the whole poem; and instead of flattering the fellow in that way, she ought to have given him a sharp dig with her keenest arrow for having the abominable bad taste to call her lunar lips " slippery blisses." By-the-by, what think you of " nectarous camel-draughts " ? Is it not enough to horrify the very genius of osculation into a fit ? Surely, after a *camel-draught* of nectar, Glaucus might have found the contents of the " black, dull, gurgling phial " an agreeable change, and after such a drench of roses and ambrosia, who would not cry aloud for camomile and wormwood ?

These are your omissions. Then, in the way of commission, you put a stroke of approval at these lines—

> " Old Œolus thy foe
> Skulks to his cavern, 'mid the *gruff* complaint
> Of all his rebel tempests.
>   Dark clouds faint
> When, from thy diadem, a silver gleam
> Slants over *blue dominion*."

Gruff is a ludicrous word; and if we may talk about *blue dominion*, I know not what classes of words there are that may not intermarry with every other class.

You approve also this—

> " While ocean's tide
> Hung swollen at their backs, and *jewell'd* sands
> Took *silently* their footprints."

Ocean's tide hangs swollen from a dyke, which keeps it back; but does it ever thus hang from a sandy beach, and how should sands be *jewelled*, and why should it be noticed that they took footprints *silently*?

It seems to me that Keats not only falsifies language very frequently, besides *making* words, such as orby, serpenting, etc., ad libitum, but that he also falsifies nature sometimes in his imagery. He turns the outer world into a sort of raree show, and combines shapes and colours as fantastically and lawlessly as the kaleidoscope. The kaleidoscope certainly has a law of its own, and so has the young poet, but it is not nature's law, nor in harmony with it. The old masters, in all their vagrancy of fancy and invention, never did·thus. They always placed their wild inventions in the real world, and while we wander in their realms of faëry, we have the same solid earth and blue sky over our heads as when we take a walk in the fields to see Cicely milking the cow. This I think is occasionally the fault of Keats, and another is that sameness of sweetness and over-lusciousness of which I have already spoken. Reading the Endymion is like roaming in a forest of giant jonquils. Nevertheless, I take great delight in his volume, and thank you much for putting it into my hands.

XII.

On the Sudden Death of her Mother.*

To Hon. Mr. Justice COLERIDGE.

Chester Place, September 26th, 1845.—My dearest John, —Thank you for your most kind letter. My soul is indeed very sorrowful. The death-silence is awful. I had to think

---

* At Chester Place, on the 24th of September, during my mother's absence on a visit to the Rev. Edward Coleridge at Eton.—E. C.

of her every minute of the day, to be always on my guard against noise; and she was one that made herself *felt*, dear creature, every hour in the day. *I* shall never be *so* missed by any one, my life is so much stiller, and more to myself.

I feel more than ever the longing to go and join them that are gone—but for my children. But the greatest tie to earth is gone from me, for even the children could do better without me than she could have done.

All that Nurse tells me of her last days is soothing. She wrote contentedly, thankful for Nurse's devotion to her, and speaking even of Caroline's desire to please her. She had said to me, as I was going away, "This is the last time you must leave me." I said, "If you are in the least ill, let me know, and I will return directly." I knew it would only vex her to give up the visit *then*.

I always looked forward to nursing her through a long last illness. I know not how it was, I could never help looking forward to it with a sort of satisfaction. I day-dreamed about it—according to the usual way of my mind —and cut it out in fancy all in my own way. She was to waste away gradually, without much suffering, and to become more and more placid in spirit, and filled with the anticipation of heavenly things. I thought, too, that this would help to prepare me for my change. Now I seem as if a long-cherished prospect had been snatched away from me. I thank God I was not thus suddenly separated from Henry.—Ever your very affectionate sister,

SARA COLERIDGE.

XIII.

Peculiar Sense of Solitude arising from the loss of a Parent—Editorial Labours on the "Biographia Literaria"—A Giant Campanula.

To the Hon. Mrs. HENRY TAYLOR.

10, *Chester Place, December 8th*, 1845.—Your kind invitation I feel quite grieved to decline, but I must decline

it, as I have done many others that have lately been made
me. I do not feel sufficiently equable in spirits to leave
home *now*, and cannot agree with my friends in general
that I should regain this quietude better elsewhere than at
home. But I hope to see more of you, dear Mrs. Taylor,
some time hence. The death of my mother permanently
affects my happiness, more even than I should have anticipated, though I always knew that I must feel the
separation at first as a severe wrench. But I did not
apprehend, during her life, to what a degree she prevented
me from feeling heart-solitude, and the full forlornness
of a widow's state. Her age and infirmities, though they
caused me great uneasiness, had not made any sensible
alteration in her mind or heart. I lost in her as appre-
hensive a companion, and one who entered as fully into
life, as if she had died at fifty. She had a host of common
remembrances with me and interests which my children
are strangers to. They cannot connect me, as conversation
with her so constantly did, with all my early life. But
the worst is the loss of cares and duties, due to her, which
gave additional interest to my existence, and made me
feel of *use* and important.

I am not, however, brooding over grief, from want of
employment. I am just now, indeed, *absurdly* busy. I
have to edit my father's fragmentary work, the "Biographia
Literaria," or at least to continue the preparations already
made for a new edition. To carry on these upon the
plan on which they were commenced, and to do for the
Biographia what has been done for "The Friend," and
other works of my father, I have found, as I advanced into
the first volume, *for me*, exceedingly troublesome. A clever
literary man, who reads and writes on a large scale, would
make nothing of the business, but it makes me feel as if
I had no rest for the sole of my feet, and must be continually starting up to look into this or that volume, or

find it out in some part of Europe. As little boys at school do' *so* wish that Virgil and Livy would but have written *easily*, so I am sometimes tempted to wish that my father would just have read more *commonplace-ishly*, and not quoted from such a number of out-of-the-way books, which not five persons in England, but himself, would ever look into. The trouble I take is so ridiculously dispro-portioned to any effect that can be produced, and we are so apt to measure our importance by the efforts we make, rather than the good we do, that I am obliged to keep reminding myself of this very truth, in order not to become a mighty person in my own eyes, while I remain as small as ever in the eyes of every one else.

Then my father had such a way of seizing upon the *one* bright thing, out of long tracts' of (to most persons) dull and tedious matter. I remember a great campanula which grew in a wood at Keswick—two or three such I found in my native vale during the course of my flower-seeking days. As well might we present one of these as a sample of the blue-bells of bonny Cumberland, or the one or two oxlips, which may generally be found among a multitude of cowslips in a Somersetshire meadow, as specimens of the flowerhood of the field, as give these extracts for proof of what the writer was generally wont to produce.

XIV.

"S. T. C. on the Body"—The Essential Principle of Life not de-pendent on the Material Organism—Teaching of St. Paul on this Point—The Glorified Humanity of Christ—Disembodied Souls—Natural Regrets arising from the Thought of our great Change.

To AUBREY DE VERE, Esq.

"What did Luther mean by a body? For to me the word seemeth capable of two senses, universal and special; first, a form indicating to A. B. C., etc., the existence and finiteness of some one other being, *demonstrative* as *hic*, and *disjunctive* as *hic et non ille*, and in this sense God alone can be without body; secondly, that which is not merely *hic distinctive*, but *divisive;* yea, a product divisible from the producent as a snake from its skin, a precipitate and death of living power, and in this sense the body is proper to mortality, and to be denied of spirits made perfect, as well as of the spirits that never fell from perfection, and perhaps of those who fell below mortality, namely, the devils."*

What did S. T. C. mean by a *form*, not material? A material form is here *divisive* as well as *disjunctive*, and this he denies of the essential body or bodily principle. Did he conceive the body in essence to be supersensuous, not an object of sense, not coloured or extended in space? Of the bodily principle we know only this, that it is the power in us which constructs our outward material organism, builds up our earthly tenement of flesh and blood. Can this power, independently of the organism in and by which it is manifested, be conceived of as a *form* indicating the existence and finiteness of some one being to another? I believe that with our present faculties we are incapable of conceiving how a soul can be embodied, otherwise than in a sensuous frame, but knowing as we do, that our fleshly case is not a part of ourselves, but that there is a something in ourselves which thus clothes us in matter, I think we may infer that the human body in the deepest sense is independent of matter, and that it may, in another sphere of existence, be our *form*, that which indicates to other beings our finite distinct individual being, in a way which now we are not able to know or imagine.

But what did St. Paul mean when he declared so emphatically, "Now this I say, brethren, that flesh and blood cannot inherit the kingdom of God." Is he not to be understood literally? Must we suppose him to have

body

* Coleridge's "Notes Theological, Political," etc., page 49.—E. C.

meant only this, the carnal mind, or the man in whom the lower animal nature has the upper hand cannot inherit the kingdom? But how will such an interpretation suit the context? St. Paul has been speaking not of holiness and unholiness, but of soul and body and the state after death, when this mortal tabernacle shall have been dissolved. In reference to this subject he affirms that as we have borne the *image of the earthy*, that is a material body, we shall also bear the image of the heavenly, and then straightway adds that flesh and blood shall not inherit the Divine kingdom. To this, indeed, he adds again, " Neither doth *corruption inherit incorruption*, evidently identifying flesh and blood with the corruptible, not introducing the alien topic of spiritual corruption. Jeremy Taylor affirms in reference to this passage in Corinthians, that "in the resurrection our bodies are said to be spiritual, not in substance, but in effect and operation;" upon which my father observes, " This is, in the first place, a wilful interpretation, and secondly, it is absurd, for what sort of flesh and blood would incorruptible flesh and blood be? As well might we speak of marble flesh and blood. In the sense of St. Paul, as of Plato and all other dynamic philosophers, flesh and blood is *ipso facto* corruption, that is, the spirit of life in the mid or balancing state between fixation and reviviscence. ".Who shall deliver me from the body of this death " is a Hebraism for " this death which the body is." For matter itself is but *spiritus in coagulo*, and organized matter the *coagulum* in the act of being restored, it is then repotentiating. Stop its self-destruction as matter, and you stop its self-reproduction as a vital organ."*

St. Paul declares that in the resurrection we are to be clothed with a spiritual body, and to leave behind the natural body which we had from Adam. Now what is a

* " Notes on English Divines," vol. ii. p. 284.—E. C.

body: not spiritual

spiritual as opposed to a *natural* body? Surely the latter is a material and fleshly body, and no body of flesh and blood can be otherwise than natural, or can be properly spiritual. Make the flesh and blood ever so thin, fine, and aerial, still the difference betwixt that and any other flesh and blood will be one of degree, not of kind. But the Apostle does not promise us a body of refined flesh and blood, such as, according to some theologians, Adam had before the fall, but sets aside our Adamite body altogether, and seems indeed to imply that the first man had no spirituality at any time, for he is opposed to the second man as being of the earth, earthy, as if in his character of the *first man*, and not as fallen man, he was the source of earthiness, the Lord from Heaven alone being the foundation of the spiritual.

There are some who believe that the Lord from Heaven is now sitting at the right hand of the Father in a material and fleshly body, such as He wore upon earth, and appeared in after the Resurrection,—a *metaphorical* right hand, as Pearson explains it, but the body of Him who sits thereat, of flesh and blood. It is quite natural for such believers to expect that the bodies of the saints in the resurrection will be fleshly too. As the first fruits, so they must think will be all that follow. This argument, however, seems to prove too much for those who contend that our bodies in the future world are to be of flesh and blood, but refined and glorified, and no longer natural. For the body in which our Lord ascended was the same as that which He had before He rose from the dead. It was certainly a natural body, that could be felt as well as seen, and which ate and drank.

But my father believed that there will be a resurrection of the *body*, which will have nothing to do with flesh and blood; he speaks of a *noumenal* body, as opposed to our present phenomenal one, which appears to the senses, " no

visible, tangible, accidental body, that is, a cycle of images
and sensations in the imagination of the beholders, but a
supersensual body, the *noumenon* of the human nature."*
In truth, he considered *this* body inseparable from the being
of man, indispensable to the actual existence of finite
spirits ; the notion of disembodied souls floating about in
some unknown region in the intermediate state, after the
dissolution of the material organism, and before the union
of the soul with a celestial, incorruptible flesh-and-blood
body, he looked upon as a mere dream, a chimera suited
only to the times when men were wont to convert abstractions into persons, and to ascribe objective reality to
creatures which the intellectual and imaginative faculty
engendered within itself. He laughed at the notion of the
separability of the *real* body from the soul, the arbitrary
notion of man as a mixture of heterogeneous components.
"On this doctrine," he says, "the man is a mere phenomenal result, a sort of brandy-sop, a toddy-punch, a
doctrine unsanctioned by, indeed inconsistent with, the
Scriptures. It is not true that body plus soul makes man.
Man is not the syntheton or composition of body and soul,
as the two component units. No—man is the unit, the
prothesis, and body and soul are the two poles, the positive
and negative, the thesis and antithesis of the man, even as
attraction and repulsion are the two poles in and by which
one and the same magnet manifests itself." †

I continually feel sorrowful at the thought of never again
beholding the faces of my friends, or rather, about to be
sorrowful. I come up to the verge of the thought ever and
anon, but before I can enter into it am met by the reflection,
"O vain and causeless melancholy!"—whatever satisfaction and happiness I can conceive as accruing to me in
this way, cannot the Omnipotent bestow it upon me in some

* "Notes on English Divines," vol. ii. p. 52.—E. C.
† Ibid., vol. ii. p. 96.—E. C.

other way, if this is not in harmony with His Divine plan?
The loss, the want, is in this life only, for whatever that
other sphere of existence may be, I shall be adjusted to it.
Still in this life it is a loss and a trial to feel that we cannot
image or represent to ourselves veritably the state and
happiness. We long to see again the very faces of our
friends, and cannot raise ourselves to the thought that in
the other world there may be no seeing with the visual eye,
but something better than such seeing, something by which
it is absorbed and superseded. The belief that the future
world for man is this world reformed, exalted and purified,
is one which I cannot reconcile with reason.

CHAPTER XIV.

LETTERS TO AUBREY DE VERE, ESQ., HENRY TAYLOR, ESQ., MISS MORRIS, MRS. H. M. JONES, MRS. RICHARD TOWNSEND : 1846.

I.

The Conviction of Sin—Exaggerated Self-Accusations of the Religious —Substantial Agreement amongst Christians of all Denominations.

To Miss MORRIS, Mecklenburg Square.

January 14th, 1846, 10, *Chester Place.*—I will at once tell you the thought or two that occupied my mind as I read your letter, on the subject of the comparative sense of sin. I quite agree with you that the *sentiment*, the feeling is natural, and, perhaps, necessary, in an awakened or awakening state of mind, respecting sin, its odiousness, and its danger. But, then, I think it is capable of being modified or balanced by the representations of the reasoning mind. This latter must tell most sinners, whose overt acts are not of the most flagrant description, that, in all probability, if they saw the hearts of others as they see their own, they would behold a very similar train of goings on to that which they discern by inward inspection. And when they hear so many of those, who appear to be trying to please God, express this opinion of their own *superior* wickedness in terms equally strong,—as strong as human language will admit,—how can they, without suspending the use of reason, avoid drawing the inference that it is no more to be relied on as absolute truth, than the unawakened Pharisee's notion, that he is *holier* than other men ?

The feeling in itself I believe to be a good one, but I do think it is plainly the intention of our Maker that man should not be guided by feeling alone, or by his intellect

alone, but that he should be kept in the right path by the
alternate or mingled action of the two. The sense of
being worse than any one else, if thus kept in its sphere
by reason, will be nothing more than a keen spiritual
sensibility ; if it went further and clouded that inward eye
which makes us acquainted with *truth*, we know not what
perversions might follow, what evil reactions and corruptions, even of the spiritual mind by means of the understanding.   How often has it appeared as if excessive
spiritual humility passed over into spiritual pride, and the
very man who was calling himself a worm, and really
fancying himself such, has shown by his acts and words,
that he considered every soul alive that did not embrace his
notions of election, justification, and such parts of theology,
as far beneath himself, in the eye of God, as a soul that is
and is to be cast out for ever, is beneath a soul that is to
be saved. Yet this same self-deceiver, as he referred to
feeling alone, felt sure that he was really humble. Had he
tried himself by all the different criteria whereby we may
arrive at a knowledge of ourselves, by the state of his heart
and by his outward course of action, by the conclusions of
his judging and comparing faculty, as well as by his
emotions, he could hardly have been thus ignorant what
spirit he was of.

My clergyman friend, who is to spend this evening with
me, speaks strongly and sadly of the mutual misunderstand-
ings that prevail amongst Christians, and I own I daily
more and more lament these *dogmatic* differences. I know the
parties on both sides insist that they are substantial and
not merely logical (*ens logicum*) differences, but I do believe
that most persons, who have gone between various parties
as I have done, not merely *read* on both sides, that is by no
means enough, but eat and drunk and slept, and talked
confidentially and interchanged, not only courtesies, but
heart kindnesses on both or all sides, would have very

much the same impression with myself, that though logical truth is one, and cannot belong equally to those who logically differ, yet that the life and soul and substance of Christianity may be pretty equally partaken by those who logically differ. And to confess the truth, my own belief is that the whole logical truth is not the possession of any one party, that it exists in fragments amongst the several parties, and that much of it is yet to be developed.

II.

Originality of Milton's Genius—Love of Nature displayed in his Poetry.

To AUBREY DE VERE, Esq.

1846.—Milton " not *characteristically* one of *nature's great men ?* " *Every* great man is characteristically *nature's* great man. When did art or learning ever make the most distant approximation to a Milton? Learning may be the form of Milton's poetry, but nature is its matter—or at most, learning is the body, while nature inspires the soul. Book-knowledge was more to Milton, world-knowledge to Shakespeare; but I believe that the latter owed as much to what he acquired, what he took into his mind from without, as the former. But book-knowledge, after all, was less to Milton than observation of external nature. It is this lore surely which forms the master charm of Comus, Lycidas, the Allegro and Penseroso, the descriptions of Eden, which are the most perfect part of the " Paradise Lost." Wordsworth has *humanized* nature; but Milton glorified it, out of itself, in showing how divine a thing it is, in its own, and none but its own loveliness, how evidently the work of God. Here he is, as you, and Wordsworth before you, say, essentially Hebraic, so far as the Hebraic mind appears in the Old Testament. Hence his sublimity,—his simplicity and grandeur, as to the nature of his theme, which the classical ornature by no means injures or misfits. He never is *so* ornamental as not to be " sensuous and impas-

o

sioned," for his ornaments are all, in themselves, the fresh products of nature, and the use that has been made of them, since they were first gathered, has deadened in no least imaginable degree, their everlasting verdure.   Milton is more profusely, more thickly and richly poetic than Wordsworth, his felicities of diction and brilliancies of imagination are more uniformly spread over the mass of his productions. As for the Homeric poetry, it is perfection in its way ; but in regard to *thought*, the work of the intellect-evolving reason and the spirit, it displays the childhood of the human race, and that under an imperfect, obscured, and broken revelation.

III.

Unfair Criticism of Mr. Coleridge's Religious Opinions—His MS. Notes—Care taken of them by Mr. Southey.

To HENRY TAYLOR, Esq., Mortlake.*

February 26*th*, 1846.—I would always invite and welcome for my father, as he did for himself, the closest examination of the character and merit of his writings.   The sooner they are clearly understood, both for praise and for usefulness, or for detection of delusive appearances of truth and excellence, the better.   His complaint always was that nobody would question his views in *particulars*, that nobody would fight with him hand to hand, but that random missiles were discharged at him from a distance, by men who fled away while they fought.

I do not know how any of the Notes came to be effaced, never having seen the copy of the " Life of Wesley," in which they were written by my father himself.   He did sometimes forget to finish a note, in some instances most tantalizingly.   Perhaps he broke off to think, and then either did not satisfy himself, or forgot to record his conclusions.   Some of his *marginalia* have been cruelly docked by binders, some rubbed out.   My Uncle Southey

* Author of " Philip Van Artevelde," now Sir Henry Taylor.—E. C.

used to ink over his pencilled notes, " that nothing be lost,"
as he said, with his usual diligence. When shall we see
such diligence again, such regularity with such genius and
versatility ? I think if he had not been a poet, he would
have been called a plodder, and have become a respectable
and useful writer by sheer industry.

IV.

Beauties of Crabbe.

To Mrs. RICHARD TOWNSEND, Springfield, Norwood.

Chester Place, June 17th, 1846.—I am glad that you enjoy
Crabbe. Sir Francis Palgrave praised him most warmly,
and was pleased and rather surprised to have a warm
response from me the other day, at Mr. Murray's. The
" Tales of the Hall " are what I now like the best of all his
sets of poems. In my earlier days I did not perceive half
their merits, the fine observation of life, the tender sympathy
with human sorrow, the gentle smile at human weakness,
the humour, the pathos, the firm, almost stern morality, the
excellent, clear, pure diction, and the touches of beauty (as
I think) interspersed here and there. The Songs I much
admire : the descriptions of Nature are decidedly poetical in
my opinion, though they bear the same relation to Milton's
and Wordsworth's descriptions as the expression of Murillo's
pictures does to that of Raphael's and Leonardo's.

V.

Reflections of an Invalid—Defence of Luther—Charges of Irreverence
often unjustly made—Ludicrous Illustration found in a Sermon
of Bishop Andrewes—Education : how far it may be Secular
without being Irreligious—Mr. Keble's " Lyra Innocentium "—
Religious Poetry ought to be *poetical,* as well as religious.

To Miss ERSKINE.

July 23*rd,* 1846.—My dear A——, I thought to have
answered your letter very soon ; but I have been ever
falling from one poorliness into another, each slight in
itself, but producing a general weakness in me which is no

slight evil, or rather it is the general weakliness which rendered me liable to those little attacks, and the attacks make it worse. But I am making the vestibule of my letter a doleful sick room, in which the most interesting and refreshing objects that present themselves are bottles from the apothecary's shop full of tonics, sedatives, liniments, gargles, and so forth. Your letter, on the contrary, was full of fresh air, and made me think of you both when I read it, and from time to time ever since, riding away on a spirited pony, with most *countrified* cheeks and eyes, and a very light heart and mind *less* light than ever. I could wish your heart and mind to be like two buckets, the latter to be ever filling, fuller and fuller, with the streams of sacred and all other lore, pure as water and rich as wine—while the former grows constantly more and more empty of earthly cares and troubles. I hope that your dear mother continues well and does not walk too much. She is rather apt, I believe, not to think of herself, when others are concerned. There are so many depôts, of the largest possible extent, where selfishness and self-preservativeness may be borrowed to any amount, that if she can but be persuaded of the necessity, she might readily furnish herself with a little of the needful article. But this I have said, as it were, with one eye open and the other shut, for, though there are in every street and lane and country village such vast stocks of selfishness to be found, yet those who are in want of the article never know how to get at any of it. Every particle clings to its native place like petrifactions in marble. But all this moral reflection is enough to petrify you by its stupidity, and, in order to put a little life into both of us, I must e'en turn for a while to controversy.

How say you, my A——, that you are not *growing in love for Luther*, but rather becoming hardened in a *Tracts for the Times*-y view of that great and good man, the noblest divine instrument, in my opinion, which the world has seen

after the prophets and apostles ? *Coarse ?* What is coarseness in *such a man*, of such dimensions, of such mental and
spiritual thews and sinews, with such a heart and soul and
spirit, and such a mighty life-long work as he had to perform, and performed most heroically ? If Luther had been
a " nice man for a small tea-party," if to write a few Tracts
for the times, or publish a few volumes of sermons, or to
put a church in proper ecclesiastical order, after a modern-
ized-primitive fashion, had been all his vocation upon earth,
then truly a little coarseness would have quite spoilt him.
But he was, as Julius Hare says, " a Titan," and " when a
Titan walks abroad among the pygmies, the earth seems to
rock beneath his tread."   It is vain to tell me that Luther
could not have been spiritual-minded, because he used rough,
coarse, homely expressions.   His whole life, public and
private, the general character of his writings, so far as I
know them, prove to me that he was a spiritual-minded man
and the most deeply convinced of sin that ever lived.   That
Luther was profane I cannot admit.   I have always thought
that the language of the Oxford theologians respecting pro-
faneness in religion had much in it that was both narrow
and uncharitable.   They confound want of good taste with
want of piety, homely breeding with that irreverence which
springs from the heart ; in the mean time *they* are teaching
doctrines and expressing opinions which appear to many
earnest and thoughtfully-religious minds in the highest
degree derogatory to God and Christ and Christianity.
Every one is profane who does not adopt their peculiar
ceremoniousness in religion, who cannot specially revere all
that they have made up their minds to think worthy of
reverence.

Think of this comparison from the pen of Bishop
Andrewes, one of their highest favourites amongst our
Anglican divines : " Are they like to *buckets ?* one cannot
go down, unless the other go up."   The " *buckets* " are the

Saviour and the Comforter! Now, would not this be pronounced highly profane by the Luther-haters, had it been
found in a book of Luther's? Yet Andrewes is considered
the *beau idéal* of a reverential spirit, by the Oxford writers,
and I have no doubt that he never for a moment lost the
feeling of reverence out of his heart. Yet, with all Luther's
occasional scurrility and violence, I doubt whether an
example so unworthy of the highest of all subjects could be
found in his works. That instance from Andrewes is
brought forward in a long note in the new work of Archdeacon Hare, "The Mission of the Comforter, and other
Sermons." The second volume is twice as long as the
other, and full of notes. Note W. contains a most warm,
thorough, searching, resolute defence of Luther against all
his modern censors. It is not to be expected, indeed, that
they who dislike the work which Luther did can ever like
the workman; still they should not bring up again the
refuted slanders of Romanists, and quote his writings out
of the books of his Romish adversaries instead of out of
his own.

Yesterday I discussed with Mr. M——, or rather, he with
me, Dr. Hook's remarkable pamphlet on National Education. M—— contends that no part of education should be
dissociated from *religious* education, that we ought not to
divide our life or our teaching into secular and religious,
and that such a plan as the one proposed would clamp and
rivet a wrong principle of education and prevent the arising
of a higher and more deeply religious system.

I think certainly that no man could teach *history* in
an effective, living manner, without infusing into it the
tone and principle either of Socinianism or Trinitarianism.
But I believe that in the routine of the National School,
except where religion is formally introduced, the spirit of
Christianity is not felt at all. And certainly a man may
teach reading, writing, spelling, and arithmetic without

letting it appear whether he is a Mahometan or a Christian —nay, more, I do not see how he could keep steadily to his business in teaching these branches, without keeping his peculiar form of religion in the background. Still, I believe that M—— is right, and that we who embrace with our hearts the Divinity of Christ, should not allow a disbeliever even to teach our children to cypher; though I would by no means admit that we ought to keep *out of all intercourse* with such disbelievers, and that is another point on which I think the Oxford teaching injurious.

I meant to talk with you a little about the *Lyra Innocentium*, but have hardly left myself room. I am doing it all possible justice, for I read it slowly, two or three poems a day, and some two or three times over. I like best "Sleeping on the Waters" and the "Lichgate." Still it would be quite insincere to say that I either like or approve of it, upon the whole, either as religion or poetry, though there are beautiful passages. I hope you do not wholly approve of it as religion. Surely the Marianism is far more than our best and greatest divines would approve. The article in the "Quarterly" is the article of a friend, and in the main a partisan; the reviewer mentions some important faults in the volume as poetry, but to my mind there is a deeper fault than any he mentions, namely, want of truth and substance, and not only of doctrine, but of human child-nature. The incidents recorded are quite insignificant in themselves, they add nothing to our knowledge, no richness to our store of reflections. They are used as mere symbols, suggestive of analogies. They are just so many pegs and hooks on which Mr. Keble can hang his web of religious sentiment. The reviewer says that to *excel as a poet* is not Mr. Keble's aim. This seems to me something like *goodyism*. He who writes poetry surely should aim to excel as a poet, and the more if his theme is religion, and his object to spiritualize and exalt. Every great poet has a higher aim, of course, than that of merely obtaining admiration for his poetic power and skill. Wordsworth's aim was to elevate the thoughts of his readers, to enrich and purify their hearts, but he sought to excel as a poet in order that he might do this the more effectually. I believe that Isaiah and Ezekiel sought to excel as poets, all the more that their poetry was the vehicle of divine truth, of truth awakened in their souls by inspiration.

VI.

Comparative Merits of the Earlier and Later Poems of Wordsworth—Burns.

To AUBREY DE VERE, Esq.

1846.—Your scheme of a critique on Wordsworth would be very noble and comprehensive, if adequately executed. The difficulty would be to avoid obscurity and vagueness. I agree to all your characteristics, so far as I understand them, except those of the later poetry, of which I take a wholly different view from that expressed in your prospectus. You have brought me to see more beauty in them than I once did; but when you say they have more *latent imagination*, are more *mellow*, exhibit "faculties more perfectly equipoised," you seem to me to have framed a theory apart from the facts. They have more *fancy*, but surely not more imagination, latent or patent. They can hardly be mellower, for they have not the same body; their substance is thinner; and some of the author's poetic faculties are, to my mind, not *there* to be equipoised. What! are any of the later poems, in the blending and equipoise of faculties, beyond "Tintern Abbey," "The Leech-gatherer," "The Brothers," "Ruth"? Did the instrument become mellower than in "Three Years She Grew," "The Highland Girl," "The White Doe"? Surely there is far more real strength in the "Sonnets to Liberty," "Song at the Feast of Brougham Castle," "Platonic Ode," "Rob Roy's Grave," than in anything the author has produced during the last twenty years.

That is a good distinction of meditative and contemplative.

Your characteristics of Burns are excellent. I agree to them all heartily. I am glad you are not too *genteel* to like Burns.

VII.

Critique on "Laodamia"—Want of Truth and Delicacy in the Sentiments attributed to the Wife in that Poem—No Moral Lesson of any Value to be drawn from such a Misrepresentation—Superior Beauty and Fidelity of a Portrait taken from the Life—Leading Idea of Shelley's "Sensitive Plant."

REASON FOR NOT PLACING "LAODAMIA" IN THE FIRST RANK OF WORDSWORTHIAN POETRY.

Laodamia is, in my opinion, as a whole, neither powerfully conceived nor perfectly executed. I venture to say that there is both a coarseness and a puerility in the design and the sentiments. I see a want of feeling, of delicacy, and of truthfulness, in the representation of Laodamia herself. The speech put into her mouth is as low in tone as it is pompous and inflated in manner. Would even a Pagan poet, would Homer have ascribed such an address to Andromache or Penelope? Would he have made any virtuous matron and deeply-loving wife address her lord returned from the dead so in the style of a Medea or a Phœdra? Surely in Ovid's "Epistle of Laodamia to Protesilaus," there is nothing so unmatronly and unwifely, bold and unfeminine. Not only does the poet make Laodamia speak thus—he clenches the imputation by a commentary. He ascribes to her *passions* unworthy of a pure abode, *raptures* such as Erebus disdains—implies that her feelings belong to mere sense, the lowest part of our nature. By what right does he impute to the spouse of Protesilaus such grossness of character, and how can he do so without representing her as quite unworthy of that deep sympathy and compassion which yet he seems to claim for her? "O judge her gently who so deeply loved." *Deep* love is utterly incompatible with such passions and raptures as Erebus can have any pretence to disdain. Even where they existed, they would be consumed, burnt up as a scroll, in the strong, steady fire of conjugal affection. After all, what is the moral of this much-pretending, lofty-sounding poem? What is it that the poet means to condemn and to warn against? To judge by his words, we must suppose him to be declaiming against subjugation to the senses, because these things earth is ever destroying and Erebus disdaining. Now, if Laodamia really longed to be re-united with her husband only for the sake of his "roseate lips" and blooming cheeks, she would deserve censure and contempt too, but the true reason of her sorrow and reluctance to part with him is this, that *she* is chained to the sphere of outward and visible things, while he is gone, Heaven knows whither, and that, except through a sensuous medium, she can have no communion with him, none of which she can be conscious, not the highest and most spiritual. Love can have no other fruition than that of union. The fervent apostle longs to be dissolved and to be with Christ. The poet's machinery, too, is extremely ill-adapted for bringing out any deep or fine thoughts on such a subject. His heaven itself is a heaven of *sense*, Elysian fields, with purling brooks and lilied banks, "purpureal gleams," and all that we have here on a brighter and larger scale, where the pride of the eye, by far the strongest and most seductive of all the senses, is to be oceanically gratified. But is submission to the will of God, and a patient waiting to be made happy in His way, true faith and trust in the Author of our being, that He who gave us our hearts and the objects of them, can and will give us the feelings and the fruitions best adapted to our eternal well-being, if we rely upon Him

with an energy of self-abandonment and patience, what the
·poet meant to inculcate ?   I can only say that if this be the
case, nothing can be more circuitous and misleading than
the way which he takes to arrive at his point; all along, if
he aims that way he shoots another.

In this poem Mr. Wordsworth wilfully divested himself of
every tender and delicate feeling in the contemplation of
the wife and the woman, for the sake of a few grand
declamatory stanzas, which he knew not else how to make
occasion for.   Of course a poor woman is glad to see the
external form of her husband after a long and perilous
absence, right glad, too, to see him with a ruddy cheek,
thankful under such circumstances to receive ever so dis-
locating a squeeze—a thing to the mere sense unluxurious,
nay, painful, but comfortable to the heart within, as making
assurance doubly sure that there he is, the good man himself, no vision or spectre like to vanish away, but a being,
confined like herself within the bounds of space, and likely
for many a day to be perceptible within that portion of
space which is their common home ; proof also, or at least
a strong sign,—that whether or no he be as glad to rejoin
her as she is to have him back, at all events he is more
glad than words can express.

Why did Mr. Wordsworth write in this hard, forced,
falsetto style of Laodamia ?   Was this a sketch taken from
very nature ?   Was it drawn by the light of the sun in
heaven, or by real moonlight in all its purity and freshness?
No ; but by the beams of a purple-tinted lamp in his study,
a lamp gaudily-coloured, but dimmed with particles of
smoke and fumes of the candle.   Compare with this the
thoughts and feelings embodied in that exquisite sketch,
" She was a Phantom of Delight," the fine and delicate
interweaving of the outward and sensuous with the things
of the heart and higher mind in that poem.   Can we not
see in a moment that the poet had been gazing on the deep

and manifold countenance of Nature herself, of Truth and
Reality, when he threw forth those verses; that he had been ·
seeing, not inventing? Yet is it not far more finely
imaginative than the other? Would any but a great poet
have so seen the face of Nature, or so pourtrayed it? Mrs.
Wordsworth lies, in essence, at the bottom of that poem.
How angry would the bard be to have her connected in
any way with the other, and its broad, coarse abstractions!
So long as sense is divorced from our higher being, it is,
indeed, a low thing; but may it not be redeemed, and by
becoming the minister and exponent of the other, be purified and exalted? I have ever thought those doctrines
that seek to sever the sensuous from our humanity, instead
of retaining and merging it in the sentimental, the intellectual, and the spiritual, " a vaulting ambition that o'er-
leaps itself and falls on the other side."

I have received more consolation from Mr. Wordsworth's
poetry than from any sermons or works of devotion at
different times of my life, but I must have more truth and
freshness than there is in Laodamia to be either highly
gratified or consoled. I would not have poetry always
dwell in the *common* world, but still it must always have
truth at the bottom. I admire, for instance, and see great
truth in Shelley's " Sensitive Plant." It is wild, but there
is nothing unreal or forced about it. I look upon it as a
sort of apologue, intended, or at least fitted, to exhibit the
relations of the perceptive and imaginative mind, as modified by the heart, with external nature.

CHAPTER XV.

LETTERS TO AUBREY DE VERE, ESQ., REV. HENRY MOORE, MISS FENWICK, MRS. FARRER, MISS MORRIS: July—December, 1846.

I.
Mr. Ruskin's "Modern Painters."
To MISS MORRIS.

1846.—A book which has interested me much of late, is a thick volume by a graduate of Oxford, whose name is Ruskin, on the superiority of the modern landscape painters to the old masters in that line. The author has not converted, and yet he has delighted me. I think him a heretic as regards Claude, Cuyp, G. Poussin, and Salvator Rosa; but his admiration of Turner, whom he exalts above all other landscape painters that ever lived, I can go a great way with; and his descriptions of nature in reference to art are delightful—clouds, rocks, earth, water, foliage, he examines and describes in a manner which shows him to be quite a man of genius, full of knowledge and that fineness of observation which genius produces.

II.
A Talk with Mr. Carlyle—Different Effects of Sorrow on Different Minds—Miss Fenwick—Milton Good as well as Great.

To AUBREY DE VERE, Esq.

Carlyle, I think, too much depreciates money as an instrument. I battled with him a little on this point when I saw him last. He is always smiling and good-natured when I contradict him, perhaps because he sees that I admire him all the while. I fought in defence of the mammonites, and brought him at least to own that the labourer is worthy of his hire. Now, this contains the pith of the whole matter. The man who devotes himself to gain riches deserves to have riches, and like Hudson, to have a monument set up to him by those whom he has enriched; and if he strives for riches, to spend them nobly or kindly, then he deserves to have the luxury of *that sort* of doing good. A Burns or a Berkeley aims at, and works for, and ought to find his reward in, other harvests. But Carlyle seems angry because the Burns or the Johnson or the Milton has not the same honours, or from the same men, as millionaires and fashionists, because the whole world—unphilosophical and unpoetical as the main part of it is—does not fall down and worship them, and cast forthwith into the sea or some Curtius gulf all the gauds and playthings which *they* do not care about. This is overbearing and unfair. Let him teach the world to be philosophical and poetical as fast as he can; but till it is so, let him not grudge it the rattles and sugar-plums and hobbyhorses of its infancy. . . . . .

Your last letter, received at Herne Bay, gave a delightful account of your mother and her consolations. Soon after reading it, I saw a fine appearance in the sky—for then I was always watching sky and sea and atmosphere spectacles —the sun and moon in a mist, the latter pallid and sickly, while the former burned through the veil, and converted all the vapour around it into a vehicle of golden radiance. This seemed to me an apt image of the diverse effect of sorrow on different minds. To a warm and deeply benevolent spirit it becomes the means of a more diffusive charity and kindliness; the sorrow itself is pierced through and overpowered, yet serves to spread abroad and augment the benevolence which it cannot damp or extinguish; while to those who have but a comparatively scanty stock of love belonging to them it is the extinguisher of all social amiability, it renders them dull and cold, the mere ghosts of their former selves. . . .

I take great delight in Miss Fenwick and in her conversation. Well should I like to have her constantly in this drawing-room to come down to from my little study upstairs—her mind is such a noble compound of heart and intelligence, of spiritual feeling and moral strength, and the most perfect feminineness. She is intellectual, but— what is a great excellence—never talks for effect, never *keeps possession of the floor*, as clever women are so apt to do. She converses for the interchange of thought and feeling, no matter *how*, so she gets at your mind, and lets you into hers. A more generous and a tenderer heart I never knew. I differ from her on many points of religious faith, but on the whole prefer her views to those of most others who differ from her. Once she said something against Milton, which made me feel for the moment as Oliver Newman did, when Randolph denounced the " blind old traitor,"

> " With that his eyes
> Flashed, and a warmer feeling flushed his cheek."

" Time will bring down the Pyramids," he said, and so forth. Randolph's respondent did but defend Milton on the score of his poetry. But I think he was great as a *man* and a *patriot*, very noble in the whole cast of his character, and very far from being what she thinks him, for his writings against that weak, wily (or at least *un*-straight-forward, not ingrainedly honest) despot, King Charles I.,— " malicious." It is seldom that so brave, so public-spirited a man as Milton harbours malice in his heart, he too who had " never spoken against a man that his skin should be grazed." So, like Oliver, though I kept " self-possession as a mind subdued," yet was I " a little moved."

III.

Danger of Exclusiveness in Parental Affection.

To the Hon. Mr. Justice COLERIDGE.

Chester Place, August 5th, 1846.—It is certainly right that parents should form, as much as possible, a friendship with their children, and seek mental association with them; but it seems to me that their desire for this, and endeavour after it, should not be without limits. Parents and children cannot be to each other as husbands with wives and wives with husbands. Nature has separated them by an almost impassable barrier of time; the mind and the heart are in quite a different state at fifteen and at forty.

Then, too, we must consider, that though so many difficulties attend the comfortable marriage of young people in our rank of life; yet, marriage, somewhere between seventeen and thirty, is what we should look to for them, as a possible and, upon the whole, desirable event for them in ordinary cases. This probability alone must interfere with our forming such habits of *continual* intercourse with them and dependence upon them for hourly comfort and amusement, as it would be very painful to break off in case of their doing what it is certainly most for their life-long happiness that they should do, — forming a marriage connection which may endure when we are gone to our rest. Whatever is most *natural*, so that it be not of the nature of sin, is in all ordinary cases the best and safest. I have seen and heard of a great deal of distress and misery arising from parents setting their hearts too much on the society and exclusive or paramount love of their children; and have always felt, especially since I have been a widow, that this was a rock which I had to avoid.

IV.

St. Augustine's College—Holiday Tasks—The Evening Grey, and the Morning Red.

To Miss FENWICK.

St. George's Terrace, Herne Bay, August 20*th,* 1846.— One day last week we drove to Canterbury, to visit the rising Missionary College of St. Augustine, which will be completed and set agoing,—made alive, as it were, before the end of next spring, as is now expected. I was much struck with the true collegiate air of the pile of buildings, and the solid handsomeness and appropriate beauty of the separate parts. I was particularly pleased with a long gallery running between the two ranges of fifty students' rooms; it will be such an excellent walk for the meditative student in bad weather, and at all times when he wishes to relieve his sitting posture. There he may untie many a knot, occurring in his studies, which has *stuck him up,* as the boys say, while he was sitting on his chair. There he may cast his eye over his future prospects,—though, perhaps, as to some part of them, it may be as well not to "proticipate," to use Mrs. Gamp's expression, for hardships seem still harder at a distance, I think, than close at hand.

Derwent and M., and their sweet chattering C——, who looks, when in a madcap wilful mood, even prettier than when she is good,—like a little wild cat of the woods, or kitten ocelot in a playful fury,—returned to St. M—— some days ago. They left their son for some time longer to be Herbert's companion. I cannot say that I have an absolute holiday even here, as I am bound to read Homer and Æschylus with these youths (of whom my son is to be sixteen, my nephew eighteen, in October) every day, and though their lessons at present are not long,—yet to rein them in when they are galloping on, leaving sense and connection of thought in the far distance;—and to have my own way about the disputed passage, when I *am* in the right, and let

P

them have theirs and their little triumph when *Ma* has
proved to be a "verdant creature," as my boy has the
coolness to call me when I have betrayed an ignorance of
something that he knows,—is to me some little exertion ;
—but not too much, for I see very little good in entire
holidays, especially when there are so many sad remembrances in the background of the mind as there are in
mine, ever ready to come forward when the foreground is
not well filled up. Sad indeed they are not, by this time,—
at least, not always and wholly. They begin to lose their
blacker hue, and to be tinged with the soft though sober
grey of thought and meditation on things to come, with
which they blend, and in which they seem to sink, and at
times almost to be absorbed. Still, I am glad to have my
eyes turned for awhile towards brighter objects, and the rosy
dawn of youth, and health, and gladness. These young
ones are as hoity-toity and fantastical, and *crest-perky* as
boys who have never known care or want, and are full of
health and strength (if not naturally of very sedate
dispositions), usually are. They are fond of chattering about
the pretty girls they meet and fascinate. M. and I make
a point of thinking the young ladies they admire particularly plain and vulgar, and assuring them, on our own
early life experience, that young ladies seldom have any
eyes for the charms of gentlemen, but are solely intent on
the degree of admiration which their own charms excite.
Well, this is a very motherly and auntly tale ; you will
think that these young beaux have one admirer at least,
their own mamma and aunt.

V.

"Saintism"—Untrustworthiness of Religious Autobiographies.

To Miss MORRIS.

Herne Bay, August 22*nd,* 1846.—Dear Friend,—I have read
a part of the memoir of the "Sisters," and have been much
interested by it ; but I think I do not feel about it *quite* as

you do. It seems to me to present a mixture of real pure
Christianity, and of *Saintism*, that spurious or semi-
spurious piety, which is to be found, not among Methodists
alone, but amongst Christians of all names, and sometimes
leavens the religion even of the truly religious. But why
do I feel thus ? What is there in the book that is otherwise
than pure and holy ? Dear Miss Morris, you will perhaps
think me very wrong and over-captious, but it is just this
absence of everything that is not presentable in the record,
that makes me distrust it, as not being the whole truth,
and nothing but the truth. So far as my reflection, and
experience, and knowledge of life, and knowledge of
biography go (I do not say they go far, but by such as I
have I must judge), souls seen *as they are*, without a
glorifying mist, do not look quite as those souls do in
that book—scarcely ever, if ever. Yet, if Papistical and
Methodistical and other religious biography be absolutely
trustworthy, and to be taken literally, there must be
thousands upon thousands of such white lambs in every
country. The very same sorts of things which I read there
are to be read in so many other volumes. There is too
little individuality about them, they do not read (like poor
Blanco White's Memoirs) like actual life, with all its
peculiarities ; for if every leaf is unlike every other leaf,
how much more is every soul unlike every other soul!
True it is that religion, like love, levels many distinctions ;
but yet, in every portrait of a living face we recognize a
thousand lines and expressions peculiar to itself. These
girls call themselves worms, poor sinners, as in reference to
their God, to infinite perfection. There is not much
humility in making this avowal. But see, after all, what
a fine character, what a noble, elevated character, with
none but *noble* faults, is traced of each of them in those
pages ! And by whose hands is that character traced ?
By any other than their own, and that of their memorialist,

partial and proud, as their biographer, and as their own sister? I cannot, and I never could, feel deeply impressed by such representations as these. I always feel that there may be, that there probably is, much of unconscious self-deception about them. A man's own journal, his own book of private confession, so far as it reports well of him, is not to be entirely trusted; for we cannot help drawing flattering pictures of ourselves even for ourselves, we do not give an exact copy of our own hearts, we involuntarily soften it off. We say we are evil, but we do not show it, and prove it. I admire and am often deeply affected by the goodness of many of my fellow Christians, but then it is such as I have had the means of witnessing myself in their daily acts and course of life, or such as is attested by persons not interested on their behalf, or from some record that has that life-like air about it, that natural light and shade, those *vera*, and not *ficta peccata*, of one kind or another, which I believe that every *real* life, faithfully and fully drawn, would exhibit. Still I think that Anne and Emma must have been girls of a very high stamp; the whole family of the M——s appear to me to be very superior.

VI.

Human Sorrow and Heavenly Rest—"The Golden Manual"—Blue and White, in Sky, Sea, and Land—Landor's Pentameron—Comparative rank of Homer, Shakespeare, Milton, and Dante.

To AUBREY DE VERE, Esq., Curragh Chase.

August 31st, Herne Bay.—Of all the thoughts that press upon us, on the loss of nearest friends, that which presses hardest and strongest is the self-question, "How have I done my part towards him that is gone? Is he now or has he been the worse through any fault of mine?" Then how earnestly we pray, when he is in the hands of his heavenly Father alone, in the bosom of Infinite mercy, that he may have that perfect kindness and boundless compassion shown him which we failed to show him here, even humanly and as far as we might. For, then, the double-faced glass is reversed, it magnifies all our trespasses against him, and exaggerates our shortcomings, while it reduces our efforts to serve and please, our bearings and forbearings, to narrow room, or at least takes the colour out of them, and makes them look as wan as the dear face that used to smile and glow in our sight. But I meant to have said something different from this, more calm and soothing. I was going to speak of the religious peace and firmness of your father's dying hours, the *sure and certain hope* he seemed to feel of mercy through the "Merits and Death of his Redeemer." These are remembrances on which the mind may repose, as on a bed of balm—more lasting in their fragrance than any balm that ever grew in Arabia, for they will yield fresh odours from time to time as long as they are pressed upon. As those dying hours of our dearest ones can never be far out of mind, it is a blessing indeed, when they have more of the rest of heaven in them than of the sting of the grave. Those you spoke of to me remind me of my own father's. He, too, was calm and clear to the last, till he fell into the coma that so often precedes death, and neither afraid nor grieved to depart, and he was thoughtful for others still struggling with the world when he was leaving it. Perhaps it is easier to die at sixty (he was near sixty-three) than at forty. It ought to be so, if we make use of our time. A man who reaches that age may feel that he has done a day's work ; and then life, as it runs on, changes its colour and aspect, just as the natural day changes from meridian light to afternoon mellowness, and then to evening grey. It seems right and fit to go hence in that evening grey, when the shadows are falling on all things here to our altered eyes, not to leave the full sun behind us when we enter the darkness of the tomb. It is true that this darkness exists but in our imagination ; we transfer to the state of the departed the obscurity of our minds respecting it, or, at least, our incapability of beholding it visually as we behold this present world; still, it has a real influence upon our feelings, although by efforts of thought we can dispel those shades of Hades, and bring before us that place where there is neither sun nor moon—no need of them, for the glory of God will lighten it, and the Lamb be the light thereof. May we more and more dwell upon that place and state, remembering that, whatever be the form and outwardness of it, whatever be its relation to the beauty of this world in which we now dwell, it is to be a spiritual state more fully than that which we abide in here, and yet that here we must be prepared for it, and, in part, conformed to it. I am at this time reading a little book of mystic divinity, the Theologica Germanica, or little "Golden Manual," a great favourite with the Platonist divine, Dr. Henry More. It contains very high spiritual doctrine, and dwells on the necessity of setting aside all "selfness and egoity," and serving God purely for love's sake alone, without respect to even a *heavenly* reward.

We are just come in from a seaside walk, driven home by the glaring sun. Scarce a breath is stirring, sea and sky are all one hue, and the air is heavy. The sunniest day in last week was fresher than this,—then there was one light wreath of white but shaded clouds rolled along the horizon, and to match it there was a fringe of still whiter foam along the edge of the retiring sea,—all else of the sea and sky was brightly blue. Herbert reminded me of Homer's expressive phrase, about spirting off the divine sea, which sounds low in English, but is not so felt in the Greek ἀποπτύει ἅλα δῖαν. The seaside plants and insects, too, all do their part of brightness on these sunny days, none more than that shiny blue flower, which grows upon a shrubby stem and emulates the sky so boldly.* Veronicas

* See Postscript.—E. C.

make a fine show of azure in the mass, as they creep over
a bank, and beds of harebells are earth skies in the clear
spaces of the wood, but the single blossoms of this plant
are each a little sky of itself.   Quite as lovely and as
lustrous in its way is the foam-white convolvulus, which
looks so exquisitely soft and innocent, as it gleams amid
the brambles and nettles which its lithe stem embraces.
Critics have made a "mighty stir" to find out what Virgil
meant by his *ligustrum.*

Alba ligustra cadunt, vaccinia nigra leguntur.

Surely, he must have meant this snowy-blossomed bind-
weed.   Privet is out of the question.   It is neither very
white nor very caducous.   The flowers of the bind-weed
are especially so ; they soon sink into a twisted roll, and
fall to the ground, though not wafted away so early as the
petals of the anemone and gum-cistus.   Then near the sea
there are always blue and white butterflies, hovering over
these blue and white flowers.

I have just finished reading Landor's Pentameron.   It
is full of interest for the critical and poetical mind, but is
sullied by some *Landorisms,* which are less like weeds in a
fine flower bed, than some evil ingredient in the soil,
revealing itself here and there by rankish odours, or stains
and blotches on leaf and petal.   The remarks on Dante,
severe as they are, I cannot but agree with in the main.   I
believe you expressed some dissent from them.   I think
that Dante holds the next rank in poetic power and
substance after Homer, Shakespeare and Milton, perhaps
above Virgil, Ariosto and Spenser, but there is much in his
mind and frame of thought which I exceedingly dislike,—
and I have ever *felt* much of what Landor expresses on the
subject, though without speaking it all out even to myself.
It happened that just after I had been declaring to Derwent
my opinion of Milton's superiority to Homer, and he had

been upholding the paramountcy of the latter, I came upon
Landor's sentence on the subject. *He* pronounces Homer
and Dante both together only equivalent to Milton " shorn
of his Sonnets and Allegro and Penseroso." I suppose he
thinks that the objectivity of the one and subjectivity of the
other (which, however, is not equal to that of still later
poets) blended into one might come up to the epic poetry
of Milton; and truly in poetic matter and stuff of the
imagination, they might even surpass it : but there is to
my mind, in the latter, a tender modern grace, a fusion of
sentiment and reflection into the sensuous and outward,
which is more exquisite in kind than anything you would
obtain from Homer and Dante melted together. I must
tell you, however, that Mr. Wordsworth considers Homer
second only to Shakespeare, deeply as he venerates Milton.

VII.

Age and Ugliness—" Expensive Blessings "—Æschylus—Principle of
    Pindaric Metre, and Spirit of Pindaric Poetry—Physical and
    Intellectual Arts of Greece.

To the Rev. HENRY MOORE, Eccleshall Vicarage, Staffordshire.

Herne Bay, September 5th, 1846.—You kindly renew your
invitation, and put it in a new shape. I can only thank
you for it, alas ! and try to keep alive a hope that I may
enjoy your hospitality some future autumn. We read much
in books, amongst other things about women which to
many of our sex are altogether new and surprising, that
the softer sex are apt to toughen as they lose the graces of
youth. Really, if this were the case, it would be such a
set-off against grey hairs, and withering roses and lilies,
and all those ugly, unflourishing dells which time gradually
introduces into our face-territory, that we might behold
those changes with at least half-satisfaction ; but I should
say from experience that, on the contrary, we grow weaker
and more sensitive in advancing life, quite as fast as we

motherhood

grow uglier. Then women who are so *unfortunate* as to have a boy and girl growing up under their eyes, are reminded of their age and weakness continually. It is a miserable thing, to be sure! and then how much money it costs! Why, if it wasn't for these plagues, I should be quite rich, and should not have to cast an anxious eye towards railways, or be tossed up and down in soul and spirit with the fluctuations of the money-market. I need never care whether I got 5 per cent. or only 3½. I *was* rather pleased, certainly, when my fellow-lodgers expressed their astonishment that I should be the mama of "that fine boy." They expected to see a buxom dame, after seeing him first. But matters are not always ordered so; and, even in this way, the race is not always to the swift, nor the battle to the strong.

During Herbert's stay here, before he left us to return to Eton, he read with me the Eumenides of Æschylus, and great part of the Chœphorœ, and the Olympics of Pindar. The drawback to pleasure in reading the former is the corruptness of so many of the choruses. You may read Latin, German, French, English translations of those compositions, all different and all unsatisfactory. Pindar is much easier; one can make him all out at last, bring him back from his long excursions to the spot whence he started, though not without some trouble. But the drawback to pleasure in reading *him*, for me, is the impossibility of realizing to my ear his strange metre, so strictly regular, yet of a regularity so varied and complex, that it seems like lawlessness and wild extravagance to those who cannot feel, though they may understand, the law of it. To judge from the eye, I should say that its flow somewhat resembled the sea with its waves, growing ampler and ampler, for a while, then sinking back again, and that this suits well with his style of thought and imagery, that combination of impetuosity with a majestic gravity—a tempered enthusiasm, controlled and regulated by the law of reason, and a

deep spirit of reverence for the Supreme and the Invisible,
—the things that are above us, and at the same time are
lying at the very depths and foundations of our nature.

What a high rank bodily exercises held in those ancient
days! A man's feet or fists, or skill in horsemanship or
driving, lifted him to renown, and wreathed his brow with
laurel,—and yet, in those same days, the intellectual arts
had reached a point in some respects (in execution, certainly) unsurpassed. The celebrated race-hero now lives
in memory of man only in virtue of the poetry devoted to
his celebration. Pindar seems but half to have foreseen
this when he intimates that the mighty man of feet or of
fists would have had but a brief guerdon but for his glowing
strains. It is some exertion for me to keep pace with
Herbert's Greek now; his eye is rapid, more so than mine
ever was,—I wish he would unite with this a little more of
my pondering propensities and love of digging *down* as far
as ever one can go into the meaning of an author;—though
this is sometimes unfavourable to getting a given thing
done for immediate use,—it takes one off into such wide
and many-branched excursions. As long, however, as I
can keep pace with the youth, I shall be able, in virtue of
my years and experience, at least for some time, to shoot
ahead of him when we come to any really hard passage, in
which it is not so much the knowledge of one particular
language, but of thought in general, that is required for the
elucidation. John often exhorts me to let my mind *go to
grass*; but who can do this while their mind can do any
sort of good in harness? After all it is a gain, even for our
own mental enjoyment, to be led back to these evergreen
haunts of the Muses, which, but for the sake of accompanying our children, we might never revisit; and I am
thankful that the limbs of my mind are still agile enough for
these excursions, and that I am not aged for rambling in
those literary fields, or for enjoying myself there, which in

some respects I am able to do far more than when I first
entered them.

VIII.

Miss Farrer.

To Mrs. FARRER.

10, *Chester Place, September 21st,* 1846.—My dearest Mrs.
Farrer,—Since I read the last pages of your kind and
interesting letter, I have been thinking almost continually
of dear Miss Farrer.* I feel as yet as if I could scarcely
understand or *reconcile* myself to her death. The event
is so unexpected, as well as unwelcome. When I first
saw her, she struck me as one full of firmness and vigour,
in rich and undeclining autumn. To say I shall never
forget her is nothing. I might *remember* a far less impressive person; but she will remain in my mind as one
of the most marked and interesting persons whom I have
met with in my walk through life—one of those who most
made me feel that religion is an actual reality—not merely
a system, but a vital influencive truth, which, even in this
world, can give such happiness as the world cannot give. I
am unable to remember many of her sayings, but I well
retain the spirit of her discoursings, and her deep, glad,
earnest voice will often sound in my ears. How graceful
and persuasive too she was in her gestures! These are the
outward things, and it seems wronging her who had such
riches within, such a depth of heart and spirit, to speak of
them; but they were a part of her here, and they bring her
vividly to mind, such as she was altogether, outwardly and
inwardly; and never was any one's outward part, countenance, carriage, and even bodily form, more expressive
of the soul within than hers was.

How many must there be, and in what distant quarters

---

* This lady, whose acquaintance my mother made in the autumn of 1843,
is mentioned in one of the letters of that date, in which her interesting and
remarkable character is dwelt upon with cordial admiration.—E. C.

of the world, that will truly mourn her death! I am sure
she must have a large interest in the heavenly habitations.
How many years she was doing good, and how steadily she
trod the path of Christian charity and bounty! I think
she was not clear-sighted on some points, and that she
fixed her eyes too exclusively on one side of truth, though
she sought so earnestly to look upon all who call on the
name of Christ as belonging to one fold under one Shepherd, let them shut themselves up within walls and hedges
of partition as much as they might. She would have
embraced all *believers* with the arms of her charity, but
did not always do full justice, I think, to the *belief*. She
was, however, a sincere and bountiful Christian. Her
example has been a burning and shining light, and will,
I trust, be remembered for good long after the tears are
dried that will be shed for her. What attracted me so to
her was to see her, wide as her charities were, so warm and
liberal and loving in her own family. I mean by *liberal*, so
full of sympathy, so ready to see all things in the best
light, and to promote all that is gay and gladsome and
beautiful. There have been philanthrophists, and sincere
and noble ones too, who have been oppressive and incon-
siderate and morose in their own families. Some who do
good abroad from selfish, ambitious motives, are selfish,
even cruel at home. But she was so faithful and tender
and affectionate.

IX.

On the Establishment—The Church Supported by the State, not in its
    Catholic, but in its National Character—Bishops in Parliament.

To AUBREY DE VERE, Esq.

What Dr. Hook says on the Establishment in his pamphlet on the Education of the People, I rather admire. A
correspondent of mine exclaims with indignation, " Conceive his asserting that the State is no more bound to the
Church than to Methodists, etc., and asking, if it is, by

what Act of Parliament? As if the Church were not an estate of the realm, as much as the monarch is, or either House of Parliament." I cannot quite understand what my friend means by this. Our Church, with the sovereign at its head, and with its present formularies, dates only from the sixteenth century. Dissolve its present connection with the State, and merge it in the Church of Rome, still the State remains essentially the same; but take away the monarch, or either House of Parliament, and you, at least organically, derange the State. It will remain, but as a different thing, with its character quite altered. Dr. Hook seems to mean only this, which seems to me undeniable, that the British nation is not of one form of Christianity, but of several, and that the State, which surely must conform itself to the nation, acting through Parliament, does not, and must not, protect, support, and, so far, help to *establish* one form alone, but as many as the nation embraces. It is true that the Church of England has some special relations to the State, which other bodies of Christians have not. But how has she obtained these? Is it simply from her being spiritually the Church of Christ, apostolically descended, while those other bodies are not the Church of Christ, or any part of it? It seems to me chimerical to say so. The special relations of the Church of England to the State, as I understand the matter, are of a temporal character, derived from her having once been the Church of the whole nation, still being the Church of the majority, and consequently having a greater amount of property than other religious communities, and that in a more imposing and dignified form. The council of the nation may be filled with Dissenters and Papists. It never, therefore, can be the duty of that Council, *as such*, to support the Church of England more than other religious bodies, except in proportion to numbers. The bishops do not represent that Church in Parliament, for they sit there as temporal peers. I believe that Christianity, religion in its deepest form, is interwoven with the State, and every state, in a vital and intricate manner. We know of no civilized state that was not in alliance with religion ; but I cannot think that one particular form of Christianity, though it be the truest form, is a component and essential part of the State, while the large body of Methodists, with Quakers, Independents, and others, are in a totally different predicament. I cannot think Dr. Hook so far wrong for asking in what real, substantial sense is the Church of England *established* here, or how has it a right to peculiar State support and protection, to be supported as the *Church of England*, not merely as a part of the Christianity of the land. Of course it is still formally the Established Church, and long may it be.

X.

The Divina Commedia—Barbarous Conception of the World of Fallen Spirits exhibited in the " Inferno "—Dante compared with Milton, Lucretius, and Goethe—Dante as Poet, Philosopher and Politician.

To AUBREY DE VERE, Esq., Curragh Chase.

October, 1846.—I cannot quite agree with you (*yet*, at least) on the superlative merits of Dante, whom you seem to me to view through a glorifying glass, bigger than that with which Herschel inspected the sun; but your reflections on the state of your country are full of that heart-poetry and spiritual wisdom, which, methinks, you " half-create," and do but half, or scarcely half, " find," in the great Epic Poem of the Middle Ages. What you say of hungry people, that they should not be convened in multitudes, is a part of this wisdom. The clamours of the *Times*, and the mingled yells and hisses of the *Dublin Review*, are—a disgrace to a Christian country. This is quite a bathos. I had something in my mind much more energetic, which I forbore to utter, lest you should think that I had had a little bite of

Cerberus myself, and that my preference of the "Inferno" to the other parts of Dante's poem arises from a fellow-feeling with those amiable gentlemen in the City of Dis, who shut the gates in the face of Virgil.

How graphic all that is! How one can enter into the *spitefulness* (if Dante had not been spiteful, he couldn't have written it) with which they proposed that Virgil should stay with them, and Dante find his way home by himself; how one can see them tearing off as hard as they could go, to bar the entrance! Milton could not have conceived this *intensity* of narrow malice; he could not have brought his rich genial mind, his noble imagination, down to it. It may truly be said that Dante brings the violence and turbulence of the infernal world into heaven— witness his 27th canto of the "Paradiso," which is all denunciation after the splendid introduction, yet comprises, to my mind, with slight exceptions, almost the whole power of the "Paradiso," on the merits of which, as at present advised, I quite agree with Landor; while Milton invests even the realms below and their fallen inhabitants with a touch of heavenly beauty and splendour. And is this in an irreligious spirit? Oh! far from it. This is consonant with religious truth and with the Bible, which leads us to look upon the world of moral evil as a wreck, a ruin, rather than a mere mass and congeries of hideous abominations. It is this which renders Milton's descriptions so *pathetic:* sympathy with human nature, with fallen finite nature, pervades the whole. If this be "cotton-wool," then cotton-wool for ever, say I. But this cotton-wool I believe to be a part of the substance of Christianity. For pure, unmixed wickedness, we can have no feeling; we can but shudder, and turn away. Dante utterly wants this genial, expansive tenderness of soul; wherever he is touching, it is in the remembrance of something personal—his own exile, or his love for little

Beatrice Portinari, or the sorrows of his patron's daughter,
Francesca. Let him loose from these *personal* bandages,
and he is perpetually raging and scorning, or else lecturing,
as in the "Paradiso." How ferociously does he insult the
sufferers in the "Inferno"—actual individual men ! You
say this is but imagination. Truly, if it were not, the
author would have been worthy of the maniac's cell, chains,
and darkness ; but surely the heart tinctures the imagination. I know my father's remark upon this very point,
and admit its truth as a general remark ; but I think it is
not strictly applicable to Dante. His pictures *are* like the
visions of heart-anger and scorn, not mere extravagant
flights of merry petulance, or pure, high-flown abstractions,
but have something in them deep, earnest, real, and
individualizing. It is a *hard* turn of mind, to say the best
of it. Carlyle does Dante more than justice—rather say,
generous *in*justice—on this point, when he tells us of his
softness, tenderness, and pitifulness, at the same time
extolling his rigour. Rigour is all very well in the right
place ; but such rigour as Dante's could scarce be approved
by Him who said, "Judge not, lest ye be judged." It is
well enough to be rigid against the *passion of anger*, but not
to stick a certain Filippo Argenti up to the neck in a lake
of such foulness as few men could have conceived or
described, and then to express a "fearful joy "—or what is
fearful to the reader, rather than himself—in seeing the
other condemned ones fall furiously upon him, and duck
him in it all but to suffocation ! And he makes Virgil (who
would have been above such schoolboy savagery) hug and
kiss him for it, and apply to him the words spoken of our
Blessed Saviour—Luke ii. 27 ! Dante ought to have
looked upon the tortures of the lower kingdom with awe
and a sorrowful shuddering, not with triumphant delight
and horrid mirth. But the whole conception was barbarous,
though powerfully executed.

You must not think that I am wholly an armadillo or rhinocerean, insensible to the merits of Dante, from what I have said. I think that his "Divina Commedia" is one of the great poems of the world; but of all the great poems of the world, I think it the least abounding in grace, and loveliness, and splendour. There is no strain in it so fine as the address to Venus at the beginning of Lucretius' great poem; scarce anything so brightly beautiful as passages in Goethe's great drama. I think, certainly, that the religious spirit displayed in it, especially in the "Purgatorio," is earnest and deep, but far from pure or thoroughly elevated. If you set up a claim for Dante, that his is the great Catholic Christian mind, then ἀφίσταμαι— I am off, and to a great distance. The following description of Carlyle seems to me to point at what is Dante's characteristic power :—" The very movements in Dante have something brief, swift, decisive—almost military. The fiery, swift Italian nature of the man—so silent, passionate—with its quick, abrupt movements, its silent, pale rages—speaks itself in these things." Yes; it is in this fiery energy, these " pale rages," that Dante's chief power shows itself, as it seems to me, not in genial beauty and lovingness, not in a wide, rich spirit of philosophy. You compare a passage in the " Aids to Reflection " to the conclusion of Canto I. of the "Paradiso." They are indeed in a neighbouring region of thought; but as neighbours often quarrel violently when they come into close contact, so I think would these if strictly compared. S. T. C. in this passage speaks of the *scale* of the creation— how each rank of creatures exhibits in a lower form what is more fully and nobly manifested in the rank above. Of this, Dante says not a word. How should he? The thought is founded on facts of natural history unknown in his day, and a knowledge of zoology in particular, to which his age had paid no attention. The chief beauty of

Q

my father's aphorism consists, I think, in the striking manner in which instances of his remark are particularized, and the poetic elegance with which they are described. Then he proceeds to a concluding reflection, which is spiritual indeed—no mere fancy, but a solid truth. But Dante's passage ends with that confusion of the material and the spiritual which my father made it his business to drive out of the realms of thought as far as his eloquence could drive it. The next canto—the Beatrician lecture on the spots in the moon—I think now, as I thought when I first read it, the very stiffest oatmeal porridge that ever a great poet put before his readers, instead of the water of Helicon. If it were ever such sound physics, it would be out of place in a poem ; and its being all vain reasoning and false philosophy makes it hardly more objectionable than it is on another score.

October 29.—For saying that Dante's spots-of-the-moon doctrine is, as the commentators say, a mere *fandonia* and *garbuglio*, we have no less authority than Newton. Canto III. you put your own opinions into. But I must not enter the field of Spirit *versus* Matter. I only beseech your attention to this point. God is a Spirit, and yet He is Substance, and the Head and Fountain of all Substance, and the Son is of one Substance with the Father. If the tendency of the whole creation, when not dragged down by sin, is upward to the Creator, then surely there is a progress away from matter into spirit. This I believe to be Platonism, and this Platonism Schelling, Coleridge, and others have tried to revive. You oppose to them Mediæ-valism, or the semi-Pagan doctrine of the primitive Christians, *converts from Paganism*, and both parties appeal to Scripture. We think the Bible plainly teaches that flesh and blood, however *smartened up*, cannot enter into the kingdom of Heaven, but that things, such as eye of man hath not seen, nor ear heard, are prepared by God for them that love Him. It is true we cannot here, in this life, *image* to ourselves that kingdom. God Himself tells us that we cannot, both in Gospel and Epistle. However, few new books would give me so great delight, as a full, wide particular criticism from your pen, of Dante, Milton, (yes, I would trust you with him, you could not but do him glory and honour, in spite of yourself, when you took him up, though you might have thought you were going to depreciate him), and Wordsworth.

Herbert keeps me busy. He writes continually about his studies, asking for explanations, advice, and so forth. He is learning Icelandic, of which he brags greatly, and is reading Dante, Tasso, and Ariosto. I sent him a sheet of Dantian interpretations lately. I take the political view of the beasts in the 1st Canto, instead of the merely moral. Dante's politics are very remarkable. Born a Guelf, he became the most intense and vehement Ghibelline. It was Ghibellinism that perverted his mind into that strange judgment of Brutus and Cassius.

CHAPTER XVI.

*LETTERS TO AUBREY DE VERE, ESQ., MISS FENWICK,
    MISS ERSKINE, MISS MORRIS, MISS TREVENEN:
    January—July, 1847.*

I.

Characters of Milton, Charles the First, and Oliver Cromwell.

To AUBREY DE VERE, Esq., Curragh Chase.

Chester Place, January, 1847.—To rebel against a tyrant,
himself a rebel against the laws and liberties of his
country, and a traitor to its constitution, is no disgrace
to Milton's memory. Both parties were wrong and both
were right in my opinion—the struggle was to be, and
on either side there was much error and much wrong-
doing, from a blindness, under the circumstances, scarce
avoidable. Charles I pity, admire, but do not deeply
respect. Cromwell I respect more, but do not venerate.
He was a man of great firmness, courage, ability. Charles
had personal not moral courage—*he* had both. I think
he was sincere and patriotic at first, but became in some
measure corrupted, just as Artevelde became corrupted in
the course of his career.

II.

A Visit to Bath—Her Son's Eton Successes—Schoolboy Taste—The
    Athanasian Creed—Doctrine of the Filial Subordination not con-
    tained in it—The Damnatory Clauses—Candour in Argument.

To the Hon. Mr. Justice COLERIDGE.

8, Queen Square, Bath, March 20th, 1847.—My dear John,
—Here we are at Bath, in the commodious temporary abode
of Miss Fenwick, with my dear old friends, Mr. and Mrs.
Wordsworth. Our journey on Thursday was a bright and
pleasant one. Mr. and Mrs. Wordsworth were waiting to
welcome us at the station, and most affectionate was their

greeting. Mr. Wordsworth has always called me his child, and he seems to feel as if I were such indeed. . . .

Since I wrote the first page of this letter, I have had to answer two notes from Edward on a very pleasant occasion; the first told me that Herbert was in the number of the select, and also that he had gained the essay prize in a very distinguished manner; the second announced, with very hearty congratulations, that he had been declared the medallist, Whymper being the Newcastle scholar. I could not help thinking with special keenness of feeling on those who are gone, who would have shared with me and E. in the pleasure of this success; but it is best, for my final welfare at least, that all is as it is, and that the advantages of this world and its drawbacks have ever been mingled in my portion. It is a great addition to the pleasure to feel that Herbert's success gives real delight to others besides myself. Anything of the kind is received at St. M——s quite as a little triumph. Edward says that to Latin composition and the general improvement of his *taste* he must chiefly address himself during the next year. His taste will certainly bear a great deal of improvement during many a year to come, for the formation of a sound literary taste is a matter of time. His taste, taking the word in a positively good sense, as the appreciation of what is excellent, is now in fragments, not a general embryo, apparently, but much more developed in parts than on the whole. He has a much better notion of the true merits of ancient writers than of modern ones — modern *subjectivity* he does not understand in the least, hence his preference of Southey's poetry to that of Wordsworth.

. . . Mr. Dodsworth asked me in his last call what I thought of the article on Development in the "Christian Remembrancer." I mentioned to him, among some other part objections, a statement toward the end which seems

to me rather awkward for those who hold by the Athanasian Creed — I mean those who not only believe the
doctrine of the Trinity and Incarnation which it sets forth,
but defend the imposition of it upon the Church and the
propriety of its expressions from beginning to end. The
statement is that the Subordinateness of the Son, *as the
Son*, to the Father, " an awful and sacred doctrine," taught
by the early Fathers, had been suffered " to fall into the
shade," " to become strange to modern ears," and thus
(according to the writer's own argument, that mere implicit knowledge is practical ignorance) to remain unknown
to the mass of Christians, Christians who are anxiously
instructed by their pastors in all the most subtle mysteries
of the faith, except this (as for instance that Our Lord
had *two wills*, against the Monothelite heresy), that on
account of its tenderness as a matter of theological handling, the Church had discouraged any handling of it at
all. It is natural to ask, can that be *the Church*, led and
enlightened by the Spirit of Christ, which shrinks from
the statement of any true and sacred doctrine, which is
unequal to guard it from running into heresy, and actually
sets forth a creed which virtually denies it ; for the expressions of the Athanasian Creed, " none is afore or after
other," " none is greater or less than another " (although
Christ said " my Father is greater than I," and Bull
applies this to the Filial Subordination—indeed, as applied
to the human nature, it would be a *truism* inconceivable
for Our Lord to have uttered), unaccompanied by the
admission of *any* sense in which the Father is before
the Son, are to all intents and purposes a denial of
the doctrine. Nor does the Nicene Creed remedy the
defect, as the article seems to insinuate. It expresses the
Origination, as the Athanasian does also, but not the
Subordination ; and if the latter be a direct and necessary
inference from the former, is it not the extreme of faithless

cowardice to be *afraid* of a direct and necessary inference ?
After all, what I most object to in the " pseudo-Athana-
sian" Creed, is the damnatory clauses, which I take
according to the common sense of mankind, and consider
to be a positive assertion of what no man *now* believes,
though when that creed was written the belief was common enough. To go back to Mr. Dodsworth, he agreed with
me, as I understood him, in this and some other objections
to the article, interesting and suggestive as it is, and
in some parts satisfactory. Mr. Dodsworth is remarkably
candid in discussions of this sort. Most persons, if an
objection to their view is stated, which they know not how
to meet, will oppose it by a general non-admission, waiting
in hope that something will turn up to justify that which
they hold as part and parcel of their creed; but he always
says frankly at once "that is very true," to any point which
he may have at first denied, if reasons are alleged in favour
of it which seem to him sufficient.

III.

Mr. and Mrs. Wordsworth—Walks and Talks with the aged Poet—
His Consent obtained to a Removal of the Alterations made by
him in his early Poems.

To AUBREY DE VERE, Esq.

April, 1847, *Bath.*—I have made an effort to come hither,
availing myself of Miss Fenwick's most kind invitation,
although it separates me from Herbert during his holiday
time; because I felt that the opportunity of being once
more under the same roof with my dear old friends was
not to be neglected. I find them aged since I saw them
last in many respects; they both look older in face, and
are slower and feebler in their movements of body and
mind. Mrs. Wordsworth is wonderfully active; she went
three times to church on the Fast Day,* and would have

---

* The Day of Fasting and Humiliation, appointed on account of the Irish
Famine. This occasion gave rise to the general remarks on fasting, as a
religious exercise, in the ensuing letter to Miss Trevenen.—E. C.

fasted almost wholly, had not Mr. Wordsworth, in a deep, determined voice, said, "Oh, *don't* be so *foolish*, Mary!" She wisely felt that obedience was better than this sort of sacrifice, and gave up what she had "set her heart upon," poor dear thing! She is very frail in look and voice, and I think it very possible that a real fast might have precipitated her downward progress in the journey of life, —I will not say how many steps. Mr. Wordsworth can walk seven or eight miles very well, and he talks a good deal in the course of the day; but his talk is, at the best, but the faintest possible image of his pristine mind as shown in conversation; he is dozy and dull during a great part of the day; now and then the dim waning lamp feebly flares up, and displays a temporary *comparative* brightness —but *eheu! quantum mutatus ab illo!* He seems rather to recontinue his former self, and repeat by habit what he used to think and feel, than to think anything new. To me he is deeply interesting even in his present state for the sake of the past; the manner in which he enters into domestic matters, the concerns and characters of maids, wives, and widows, whether they be fresh and gay, or " withering on the stalk," is really touching in one of so robust and manly a frame of mind as his originally was, and, in a certain way, still is. We sit round the fire in the evening, his aged wife, our excellent hostess, your friend S. C., Louisa F., a very handsome and very sweet and good girl, and my E., and talk of our own family matters, or the state of the nation, or the people of history, Tudors and Stuarts, as subjects happen to arise, Mr. W. taking his part, but never talking long at a stretch, as he used to do in former years. Sometimes we walk together in the morning, and one day I had the satisfaction of hearing him assent entirely to some remarks which I ventured to make upon the alterations in his poetry, and even declared that they should be restored as they were at first. I say "they," but it remains to be seen to what extent he will do this. He promised, in particular, that the original conclusion of the "Gypsies," should be restored in the next edition; he also seemed to assent to my view of the new stanzas in the Blind Highland Boy, that though good in themselves, they rather interfere with the effect of the poem. I would have them preserved, but detached from the poem, and the story of the tub retained with a little alteration of expression if possible. One day I contrived to draw Mr. W. out a little upon Milton, and to hear him speak on that subject in a *to me* satisfactory manner.

IV.
Fasting and Self-denial.

To Miss E. TREVENEN, Helston, Cornwall.

April 9th, 1847, *Bath*.—As for the sham fasts or semifasts, with a great heavy supper afterwards, which some people practise by way of obeying the Church and following the example of the ancient Christians, I cannot believe that they are of any great service to Christendom; and real fasts are so injurious to the health of a large proportion of Christians, that I can never believe them to be an acceptable sacrifice to God. However, on this point I differ from many whom I deeply respect, while I agree with some whom I deeply respect also, and I will enter into the subject no further than to say, that I believe in fasting, in a high and spiritual sense, that of abstaining from self-indulgence for the sake of doing good to others. Contracting our wants into as narrow a compass as possible, without injury to our body or mind, is a most important part of Christian duty, and no one can be a true Christian who does not practise it. They who give largely to the poor *must fast* in this sense, because they diminish their means of indulging in the pride of the eye, and all kinds of unnecessary luxuries and elegancies.

V.

The Irish Famine—Defects and Excellencies of the Irish Character—
"The Old Man's Home."

To Miss ERSKINE.

8, *Queen Square, Bath, April,* 1847.—My dear A——,—
I thank you for your kind congratulations, and for your
wish that this visit may encourage me to avail myself of
an invitation to Little Green at some future time from dear
Mrs. Erskine. I strained a point to come hither in order
to be with my dear old friends Mr. and Mrs. Wordsworth.
They are aged since I saw them last, but still wonderful
people of their age, very active in body, and in mind to me
most interesting. We have many, many mutual recollections and interests and acquaintanceships, and should
have enough to converse about, even if *news* reached us not
here. It is impossible, however, not to dwell a good deal
on the state of Ireland. I have just received a long letter
from Adare. No one has died of starvation in his neighbourhood, my friend tells me, though there is want and
trial enough. He is indignant at the abuse of Irish landlords in our papers, which he treats as absolute slander.
"People who cannot get rent enough to keep them in snuff,"
says he, " are spoken of as having £10,000 per annum,
and men who are feeding their poor on the venison of their
parks are accused of living in palaces amongst beggars,
just as if they could grind down the statues in their halls
into powder, and make the poor people live on limestone
broth." He calls the English subscriptions " magnificent,"
but says that all the good-hearted people he converses with
are dreadfully incensed at not being allowed to feel as
grateful as they would wish to feel. I believe that there
are good, bad, and indifferent among Irish landlords, as
amongst other sets of people, and that *some* are as bad as
they have been represented. We have reports of some from

persons resident among them, which describe them as most selfish and unfeeling. Surely, too, there are some besetting faults in the poor of that land; they seem to be indolent, improvident, not truthful. How much of this arises from misgovernment is hard to say, but I am inclined to think that the *circumstances* of the Irish would never have been so bad as they have ever been, had their original disposition and character not been wanting in certain elements, conducive to prosperity and well-being. They have passive courage, but they want persistent energy and activity, and steady, effective principle, though there are many excellent, amiable points of character in them, and they have produced some admirable men. Bishop Berkeley I have long thought one of the best and most-to-be-admired of mortals, and have warmly assented to that line of Pope's in which he assigns

"To Berkeley every virtue under Heaven." . . .

I have no time, or scarce any, for reading here, but have read by snatches Adams's " Old Man's Home," which is sweet and pleasing in style, but in aim and import, as it seems to me, very vague and unsatisfactory. It is difficult to see exactly what moral or maxim or sentiment the author means to enforce; if you take it one way, it seems scarce worth making a tale about, if another, then it is an untenable falsity, such as it is scarce worth any one's while to take the pains to refute. Equivoques and paradoxes I never could entertain any respect for myself, though they are often very popular; a sentiment looks well in a mist, and has a sublime air, like our terraces in the park, which look like common houses of £200 or £300 a year, instead of romantic palaces, when the vapours clear off.

VI.

Illness of Mrs. Quillinan—Answer to the Question whether Dying
Persons ought to be warned of their State at the risk of hastening
their Departure ?—Holy *Living* the only real Preparation for Holy
Dying.

To Miss FENWICK.

Chester Place, May 3rd, 1847.—My dearest Miss Fenwick,—I return to you, with many thanks, poor Mr. Quillinan's very affecting letter, which conveys the impression
that our sweet, dear Dora * has but a few weeks, perhaps
not many days, of life in this world before her.

In my reply to Mr. Quillinan, I expressed briefly my
own strong opinion against communicating to the patient
medical opinions, that destroy all hope of prolonged life.
The truth to me seems this, dear Miss Fenwick. That we
ought not to deprive our friends of a certain or even highly
probable spiritual advantage for the sake of saving them
any trial or suffering here, I most entirely agree with you ;
but I cannot help greatly doubting, as I believe James
Coleridge doubts too, that the spiritual advantage is such
as many suppose it. Have we a right to hasten death, to
destroy (as in some cases we may) a remaining *chance* of
recovery, to cut short what may be days of *real*, if not
formal preparation, to produce a state of, perhaps, unspeakable distress and terror, preclusive of that calmness and
self-possession, which are so indispensable to the best and
most efficacious spiritual reflection ? Every medical man
will say that such communications have generally a bad
effect upon the body ; can spiritual guides *assure* us that
they have a good effect upon the soul, or give us great
reason to think so ? What Mr. Wordsworth expresses seems
to me to be the simple truth ; my Uncle Southey held the
same opinion. It is very true that numbers of persons view

* Mr. Wordsworth's only daughter, whose early life was spent in sisterly
intimacy with the family at Greta Hall. She died of consumption in the
first week of July, 1847.—E. C.

the approach of death with composure, even welcome it; this
was the case with my sister Fanny Patteson; she had long
thought that she was death-stricken, and not regretted it;
when her time came she *knew* the truth, without being told
it, and great as her blessings in this life had been, was
"glad to go."   But there are other persons, equally good,
equally religious, to whom the near prospect of dissolution
is intolerable; to persons in general, I think we may say,
the shock is awful.   I fear you may not agree with me, but
I must express my doubt whether the agitated prayers which
persons offer up in this terrified state, prayers produced
more by a vague horror and dread of punishment, than a
calm, clear sense of the odiousness and unhappiness of sin
as *sin*, let it bring further consequences beyond itself or no,
are of such service, in a religious point of view, as persons
generally suppose. It seems a trite thing to say, that it is
the use we make of life and all our active powers, what we
make ourselves to *be* inwardly by the life we lead, that our
well-being hereafter depends upon, and not the thoughts of
our final change specially occupying the mind during our
last few days, and producing a special preparation.   Yet
this special preparation, if it can be brought about, well or
usefully, is by no means to be disregarded.   I am inclined
to think, however, that even where there is still hope of life,
and not an absolute coming face to face with approaching
death, there is often a most salutary discipline and real
preparation: a sense of the precariousness of life, and the
weakness and liability to suffering of this our earthly state,
must be strongly impressed on any impressible mind under
such circumstances; and to this preparation, with its
subdued yet quiet and cheerful frame of spirits, I should
trust more than to any which the prospect of speedy disso
lution brings about.   I would not go so far as to say that
true penitence may not be produced by this prospect, but I
think it is best for Christians through life to feel that if

they do not repent of sin effectively while they yet may practise it, the mere sorrow that they *have* practised it when they are on the verge of a state where only the misery of it can survive, will stand them in little stead, or at least is nothing to rely upon.

If you ask me how would I myself be dealt with under such circumstances, I scarce know what to say; only I feel *now* that if I do not now prepare to go, it will signify little then. I should be resolved to have everything temporally, as much as I can, in readiness, and as I should wish it to be were a disabling illness to come upon me, and I always pray to be prepared for my final change, and enabled *now* to realize the short interval between my present existence and that other state. I earnestly hope that I may be, as Fanny was, aware when the time was approaching, by my own inward feelings, so that friends about me will not have the pain of breaking it to me. Alas! I have neither husband nor parents to be grieved; and children, however loving and beloved, cannot feel as they feel. But, dear friend, this is not altogether to be deplored. I doubt not you feel with me that there is a calmness, even if a sadness, in this thought. We must, as Keble says, take that last journey alone; we must learn to be alone *in heart* here first. I always felt that my deep losses would make it easier to die.

VII.

A Month later.

To Miss MORRIS, Mecklenburg Square.

Margate, May 31*st*, 1847.—This place is very refreshing. The larks twittering in the fields of dwarf beans, now in fragrant bloom, and the lush green oat-crops, and the clover-beds, not yet in blossom, but soon to be, and the sight of the blue field of ocean beneath the blue sky, are all very pleasant. I think of the time when I came hither first, four years ago—a sad, sad widow. My children were with me, and their gambols and extreme vivacity were not like what any other gaiety would have been to my feelings, as " the pouring of vinegar upon nitre, and the taking away a garment in cold weather." They " sang songs to my heavy heart," without seeming to increase its burden. Then the dying bed of my beloved husband, who had ever been such a lover to me, his last illness and dying hours, were all fresh in my mind; but a little space interposed between the present and that sorrow. *Now* I have to dwell on the dying bed of one of my very earliest companion-friends, dear Dora Quillinan, once Wordsworth, who is sinking in the last stage of consumption. You know I was with her parents at Bath in March. In April they were for a week in London, were hastened home by a report that the medical man had discovered fatal symptoms in her. Now for the last fortnight she has known her prospect, that she is death-stricken, and that it is only with her a question of time, and nothing can exceed the heavenly composure, sweetness, and piety of her frame of mind. She bore the communication, which she solicited herself, with perfect firmness, seemed quite happy to go, though full of love to all around her, and no dying bed can be more full of amiable dispositions, or more perfect in its resignation than hers. I must write to Mrs. Wordsworth in reply to a detail of her beloved child's sayings and doings in this her season of death-expectancy and final weakness, which she thought due to me as her earliest companion-friend. Scarcely a day passes that I do not receive, either from Rydal Mount or from our mutual friend, Miss Fenwick, accounts of the dear sufferer. It is quite a privilege to be admitted to dwell on such a dying bed as hers. In the day my children and other interests share my thoughts with her, but at night, in my sleepless hours, I am ever with her, or dwelling on my own future deathbed, or going back to that of my dear husband, or the last days and hours of my beloved mother.

The parents are wonderfully supported, but deep, deep is their sorrow. Mr. Wordsworth cannot speak of it without tears. Poor Mr. Quillinan! But I must say no more of this, to me, engrossing sorrow.

VIII.
The Earnest of Eternal Life.

To Miss FENWICK, Bath.

Chester Place, July 1st, 1847.—Poor Mr. Quillinan's letter increases the sad feeling with which I approach in thought that sick room at Rydal Mount. But while the mind is so far from sick, these are indeed, as you say, but temporary emotions: the natural horror of continuous pain and suffering will go ; the remembrance of the sufferer's strength and sweetness will remain. We cannot need arguments and sermons on immortality ; or, at least, after being instructed in Christianity, we cannot need them to strengthen and refresh our faith when we have such living documents and earnests of Eternal Life before us as these. If the mind seemed to weaken and die with the body, we might doubt; though even then I trust the written Word might sustain us ; but up to the last breath, how brightly the light shines in some ! It would be impossible to think, even without the Word, that such a power of thought and feeling was in a few moments to cease to be for ever !

IX.
The Sister of Charles Lamb.

To Miss FENWICK.

Margate, July 6th, 1847.—I see that Mary Lamb is dead. She departed, eighty-two years old, on the 20th of May. She had survived her mind in great measure, but much of the *heart* remained. Miss Lamb had a very fine feeling for literature, and was refined in mind, though homely, almost coarse, in personal habits. Her departure is an escape out of prison, to her sweet, good soul more especially. To put off the clog of the flesh must be to the sanest an escape from a body of death.

X.

Religious Tendency of Mr. Coleridge's Writings—Her own Obligations
to her Father, her Uncle, and Mr. Wordsworth.

To Miss FENWICK, Queen Square, Bath.

Chester Place, July 7th, 1847.—Dear Friend,—I have been
extremely gladdened by what you said in your last but one,
on the use that my father's writings had been of to you.
No better compliment could be paid them, than to say that
they *sent you to the Bible;* and this exactly describes my
own feelings and experience. I, too, feel now, that though
I read books of divinity—especially of Jeremy Taylor and
our old divines—with delight, and a certain sort of advantage, I do not *want* any book spiritually, except the Bible,
now that, by my father and Mr. Wordsworth, I have been
put in the way of reading it to advantage. They, indeed,
have given me eyes and ears. What should I have been
without them! To my Uncle Southey I owe much—even to
his books; to his example, his life and conversation, far
more. But to Mr. Wordsworth and my father I owe my
thoughts more than to all other men put together.

CHAPTER XVII.

*LETTERS TO AUBREY DE VERE, ESQ., HON. MR. JUSTICE
COLERIDGE, MISS FENWICK, REV. HENRY MOORE,
MISS ERSKINE, MISS MORRIS, MISS TREVENEN,
MRS. H. M. JONES, MRS. RICHARD TOWNSEND:
July—December, 1847.*

I.
Grasmere Churchyard.
To Miss Fenwick.

August 2nd, 1847.—Your account of dear Mr. and Mrs.
Wordsworth is very consolatory. I am sure they must be
soothed and sustained by the remembrance of their blessed
child's sweet, loving, beneficent life, and of her calm, happy,
patient deathbed, so full of faith and Christian graces. I
should think that a visit to the churchyard where she lies
must, under these circumstances, be soothing. Well do I
remember Dora shedding tears when we, 'her thoughtless
companions, read aloud the names of her little departed
sister and brother in that churchyard. How little did I
think, full of life and strength as she then was, that she
would be laid there herself while I survived, and her own
parents still lived to lament her loss !

II.
The Installation Ode—The Triad.
To the Rev. Henry Moore, Eccleshall Vicarage, Staffordshire.

Chester Place, August 4th, 1847.—The visit to Bath was
very interesting, though I saw in Mr. Wordsworth rather a
venerable relic, so far as his intellectual mind is concerned,
than the great poet I once knew; and I do not agree with
H. T. in thinking highly of his Installation Ode.* It is
only so far Wordsworthian that it is not vulgar, not decked

* Written on occasion of the Installation of the Prince Consort as Chan-
cellor of the University of Cambridge.—E. C.

out with a second-hand splendour that may be bought at
any poetry-mart for the occasion. But the intercourse
with my dear old friends was saddened by the bad news
they were receiving of their beloved daughter. A week after
they came to town they received a report of her which
hastened them home, and now she is in her grave,—has
been in her grave for some weeks. She is one of my
earliest friends, and her death has saddened this summer
to me. Never was there a more blessed deathbed than hers,
—one fuller of faith, and love, and fortitude, and every
Christian grace. Still, it is sad for those who knew her
from childhood to see her light go out in this world. Look
at " *The Triad*," written by Mr. Wordsworth four or five
and twenty years ago. That poem contains a poetical
glorification of Edith Southey (now W.), of Dora, and
myself. There is *truth* in the sketch of Dora, poetic truth,
though such as none but a poet-father would have seen.
She was unique in her sweetness and goodness. I mean
that her character was most peculiar,—a compound of
vehemence of feeling and gentleness, sharpness and lovingness,—which is not often seen.

III.

Intellectual Ladies, Modern and Ancient.

To AUBREY DE VERE, Esq.

Chester Place, August 20th, 1847.—I had a very interesting talk last night with Mr. H. T., who is looking remarkably well. He put in a strong light the unattractiveness of
intellectual ladies to gentlemen, even those who are themselves on the intellectual side of the world—men of genius,
men of learning and letters. I could have said in reply, that
while women are young, where there is a pretty face, it
covers a multitude of sins, even intellectuality ; where there
is not that grand desideratum to young marrying men, a
love of books does not make the matter much worse in one

way, and does make it decidedly better in the other : that
when youth is past, a certain number of persons are bound
to us, in the midst of all our plainness and pedantry ; these
old friends and lovers cleave to us for something underneath
all that, not only below the region of good looks, skin, lip,
and eye, but even far deeper down than the intellect, for
our individual, moral, personal being, which shall endure
when we shall be where all will see as angels ken, and
intellectual differences are done away : that as for the world
of gentlemen at large—that world which a *young* lady desires,
in an indefinite, infinite way, to charm and smite—we that
are no longer young pass into a new, old-womanish, tough
state of mind; to please them is not so much the aim, as to
set them to rights, lay down the law to them, convict them of
their errors, pretences, superficialities, etc., etc. ; in short,
tell them a *bit of our mind.*   This, of course, is as foolish
an ambition as the other, even more preposterous ; but it is
so far better, that even where the end fails, the means themselves are a sort of end, and a considerable amusement and
excitement.   So that intellectualism, if it be not wrong in
itself, will not be abandoned by us, to please the gentlemen.

God bless you, and prosper you in all your labours, for
your country's sake and your own.   But do not forget the
Muses altogether.   Those are intellectual ladies who *have*
attractions for gentlemen worth pleasing, and who retain
" the bland composure of perpetual youth " beside their
refreshing Hippocrene.

IV.

Sacred Poetry : Keble, Quarles, and Crashaw.

To Mrs. Richard Townsend, Springfield, Norwood.

Chester Place, September, 1847.—I am much pleased to
hear of your undertaking,* and feel provoked that I cannot

* A collection of sacred pieces, chiefly from the elder English poets, entitled " Passion Week ; " and followed by " Christmas Tyde."—E. C.

aid you in it—poet's daughter, and niece, and friend, as I am—I mean in the way of pointing out some green haunts of the sacred Muses which you have not yet found out. But though sacred poetry abounds, good sacred poetry is more scarce than poetry of any other sort. I do but half like the "Christian Year," I confess; but this you will think bad taste in me, though I could quote some poetical authorities on my side. I admire some stanzas and some whole poems in the collection exceedingly, but they seem to me quite teasingly beset with faults, both of diction and composition. Of these, the former annoy me most, and most interfere with my pleasure in reading them. I know no other mass of poetry so good, that is not at the same time better, showing more poetic art and judgment.

I can only mention to you Quarles, a great favourite with my Uncle Southey, and Crashaw,* whose sacred poetry I think more truly poetical than any other, except Milton and Dante. I asked Mr. Wordsworth what he thought of it, and whether he did not admire it? to which he responded very warmly. My father, I recollect, admired Crashaw; but then neither Quarles nor Crashaw would be

---

* Richard Crashaw, a contemporary of Herbert, Quarles, and Vaughan, became a Roman Catholic during the troubles of the Civil War, and died a canon of Loretto, A.D. 1650. His poetry is marked by a dreamy, fanciful sweetness and devotional fervour, which give it a peculiar charm. The following elegant little poem, "On Mr. George Herbert's Book, intituled the Temple of Sacred Poems, sent to a Gentlewoman," must surely have been prized by the receiver, as adding to the value of the gift:—

> "Know you, Fair, on what you look?
> Divinest love lies in this book,
> Expecting fire from your eyes
> To kindle this his sacrifice.
> When your hands untie these strings,
> Think you've an angel by the wings—
> One that gladly will be nigh
> To wait upon each morning sigh,
> To flutter in the balmy air
> Of your well-perfumed prayer.
> These white plumes of his he'll lend you,
> Which every day to heaven will send you,
> To take acquaintance of the sphere,
> And all the smooth-faced kindred there!"—E. C.

much liked by the modern general reader. They would be thought queer and extravagant.

V.

The Art of Poetry—A Lesson on Metre.

To Miss MORRIS.

1847.—My Dear Friend,—I may not on Wednesday, or before, for I hope we shall meet again before, be able to squeeze in a word about the Art of Poetry; and so I will write a few lines on the subject now, only as a prelude to much talk on such subjects, which I hope to have with you from time to time.

I must begin with telling you that I never wrote blank verse in my life, and smile at myself when I think that I am about to attempt giving instructions, or even hints on metre. I always, in attacking Wordsworth's later poetry with Mr. de Vere, admit that, from his far greater practice in verse-making and executive skill in poetry, he is more alive to delicacies of metre and elegancies of diction than I am. However, though I never wrote Latin verses myself, I could often inform Herbert of the faults of his; and so in regard to your lines. I can perceive that some of the lines have not quite the right metre, without too much humouring.

You know that blank verse consists of ten feet, called iambuses, each foot containing a short and a long syllable, represented in the symbols of ancient prosody thus: ⏑ –, as forbēar.

This heroic measure is called pure when the accent rests upon the second syllable through the whole line, as—

But who | can bear | th' approach | of cer | tain fate.

Still it would be very wearying and tame if the accent was never transposed in the course of a composition. Very often spondees are introduced in the place of the iambus;

—the spondee is a foot formed of two long syllables, as wāx-líght;—or a trochee, a long and a short, as dáily.

Here Lóve | his góld | en shafts | emplóys | here líghts |

His cón | stant lamp | and waves | his pur | ple wings—
Reígns hére | . . . .

In the second line you see the iambic measure is pure, in the others mixed. (I should have said above, that the ancients have *syllabic* quantity, their short and long syllables depending upon the number and position of the consonants, and the time taken up in pronunciation; we have only *accentual* quantity, at least as an absolute rule, though some attention to the length of syllables is also paid by every fine versifier.) Milton often crumples two short syllables into one for the last half of his iambus at the end of a line, as—

Yōur bō | dīes māy | āt last | tūrn āll | tŏ spirĭt.

Equivalent in time to a short and a long, for two shorts are equal to one long.
So again :—

Ētēr | nāl Kĭng, | thĕ aŭth | ŏr ŏf | āll bĕīng

In this line there is a pyrrhic in the fifth place, and a dactyl (– ˘ ˘) in the last, which forms a very agreeable variety. Here you see the time is equal to that of the pure iambic, if you take the two last feet together, because the long syllable " all " is in the place of a short syllable. The time in the two last feet is the same as six shorts, or three longs, or two shorts and two longs, which is the usual distribution. Only the change of arrangement, introduced but very seldom, and in an appropriate place, is a beauty. Do just mark the exquisite metrical variety in the passage —Book III. l. 844-871,—especially from "With these that never fade," to the end of the paragraph.

By way of practice you ought to scan Milton's Paradise
Lost. That is, read passages, attending principally to the
metre, and putting them on paper with the prosodiacal
marks, as—

Pāvemĕnt | thăt lĭke | ă sēa | ŏf pūrp | lĕ shōne

and mark in a paragraph the varieties of accent and their
relation to the sense and the feeling of the verse. Does it
not seem brutal thus to anatomize and skeletonize poetry?
but so painters learn to paint, and so poets must learn to
poetize, I believe.

It is the sense of the great difficulty of writing blank
verse that has always kept me from attempting it. In
rhymes and stanzas there is a mechanical support, a sort
of *framework* of poetry which my weakness rests upon. But
some person's thoughts (probably yours are such) naturally
flow into that form more than any other.

I have criticised you as freely as I do many of my other
friends. I think that writing verse is useful in a secondary
way, as learning music is also; it teaches us to feel doubly
the excellencies of the great poetic artists, as musical
practice to understand fine playing.

VI.

Modern Novels : "Grantley Manor," "Granby," The "Admiral's
Daughter."

To Miss FENWICK.

Fort Crescent, Margate, October 2nd, 1847.—We have
both read "Grantley Manor," with which we have been
rather disappointed after the ecstatic reports of it which we
received. The story proceeds languidly, though never devoid
of interest, till the middle of the third volume, and whether
or no it was Anglican prejudice, but so it was, that the
heroism and oft-repeated agonies and anguishful trials of
the Romish heroine, were to me more wearying than

affecting. It was so easy to give the fine, elegant, heavenly-minded, firm-souled, poetical sister to the Church of Rome, and the little short, half-worldly, half-coquettish, pretty, but cross-mouthed sister to the Church of England! The trap for admiration is too palpable. We see it afar off, and will not walk into it. Still there is much to admire in this book, and some scenes are extremely good. There is every wish on the part of the authoress to be candid, and in Ann Neville she has portrayed a character quite as excellent and admirable as Ginevra, and given her to our Church.

But I confess, fond of the poetical as I am, and of reflection and sentiment, I do not like so much of this sort of thing *in a novel*, as Lady Georgiana Fullerton gives us. At least I think the best sort of *novel* is that which deals chiefly in delineation of character, dialogue and incident. I have been much pleased, more than I expected to be, with a novel by Mr. Lister, "Granby." The *ease* with which it is written throughout is admirable. This ease is quite inimitable. It results from birth, breeding, and daily association with that sphere of thorough gentility where the inhabitants have little else to do than to be refined, and are cut off from all particular occupations that give a particular cast and impress to the manners. Dickens could as little give this air to his dialogue by letters or narrative as the author of "Granby" could have produced Sam Weller and his father, or Ralph Nickleby, or Sairey Gamp. Do you like Mrs. Marsh's books? The "Admiral's Daughter" seems to me one of the best tales of the day. It is deeply pathetic, and the scenes are admirably well wrought up.

VII.

"Marriage," by Miss Ferrier—Novel Writing.

Margate, October, 1847.—I am now engaged with
"Marriage" by Miss Ferrier, which I had read years ago.
It is even better than I remembered. The humour reminds
me of that of our good old plays. Lady Maclaghlan and
Sir Simpson are excellent, and there is an easy air of high
life in Lady Juliana which makes it bearable to dwell so
long on a heartless childish creature. To read novels is all
very well; but to write them, except the first-rate ones,
how distasteful a task it seems to me ! to dwell so long
as writing requires on what is essentially base and worthless !

VIII.

Mrs. Gillman of Highgate.

To Miss FENWICK.

Chester Place, October 30th, 1847.—I was much pleased
to see my dear old friend, Mrs. Gillman, at Ramsgate,
looking far better, and evidently in better health than
several years ago. She is wondrously handsome for a
woman of seventy, far more interesting than I remember
her in middle age,—for she has more colour and becomes
the fine cap close to her face, all hair put away, more than
her more commonplace head costume of former days. Her
profile is quite Siddonian, and her black eye is bright; the
only drawback is rather too keen an expression, inclining
almost to hard and sharp, when she is looking earnestly
and not smiling. She is still lame from the effects of a fall
which, I think, she had in running once hastily to my
father when he was ill. It was interesting to me to see her
surrounded with portraits of old familiar faces, now past
away from earth, and pictures that I used to know at
Highgate.

IX.

**The Salutary Discipline of Affliction—Intellectual Resources—Earthly
Enjoyments and Heavenly Hopes.**

To Miss Morris.

24, *Fort Crescent, Margate, October 6th*, 1847.—My dear
Friend,—Most sincerely do I thank you for your letter,*
which affected me deeply,—affects me, I may say, for I
cannot look at it, or think of it, without feeling my eyes
fill with tears. It contains a record which will ever [be
precious to me,—a testimony to the power of faith, one of
those testimonies which make us feel with special force that
Christianity is no mere speculation or subject of abstract
thought, but a blessed and glorious reality,—the *only*
reality, to speak by comparison. But I believe it impossible for us in this earthly sphere to realize religion without
an attendant process of destruction; while this destruction
of the natural within us goes on gradually we do not note
it,—but in great affliction, when much work is done at
once, the disruption is strongly felt; and the body for a
time gives way.

After a while, even the body seems to gain new strength;
it has adjusted itself to a new condition of the soul. It
remains attenuated, but firm. We seem to have passed
into a partly new state of existence, a stage of the new
birth. One coat of worldliness has been cast off; the
natural is weaker and slenderer within us, and the spiritual
larger and stronger. I seem to myself scarce worthy
to talk of such things. I have not profited by affliction
as I ought to have done. Better than I once was, possessed of a far deeper sense of the beauty and excellence
of Christianity, I do humbly hope that I am. But I have
had perhaps too much worldly support, *earthly* support,
I should rather say. Things of the mind and intellect
give me intense pleasure; they delight and amuse me, as

* Containing the account of a sudden and severe affliction in the writer's
family, and of the Christian resignation with which it was borne.—E. C.

they are in themselves, independently of aught they can
introduce me to instrumentally; and they have gladdened
me in another way, by bringing me into close communion
with fine and deep minds. It has seemed a duty, for my
children's sake and my own, to cultivate this source of
cheerfulness, and sometimes, I think, the result has been
too *large*, the harvest too abundant, of inward satisfaction.
This is dangerous. How hardly shall the rich man enter
into the kingdom of heaven! and these are the richest of
earthly riches. They who *use* intellect as the means of
gaining money or reputation, are drudges, poor slaves,—
though even they have often a high pleasure in the means,
while they are pursuing an unsatisfactory end. But they
who live in a busy, yet calm world of thought and poetry,
though their *powers* may be far less than those of the
others, may forget heaven, if sorrow and sickness, and
symptoms of final decay, do not force them to look up, and
strive away from their little transitory heaven upon earth
to that which is above. Bright, indeed, that little heaven
continually is with light from the supernal one. But we
may rest too content with those *reflections*, which must fade
as our mortal frame loses power. Hope of a higher existence can alone support us when this half-mental, half-
bodily happiness declines.

X.

Controlling Grief for the Sake of Others.

To Miss ERSKINE.

Chester Place, October, 1847.—I have always gone upon
a plan of avoiding all excitement and agitation on the
subject of my own deep irretrievable losses. This for me
was an absolute necessity; had I not kept sorrow at arm's
length, as it were, with my very irritable state of nerves,
I should have been perpetually incapacitated for doing my
duty to my children. In early youth one thinks it impossible to keep grief at bay. To banish it is indeed im-

possible; keep it off as far as we may, there it stands dark and moveless, casting its shadows over our whole life, tinging every thought and action, and every would-be sunny prospect with at best a twilight evening hue. But this is far better than to be for ever at close quarters with sorrow, continually plunged in tears, and stung with keen regrets. I take no credit to myself for what I have done in this way, because it was not I that did it, but my circumstances. I had children to consider and to act for; and the sense how cruel and selfish it would be to shadow their young lives by the sight of a mother's tears, was a motive for exertion in cultivating all cheerful thoughts, which I could never have supplied to myself. Hence, as soon as possible, I did away all the special reminiscences of my past happy wedded life which lay in my daily path; this was not to diminish the remembrance of the departed; that remains vivid as ever without a hue faded or a line erased, but it prevented me from continually beholding the image of the departed in the midst of my daily work, when I could not afford to stand still and gaze upon it, and forget the present in the past.

XI.

"Anti-Lutherism"—Charges made against Luther of Irreverence, Immorality, and Uncharitableness—Luther's Doctrine of Justification adopted by the English Church—"Heroes," and the "Worship" due to them—Luther's Mission as a Witness for Gospel Truth.

To AUBREY DE VERE, Esq., Curragh Chase.

Margate, October 12th, 1847.—I regret our difference of feeling and opinion concerning Luther more than on any other subject, but differences on persons are not such discrepancies as differences on things. Did I conceive the old Reformer as you conceive him, I should admire him no more than you do. But a totally different person is before my eyes, when I think of him, from what you present. I marvel how you can admit him to be a *hero*, if you believe his strength to have been "of a very physical kind,"—look upon him as a religious demagogue, a "self-intoxicated man." It seems to me that you do by Luther what has so often been done by my father,—that is, that you present an exaggerated image of the mere surface of the man—the outside of his character—for the man himself. I believe that Luther was not that mere tempestuous struggler for liberty, that coarse, bold, irreverent, self-deceiving fanatic whom you present to me.

The truth is, your view of the objects of Luther's warfare, the things for which and against which he strove, determines your view of his personal character. You call him irreverent. Why? Because he did not revere much that you look upon with veneration. But has it yet been shown that Luther wanted reverence for the objects of faith and religious awe to which there is a clear testimony of reason and the spiritual sense,—which are *Christian*, not mediæval? He had no reverence for the priesthood, considered as the possessors of mystic gifts and ecclesiastical privileges—*pseudo*-ecclesiastical, I should say. I confess I have just as little as he. I think no one can exceed me, according to the powers and energies of my mind, in love and respect for the Christian pastorate. I honour the minister of Christ both in his office, and still more, when he is what he ought to be, for his personal gifts and graces. I look with deep interest and gratitude to God on the succession of Christ's shepherds from the Apostles to the present day, but the Succession *dogma*, taught in the "Tracts for the Times," I cannot behold with any respect whatever; just because it seems to me absolutely devoid of evidence, and secondly, a mere spiritual mockery, which adds nothing to religion but a name and a notion.

It is true that Luther, in the beginning of his career, spoke rashly of St. James's Epistle; but I cannot permit this fact to nullify for me all the evidence of deep religious feeling which I see in his writings and in his life. As for his want of charity, I do not defend his language; but vehement language alone can never convict him or any man of an uncharitable heart. Luther began with great moderation, but the murderous malice and violence of his enemies, who would have martyred him ten times over, and would be content with nothing but absolute renunciation of what he held to be the truth of God, goaded him to a degree which a writer of " Tracts for the Times," sitting quietly in his study, does not fairly allow for.

What are those moral enormities, those *thicks and thins* that Mr. Hare *defends ?* There is but one moral offence of any magnitude that has ever been brought home to Luther, —the affair with the Landgrave of Hesse,—and surely Hare does not *defend* his part in that matter. He only shows, very ably, as I thought, all the extenuating circumstances, and exposes the ridiculous unfairness of the representation of it by his adversaries. Those Romanists, and admirers of Romanism, treat it as an unprecedented crime in Luther to have done, with deep repentance afterwards, what their infallible Vicegerents of Christ had done before, without repenting of it at all. That Luther ever meant to defend or recommend polygamy, he shows, I think, very clearly to have been one of the ten thousand calumnies uttered against him by his untruth-telling foes. He said, I think justly, that we ought not to look upon polygamy as *essentially* a crime. What God has once sanctioned (surely the words of Nathan to David show that it was sanctioned) cannot be compared with sins against which there is a fiat of the Eternal.

Do you think that I admire Luther's doctrine for its energy and spiritual boldness? No; I admire the energy and boldness for the sake of the doctrine. What are those most vehement assertions of his which you consider heterodox? The great assertion of Luther's life as a theologian was justification by faith alone. Is this heterodox? Then is the Church of England heterodox in her Articles and her Homilies. It is vain to say that they teach Melancthon's doctrine. There is no real difference, I believe, and I have studied the subject a good deal, between Luther's view of the subject and that of his bosom-friend Melancthon. But Philip was a mild, calm man. He explained the doctrine, and put it into language less liable to be taken by a wrong handle, though far less calculated to make way for it in the first instance. The Commentary on Galatians was spiritual thunder and lightning. That it reads as well as it does now, when we consider the sort of work it did, and compare it with other such instruments by which great changes are made suddenly in masses, we may see, and ought, I think, to acknowledge, that if Luther was a spiritual demagogue, he was of the first order of such after inspired men. Indeed, my father, as appears in the "Remains," put him in the next rank after St. Paul and the Apostles. That article of our religion which the Commentary on Galatians is specially devoted to set forth, the manner of our justification, he thought more clearly seen, with greater depth of insight, by Luther than by any other man after the Apostle to the Gentiles. Such are his and my heresies.

As for hero-worship, if by *Hero* you mean only a strong man, able to produce great changes and make a sensation, and by *worship* such homage as Romanists pay to the Virgin and the Saints—which I believe to be too near that which belongs to God alone—I am as little a hero-worshipper as you are. I mean by a Hero a great, good man, endued with extraordinary gifts by the Father of Lights, which he employs for the benefit of mankind. Ought we not to *worship*, that is, honour and praise, and listen to such men? It seems to me that Luther's ends were great and noble, and that his motives were always disinterested, high, and pure. In some instances his means were blame-worthy. He was embarked in a mighty and most perilous, laborious, and difficult enterprise; and if, in the conduct of it, he sometimes, through fear of losing what had been gained, departed from the strict rule of right, surely a liberal and charitable judgment will not deny him the praise due to a benefactor of men. That he was a true religious enthusiast, not one who makes religion either a source of self-glorification or worldly advancement, seems clear from his dedication of himself at first, before the struggle with Rome began. He was raised up, as I fully believe, by Providence, to resist the practical corruptions of the Church, and to bear witness to the truth that it is the state of the heart, and not any number of outward acts or course of observances, on which our spiritual prospect depends.

XII.

Church-Ornamentation.

To AUBREY DE VERE, Esq.

December, 1847.—Mr. —— is raising a subscription for a painted window; and I scarce know what to do about it. I must confess, though here again I am out of sympathy with most of my friends, for, like Mr. M——, I am ever protest-ing against my own party, that is to say, the party which to my mind embraces *most* of the truth, and with whom I can in general concur in all that is practical,—but I must confess that I have scruples about giving spare money for painted windows when there is spiritual destitution still to provide for. "Oh! the more is given in one way, the more will be given in the other," is the cry. This seems to me an equi-voque. The same spirit which excites one kind of giving will excite both; but that any man who gave *all* he pro-perly could and ought for the higher object would have anything left for the lower I cannot believe; and thus,

s

while some churches are smartened up (and there is no limit to the expensive smartness that may be lavished upon a single edifice), others are erected of the meanest description. I do not feel quite satisfied that church grandeur was ever based on pure gospel *faith*, as Keble and others maintain. Pure faith does so much *else* for God, so much for her neighbour during lifetime, that she leaves not great sums behind to build a temple, to make up for the temple to God's honour and glory that she did *not* build, while she might, with her own hands. Then our modern church splendour is so poor, and petty, and equivocal; so vulgarized by patterns displayed in shops, and all kinds of trade associations. It does not flow from any great universal spirit which will last, but is supported by an effort of a busy section, running counter to the age instead of concurring with it.

XIII.

Dr. Hampden.

To Mrs. H. M. JONES, Hampstead.

1847.—Hampden has offended the bigots and zealots of all parties, Romanistic and Puritanical, by his charitable and conciliative sentiments, by daring to say that good and well-disposed men, with sound heads and sound hearts, who hold in their hands the one Gospel of Christ, believing it all to be the Word of God, cannot and do not differ substantially, in their vital operative faith, as much as they appear to do in dogmatical statements and intellectual schemes of belief. This has given far more deep and bitter offence than if Hampden had been really a disbeliever in any of the truths generally acknowledged in Christendom; the self-styled orthodox love to think themselves up in heaven, those who differ from them in the gulf below,— themselves to be the soft, snowy, lovely, innocent sheep, others the great coarse, rough, ill-scented goats. Hampden's doctrine partly fills up the gulf, the wide chasm which they would establish betwixt themselves and all who are not ready to swear to all their articles, and embrace what the Middle Ages determined on matters of faith by the mouths of uninspired Ecclesiastics, with implicit faith.

XIV.

Dr. Hampden's "Observations on Dissent."

To Miss ERSKINE.

1847.—What is considered such a crime in Hampden is his having dared to proclaim what are simple facts, of which proof has been given, and which have never been disproved; as, for instance, that the phraseology commonly used by Divines in theological statements has been established by dialectical science; that the *forms* of doctrine have been determined by the psychological philosophy of the period when they arose; and that the doctrine of the Sacraments (that is the Scholastic theories concerning them) is "based upon the mystical philosophy of secret agents in nature Christianized."

CHAPTER XVIII.

LETTERS TO AUBREY DE VERE, ESQ., REV. HENRY MOORE, MISS MORRIS, MRS. H. M. JONES, MRS. RICHARD TOWNSEND, MRS. GILLMAN, C. B. STUT-FIELD, ESQ.: 1848.

I.

Her Son's Preparation for the Newcastle Examination—School Rivalries.

To Mrs. GILLMAN, Ramsgate.

Chester Place, March, 1848.—Herbert is now preparing for the Newcastle contest. On the 3rd of April it will commence, the Scholarship will be declared on the 8th, and on the 10th he returns home. He bids me have no expectation of his gaining the Scholarship. His most formidable competitor, the eldest son of Sir Thomas F——, is nearly a year older than he, very clever, and very desirous to conquer, and has had much instruction during the holidays,—more than H. has.

It is a comfort to see what an excellent state of feeling exists between him and F——, not a shade of jealousy, I am sure. Indeed, I think that rivalry at public schools and at college is not the source of evil generally. Boys are generally inclined to like and respect those whose pursuits are similar to their own, and who exhibit talent in the line in which they are trying to distinguish themselves. They are oftener unjust to those of different habits, pursuits, likings, and dislikings, are apt to set them down as "brutes" and "asses," and to be perfectly blind to their abilities and good parts.

II.

The Newcastle Scholar—The Chartist Demonstration—Lowering of the
   Franchise ; its probable Result—Moral and Material Improvement
   the real Wants of the Poor, not Political Power.

To AUBREY DE VERE, ESQ., Curragh Chase, Ireland.

April 14th, 1848, *Chester Place.*—The news of Herbert's
success, on which you congratulate me in a manner which
adds greatly to the pleasure of it, was indeed very pleasant.
He darted in upon us like a beam of light on Saturday
afternoon, and received from us an awful account of the
Chartist preparations for insurrection and violence. You at
a distance, except by comparing our troubles with your
own, not by reports, can hardly have a notion of the alarm
and excitement that was produced all in a day or two. I
had been thinking of the matter a week or two before, and
consulted our intelligent neighbour, Mr. Scott, whose
opinion with regard to the state of the poor I thought
more important than any other. He told me that he had
been trying by private letters to rouse people in authority
to a sense of the necessity of making a determined show of
power and will to put down violence. The middle or shop-
keeping class, he said, think all these points of political
arrangements and government very much the gentry's affair.
Still, they will side with the gentry, feeling them to be
their natural protectors, and the class with whose interests,
in the present state of things, theirs are interlinked,
if they feel that the gentry can stand up for themselves,
and present a bold front to the insurgents ; otherwise,
having no *principle* to guide them one way or the other,
and not being given to theories or abstractions, or to go
beyond the present hour, they might throw themselves into
the arms of the mob, as did the shopkeepers and National
Guard, who are so much composed of that class, in Paris.
But then the army ? Well, he did not think we could be
certain of the army. There was no knowing how they

might act if the Chartists proved very formidable. He
thought the danger lay at present in the apathy and in-
activity of the upper classes, who carried a good principle
of not interfering with the liberty of the people much too
far. At this time no one was alarmed. Nothing was said
about the Chartists in the large print part of the *Times*.
On Saturday people began to be frightened. I was resolved,
though the maids were terrified, and we had no man-
servant, not to go away. The gentlemen of the neighbourhood—several of them—called on me on Sunday
morning, to tell me all the arrangements for the defence of
the Park, to offer protection, etc. On Sunday evening I
went to St. Mark's College. The young men brought
alarming reports from the city. The Bank and other
offices were bristling with artillery,—it was reported that
the Government had received bad news. Now, for the
first time, I did feel a little alarmed. The report was
(quite false, as it turned out) that two regiments were
disaffected. I did not wholly believe this. I hoped it was
not so, but Miss T. had heard the report about the Cold-
stream Guards at Plymouth,—and it seemed to me that if
the Duke of Wellington *was* unpopular, as was said, and
the troops *were* discontented, and should refuse to act
against the people, there might be a revolution. Still, I
should have stayed in the Park (for how was one to run
away from a revolution that would reach one in Cumberland) had I not received a letter from Eton, pressing me to
go thither with plate, etc. I accepted this offer, because I
feared that otherwise Herbert would hardly be prevented
from coming home on the dangerous Tuesday. So we flew
to Eton on Sunday morning, and at Eton heard the happy
event of the dreaded Chartist demonstration. Now all feel
that the attempt has been a blessed thing for the country,
since it has plainly discovered the weakness of the physical-
force party and the power of that body in the State who

are interested in the preservation of our present constitution. I really feel with the *Times* that our country has afforded a "sublime spectacle" to Europe on the late occasion. The arrangements of the Duke for the preservation of the metropolis were worthy of the hero of Waterloo, and how merciful thus to preclude, by the formidable and complete nature of the preparations, any attempt on the part of the misguided Chartists. Even if their demands were in themselves reasonable, or such changes as they propose could benefit the people at large, the *manner* of making them is contrary to all government whatsoever, and if yielded to must lead to pure anarchy alternating with despotism. Some think that these events will lead to an extension of the franchise. It does not seem at all clear to me that there would be the slightest use in giving votes to more and poorer men, without bettering their condition or improving their education beforehand. They say not more than a fourteenth part of the population is represented. I do not see the grievance of not being represented *per se.* What the poor really want is to be better off; they care not for more representation except as that may favour their pockets. An extended representation cannot produce more bread and cheese. As it is, taxation does not affect the very poorest people. The income-tax is hard upon professional and trading persons, who make only just enough for their wants. Hardly any of these persons are Chartists. I believe the Chartist body to be composed principally of men who have nothing to lose, are not doing well in any trade or calling, for the humblest charwoman who has work is furious against them, and looks to the upper classes for support. A great proportion of them are sufferers by their own fault, though there may be some bodies of men thrown suddenly out of employment, who are in great distress through pure misfortune, and who become Chartists in pure ignorance, with a blind hope of bettering their state by changing the present order of things.

III.

Youth and Age.

To Miss FENWICK.

1848.—I am glad, dear friend, that you have had some enjoyment at Teignmouth. I feel a good deal as you do, that there is not so much greater proportion of happiness in youth (and, I would add, still less in childhood) than in more advanced periods of life, when thought and experience have brought more knowledge (of all that it concerns us most to know) and more tranquillity. Youth and childhood are indeed beautiful and interesting to look back upon; but I feel as old Matthew did about the lovely child, *I do not wish them mine*—mine to go over again.

IV.

Early Marriage.

To C. B. STUTFIELD, Esq., Hackney.

Chester Place, 1848.—I have been much interested by your note; it really gives the *pith* and *marrow* of the case in *pithy* language. I agree to it all without reserve, except a partial one on a single point. You say that a "young man much occupied, will not generally think of marriage till past thirty." I know a good many exceptions to that rule, I think. It seems to me, I own, that the time to form a marriage engagement, in an ordinary case, for a man, is between twenty and thirty. It is not so naturally, easily, or well done, afterwards. D——, who has had some experience of youth, laments exceedingly the difficulties in the way of early marriage for men, and my Uncle Southey was of the same mind. But the difficulties are often insuperable. What I like is to see a young man ready to work hard, and ready to be married. Energy, energy, that is the thing, if it be kept in order by a religious mind.

V.

Charms of our Native Place—Country Life and Town Life—Portraits
of Middle-aged People.

To Mrs. RICHARD TOWNSEND, Norwood.

Chester Place, July 7th, 1848.—It strikes me, dear Mrs.
Townsend, that you would be better off, as regards your
health and spirits, if you resided in Regent's Park, or some
airy part of London, than at Norwood, sweet and (for a
summer-spell) enviable as Norwood is. Your husband
seems to be much engaged, and the society of any country
place is necessarily limited. Our native place is quite a
different affair. *There* every stick and stone, or at all
events, every nook and woody clump, and turn of the
well-known river, whose sounds were the first that struck
upon our infant ears,—*there,* all the old familiar faces,
however hum-drum or even unpleasing to strangers, are
full of interest from old association. We see in these
objects not simply their present selves, but a host of past
impressions, which, as it were, illuminate them,—impart
to them both a general luminous glow, and a rich mosaic
embroidery, which render them far more interesting in our
eyes, than new ones though infinitely more striking, as seen
for the first time.

Here I have almost too much excitement from intercourse with interesting people. I feel the charm of London
society deeply, but my nervous system is so weak and
irritable, that I seem always on the verge of being outdone,
even though I keep quite on the outskirts of the gay, busy
world, and go out little in comparison with most of my
friends,—very seldom (never if I can help it) two nights
consecutively.

I am now sitting to Mr. L—— for my dear old friend
Mrs. Stanger. E. thinks that the picture promises well.
Some of my friends decline sitting because they are middle-
aged, and middle-age is neither lovely nor picturesque. *My*

objection is not the plainness of the stage of life, but the
variability of my nervous state, and consequently of my
looks.   Sometimes the artist is forced to work away at the
gown (at least Mr. R—— was sometimes) because the *face*
is actually gone away *pro tempore*.

VI.

Teaching Work—Dickens as a Moralist for the Young.

To Mrs. H. M. Jones.

Herne Bay, August 17th, 1848.—My sister and C—— left
us last Monday; young D—— remains with us till Friday.
He reads Homer to me, and this with H.'s readings, and
E.'s, is as much in that way as my nerves will stand; for
I can do everything that I ever could, *a little,* but nothing
much or long.   The hundred lines with each youth, and
sometimes Pindar or Horace beside, which seems nothing
to my brother, is a good deal to me.   They like to talk
with me and each other about "Harry Lorrequer" and
other military and naval novels, and above all about the
productions of Dickens, the never-to-be-exhausted fun of
Pickwick, and the capital new strokes of Martin Chuzzlewit.
This last work contains, beside all the fun, some very
marked and available morals.   I scarce know any book in
which the evil and odiousness of selfishness is more forcibly
brought out, or in a greater variety of exhibitions.   In the
midst of the merry quotations, or at least, on any fair
opportunity, I draw the boys' attention to these points, bid
them remark how *unmanly* is the selfishness of young
Martin, and I insist upon it that Tom Pinch's character, if
it could really exist, would be a very beautiful one.   But I
doubt, as I do in regard to Pickwick, that so much sense,
and deep, solid goodness, could co-exist with such want of
discernment and liability to be gulled.   Tigg is very clever,
and the boys roar with laughter at the "what's-his-name
place whence no thingumbob ever came back;" but this is

only a new edition of Jingle and Smangles. Mark Tapley also is a second Sam Weller. The new characters are Pecksniff, and the thrice-notable Sairey Gamp, with Betsy Prig to show her off.

VII.

Mr. Coleridge's Philosophy inseparable from his Religious Teaching—
His View of the Inspiration of Scripture.

To Miss MORRIS.

1848.—I doubt not that though your American semi-Coleridgian, or rather Coleridgian only in fancy, imagines my father a " Heretic," in his *formal divinity mind*, yet that his heart and spiritual being, if he really have benefited in any way or degree worth speaking of, by his writings, is making a far different report. Why should a fine intellect (and most men allow my father that), united with a disposition to believe, and strong desire to be in sympathy with the religious, become suddenly effete and worse than useless, when applied to the discernment of religious truth? I know how vain it is to argue. But I say this to show you my own state of mind on these matters, not in any expectation of altering yours, or that of any of those who see the subject of religious belief, or rather *the theory of faith*, as you do. My father's religious teaching is so interwoven with his intellectual views, as with all deep and earnest thinkers must ever be the case, that both must stand or fall together; and in my opinion those persons dream who think they are improved by him intellectually, yet consider his views of Christianity in the main unsound. There are some portions of his theology on which I feel unresolved, some which I reject; but in the mass they are such as both embrace me and are embraced by me. His view of Inspiration, as far as it goes, I do entirely assent to; and it is my strong anticipation, as far as I have any power to anticipate, that after a time, all earnest, thoughtful Christians will perceive that such a footing, *in the main*, as that on which he places the Inspiration of Scripture is the only safe one,—the only one that can hold its ground against advancing thought and investigation. I refer not so much in this to examination of outward proof, but to reflection on the nature of the thing in itself, the discovery of the internal incoherency of the ordinary schemes of belief on this subject. I think it will be found how satisfyingly spiritual it is.

VIII.

Mr. Spedding's Critique on Lord Macaulay's Essay on Bacon— The Ordinance of Confirmation—Primitive Explanations of its Meaning and Efficacy.

To AUBREY DE VERE, Esq.

1848.—I am delighted and interested in a most high degree by the vindication of Bacon. It seems to me no less admirable for the principles of moral discrimination and truth, and accuracy of statement, especially where character is concerned, which it brings out and elucidates by particular instances, which as it were substantiate and vitalize the abstract propositions, than for the glorious sunny light which it casts on the character of Bacon. Then how ably does it show up, not Macaulay's character individually and personally, so much as the class of thinkers of which he is the mouthpiece and representative. There are numbers who dislike and suspect that anti-Bacon article, and would take in with avidity the refutation.

But can it be true that Bacon doubted whether Confirmation were a *subsequent* to Baptism? How can it be doubted by any one who knows what Confirmation is, what are the purposes of it?

There can be no doubt that Confirmation was in the beginning considered, if not a component part of the whole sacrament of Baptism, yet certainly a sacrament in which the regenerative Spirit was received. The two were united in time, and formed one double rite. Confirmation, or

Imposition of Hands, was performed directly after Baptism ; and Tertullian affirms that men are prepared for the Spirit, or purified by the Baptismal rite,—that they receive the Spirit by Imposition of Hands.

I think we may argue from this, and many like dogmas of the early Fathers, that it is not possible to follow out the primitive rationale of Sacraments on all points. The Church afterwards separated Imposition of Hands from Baptism, and taught that the gift of the Regenerative Spirit appertained to the latter. Still Confirmation is surely a complement of Baptism, has a special reference to it, though it be not necessary to salvation, or an essential part of Baptism. The term " subsequent to Baptism" is ambiguous. Confirmation is not to confirm the Baptism, but to confirm or corroborate the baptized in the graces and spiritual edification originally received in baptism.

IX.

Pindar—Dante's " Paradiso "—" Faustina," by Ida Countess Hahn-Hahn—Haziness of Continental Morality—A Coquette on Principle—Lord Bacon's Insincerity.

To AUBREY DE VERE, Esq., Curragh Chase, Ireland.

Chester Place, 1848.—One feels proud of reading Pindar. It is like being at a fountain-head, at the fresh top of a lofty aerial mount, a wide prospect of the land of beauty spread out before one. The Second Pythian Ode contains one of those Scripture-like passages which one seems to have read somewhere in the Old Testament, but knows not exactly where,—perhaps in the Psalms, in Job, or Isaiah. . . .

Canto V. of the " Paradiso " is in the main rather dry, sententious, and unsensuous, but it reads impressively, and I feel this time, more than before, how finely the light *keeps growing* as one goes on in the " Paradiso," how the splendours accumulate, the glory deepens, the colours glow out more and more in ever richer variety.

I was very glad, however, to conclude the evening with Countess Ida; and now I have read her story carefully to the end, and what do I think of it? Why, that it is in the style of execution very exquisite, full of grace, beauty, light rich fancy; but that it is as strong an instance as I ever met with of that pseudo-morality, that vague, slippery, luminous-misty view of right and wrong, which it would be unfair to call German, as if it belonged to the Germans more than to the French, Italians, Danes, or Swedes, but which we may certainly call *un-English*. If the plant appears amongst us it is recognized as a foreigner at once. Goethe's morality has been much questioned amongst us, but there is nothing in his tales surely of worse tendency than this "Faustina," more false and insidious. The conduct of the heroine is that of an unprincipled coquette, —a frail, fickle, faithless, self-indulgent, passionate creature; nay, more than that, heartless and cruel in the extreme. Yet, forsooth, we are assured that these acts in *her* proceed from superlative *purity of heart!* the simplicity of genius,— an innocent desire to *mould her being*, to take to herself whatsoever is beautiful, noble, and excellent; to keep it as long as it suited her, and then fling it away like a sucked orange, or let it fall, as she does the wild flowers, when she is tired of them! It is a libel, a shocking libel, on purity of heart and genius, to lay such sins as these at their door, or even to suppose them compatible in any way with the former. No woman that united a fine intellect with a generous, noble, and tender heart, or even a heart of tolerable goodness, could have acted the part of Faustina, even suppose her to have been ever so badly educated; so at least it strikes me. I complain of the whole representa- tion as radically *false*, and cannot be reconciled by the delicacy and beauty of the execution, to what is so deeply wrong in the main conception. "Faustina" is entirely a woman's book, a continental woman's book, as "Jane

Eyre" is that of an English *man*.* And oh! how vastly superior in truth and power is the latter, coarse and hard in parts as it certainly is. Faustina is false in another way too, I think. She does nothing but what any exquisitely beautiful and graceful woman might do. Hers are not, as seems to be pretended, the triumphs of genius. Jane Eyre, without personal advantages, gains upon the mind of the reader by what she does, and we can well understand how she fascinates Rochester. We *see* that she is heroic, we are not merely *told* so. "Faustina" reminds me of two novels by women,—"The History of a Coquette," by a daughter of the well-known Bishop Watson, and "Zoe," by Miss Jewsbury. The latter is less refined than Faustina, but contains greater variety,—I should say exhibits more power upon the whole. It has the same moral falsity that strikes me in "Faustina,"—that of uniting noble qualities of head and heart with conduct the most unworthy and unvirtuous. T. F. warmly defends "Zoe," declaring it to be but a true picture of life. If I could think it a true picture, I too would defend the representation. But I believe that such compounds as "Zoe" and "Faustina" are to be classed with the griffins and sphinxes of ancient fable. Nay, those have at least subjective truth; in these I can see none at all.

.   .   .   .

I dissent from Spedding's defence of Bacon's slight dissimulation about the calling of Parliament. Silence is one thing, but untruth, ever so slight, will never do.

* My mother's critical discrimination was at fault here. She felt sure that the mysterious "Currer Bell" was a *man*; and used to declare that she could as soon believe the paintings of Rubens to have been by a woman, as "Jane Eyre."—E. C.

CHAPTER XIX.

LETTERS TO THE REV. HENRY MOORE, AUBREY DE VERE, ESQ., MISS FENWICK, THE REV. EDWARD COLERIDGE: 1848 (continued).

I.

Dr. Arnold's School Sermons—His Comment on the Story of the Young Men who mocked Elisha—Individuals under the Mosaic Dispensation dealt with as Public, not as Private Characters—Dr. Hammond's proposed Rendering of 2 Peter i. xx.

To the Rev. HENRY MOORE, Eccleshall Vicarage.

1848.—I must write a line to thank you for giving to my boy those excellent sermons of Dr. Arnold's, more comfortable to my spirit than most of the sermons addressed to men. I think in his application of the judgment on the young people who mocked Elisha, he seems not sufficiently to bear in mind that they were punished for contemning the character and authority of an Envoy of the God of Israel, not for teasing an old man. The judgment would be frightfully disproportionate if we did not look upon it thus nationally, in analogy with the whole sacred history. In the Old Testament individuals appear to be dealt with not primarily in reference to their own merit or demerit in the sight of God, or their own private destiny, but as they are parts and instruments of one comprehensive scheme for the advancement of the human race by their Creator. Now, I say that Carlyle, in his History of the French Revolution, whether consciously or otherwise, has in some sort written upon the Scriptural plan. He looks at the French Revolution, in all its horrors and miseries, as an awful retribution for the accumulated crimes of selfishness, cruelty, and profligacy of the wealthy and powerful classes,—a long-delayed vengeance,—to be a grand beacon and instruction for the ages to come, and, at the same time, the preparation for a new and better state of things. The actors in the Revolution he considers *principally* as instruments of this divine work, and he therefore views them chiefly in reference to their *powers.* What he says of Mirabeau's powers, his wisdom, and insight, I believe to be quite true. There is a sketch of the life and character of Mirabeau by my husband in a periodical work, written before Carlyle's book appeared, which contains in substance all that Carlyle maintains on that point. Mirabeau had, however, not only *powers,* but virtues, though mingled with great vices, and it is not true that Carlyle disguises or disregards the vices; he speaks of them as to be lamented and wept over with bitter tears.

.   .   .   .

I am looking at Horsley's Sermons on 2 Peter i. 20, 21.* But he appears to me to have, to a certain degree, a wrong notion of the drift of the text from neglecting Hammond's explanation. Hammond says that ἐπίλυσις is an agonistical word, and signifies the starting or watchword upon which the racers set out in their course. According to him the passage has nothing to do with *interpretation* whatever, no bearing of any kind upon *private judgment,* as it has been a million times quoted for or rather against. I think if you consult Scapula or Passow, you will find that the good doctor is right, and that ἐπιλύσεσθαι means to let loose as dogs or hunting leopards from a leash (though it also means to solve or explain), and *this* is more accordant with the context. " No prophecy is ἰδίας ἐπιλύσεως—*for* the prophecy came not in old time by the *will* of man, but holy men of old spake *as they were moved* by the Holy Ghost." Now, is it not better sense if we render the Greek, " of his own

* " Knowing this first, that no prophecy is of any private interpretation. For the prophecy came not in old time by the will of man; but holy men of God spake as they were moved by the Holy Spirit."—St. Peter, 2, i. 20, 21.

T

starting," "without particular mission from God," than if we understand it of private *interpretation*, which has nothing to do with what goes before, or what comes after? St. Peter was not warning men against self-willed un-catholic *views* of prophecy, but simply exhorting them to *trust* to prophecy, because it was from God.

II.

Mr. Longfellow's "Evangeline"—Hexameters in German and English —"Hyperion," by the same Author—"Letters and Poetical Remains of John Keats."

To AUBREY DE VERE, Esq., Curragh Chase, Ireland.

Chester Place, September, 1848.—Thank you much for Evangeline, which is full of the beautiful, and is most deeply pathetic, as much so as the story of Margaret in the Excursion. Perhaps you will think me paradoxical (no, *you* would not, I believe, though many would), when I say that this deep pathos is not the right thing in a poem. I could not take the story and the poetry together, but was obliged to skim through it, and see how the misery went on, and how it ended, before I could *read the Poem*. I think a poem ought not to have a more touching interest than Spenser's "Faerie Queen," Ariosto, and Tasso. The agitations of the Drama may be quoted against me. I can but say that I feel the same objection to Romeo and Juliet; but then the edge of the strong interest is rubbed off after a first perusal, and we recur to it as to a poem;—and so we may in any other case. But those fine old dramas contain so much *more* than the mere story, even in the material; so much wit, and display of character and humour and manners, that they are hardly to be compared with our modern affecting metrical tale.

It does not clearly appear why Gabriel should lose sight of Evangeline on leaving Acadia. Perhaps we shall be told, as we are of the story of Margaret, that it is matter of *fact.* This would not excuse it, if it *looks* improbable; and depend upon it *in the fact* there was something different, something that prevented the difficulty which suggests itself in the written tale. Evangeline seems to be, in some sort, an imitation of Voss's Luise. The opening, especially, would remind any one who had read the Luise, of that remarkable Idyll. It is far inferior to that, I think, both in the general conception, and in the execution. Voss's hexameters are perfect. The German language admits of that metre, the English hardly does so. Some of Longfellow's lines are but quasi-metre, so utterly inharmonious and so prosaic in regard to the diction. I do not think there will ever be a continuous strain of good hexameters in our language, though there may be a good line here and there. Goethe's hexameters are excellent; those of Schiller in Der Tanz, a poem in longs and shorts, exquisite.

You should read Longfellow's Hyperion, which is an imitation of Jean Paul Richter, in the same degree, perhaps, that Evangeline is an imitation of Voss. It is extremely refined and pleasing. It is, however, a collection of *miscellanea* strung together on the thread of a Rhine tour, with very little of a story, only an event to begin with and an event to end with.

The "Letters and Remains of Keats" are highly interesting. The "Eve of St. Mark" is an exquisite fragment; "Otho the Great" an utter failure, in my opinion. I do not agree with Milnes about the "splendour and glory of the diction." There is a speech or two that might have suited Lamia or Endymion, but nothing of proper *dramatic* force or beauty, from beginning to end; and the blank verse is poor.

Severn's journal of poor Keats' last days is deeply affecting. But how sadly he wanted fortitude. He was manly in some respects; but in others he was but "five feet high" after all.

Compare the death-bed of the Deist Blanco White with that of poor Keats, and I think it must be admitted that both in faith and fortitude the former has immeasurably the advantage. It ought, however, to be recollected that Blanco White was older, and had had more time to gain strength of mind. But he was also of a more religious turn from the first.*

III.

Justice and Generosity—"Vanity Fair"—The World, and the Wheels on which it moves—Thackeray, Dickens, and Currer Bell—Devotion of Dobbin to Amelia.

To Miss FENWICK.

November, 1848.—It is commonly thought that justice and generosity belong to different characters, but it seems to me that a want of both often goes together, and that people are seldom thoroughly *just*, who are ungenerous. But perhaps

* [The following lines written in 1845, with a marginal note added later, will find an appropriate place here.—E. C.

BLANCO WHITE.

Couldst thou in calmness yield thy mortal breath,
Without the Christian's sure and certain hope?
Didst thou to earth confine our being's scope,
Yet, fixed on One Supreme with fervent faith,
Prompt to obey what conscience witnesseth,
As one intent to fly the eternal wrath,
Decline the ways of sin that downward slope!
O thou light-searching spirit, that didst grope
In such bleak shadows here, 'twixt life and death,
To thee dare I bear witness, though in ruth—
Brave witness like thine own—dare hope and pray
That thou, set free from this imprisoning clay,
New clad in raiment of perpetual youth,
May'st find that bliss untold 'mid endless day
Awaits each earnest soul that lives for Truth.—S. C.

I have never defended Blanco White, but I do insist on looking at his virtues, and struggles, and powers of mind with the naked eyes, and not through the glass of an opinion concerning his religious opinions. In thus dealing I put forth no new view of Christian justice and toleration. I do but carry out the received view consistently, and without vacillation. Men *will* not believe that B. W. died a firm believer in a Moral and Intelligent Creator and Governor, to whom our homage and submission is due, because he rejected outward Revelation, and was unconvinced of the resurrection of man's soul to conscious existence.—S. C.

the truth is that the ungenerosity to which I allude is a sort of injustice—the temper that grudges not only the outward things of this life, but cannot bear to bestow praise, honour, and credit where they are due, and where perfect justice would award them.

I believe " Vanity Fair " presents a true view of human life,—a true view of *one aspect and side of it.* We cannot live long in the world, I think, with an observant eye, without perceiving that pride, vanity, selfishness, in one or other of its forms, together with a good deal of conscious or unconscious *pretence,*—pretence to virtue and piety especially, but also to intellect, elegance, and fashion,—to disregard of praise and admiration and various other supposed advantages,—are among the great main wheels which move the social machine. Still, these are uneasy reflections, and perhaps we are not in the best frame of mind, when such things present themselves to us very strongly. I hope that " Vanity Fair " presents but one side of the author's own mind, else it must be a most unhappy one. Still I must say, I think very highly of the book. None of the kind ever exceeded my anticipations so much. In knowledge of life and delineation of character, it seems to me quite equal to " Jane Eyre," though it has never been so popular, and I cannot but think that it afforded some hints to that celebrated novel. Thackeray is not good where he imitates Dickens, where he describes houses, for instance. The *still* part of his descriptions is often tedious ; whereas in " Jane Eyre," the landscape painting is admirable, and Dickens shines in Dutch pieces, descriptions of interiors, and so forth. But Thackeray has a vein of his own, in which he is quite distinct from his predecessor and successor in the novel-writing career, and it is a keen and subtle one. I believe the description of Sir Pitt Crawley is hardly an overdrawn picture of what may have existed fifty years ago.

Dobbin's devotion to a weak woman like Emmy is perfectly natural. That sort of devotedness is seldom bestowed
on very worthy objects, I think, for they do not excite
tenderness in the shape of pity, are more independent, and
turn the admirer's thoughts into a better and higher
direction.

IV.

Mr. Carlyle on Hero-Worship—Ceremonial, in his View, the Husk of
    Religion; Veneration its Kernel—Veneration rightly bestowed on
    Mental Power as an Image of one of the Divine Attributes—
    Voltaire justly Admired by the French for his Native Genius—
    Association of Goodness with Wisdom, and of Poetry with
    Philosophy—Mr. Carlyle's Heroes described by him as Benefactors,
    not merely Rulers of Men—Instances of Voltaire, Rousseau, and
    Cromwell—A True Sense in which " Might is Right "—Character
    of Mirabeau—Comparison of Mr. Carlyle as a Moralist with Lord
    Byron, as an Historian with Lord Macaulay—Aim and Spirit of
    his History of the French Revolution.

To Rev. EDWARD COLERIDGE.

REPLY TO STRICTURES OF THREE GENTLEMEN UPON CARLYLE,
    SUPPORTED BY A REFERENCE TO CERTAIN PASSAGES IN HIS
    WORKS.

In order to do justice to the views of an author, especially
such an author as Carlyle, who less than most men can be
understood in fragments, a want of finish in the parts being
the characteristic defect of his style, we must take care to
place ourselves in his point of view, to possess ourselves of
his aim. Now, Carlyle's great theme in the work before
us is worship—the instinct of Veneration in man; (but see
his limitation of the term, p. 381,—or intimation that he
has been using it in a limited sense). The religion of
nations, as to its superficial and outward part, he considers
to be, in great measure, a system of empty forms, dead
conventionalisms, and lifeless ceremonies,—the worthless
remains of a something which once had life. On the other
hand, he believes that in all religions which have ever held

sway over masses of men for a considerable time, there has
been at bottom a living and life-exciting principle. This
principle, which he sets up as the *work of God*, against the
arte-facts of men,—vain substitutes for genuine gifts from
on high,—he maintains to be *Veneration*—the principle or
feeling which leads men to bow down before the image of
God in the soul of man. Power is an attribute of God,—
Carlyle maintains that the instinct whereby we are impelled
practically to adore and obey mental power, wherever we
behold it, is a salutary and high instinct, which instrumentally redeems mankind from the dominion of sense and
the despotism of moral evil. (But power in God is joined
with benevolence, and so it is in all whom Carlyle sets up
as objects of "worship.")

In the first passage referred to (*Hero-worship*, pp. 22, 23),
Voltaire is spoken of as a *kind* of hero, a man gifted by God
with remarkable *powers* of thought and expression, and
who, whatever evil he may have done,—exceeding any good
that can be ascribed to his authorship,—was nevertheless
believed by those who "worshipped" him to have devoted
his life and abilities to the "unmasking of hypocrisy," and
"exposing of error and injustice." Carlyle's proposition
seems to me to be simply this,—The French nation being
such as they were, that is to say, in a comparatively low,
dark, unspiritual state, their enthusiasm about Voltaire was
a favourable symptom of their mental condition,—the
spirit evinced therein a redeeming spirit (in its degree)—
their feeling of admiration and veneration for one whom
they thought *above* them, in its own nature a noble and
blessed feeling. Poor and needy, indeed, must that people
be who have no better object of such a feeling than Voltaire.
Our author means only to affirm that Frenchmen were
better employed in "worshipping" him even for suppo-
sititious merits than in grovelling along in utter worldliness,
pursuing each his own narrow selfish path, without a

thought or a care beyond the gratification of the senses. Here is no intention to set the intellectual above the moral, or to substitute the one for the other, but to insist on the superiority of *natural gifts*, as means of bettering the souls of men, to the vain shows and semblances which commonly pass for religion in the world, according to the author's opinion.

The second passage (pp. 166, 167) I remember noting when I first read the work in which it is contained, as announcing a doctrine either wrong in itself or wrongly expressed. But I cannot see that it is erroneous by the exaltation of intellectual power above goodness, but rather by too bold and broad an affirmation that the former is the measure of the latter. So far I agree with Carlyle, that I believe the highest moral excellence attainable by man is ever attended by a certain largeness of understanding; not that intellectual power is a part of goodness, but that moral goodness cannot be evolved, to the greatest extent, without it. Men of high virtue and piety are ever men of insight, the moral and intelligential in their mixed nature reciprocally strengthening and expanding each other. To transfer these remarks to a lower subject, every *great* poet must be possessed not merely of a fine imagination, a lively fancy, or any other particular intellectual faculty, but of a great understanding; he must be one whose mental vision is deeper and more acute than that of other men, who sees into the truth of things, and has a special power of rendering what he sees visible to others. He must be *practical* as well as percipient, else he is not a *poet*, a maker or creator; —he must see keenly and (if the expression may be allowed) *feelingly*, else his poetic faculty has no adequate materials to work upon. Shakespeare was, inclusively, a great philosopher. Lear, Hamlet, and Othello could never have been produced by one who did not see into the human mind deeply, and survey it widely. But to be a Shakespeare a man must have certain *peculiar* gifts of intellect added to this great general *powerfulness;* or, to express myself more distinctly, his mind must be specifically modified, and that from the first—*à priori*. I cannot at all agree with Carlyle in thinking that the sole original qualification of every great man of every description is a strong understanding, and that where there is this common base, circumstances *alone* determine whether the possessor is to be a Cæsar or a Shakespeare, a Cowley or a Kant, a Wellington or a Wordsworth. To return to the moral side of the subject, I think that Carlyle expresses himself too broadly when he says, "that the degree of vision that dwells in a man is the correct measure of the man," and illustrates his meaning by a reference to Shakespeare. Was Shakespeare as much better than other men as he was deeper and clearer sighted? The truth is, that *vision* considered in the concrete, as found in this or that individual, is always *specific*. The saints and servants of God have a vision of their own—but here let me pause, for I am at the mouth of a labyrinth. Lord Byron, to whom Mr. A—— refers, was a very *clever* man; but I think that Carlyle would not allow him any very remarkable " degree of vision;" his " superiority of intellect," *sensu eminente*, he would plainly deny, and, in my opinion, with justice. But still Byron had a stronger understanding than many a better man, though his fame during life may have been no " correct measure " of his intellectual size (in literary and poetical circles his fame is now fast shrinking into more just proportion therewith). Carlyle's statement is, at best, confused and inadequate, probably because he had not properly thought out the subject, when he undertook to speak upon it.

Much waste of words and of thought, too, would be avoided if disputants would always begin with a clear statement of the question, and not proceed to argue till they had agreed

upon what it was that they were arguing about.   The proposition which I understand Mr. A—— to maintain (when he
censures Carlyle as a worshipper of intellect, implying that
he worships it in a bad sense), and which I venture to deny,
is this: That Thomas Carlyle, viewed in his character of
author, as appears upon the face of his writings, exalts
intellect taken apart from the other powers of the mind,—
that he sets up mere intellect as the ultimate object of
esteem and admiration, and represents a man as truly
great and worthy of all honour, purely on the score of
intellectual gifts, without reference to the use he makes of
them.   In disproof of this position (or by way of attempting
to disprove it) I appeal to the fact, that all his heroes,
whom he describes as being the deserving objects of what,
"not to be too grave about it," he chooses to call "*worship*,"
are represented by him as benefactors of the human race,
just in proportion as they were *deserving* objects of worship.
He describes them as men whose powers have been employed
by God's will and their own, for good and noble purposes
on a large scale, chiefly for the purpose of leading men,
directly or indirectly, from earth to heaven, from the
human to the divine.   This indeed is the keynote of
Carlyle's writings, it is the beginning and the end of his
whole teaching, it is this which gives a character of elevation to all the productions of his mind, and renders him so
widely influential, as, with all his bad taste and frequent
crudity and incompleteness of thinking, he certainly is, that
in all he puts forth there is an immediate reference to
man's higher destiny, under the power of which thought all
his other thoughts are moulded and modified.   His vocation
is that of an *apostle*, in the sense in which the title may
truly and reverently be bestowed upon uninspired men.   If
it be objected to this view of his drift and purpose, that
Voltaire and Rousseau are mentioned among his heroes, I
reply that he has done this, not from blindness to their

faults and deficiencies, but from the supposed perception of a certain degree of merit in them not commonly recognized by admirers of goodness. This supposition may be well or ill founded,—he may be wrong in supposing those writers to have exerted any beneficial influence; but the character of his aim is to be determined by the supposition and not by the fact. He places them very low in the scale of benefactors, and brings them forward rather as illustrations of his meaning in the lowest instances, than as considering them worthy to be placed by the side of the best and greatest men, in the scale of moral greatness. His account of Cromwell I think very fine as a sketch, and very well framed as an exponent of his doctrine; with regard to its truth in fact my judgment is suspended. Be that as it may, Carlyle's heroes are all men who have striven for truth and justice, and for the emancipation of their fellow-mortals. He represents them as having been misunderstood by the masses of mankind, in the midst of all their effectivity and *ultimate* influence, simply because the masses of mankind are not themselves sufficiently wise, and good, and perspicacious to understand and sympathize with those who are so in an eminent degree. There is some originality in Carlyle's opinions; but he seems to me to be more original in manner than in matter; the force and feeling with which he brings out his views are more remarkable than the views themselves.

Carlyle has somewhere spoken as if he thought that bodily strength gave a just claim to the possession of rule and authority, and this passage has been quoted against him with considerable plausibility. But is it not true that superior strength of body and mind have ever enabled the possessors, sooner or later, to command the herd of their inferiors? This is a fact which Carlyle does not invent, but only reasons upon, and his reasoning is, that, native strength and other personal endowments, conferred directly

by God, without man's intervention, convey a better claim
to the obedience and service of men, and are a safer ground
whereon to erect sovereignty, than arbitrary human distinctions and titles established conventionally, which, by a
certain theory of theologians, are made out to have been
instituted by God Himself.   The only divine right of kings
which he will acknowledge is *native might*, enabling a man
to rule well and wisely, as well as strongly.   Hereditary
sway, pretending to be divine, he looks upon as a mere
human contrivance, one that has never adequately answered
its purpose, that arose originally from false views and bad
feelings, and as it had in it, from the beginning, a corrupt
root, is ever tending to decay and dissolution.   For myself,
if it is worth while to say what I think, I cannot clearly
understand the *divine right* of kings as taught by High
Churchmen, but neither do I believe that Carlyle has seen
through the whole of this matter, or that there is not much
more to be said for conventional sovereignty than appears
in his notices of the question.   If all men were at all times
wise enough to chose the best governors, there need be no
such contrivance as hereditary sway,—but, till they are,
elective sway is no better ; and in the mean time, according
to Carlyle's own admission, native strength has a sphere
of its own, in which it governs with more or less effect,
according to its intensity.

Carlyle's *manner* of describing the character of Mirabeau
is, perhaps, the most questionable part of his writings, yet
even here, I think, his main drift is quite consistent with
morality.   He is not judging the eminent Frenchman as a
divine, or examining him as a moralist.   His theme is the
French Revolution, which he regards as a tremendous
crisis, the result of a long series and extensive system of
selfishness, cruelties, and injustices, and he views all the
persons of his narrative principally in reference to the part
they acted, and the effects they wrought, in this great

national convulsion. Whatever Mirabeau's private character may have been before God, yet as far as he was a powerful and conspicuous agent in carrying forward the work of the Revolution, Carlyle was justified, as it seems to me, in setting him forth as an object of interest, and even of admiration, proportioned to the amount and rareness of the gifts which rendered him a potent instrument in the hands of Providence, for a particular purpose; and this he might have done without calling evil good, or good evil. But it is abundantly evident that Carlyle did *not* consider Mirabeau's mind and disposition, as *upon the whole*, morally bad; he ascribes to him high purposes and public virtues, that is, virtues specially calculated to benefit the public. Whether his account of him be true in fact, or whether it is a fiction, our argument does not require us to consider. The question only is, does Carlyle's language respecting Mirabeau confound the distinction betwixt virtue and vice, —does it tend to dim the lustre of the first, and to surround the last with a false and falsifying splendour? Now, I am inclined to answer this question in the negative, both from consideration of Carlyle's general turn of mind, as displayed in his books, and from a survey of all that he says of Mirabeau, taken in connection with the spirit and principles of the work in which it appears, though I admit that he has not taken sufficient pains to prevent his sentiments from being taken for that which they are not. The writings of Lord Byron are really open, in some measure, to such a charge, because they array in attractive colours imaginary personages to whom no really good or noble qualities are ascribed; they are not reprehensible for that they represent men as worthy to be admired in spite of great vices, but because they tend to produce admiration of the very vices themselves,—to detach it from virtue altogether, and place it on inferior objects. Lord Byron's heroes have no higher merits than gallantry and courage; they are invested with a

kind of dignity from romantic situation, and the possession
of outward elegance, not dignified by their instrumentality
in great and important events. Such representations are
essentially mean and worthless, but such is not Carlyle's
representation in the present instance. He describes
Mirabeau, not only as a man of vast energy and amazing
political sagacity, but amid much personal profligacy and
unruliness of passion, as being possessed, like his father
before him, of a philanthropic spirit, high, disinterested
aims, and a zeal to serve his country. He affirms, and in
this, whatever Macaulay's opinion may be, he is borne out
by other authorities, that Mirabeau took a right view of the
political needs of the French people, that he sought to bring
in a limited monarchy, on the English model, knowing it to
be the only form of public liberty for which the French nation
was fit, and that, had God spared his life, and permitted
him to go on in the career which he had commenced, he
would have been the saviour of his country, so far as this,
that without the horrors of the Revolution he would have
established all that the Revolution ultimately brought
about in so violent and calamitous a manner. Such,
according to Carlyle, was Mirabeau's aim; such his insight.
That he was in many respects a bad man, cannot make
such an aim not to have been good, the sagacity with which
he directed it, and the resoluteness with which he pursued
it, not to have been admirable;—and to *deny* this character
of excellence appears to me.to be a confounding of good and
evil; not to *affirm* it. Would it not be an approach to the
ill practice of lying for God, if we were to refuse all honour
to the name of Mirabeau, on account of that bad side of his
mind and actions, supposing Carlyle's account of him to be
correct? Carlyle represents this remarkable man as a
voluptuary and a libertine. Libertinism is of the nature of
wickedness, but mere libertinism, though it may be accompanied by, and though it tends to produce, hardness of

heart, and is a contempt of God's Word and command-
ments, does not alone constitute the man who is guilty of it
" an atrocious villain." It may be villainously pursued,
but it is not in itself the same thing as villainy ; for a
villain, according to the common acceptation of the word, is
a man basely malignant as to his general character,
incapable of generous thoughts and actions ; but libertinism
is not absolutely incompatible with generosity and benevolence, however it may *tend* to weaken and fret away all that
is better than itself in the mind of the libertine. Again, a
mere voluptuary is a contemptible being. But Mirabeau,
according to Carlyle, was much else beside being a
voluptuary. He seems rather to have acted the rake, as a
form of activity, than through a slavish subjection to mere
sensual appetite, and Carlyle brings forward his exploits in
this line, rather to show his multifarious energy,—how
many different kinds of things he was able to do at once,
and with the force of a giant, than with any intention of
admitting that he was a selfish sensualist in the main ; that
this was his distinguishing character. I am afraid his way
herein was made all too smooth before him, and that the
women sank before his genius with fatal facility. They are
too apt to yield their whole heart and mind to men of power
and distinction, let their other qualities be what they may,
and there was little Christianity in Paris, during Mirabeau's
career, to keep such a disposition in check. However, I am
far from defending the *tone* in which Carlyle deals with this
part of his subject ; there is a something of exultation in it
highly reprehensible. As a defender of truth he should not
have referred to such things without a mark of reprobation,
nor as a pretender to refinement and elevation of feeling
should he have touched upon them without expressions of
disgust and contempt.

On one other point, however, I do think Carlyle may be
defended without sophistry or straining. It was said, as I

understood, that whereas this writer treats his own favourites
with undue indulgence, he displays a bitter and vehement
spirit against their adversaries, and generally all who are
not of his school and party. I should say, on the contrary,
that Carlyle treats all historical characters that come under
his cognizance with leniency ; he speaks admiringly and
indulgently, for instance, of Marie Antoinette; and I can
perceive no *scorn* in his exposure of the weakness and
dulness of her husband,—which who can deny. In speaking
of Laud, he less decries the *man* than the circumstances of
which he was the creature. One of Carlyle's opinions,
whatever his candour, could not look upon Laud as a large
and free-minded man, a martyr in a wholly good cause.

Carlyle is a satirist, but he is not given to satirize
individuals, or even parties of men. The object of his
satire, as it appears to me, is the weakness and wickedness
of *mankind,*—systems of opinion, not bodies of believers.
He speaks occasionally with contempt, though not always
with unqualified contempt (see his last work, " Past and
Present "), of Puseyism, as a resurrection-system of defunct
things ; but he says nothing of any of the resurrection-men,
nor has he ever joined any person or party, that I am
aware of, in impeaching the conduct of the Puseyites, considered as a party.

Macaulay's opinion of Mirabeau is cited by Mr. A——.
Macaulay may be more correct than Carlyle as to the facts
of the case (though I do not see that this has been proved),
but I cannot think him fit to be trusted with the character
of any great man. He is a thorough Utilitarian and anti-
spiritualist, and though he makes judicious remarks upon
this person and upon that, yet scarcely sees at all that
element of greatness, that spark of the divine in these
marked agents of Providence, which Carlyle sees too exclusively. Macaulay finishes fully, but his conceptions are on
a confined scale. Carlyle aims at something higher and

deeper, his views are more novel and striking, but they are
hastily and often inaccurately set forth.   Carlyle writes
paradoxically about great men.   Macaulay on similar subjects, is liable, in my opinion, to write untruly, from defec-
tive perception of a certain side of greatness.   I would refer
to Carlyle's character of Johnson, in his Essays, as a most
interesting sample of his style and mode of thinking.

   In the comparison of Byron and Carlyle, with regard to
the moral tendency of their writings, I would add, that if
the latter had *invented* the character of Mirabeau, or if the
character thus invented was untrue to nature, in representing high and noble qualities in combination with evil ones,
so as they never appear in actual life, he might justly be
accused of depreciating the former and varnishing over, or
softening off the latter.   But Carlyle has not been found,
I believe, to have misrepresented the life and actions of
Mirabeau, nor has it yet been shown that he has misrepresented human nature in his account of them.   Neither
this nor that, indeed, is the charge against him; but rather
that he has described him as a wicked man, and yet has
held him up to honour and admiration, on the score of
marked talents and striking qualities, apart from virtue.
This charge is unsupported, I think, by sufficient evidence;
Carlyle has not exalted him as a *man*, still less as a subject
of the *Prince of Life*, but as an actor in a great historical
drama; nor has he held up worse actions to positive admiration, he has but given them a place beside his worthier
ones, without drawing the line betwixt them with sufficient
sharpness.   But he was not called upon by the nature
of his undertaking to sum up all the points of Mirabeau's
character, and decide whether it was good or bad in the eye
of God.   He had undertaken to describe and to moralize
and philosophize, implicitly rather than expressly, upon the
French Revolution; and this I think he does in a deeply
religious spirit, ever bearing in mind and bringing before

                                                    U

the minds of his readers, that there is a God that both
ruleth and judgeth the world, and exposing the *moral* bearings of his subject, whether justly or not, yet with a
constant regard to the law of conscience, and the inward
revelations of the Spirit. It was not his province to censure
the private vices of Mirabeau (I mean that this was not
within the scope of his principal design, though I admit that
he ought not to have spoken of them without noting his
disapprobation of them more clearly). It was his province
to show how the selfishness and godlessness of *numbers,* how
spiritual wickedness in high places, gradually reared up a
pile of misery and mischief, and how this mass of evil, when
at last it exploded with ruinous violence, was at once a
remedy from God and a retribution.

CHAPTER XX.

*LETTERS TO MISS FENWICK, MISS MORRIS, MRS. J.
STANGER, MRS. R. TOWNSEND, MRS. PLUMMER,
AUBREY DE VERE, ESQ., HON. MR. JUSTICE COLE-
RIDGE, EDWARD QUILLINAN, ESQ., REV. EDWARD
COLERIDGE: January—July, 1849.*

I.

A sad New Year—Alarming Illness of her Brother Hartley.

To Miss Fenwick.

Chester Place, January 7th, 1849.—My dear Friend,—You
may perhaps have heard from the north of my present
sorrow and anxiety, but whether you have or not I must
write to tell you of it. On Christmas Day came from dear
Mrs. Wordsworth an alarming report of my dear brother
Hartley. Several other reports were still worse, and after
one of them I almost mourned him as dead. Then a report
that he had happily passed the crisis, as was hoped, assured
me for a while of his restoration. When the news worsened
again, Derwent went to him. The news he sent was cheer-
ing at first, but ever since the first has been worsening.
On Wedneseday night he grew faint, his countenance
changed, and Derwent thought his last hour was approaching. Derwent gave him brandy and water; . . . he revived
upon this, and conversed a good deal; talked on Pindar,
Cary, Dante, on Ireland and such topics. . . . Yesterday's
report was that he was no better, weaker if anything. . . .
He has every advantage of medical skill, the most excellent
and affectionate nursing, and testimonies of love and regard
from numerous friends, more than I can express. No man,
I do think, can ever have been more beloved who had no
means of attaching men to him but his mere personal
qualities.

His state of mind in regard to religious feeling is all that can be desired. Nothing, Derwent says, can be more devout, more pious, resigned, simple, and loving. But he appears at times greatly depressed, both in his mind, from itself, and by his bodily sufferings. Dear Mrs. Wordsworth's letters were all you could expect from her,—wonderfully clear and strongly written, and most kind and affectionate. On Friday Derwent wrote—" Mr. Wordsworth has seen him, and was much affected. His own appearance was very striking, and his countenance beautiful, as he sat by the bedside." . . . He took the Sacrament some days ago. I suffer greatly in being unable to be at his bedside. The journey taken at once would render me useless, and, after our long separation, for me to arrive at Rydal shattered and prostrate, would do nothing but harm. . . . His illness has brought up strongly before my mind all my past early life in connection with my dear brother. I feel now more than I had done before how strong the tie is that binds me to him. Scarce any death would make me anticipate my own with such vividness as his would do. Children and parents belong each to a different generation, but a brother, a few years older, who has never suffered from any malady, in him I should seem in some sort to die myself. I trust, if he is spared, we shall all be more serious for the future,— not more sad,—more cheerful, but more earnestly thought-ful of the true end of life, and desirous to make ready for departure.

II.

His long Absence and unexpected Death—Disappointment of long-cherished Hopes—His attaching Qualities—His Grave in Grasmere Churchyard—His last Hours.

To Miss MORRIS.

10, *Chester Place, January* 17*th*, 1849.—Many, many thanks, dearest Miss Morris, for your note. I am so thank-ful that you can anticipate my deep grief! We had long been separated from each other, as to outward sight, but oh! how much he occupied my thoughts, and how dear he was to my heart!—never till now did I know how dear.

There were three who loved me best in this wide world, to whom I was most dear, most important. Now all three are gone, and I feel, even from earthly feeling, as if that other world were more my home than this.

I never thought of surviving him. I always thought he would live to old age, and that, perhaps, in our latest years, we might cherish each other; meantime, that I might see much of him, in some long visit to the north, when I might make my children known to him.

It seems as if he were snatched away from me all on the sudden, and all the thoughts and visions of so many, many years are swept away all at once. This has brought my mind into a strangely agitated state. I have felt worse since yesterday evening than I did before. Dear friend, I cannot as yet reconcile myself to this loss. For a time I feel resigned,—then comes back a tide of recollections which deluge me with tears. It is so grievous to me that I could not attend on him in his last illness. That was impossible. The sight of me, after so long a separation, would have agitated him, I knew, and been too injurious. I thought to go with Nurse had the illness continued. He was the most attaching of men; and if tributes of love and admiration from those who knew him well, and tears shed for his un-looked-for death, could remove or neutralize sorrow, my cup would have lost its bitterness. Never was a man more loved in life, or mourned in death; indeed, within the circle of my acquaintance, I might even say, *so* loved and mourned.

It soothes me to think of all the love and sorrow of the Wordsworths, and that by their wish—it would have been his too—his remains are laid as near as possible to the spot where they are to lie, in the south-east corner of Grasmere churchyard, near the river, amid the cluster of graves which belong to the Wordsworths,—dear bright-minded, warm-hearted Dora, who never spoke of him but with praise and affection,—and others of the family still earlier removed. But oh! how little did I think that I was never to see him more!

I should like you some day to see the letters which give account of his state in illness, his dying hours, and then of the funeral. Nothing could be more gentle, loving, pious, and humble, more deeply penitent for sin. Long and severe was his parting struggle, severe both to body and mind; but at the very last, he went off gradually.

III.

Affectionate Behaviour of the Old Friends at Rydal Mount on this Occasion—Mr. Wordsworth's Opinion of Hartley's Character and Genius.

To the Rev. EDWARD COLERIDGE, Eton College.

10, *Chester Place, Regent's Park, January,* 1849.—My dear Edward,—I think you will be glad to see the letters I enclose. They will tell you more of my dear Hartley's last days than you could otherwise hear. Our old friends, Mr. and Mrs. Wordsworth, are more endeared to me and Derwent than ever, by the love and tender interest they have shown; not more, indeed, than I should have looked for from them, but all I could have thought of or hoped. "You should have heard the old man say, 'Well! God bless him!' and then turn away in tears. 'It is a sad thing for me, who have known him so long! He will be a sad loss to us; and let him lie as near to us as possible, leaving room for Mrs. Wordsworth and myself. It would have been his wish.'"

In another letter, when all was over, Derwent says,— "Mr. and Mrs. Wordsworth had been at the cottage during my absence. Mrs. Wordsworth kissed the cold face thrice, said it was beautiful, and decked the body with flowers. This has also been done by others. Mr. Wordsworth was dreadfully affected, and could not go in. Miss S—— had told her father that the face was still the same—the same countenance. 'Is it strange,' he replied, 'that death should not be able to force a mask on him, who in his lifetime never wore one?'"

It soothes me to think that my dear brother, the greater part of whose life has been spent in our dear old friends' daily sight, should in death not be parted from them—the same neighbourhood in their last homes as in the abodes where they have lived, that his remains should rest beside those of dear, bright-minded, kind-hearted Dora, who never mentioned his name but to say something of praise or affection. Her father's expressions about Hartley, when I met him at Bath nearly two years ago, have been a treasure of memory to me ever since, and ever will be. Tributes of admiration to his intellectual endowments, his winning, though eccentric manners, were plentiful as flowers in summer. This was *more*. It showed me that he was esteemed in heart by one who knew him well, if ever one man could know another—one not too lenient in his moral judgments. I valued this testimony as confirming my own belief, which, because it related to one so dear, I held tremblingly, not as making me feel what I had not felt before. "It falls to the lot of few," another old friend says, "to have been so beloved and so worthy of love as poor Hartley Coleridge." No one could be loved as he was without a great share of those qualities to which our Saviour referred when He said, "Of such is the kingdom of heaven."

IV.

Christian Use of Sorrow.

To the Hon. Mr. Justice COLERIDGE, Heaths' Court.

January, 1849.—I am sure, dear John, this most unexpected death of my dear brother is a spiritual benefit to me. Nothing has ever so shaken my hold upon earth. Our long separation made me dwell the more earnestly on thoughts of a re-union with him, and the whole of my early life is so connected with him, he was in my girlhood so deep a source of pride and pleasure, and at the same time the cause of such keen anguish and searching anxiety, that his departure brings my own before me more vividly and with more of reality than any other death ever has done. If thinking of death and the grave could make me spiritual and detached from the weaknesses of this earthly sphere, I should be so; for I am perpetually dwelling on earth and that other unimaginable state. But, alas! more is required than the sense of our precarious state here, to fit us for a better and a higher.

V.

Sensitiveness about Public Opinion.

To the Hon. Mr. Justice COLERIDGE.

Chester Place, February, 1849.—The accompanying letter shows a sensitiveness about any exposure of private matters to the public, in which I cannot *now* quite sympathize. A good deal of thought upon the subject, through a good deal of experience, has brought me to think that a serious, anxious concern on such points is hardly worth while. If we could but overhear all that people say of us, when we are supposed out of hearing, all their careless comments and detailed reports of our affairs, I believe it would cure a good deal of this anxiety, by showing us how vain it is to aim at keeping ourselves out of the reach of observation; that it is but an ostrich-like business of hiding one's head in the sand. More especially with respect to money matters and *age*, it is politic to tell our own story, for if we do not, it will surely be told for us, and always a degree more disadvantageously than truth warrants. The *desire* to be the object of public attention is weak, but the excessive dread of it is but a form of vanity and over-self-contemplativeness. The trouble we take in trying not to *seem*, would be better spent in trying not to *be*, what we would rather not appear to be. If a strain of thought is beautiful and interesting in itself, I would not generally withdraw it from a collection of poems about to be published, because it touches on private affairs. I remember the time when I felt otherwise; but now I cannot help thinking that we should so order our lives and also our feelings and expectations that we may be as far as possible independent of the opinions and judgments of our fellow-men; and that whatever is the truth on a subject of any sort of interest, can very seldom in the long run be effectively or beneficially concealed.

VI.

Visit to the Dudley Gallery—Early Italian Masters, Fra Angelico and Fra Bartolomeo—Fra Angelico and Dante.

To Mrs. PLUMMER, Gateshead.

Chester Place, February 20th, 1849.—My nieces have just sent a messenger to arrange with me about a visit to the Dudley Gallery—Lord Ward's pictures—in Brook Street. This collection I saw a little while since with the D——'s, now I wish to show it to E. and the P——'s. It contains many beautiful pictures by the older Italian masters, as well as some, *to my mind,* still greater beauties by Correggio, Guido, and Salvator Rosa. I confess I cannot feel that enthusiasm for the pictures of Fra Angelico which some mediævalists in taste as well as in doctrine tell us we ought to feel. I have seen the pictures of Fra Bartolomeo, which I admired exceedingly; they struck me as uniting some of the grace and fine finish of Raphael with that simple, severe, or serious air of devotion which characterizes many of the older painters. But the productions of the earlier school are often grotesque, feeble, wanting in richness, grace, and beauty to my eyes; and though I respect them as devotional pieces, where they really do express a religious sentiment, I cannot much admire them as works of art. The admired Fra Angelico in Lord Ward's gallery is a representation of the Last Judgment, and is to my mind more curious and interesting than beautiful. On one side is a most debased copy of a portion of Dante's Inferno, quite devoid of the pathos and sublimity of the Florentine's poetic place of retribution. Dante, amid all his mediæval grotesqueness and monstrosity, is almost always elevated or affecting. What a study his great poem is!—what a compendium of the religion, philosophy, ethics, politics, taste of the Middle Ages!

VII.

Strong-minded Women.

Mrs. JOSHUA STANGER, Fieldside, Keswick.

Chester Place, March 6th, 1849.—Young ladies who take upon them to oppose the usages of society, which, as I fully believe, are the safeguards of female honour and happiness, and supporters of their influence over the stronger and wiser sex, and have arisen gradually out of the growing wisdom of mankind, as they increase in civilization and cultivation, are generally found to possess, I think, more self-confidence than thorough good sense, intellect, and genius. Certainly all the women of firstrate genius that I know have been, and are, diffident, feminine, and submissive in habits and temper. For none can govern so well as those who know how to obey, or can teach so effectively as those who have been docile learners.

VIII.

Dean Stanley's Sermons—Study of German Theology.

To Mrs. R. TOWNSEND, Springfield, Norwood.

Chester Place, March 27th, 1849.—I am reading with great delight Stanley's Sermons, which, strange to say, I never read through till now. He brings out the distinct characters of St. Peter and St. Paul, and their different missions, quite grandly.

He speaks of the study of German theology, in his preface, in what seems to me the right spirit and the right way.

Some of the chief aids in his task had been found in "the labours of that great nation from which we should be loth to believe that theology alone had derived no light, or that whilst we eagerly turn to it in every other branch of study, we should close our eyes against it here. Until we have equalled the writers of Germany in their indefatigable industry, their profound thought, their conscientious love of knowledge, we must still look to them for help. I know not how we should be justified in rejecting with contempt the immense apparatus of learning and criticism which they have brought to bear on the Sacred Writings."

In truth, this *cannot* be. If there is light in Germany more than here, it will shine in upon us. In these days light travels fast. It is not as it was centuries ago, when light might shine in corners here and there, yet ages pass away before it had become diffused, on account of the thick masses of palpable cloud and smoke which occupied the main part of the region. What a significant fact it is, that Strauss' book was translated into French and English as soon as ever it appeared—that four translations of it were offered as soon as it came to England! The worst books— those which contain some portion of truth so presented that it has all the effect of deadliest error, half-truths, and truths without their proper accompaniments—are sure to penetrate and spread fast among us. Hare, and Stanley, and Arnold would have the German mind brought *whole* in amongst us, convinced that, as a whole, it will promote the cause of spiritual religion ultimately, and that its philosophy will counteract its pseudo-philosophy, that German error is more easily to be fought by arms from Germany than from elsewhere. Those men who declaim against German theology in the mass are sometimes absolutely ignorant of a single German author, and uniformly unable to appreciate the true meaning and value of German philosophic speculations. They never really combat German opinions, or disprove them: they do but raise a hue and cry against them. I would be a conservative, too; but is there not a kind of conservatism that is self-destructive? Such, I think, is the conservatism of T—— and P——, which leads them to attempt to stifle the products of German thought, instead of boldly accepting it, examining the mass, and winnowing the good from the evil. It is a want of faith to doubt for a moment that religious truth can maintain its ground against all that the heart of man can conceive, or the human mind imagine.

IX.

Review of Lord Macaulay's History in the *Quarterly*—Miss Strickland's Life of Maria d'Este—Remarks on Governesses in an Article on "Vanity Fair."

To EDWARD QUILLINAN, Esq., Loughrigg Holme, Ambleside.

Chester Place, March 31st, 1849.—I am awaiting with some curiosity the arrival of the *Quarterly,* in which Mr. Lockhart has dealt with Macaulay. I wonder whether he will prove him wrong in any of his points with respect to the career of James II. Since finishing Macaulay's highly attractive volumes, the second of which has an enchaining interest, I have perused Miss Strickland's Memoir of James II.'s wife, Mary d'Este of Modena. The book seems to me childishly perverted and partial in much that relates to James II., but the account of his wife grows upon one. Proud and impetuous she must have been, but certainly she must have had a heart. The history of her feelings in the first days of widowhood, and in her husband's last illness, was to me, on reading, a mere repetition of that which is written in my own memory of my own experience. Macaulay's cool way of speaking of her person, which must have been one of the finest in Europe, is one of the greatest signs of party-spirit in his book, unless it is not party warmth, but mere temperamental coldness and apathy on the subject of female charms. Yet that it cannot be, since he can use strong words enough about some of Charles II.'s good-for-nothing beauties.

Miss Rigby's * article on "Vanity Fair" was brilliant, as all her productions are. But I could not agree to the concluding remark about governesses. How could it benefit that uneasy class to reduce the number of their employers, which, if high salaries were considered in all cases indispensable, must necessarily be the result of such a state of opinion? Many governesses, as it is, receive £80 and £100 a year. When the butler has £40, and lady's-maid £20, or housekeeper £30, this is surely the average. Besides, hard and unsentimental as it may seem, I must think that the services of the ordinary tradesman's governess are not worth more than £30 a year. After all, let the governess' discomforts be what they may, is not the situation in all respects far more tolerable for a lady, or semi-lady, than that of lady's-maid or upper housemaid, or the health-destroying slavery of the milliner's or dressmaker's business, or the undignifying, if not positively degrading, place behind the counter, which really in London partakes of some of the disadvantages of the stage, so obviously are the young women dressed up, and *selected* perhaps, to attract the eyes of customers and their lounging companions? But to some one of these situations must many a destitute young woman descend, if that of governess in some family of limited means was not to be procured.

X.

"Une Femme Accomplie."

To E. QUILLINAN, Esq.

1849.—Did you ever meet Miss R—— in London? She is perhaps the most brilliant woman of the day—the most accomplished and Crichtonian. She draws, takes portraits like an artist, and writes cleverly on painting; she plays with power, and writes most strikingly on music; she speaks

* The present Lady Eastlake.—E. C.

different languages. Her essays and tales have both had great success, the former as great as possible. To put the *comble* to all this, she is a very fine woman, large yet girlish, like a Doric pillar metamorphosed into a damsel, dark and striking. No, this is *not* the *comble:* the top of her perfections is, that she has well-bred, courteous, unassuming manners, does not take upon her and hold forth to the company—a fault of which many lionesses of the day are guilty. At this moment no less than *four* rise up before me, who show a desire to talk to the room at large, rather than quietly to their neighbour on the sofa. Miss R—— is honourably distinguished in this respect. She is thoroughly feminine, like that princess of novelists, Jane Austen.

XI.

Failure and Success—Her Son's Choice of a Profession—Metaphysical Training a Desideratum in University Education—A General Council of the Church to be desired for the Settlement of Controversies.

To the Hon. Mr. Justice COLERIDGE.

10, *Chester Place, April* 10*th,* 1849.—I am glad you think it some credit that Herby obtained a second place in the "Ireland" contest. Disappointments, interposed between successes, are decidedly useful to a mind of any native strength, as are all the trials of this life; and it is a good point in Herbert that he is never so discouraged by failure as to lose a just confidence in himself, and become listless and inactive. As for my boy's prospects at the bar hereafter, it is all dimness and darkness to me. Herbert will take the law as a profession, because no other bread-making career is open to him, not because there is any particular eligibility in it for him. He is fitted for the profession by his power of application and of continuous study; but I know not whether it will suit him in all respects. I hope he will prove to have some logical ability, but I cannot judge at present whether his interest in the reasonings of

Plato is a true indication of this or no. I have thought it a desideratum in the education of our young men, that they should undergo some systematic metaphysical training, and acquire some of that learning and power of analyzing thought, of which the schoolmen display so much. Many debates would be cut short, and long webs of theory would be swept away before they had wasted the time of authors and readers, if men were regularly taught at college the import of such terms as *nature, person, matter, soul, spirit, will, reason, understanding,* and so forth. I mean, if they were but taught those principles which *all regular* metaphysicians of all schools admit, but which many writers of the present day lose sight of in their arguments, simply from being quite out of the habit of abstracting and reflecting on the processes of the mind within itself. Men who show great ability and good sense while they keep to the *practical,* often commit, as I believe, the greatest blunders, which the merest tyro in mental science could detect, when for some practical end they set up explanatory theories involving metaphysical distinctions. I think I could give some instances of this ; but I must not ask your attention to matters of this sort, exercised as you are with head-work of various kinds. In support of my remark, I will merely say that educated, well-principled men could hardly come to such opposite conclusions, one among another, as we see them do, on points which are not mere matters of taste and feeling, but seem to be altogether within the domain of logic, if they were better instructed in the meaning of the terms they make use of. I often, on this account, feel a great yearning for a General Council of the Church. Surely, if there could be even such general discussion as took place before the Council of Trent, when Cardinal Contarini—that admirable Cardinal, and other good men—sought so hard to bring about a reconciliation between the Protestants and the rest of the Western Church, *some* questions must at

least be set at rest for ever, and the range of debate somewhat narrowed. Now, every man writes what seems good
in his eyes; and if the book is eloquent, and shows some
reading, it is extolled to the skies by the party whom it
serves, even though its main arguments are such as the
reflective among them would not subscribe to were they
fairly put before them, and which, in fact, *they never notice*,
even though they form the *pith*, or at least contain the chief
point in the whole work, and that for the sake of proposing
which it was composed and published.

XII.
Modern "Miracles."

To Miss FENWICK, Bath.

Chester Place, April 13*th*, 1849.—The cases of L'Addo-
lorata and L'Ecstatica in the Tyrol are very interesting.*
But Mr. Allies' conclusion respecting the object and use of
the supposed miracles is, to my mind, very inconclusive. He
thinks they are intended to awe and impress a sceptical,
unspiritual age. But the worst of it is, that no one not
already brimful of what Allies calls *faith*, but what some
would designate superstition, would ever consider them for
a moment in the light in which he regards them, or indeed
as having any connection with religion; and no one not
already a believer in the gospel would take the least interest
in them, except as strange *physical* phenomena.

---

* This passage refers to an account, which attracted some attention at the
time, of two peasant women in the Italian Tyrol, whose prolonged trances,
and other strange symptoms, excited the wonder of their neighbours, and
were looked upon by some persons as direct communications from heaven.
—E. C.

XIII.

Lights and Shadows—" Latter-Day Pamphlets "—" Chartism "—
" Shirley "—Walking Powers not Lost.

To Mrs. H. M. JONES, Heathlands, Hampstead.

3, *Zion Place, Margate, May* 19*th*, 1849.—I enjoy the quietness of this place. Very few visitors are here. We have the cliff all to ourselves for the most part, or share it only with the carolling larks. This place is better than Herne Bay; it has a fuller sea, and the water comes up to the bottom of the cliff, along which we walk, and although the inland country is much prettier between the Kentish coast and Canterbury, yet, as I come for refreshment and bracing sea-breezes, I do not miss the shady lanes and lawns and copses about Herne, but take my two walks a day, with E—— beside me, in perfect tranquillity and contentment, if not in hilarious glee. Who can be very *gleeful*, for more·than a few minutes at a time, in such a world as this, dear friend, so full of sorrow and misery and crushing want, spiritual and physical, and so surrounded by impervious shadow, the awful mystery of the world to come ?

Have you read Carlyle's " Pamphlets " ? The last, called " The Stump Orator," contains some good things, and the *Guardian* cannot sneer it down, with all its talent at sneering. People affect to despise its *truisms*, when, I believe in fact, at heart, they are galled by some of its bold, broad *truths*, expressed with a graphic force and felicitous humour which it is easier to rail at than to hide under a bushel. Put what bushel over it they may, it will shine through and indeed burn up the designed extinguisher, as the fire eats up a scroll of paper. " Chartism," by the same author, however, is better than any of these new pamphlets, which repeat in substance a good deal of its contents. That book seems to me prophetic, as I read it now. The accounts of the poor, of the savage Irish, etc., are wonderfully powerful.

Have you read " Shirley " ? We are delighted with it.

x

The review in the *Edinburgh* made far too much fuss about its little faults of style and breeding. When you read the sentences in question, *where they occur*, they do not appear very shocking. The worst fault by far is the development of the story. Mrs. Pryor's reason for putting away her daughter is absurdly far-fetched and unnatural. No wonder the "Old Cossack" disliked her, and thought her a queer sort of maniac.

I think my sleeping is a wee bit improved, and I am very active on my legs. The country folks at Keswick, when I was a little one, sometimes called me a "lile Jenny spinner," and I can spin along yet, though my face is so pale and small, and tells such a tale of sleepless nights, a weakly wifehood, and nervous widowhood.

XIV.

Afternoon Calls—Hurried Composition—Middle-aged Looks—Simplicity of her Mother's Character.

To AUBREY DE VERE, Esq.

1849.—I find it difficult to carry on literary business, all I have to do in editing my father's books (and a long task in that way yet lies before me), and worldly business, to see about the various investments of our little property, besides domesticities and social business, the last by far the hardest to me of the three. Oh! how I do abominate the afternoon calling, to pay or to receive it! To go out *prepared* to meet our friends is pleasant enough, but in the afternoon, when one is engaged, their coming is felt as an interruption. Nothing is so fatiguing as to go through a round of afternoon visits, to initiate half a dozen different conversations in different styles, take up half a dozen different tunes, pitch oneself at half a dozen different keys, and then feel obliged to rush away just as the strain begins to have a little heart in it. However, it is not the feminine visitations (if I were to begin the list of exceptions of ladies I am always glad to see, *even in an afternoon*, I should fill up too much of my paper), it is the evening visiting that knocks me up.

I am truly sorry that you feel it necessary or desirable to compose hurriedly and within *a limited time*. It is that which makes intellectual exertion so injurious, so ruinous. It has *killed* its thousands, and invalided its tens of thousands. I hope you will have strength of mind to give it up, come what may.

You ask me how I am. Richmond asked me to sit for a chalk drawing on my return from the sea, but my phiz, to judge by the glass here, which, however, is always in the shade, because the toilet-table is covered with my books and papers, and half the only chest of drawers is filled with the same, is not improved since my stay here. It is even more hollow and hatchetty than it was. Middle-aged faces are very bad and difficult subjects. The lines and sinkings appear in them as worsenings, impairments, impoverishments, deficiencies; a few years afterwards they look like seasonable marks of time, having a grace and a meaning of their own. I remember Mama, at my age, put on quite the old woman, and the Keswick people called her "auld Mrs. Cauldridge," though her complexion was a hundred times clearer and rosier than mine is now, and her cheeks rounder. As for her hair, she cut it all off and wore a wig, when she was quite a young woman, and her everyday front (a sort of semi-wig, or wig to wear with a cap), for she was too economical to wear the glossy one in common, was as dry and rough and dull as a piece of stubble, and as short and stumpy. Dear mother! what an honest, simple, lively-minded, affectionate woman she was, how free from disguise and artifice, how much less she played tricks with herself, and tried to be and seem more and better than she was, than the generality of the world!

XV.

Early Associations with the Seasons—Vaughan, Herbert, and Crashaw.

To AUBREY DE VERE, Esq.

10, *Chester Place*, 1849.—My dear Friend,—I had great pleasure in transcribing the enclosed poem, it brought spring so vividly before me, beloved spring, which is as closely unified, to my mind, with my childhood, as autumn with my girlhood. I can scarce recall what I did as a *child in autumn*. Winter was a glorious season; summer heat I well remember, and the throng of flowers in June, with the June Pole, and all our garden and river doings in May and June. But autumn brings no visions of childhood, except of seeking for plums in an old worn-out orchard, where the plum-trees were in the last stage of imbecility and dotage, and of standing in a sweet apple-tree, eating half the apples off the boughs, carrying on a lively dispute with my Cousin Edith, who was swinging away, in the warmth of the debate, on an opposite apple-tree.

And now even my children's childhood is past away !

Do you know Vaughan's "Silex Scintillans," a collection of sacred poems, a few years younger than those of George Herbert ? They are very sweet, some lovely, but have less power and thought than Herbert's, less perfect execution than Crashaw's.

XVI.

Miss Sellon at Plymouth—Lord Macaulay's History—Cruelty of James II.

To Miss FENWICK, Bath.

Chester Place, June, 1849.—I have heard nothing of the Sellon case at Plymouth, except at second hand. Substantially the reformeresses must be in the right. But it struck me, as I heard the case stated by one quite on her side, that it was a pity she could not have done her good things after a more Protestant fashion as to externals, avoiding party-badges, however silly it may be in her opponents to consider

such externals as necessarily connected with Popery and unsoundness towards our Anglican Church in the main. The
bishop seems to have taken the lady's part with great
warmth. However, when I speak of *party-badges*, I may
speak on misinformation, and she may have used no
fashions but such as have been approved or allowed by
our authorities here.

Macaulay's History has had, and is still having, an
immense run. It is certainly a fascinating book, but in
some respects perhaps too fascinating and attractive to be
thoroughly good as a history. Dry matters are skipped,
and many important events are rather commented on than
narrated. And yet every true history that is to be a useful
and faithful record must contain much that is dry and
heavy to the common reader. His account of James II.
makes the profligate, unpatriotic despot, Charles II., appear
like an angel of light. For what can be more hideous in
the human character than implacable malice and revenge,
deliberate barbarity, and love of human suffering and
misery for its own sake?

CHAPTER XXI.

LETTERS TO MRS. J. STANGER, AUBREY DE VERE, ESQ.,
HENRY TAYLOR, ESQ., MISS FENWICK, MRS. FARRER:
August—December, 1849.

I.

" Sacred and Legendary Art," by Mrs. Jameson—Parallel between
the Classic Mythology and the Hagiology of the Roman Catholic
Church.

To AUBREY DE VERE, Esq., Curragh Chase.

1849.—I am delighted with Mrs. Jameson's two volumes
on " Sacred and Legendary Art." It interests me doubly
from its descriptions of curious and beautiful works of art,
and even still more from the picture it presents of what
may be called the *Christian Mythology.* It is very curious
to see how the saints and saintesses of the Middle Ages,
after the secular establishment and worldly enrichment of
Christianity, succeeded to the places of the Pagan Deities,
and inherited their honours, in some cases were invested
with their attributes. There are the four great Catholic
Saintesses—St. Catherine, St. Barbara, St. Ursula, and
St. Margaret. One can plainly see that the first corres-
ponded to Minerva, as Mrs. Jameson suggests, and the
second to Pallas or Bellona. The Virgin Mary, as Regina
Cœli, is a purified, elevated, glorified Saturnian Juno, the
spouse of Jove, and Queen of Heaven. St. Ursula rather
resembles one of the protective matron goddesses. " Mild
Maid Margaret," that loveliest conception of them all, in
her purity and courage may be compared with Diana ; in
her lovely gentleness and humility has no prototype out of
Christianity. Mrs. Jameson's way of treating these subjects
will not please religionists of any kind or class, except the
very Latitudinarian, whom some will call the *Ir*-religionists.

Antiquarians, and Mediævalists, and Romanizers will feel indignant at her treating the legends as cunningly devised fables, highly as she praises their devout religious spirit, and effective embodiment of moral and spiritual truth; while zealous Reformists will frown at the favour with which she regards them, and her indifference to the large amount of superstition and idolatry which they have suggested and fostered. The legends are, many of them, full of beautiful, picturesque incident, and expressive allegories and emblems. Many of them I knew before, but, like ribbons in a shop, or the different stripes in the rainbow, they set one another off, and the whole is a most interesting panorama of Devotional Art and of Christian semi-evangelical Polytheism.

II.

Hearing and Reading—Facts and Opinions.

To HENRY TAYLOR, ESQ.

10, *Chester Place*, 1849.—If it is not too greedy, what I should like is to *read* the play first, and then to *hear* it *read* by you. I do not catch very quickly by the ear, and I have got into such a slow, musing way of reading that I cannot easily follow a reader aloud of anything interesting. I am staying behind, picking flowers and finding nests, and exploring some particular nook, as I used to be when a child walking out with my Uncle Southey, whom I found it hard to overtake when thus tempted to loiter. . . .

How the *Quarterly* and *Edinburgh* contradict each other about the Dolly's Brae affair! I believe there is nothing so uncertain and slippery as *fact*. Theories and opinions, much as they differ, are scarce so different as the reports of what purport to be the same facts by the different parties.

III.

Judgment of the Privy Council in the Gorham case—Depreciatory
Tone of the "Latter-Day Pamphlets"—Pictures belonging to
Mr. Munro of Hamilton Place.

To HENRY TAYLOR, Esq., Mortlake.

1849.—My dear Mr. Taylor,—I was horrified when late
yesterday evening my eyes fell on the enclosed preface as I
was searching in a drawer for the Key to Cattermole's great
Picture of the Protest at the Diet of Spires, my print of
which I have had framed and hung up, partly in honour of
the late triumph of toleration and moderation, grand
characteristics of the Reformed Religion, in the decision of
the Privy Council in the Gorham case.   I believe two-thirds
of the clergy, had the decision been in the Bishop of
Exeter's favour, must either have given up their livings or
cures, or have retained them with *peine forte et dure* of
conscience. *Now*, where is the *practical* difference in the
affairs of the Church and interests of Churchmen ?   The
judgment has but declared that to be an open question
which has always in fact been so.   As for Lord John
Russell being the "Pope of our Church," in one sense he
is so, and, as I believe, very properly and profitably for the
country ; in another sense, the only one that concerns truly
spiritual matters, he is not aught of the kind.   Infallible
guide we have none, and do not think it possible to have
upon earth, but the doctrine of the Church of England has
always been settled by the Church interpreting Scripture.
This judgment does but declare what the law of the Church
is, what our formularies mean, and to make such a declaration is quite within the province of the learned body of
which the Privy Council is composed.   There were three
Bishops for the supply of theological information, and that
all the body were not divines was in favour of truth and
impartial justice.

. . . I wonder what you think of the "Latter-Day Pamphlets"? They are much to be admired, especially for felicity of particular expressions, and they please some persons whom the author never pleased before. But I, for my part, like all his former works better than these. The drift of "Hero-Worship," and most of his other writings, was to defend and exalt, to set in a clear light, neglected merit. In the present publications I feel as if the drift were depreciatory. I do not see why we should try to make anything from the good name of Howard. Nobody ever said that he was a brilliant man, but it was to his credit that he found his Bedfordshire estates insufficient to fill up the measure of his mind, and to satisfy his aspirations.

E—— and I have lately seen such a fine collection of Italian pictures at the house of Mr. Munro, Hamilton Place. The Candelabra Virgin, by Raphael, most exquisite. One most lovely Claude, with a mountain which Ruskin would criticise, but which (*i.e.* the picture) you ought to have engraved as an embellishment for your new play. A space in a wood with a lovely pool, a clump of tufty, waterish-looking trees, goats roaming in the afternoon sunlight under the trees, and figures in front. There was also a splendid Venice by Turner, and Watteau's darling little town-girls, a famous picture.

IV.

Scotland and Switzerland—Historical Interest attaching to the former
—Bathing in the river Greta.

To Mrs. FARRER, Greenway, Dartmouth, Devon.

12, *St. George's Terrace, Herne Bay, August,* 1849.—How I long to visit Scotland! I think there is more *romantic* interest attached to it than even to poetic Switzerland. The latter puts me in mind of my father's "Ode or Hymn in the Vale of Chamouni," and of the poem of the beautiful

Duchess of Devonshire on crossing Mont St. Gothard,* verses
that might almost have been admired for their own sakes,
and not merely as coming from the pen of a popular
Duchess and Beauty. But Switzerland has no historical
associations in my mind higher than Aloys Reding, or at
most William Tell, celebrated by the modern Schiller.
while Scotland is connected with history, from Macbeth, as
he appears in Shakespeare's play, to James I., and from
him down to the romantic, foolish, wrong-headed times of
the Jacobites. That wild heath on which the witches met
Macbeth almost symbolizes Scotland for me, or at least,
that, with the "Lady of the Lake" to fill up the picture, or
to present the picturesque of the land in another aspect.

That wooded bank of the Dart which you speak of, overlooking Torbay, takes especial hold of my fancy. I am
pleased to hear of the primitive river-bathing. It reminds
me of my Greta Hall days.

V.
Tunbridge Wells.

To Miss FENWICK.

August 28th, 1849.—I do not wonder that you are not
fascinated with Tunbridge Wells. It is a fine place to drive
out from in various directions. But there is far more
refreshment and change in a sight of the changeful ocean
while we are stationary. The lie of the country is beautiful
at Tunbridge Wells, the terrace-roads and rich, green glades,
and basin-like valleys want only running streams and herds
of deer, and kine, and sheep and goats to be delightful. But

* This poem, entitled the "Passage over Mount Gothard," forms the subject of the "Ode to Georgiana, Duchess of Devonshire," by S. T. Coleridge,
beginning—

"Splendour's fondly-fostered child !
And did you 'hail the platform wild,'
Where once the Austrian fell
Beneath the shaft of Tell?
O Lady, nursed in pomp and pleasure,
Whence learned you that heroic measure?"

—E. C.

they *do* want life and movement. There is something to
me quite depressing in their stillness. The beautiful trees
seem made in vain, with no living things to frolic around
them or lie under their shade, and the eye quite thirsts for
water. How oddly, too, the stones and rocks are seated on
the turf, as if they had been taken from their native bed,
and placed there by some giant who had been playing at
bowls with them.

VI.

Cholera and Infection—Need of Sanitary Improvements—Evening
Walks at Herne Bay—Sisterhoods — Remarks of Sir Francis
Palgrave on the Resurrection of the Body, and on the Gospel
Narratives of the Healing of Demoniacs—A Last View of Herne
Bay — Home and Social Duties — Archbishop Trench on the
Miracles—Associations with Places—Love and Praise.

To AUBREY DE VERE, Esq.

Herne Bay, September 18*th,* 1849.—Here I am still, kept
here for a week longer than I intended by the encroach-
ments of that fiend cholera, and the advice of our careful
medical friend, Mr. N——, who expressed his regret to my
servants that I should return to town when the disorder was
on the increase. I, for my part, believe that the cholera
atmosphere is all over England, and that the complaint
kills off most people where there are most people to kill,
and in the most unfavourable circumstances in regard to
diet, clothing, and the air of their dwellings. I strongly
suspect that the disorder is in some degree infectious, since
one hears so often of many dying in one house, and sometimes when there seems to be no special cause of malaria. I
have been saying to John that it is an ill wind that blows
no sort of good, and that it is to be hoped the present pesti-
lence will improve the drainage of England. Yet how little
is done and doing in this way compared to what ought
to be! If men would but expend as much energy and
ingenuity upon this subject, or half as much, as they do
upon making money fast, or adding to the sum of amuse-

ments and luxuries, what a blessed, odoriferous nation we should be! I speak feelingly, dear friend, and beg you will feel for me, and for my E—— and our good Nurse, for Herne Bay, in a high wind blowing inland, as at present, resembles a certain compartment in a certain circle of Dante's "Inferno" in point of olfactory horribleness. E—— and I have to fly like chaff before the wind, when we pass certain parts of the town, which we must pass daily to post our letters, and to strike into the two best walks of the neighbourhood. I wonder whether the drainage of this good land, and the sewerage, and all that sort of thing, will ever be so perfected as to prevent all escape of noisome vapours. I often day-dream what England will be five hundred years hence, whether it will be free from coal-smoke, from butcher's meat exhibited openly in the street, from the abominations of Smithfield market, from rookeries like St. Giles, from nuisances affecting the atmosphere of every sort and kind, and I am sure if there are seventy different species in Cologne, there must be seven thousand in London. But stop! let me turn the current of my thoughts into a better channel, or rather, let me open a different spring and display a clearer, fresher stream, which will make its own banks green and flowery, and fit for your eye to rest on.

Imagine us on our evening walk out upon the East Cliff, a mile and a half from our present abode. We have passed a rough pathway, and weary of a long, low hedge, the very symbol of sameness and almost of nothingness, have struck in by a breach which the sailors, who sit there with their observatory telescopes, have made upon the grassy cliff, and are looking upon the sea and sky and straggling town of Herne Bay. The ruddy ball is sinking, over it is a large, feathery mass of cloudage that *was* swansdown, but now, thrilled through with rosy light, resembles pinky crimson flames, and the dark waters below are tinged with rose-colour. In the distance appears the straggling town with its tall watch, or rather, clock-tower, and its long pier like a leviathan centipede walking out into the waves. This time we are home before dark. Another evening we set out later, and by the time we descend the cliff it is dark, and as we are pacing down the velvet path, as we call the smooth, grassy descent, which leads to the town, there is Nurse in her black cloak waving in the wind, moving towards us through the dusk like a magnified bat. As we pass the town, what a chrysolite sky is before us, passing off above into ultra-marine, spangled with one or two stars, and below into a belt of straw-colour and orange above the horizon, over the οἴνοπα πόντον. Then we enter our lodging and begin to feel—

> " Com 'è duro calle.
> So scendere e il salir per le altrui scale."

Thirty-six steps, steep ones, too, have we to ascend to our sleeping apartments.

Then see us on the West Cliff. Just below us is a collection of huts, where live a set of people who gain a poor maintenance by picking copperas from the beach and cliff. When I first looked upon this hovelage, think I, this is like an Irish hamlet, and the people have an Irish look about them. Afterwards I heard that they were Irish, and that the old Nelly, who so gladly received the scraps and fragments from our not very extravagant repasts, is from the good town of Cork. It seems that she went not long ago to her mother-land, and there received such unnatural treatment that she was very fain to turn her back upon it. And now she applies a transitive verb that begins with *d*, the harsher form of the verb condemn, both to Ireland in general, and to Cork in particular.

Wednesday evening.—Right glad were we this evening on the East Cliff to welcome back the moon from her " interlunar cave." Lovely gleamed her crescent in the chrysolite depth above the crimson, yellow border of the vault serene. The sea was darkly steel coloured, and all the vessels upon it looked black. How much do they lose who walk out only in the full daylight!

I am writing to dear Miss Fenwick, and wish to interest her for poor M. S——, who has lately lost her mother, and is left quite desolate and destitute. She tried a religious establishment, but found the life too hard, and fell ill there. Now she is trying another. But she complains of want of fresh air, it is evident she only remains there for a home. She has sent me a plan of hours, showing how the time of the inmates is to be spent, and indeed it must require a burning zeal to render such a life tolerable. It is not so much the hardness and laboriousness that must be trying, though it *is* hard and laborious, but the dryness, the monotony,— nothing but private devotions and public, parish visiting and teaching. The only relaxation almost is reading aloud, with the needle. It is a pity that the bow is bent so tight; or at least it is a pity that there cannot be an honourable retreat of this kind, where persons who have no home of their own, no domestic duties to fulfil, might take refuge and be useful, without being worn out by requirements more than can be well complied with by any one but the very strong, or those who gain an unnatural feverish strength from zeal, and what some will consider fanaticism. I believe that worldly people much misjudge the zealous members of these institutions, but still I think that such systems cannot answer in the long run, except by aid of superstition, if to succeed by superstition is to succeed at all. Whenever they withdraw active, earnest-minded women from home duties, or service to those with whom they are connected by blood or early intimacy, or claim of gratitude, they are doing, I think, most serious mischief, for which they never can compensate.

September 21st.—A note from Sir Francis Palgrave this

morning. He says "The Antiquarian theologian will tell you what he means by a celestial body, when the scientific philosopher of the nineteenth century shall have explained the nature of the ultimate atoms of which the matter constituting a terrestrial body is composed." Now, I had not been complaining of the Antiquarian that he does not attempt to explain the celestial body. I remarked that he does attempt, not to *explain*, but to *describe* the celestial body, or rather takes it for granted that it is describable and conceivable by our present senses and faculties,—that it is a sort of improved, brightened, subtilized, glorified, earthly body, having the same form and lineaments, visible and tangible, as our present body. The question is, whether this notion is not disclaimed by St. Paul, and negatived by reason and by philosophy.

Sir Francis says too, "The theologian of the nineteenth century, who explains away narratives of demoniacal possession in the Gospels, is on the verge of explaining away the Gospels altogether." The subject often causes me anxiety, because I feel that it is going very far to believe that our Lord spoke as if He entertained the popular belief, while the popular belief was a delusion ;—*going far*, though only on the same road that all must enter who would reconcile the language of Scripture on many other subjects with truth of science. Still the case is not so bad, not at all such as Sir Francis says it is, if by "explaining away" he means understanding the demoniacs to have been madmen possessed with a belief that they were possessed by evil spirits, or, what is common with the insane, that they were evil spirits themselves. All that is related by the Evangelists may have taken place,—a miracle been performed of which the moral purport, the use and aim, is the same as it would be on the popular supposition. Our Lord healed a madman, and sent the spirit of madness into the swine, probably in order to render the display of His power the more striking and impressive. It is unfair to call such a view an *explaining away* of the miracle, it is but another interpretation of the nature of the miracle,—all the moral effect and the exertion of superhuman power remaining the same. This is a subject that has given me anxiety; I can only say that the popular view is obviously a part of the old false philosophy, which confounds the material and the spiritual, a philosophy now obsolete, except where it is retained for the sake of retaining certain ancient interpretations of Scripture, involving not mystery, but plain contradictions, which no human mind can really receive, however the owner of the mind may blink, and fancy that he is believing. As for the view substituted by Trench and others, namely, that the afflicted persons were *influenced* by evil spirits, as the sons of God are influenced by the Holy Spirit, I own it does not satisfy me, because it is, *in fact*, as irreconcilable with the language of the Evangelist, and the reported words of our Lord, and the manner in which His words were understood at the time, as the other modern interpretation, or at least, it is quite irreconcilable by fair methods with them. I confess I have other objections to it, relating to the general view which it involves of the existence of *personal* evil spirits; but it is sufficient to say, that to my mind, it does not accomplish what it undertakes, that is, to reconcile the Scripture narrative (understood as we may suppose the narrator understood it) with that view of the state of the demoniacs which Trench deems preferable to the ordinary ancient notion of possession. But no belief that is irreconcilable with reason will stand its ground among *reasoners*, upon whom ultimately the form of the popular religion depends. In all ages the learned and thoughtful have given to religion a framework accordant with the philosophy of their times, and with the highest reason which, in their times, had manifested itself. The Antiquarian must show the reasonableness of his creed, if he seeks to defend it. If he fails in this he loses the game. But you perhaps think that he will not fail.

Friday night.—We have looked from the East Cliff down upon the sea, on one side, and the quiet inland view, with the village of Herne, upon the other, perhaps for the last time. The bright crescent of the moon was shining in the white depth, above a bank of soft blue clouds, broken into vultures' heads, and many bold promontories, and the waters looked bluish grey, while swansdown clouds, shaded as with Indian ink, were overhead.

The rapidity of agricultural operations, and continual changes going on upon the surface of the earth, give a spirit to the country. The canary, which, I believe, is raised chiefly in Kent, is a very pretty crop, looking at a distance like wheat. The ear is of the form of the hop blossom, but yellow. The grain is used for birds, and is very dear, as dear as wheat, nine pounds a quarter, I think I heard. There is more canary in this neighbourhood than any other grain.

Monday.—As soon as one returns home, even in this season of London desertedness, one is dropped in upon in such a way that leisure goes away as fast as a plumcake under the maw of a hearty, munching child. One young gentleman drowned half yester afternoon, and another took a large slice out of the evening. In the night I read Trench on the Miracles, a book with which E—— and I are delighted. The author is High Church, but in point of doctrine follows very closely the early Reformers, as, for instance, on justification by faith, and is in decided opposition to the Romish views on the Virgin Mary, on the superior sanctity of a retired and celibate life, etc. He does justice to Spinoza, even in arguing against his views, refuting the charge of atheism and impiety brought against him, but deals with Woolston, Paulus, Strauss, and

Y

the other misnamed Rationalists, with all due severity.   In his interesting section on the water made wine, he sets forth a metaphysical view which you and I anticipated in one of our searching, lengthy discussions.   "He who does every year prepare the wine in the grape, causing it to drink up and expand with the moisture of earth and heaven, did now gather all those his slower processes into the act of a single moment, and accomplish in an instant what ordinarily He does not accomplish but in many months."   This comes from St. Austin, as so many fine-spun speculations do.

Yes, Curragh Chase must indeed be full of pensive recollections.   So was Herne Bay to me.   It brought back my children's early childhood, and my own anxious, yet on the whole happy, wifehood.   You can scarce imagine the change from wife to widow, from being lovingly flattered from morn to night, to a sudden stillness of the voice of praise and approbation and admiration,—a comparative dead silence it seems.   Vanity and the affections have such a mixed interest in this that it is hard to disentangle them, and the former during a happy state of marriage grows up unperceived under the shadow of the latter, and absorbs some of its juices.

VII.

Kentish Landscapes—Scenery of the Lakes.

To Miss FENWICK.

September 19*th*, 1849.—Strode Park, near Herne Church, is very interesting in its quiet Kentish beauty.   There is a stillness in the landscapes of this county, owing to the want of water, and moving objects, which is to my feelings almost melancholy.   I can *admire* other counties beside my own native lakeland, other sorts of nature-beauty, abundantly, but I cannot thoroughly *like and enjoy* any but that in which I was born.   When in the country I am full of thoughts and longings for my native vale.   Friars Crag, and Cockshot, and Goosey Green, and Latrigg Side,—all my old haunts, I long for.   Yet, if I were there, I should find that my *youth* was wanting, and the friends of my youth, and that I had been longing for them along with the old scenes, the old familiar *faces*, and the old familiar *places* together.

VIII.

Remarks on an Article on "Tennyson, Shelley, and Keats," in the *Edinburgh Review*—Inferiority of Keats to Shelley in point of Personal Character—Connection between Intellectual Earnestness and Moral Elevation—Perfection of his Poetry within its own Sphere—Versatility ascribed by the Reviewer to Keats in Contrast to Coleridge—Classification of her Father's Poems, showing their Variety.

To AUBREY DE VERE, Esq., Curragh Chase, Adare.

10, *Chester Place, November 4th,* 1849.—My dear Friend, —I have just read your article on Tennyson, Shelley, and Keats, and can no longer delay expressing to you my delighted admiration.   I think it quite your finest and most brilliant piece of prose composition.   It is full of beautiful sayings and pithy remarks, and it does a justice to Keats, not only which was never done to him before, but I should almost say a higher justice than any poet of this age has ever yet received from the pen of another.   Nothing can be more admirable than your characterization of Keats; I was quite excited by it.   What you say of Shelley is excellent too; but this is more *entirely* new, and the whole article is worthy of you, which I think a good deal to say, for you have been rather tardy in bringing out your mind in prose writing.   However, it is all best as it is, and I am sure the richest products are those which are delayed, so that they unite the peculiar qualities of the youthful mind carried forward with the greater force of a maturer age.   I must some day soon talk with you about the article at large in detail.   I wish you could see the copy I have marked.

One general criticism I must make, which you will not admit, because the *effect* I shall notice flows from your general temper and mental complexion as its cause.   You have a propensity to aggrandize and glorify; you over-praise, both negatively and positively, by omission of faults and drawbacks, unless they are of a kind (such as Shelley's want of reverence, and Cromwell's antagonism to bishops and kings) especially to excite your disapprobation and dislike, and by the conversion of certain deficiencies into large and glorious positives. You are more displeased with Shelley's *wrong* religion than with Keats' *no* religion. That very deficiency in the mind of Keats, which prevented him from being a very good man, and must, I think, for ever prevent him from taking the highest rank as a poet, want of power or inclination to dwell on the intellectual side of things or the spiritual organized in the intellect as soul in body, or indeed to embrace things belonging to the understanding at all, do you contrive to represent in the light of a very sub-lime, angelical, seraphical characteristic. It is all very well to distinguish meditation from contemplation, and to intimate that the mind may feed on deep thoughts and soul-expanding spiritualities, when it is quite apart from the region of logic and intellectual activity. But is it not the fact, and a painful truth which must forcibly strike every reader of Keats' letters and life, together with the mass of his poetry, that Keats never dwelt upon the great exalting themes which concern our higher peace, in any shape or form? "Oh, he was dark, very dark," said Miss Fenwick to me one day about Keats, and I heard her say it with pain. "He knew nothing about Christianity." You say he had no interest in the intermediate part of our nature, "the region of the merely probable." You give him "*in-tuitions*" (of the highest things which humanity can behold implicitly), and call his nature "Epicurean on one side, Platonist on the other." I wish I could see the matter as you do, or rather I wish the matter really were as you describe. But the truth seems to me to be rather this, that by means of a fine imagination and poetic *intellect*, Keats lifted up the matter of mere sensation into a semblance of the heavenly and divine, while the heavenly and divine itself was less known to him than to the simplest Bible-reading cottager who puts her faith in Christ, and bears the privations and weaknesses, or even agonies of a lingering death with pious fortitude. The spectacle of Keats' last days is a truly miserable one, and I must say I think that, beautifully gentle as is your treatment of Shelley, if viewed in itself, yet *taken together with your judgment of Keats*, it is hardly fair. Surely Shelley was as superior to Keats as a moral being as he was above him in birth and breeding. Compare the letters of the two, compare the countenances of the two, as they are imperfectly presented to us by the work of the graver, see how much more spiritual is Shelley's expression, how much more of goodness, of Christian kindness, does his intercourse with his friends evince! Shelley, in his wild way, was a philanthropist; Keats was social, but the same spirit which led him to turn away from earnest questions which agitate the religious world, which agitated Augustine and Pelagius, Luther and Calvin, Hooker and Taylor, some of the greatest and best men that have ever lived, rendered him careless of promoting the good of mankind, or any but those individual felicities of the passing hour which added to his own earthly sensational enjoyment. He showed a pettish jealousy respecting the estimation of his works in his intercourse with contemporaries, and in his love affair he betrayed all the weakness, all the passive non-resistancy of a passionate girl of eighteen, together with the impetuosity of a young man and the sensitiveness of a poet. Again, I must say that it is a *miserable* spectacle. I have read of late numberless lives of poets, philosophers, and literary men, not one that upon the whole inspired me with so much contempt as that of Keats. His effeminacy was mournful, and his deliberate epicureanism, with the light of the Gospel shining all around, even worse

than mournful. I quite agree with you as to the excellence
of his poetry, and that he was even, upon the whole, more
highly gifted in that way than Shelley. There is even a
greater intensity in his productions, a perfection in the
medium of repose. Upon all that part of the subject you
are as just and discriminating as you are eloquent and
inwardly poetic. But when you go on to endow Keats with
all the nobler qualities of a man and a writer, and not content with showing him to be an exquisite, sensational poet,
must exalt him into a poetical seraph; why, either I am too
narrow and ill-natured, or I am too simple and straightforward and truth-requiring to accompany you to the far
end of your eulogium.

Shakespeare as little preached and *syllogized* as Keats
does. But Shakespeare was a great philosopher, implicitly.
Shakespeare furnished *material* for the contemplative, in-
quiring, discriminating intellect, and consequently intellec-
tualists like Goethe, Schlegel, and S. T. C., find a perpetual
feast in his writings, and are for ever converting into the
abstract what he presented in a concrete form. Not so will
any great thinker ever be able to do with the writings of
Keats. His flight was low, his range narrow; he kept on a
lower level; and in that poor rejected critique of mine
which Lockhart cut out of my article on *The Princess*, I
endeavoured to show what advantage he derived from his
unity of purpose, from his confining himself so entirely, and
with such a faith and complacency in his own genius,
within his native range of power and beauty. I did not
attempt to do *justice* to Keats, I knew *that* would not be
allowed in the *Quarterly*, even if I had been equal to the
subject, which I am not, for no woman can give the portrait
of a man of genius in all its masculine energy and full proportions. I did not present him with a grand chaplet of
bays, as you have done in your noble criticism, but culled
a nosegay of sweet flowers out of his own poems, and bound

it about with a silken band of subdued praise and temperate characterization.

But this is a digression. I must make an end about Keats. I was astonished at your calling the last act of that, to my mind, wretched tragedy of his "very fine." I thought, as I read it carefully more than once, that anything so poor and bad from a man of real, great poetic genius, never proceeded. I do not quarrel with it for not having the slightest merit as a drama. It has scarce any merit, as it seemeth to me, in any other way. It is as vapid as the little fragment "The Eve of St. Mark" is exquisite. Lastly, to conclude my objections on this part of the article, I do not understand why you ascribe *versatility* to Keats, and deny it to my father. What you say of my father on this head I think a deserved compliment, by which I mean, of course, not a flattery, but a just recognition of excellence. But it seems to me that you should have commenced with a *definition* of versatility, if not explicit to the reader, yet at least in your own mind. I should say that my father had shown a greater range of poetic power, that he had exhibited more *modes* of the poetic faculty than Keats has done, or Tennyson either. Let us enumerate them:—

1. The love poems, as "Lewti," and "Genevieve," which Fox thought the finest love poem that ever was written.

2. The wild, imaginative poem, treating of the supernatural, as "The Ancient Mariner" and "Christabel."

3. The grave strain of thoughtful blank verse, as "Fears in Solitude."

4. The narrative ballad, homely, as "The Three Graves;" or romantic, as "Alice du Clos."

5. The moral and satirical poem of a didactic character, as the lines on "Berengarius," and those lines in which he speaks of seeing "old friends burn dim like lamps in noisome air," and "Sancti Dominici Pallium."

6. The high, impassioned lyric, as "The Odes to France," and on "Dejection."

7. The sportive, satirical extravaganza, as the "War Eclogue," "The Devil Believes," etc.

8. The epigram and brief epitaph.

9. The drama.

I must say good-bye to you, though I shall chat with you again soon about your splendid article, which contains matter enough for four such as the *Edinburgh* has usually favoured the world with. Think of the *Edinburgh* beginning in her old age to criticise poetry poetically! "Age, twine thy brow with fresh spring flowers!"

IX.

Personal Likeness between Mr. Coleridge and Lord Macaulay.

To Miss MORRIS.

Chester Place, November 16*th,* 1849.—I met Mr. Macaulay on Tuesday at a very pleasant party at Sir Robert Inglis's. He was in great force, and I saw the likeness (amid great unlikeness) to my father, as I never had seen it before. It is not in the features, which in my father were, as Laurence says, more vague, but resides very much in the look and expression of the material of the face, the mobility, softness, and sensitiveness of all the flesh,—that sort of look, which is so well expressed in Sir Thomas Lawrence's beautiful unfinished portrait of Wilberforce. I mean that the *kind* was common to Wilberforce, but the species alike in Macaulay and S. T. C. The eyes are quite unlike—even opposite in expression,—my father's in-looking and visionary, Macaulay's out-looking and objective. His talk, too, though different as to sentiment and matter, was like a little, in manner, in its labyrinthine multiplicity and multitudinousness, and the tones so flexile and *sinuous*, as it were, reminded me of the departed eloquence.

CHAPTER XXII.

LETTERS TO EDWARD QUILLINAN, ESQ., AUBREY DE VERE, ESQ., MISS FENWICK, MRS. T. M. JONES, MISS MORRIS, MRS. R. TOWNSEND, PROFESSOR HENRY REED: January—July, 1850.

I.

Chinese Selfishness—The Irish Famine—Objects of Charity—Church Decoration, and the Relief of the Poor—Butchers' Prices—Sudden Death of Bishop Coleridge.

To AUBREY DE VERE, Esq., Curragh Chase, Adare.

10, *Chester Place, Regent's Park, January 4th,* 1850.— Some philosopher observes that not a man in Britain would make a worse dinner if he heard that the whole Empire of China was swallowed up quick. Of all people on the face of the globe the Chinese are those I should feel the least inclined to cry about, whatever befel them; and I think the reason is because I have a strong impression that less than any other people do they care what becomes of the rest of the world, that their sentiments and sympathies are of the dullest possible description. But this starving state of the Irish does occupy my mind a good deal. Here we are much better off, and yet it is dreadful to walk the streets of London, and to think that the poor wretches who moan for alms are by no means the worst off class of the community. If I happen to have left my purse at home, I am almost sure to come home unhappy about some object whom I would fain have relieved. One day I was quite upset by the piteous cry and pale sickly face of a little old woman. I had no money, and felt ashamed to ask Herbert for a shilling, knowing that there were hundreds whom he would think as deserving of charity. You must know that ever since I lost my dear mother, the sight of any feeble old woman agitates me. I felt quite glad that Lady Inglis was out, and that I had not to present my nervous visage to her. Soon afterwards I walked the same way, and luckily found the old woman. I gave her 6d., and had to give 3d. away before I got home. I will never go out again without a pence purse.

My niece Mary was talking the other day of the beautiful Ottery Church, with its groining, and arches, and painted windows. The siren drew me on, and on hearing that some of the small windows cost only £5, I cried in a fit of enthusiasm, "I *will* give a window myself," though I had signified to her father that a sovereign for the eagle lectern in our church was the last money I meant to give for church decorations. I think I shall tell her that the £5 she shall have, but that I would rather she gave it among those poor distressed underfed slaves, whose condition she had been describing to me when we last went out together to dine at Baron Rolfe's, than spend it on the coloured window.

Then what a shameful conspiracy there is among the butchers against the poor!—for such it may be called—when they are selling the inferior parts of animals to poor creatures by gas-light for 6d. per lb. My cook overheard a butcher extorting that price from a poor creature for *shin* of beef (mere *shin*) a few days ago. The farmers complain that they cannot obtain a decent price for their stock,—nay, sometimes cannot sell them at all,—and these butchers are putting into their abominable pockets all the profit, instead of lowering the price proportionably to the consumer. I have been writing notes about this to many of my friends, and all agree to make a stand. But I wish when we make a stand for ourselves, we could do something in this matter for the poor.

Our Christmas has been saddened, as you may suppose, by the sudden and most unexpected death of William Coleridge, the only son of my never-seen uncle Luke Coleridge.* He was conscientious in public and in private, doing scrupulously whatever he thought right, and in his own family he was most loving, even-tempered, and amiable. William, in person, was just fitted for a Missionary Bishop. He was *six feet* in all his proportions, not merely in height, with a stentorian voice, fit to preach on a mountain, which he has been known to do in the Leeward Isles, and with a stout, robust, but not corpulent frame. We thought he had twenty years of vigorous life in him yet. He shone in the practical more than in the exercise of the speculative intellect; he managed the clergy under him admirably, and was much beloved in Barbadoes, spite of the war he had to carry on against selfishness and prejudice.

* Luke Herman, seventh son of the Reverend John Coleridge, of Ottery St. Mary, was a surgeon at Thorverton, where he died at the early age of four-and-twenty. His wife, daughter of Mr. Hart of Exeter, was a woman of much feeling, united with firmness of character. It is related that when her only son, William, asked the consent of his widowed mother before accepting the appointment of first Missionary Bishop of Barbadoes and the Leeward Islands, she replied to him in the following letter :—"MY SON— Abraham's faith can be imitated. Go.—I am your mother, SARAH COLERIDGE."

Bishop Coleridge left England in 1825 for his tropical diocese, where his evangelical labours among the negroes, and untiring advocacy of the cause of justice and humanity, are well described by my father in his "Six Months in the West Indies," which contains an account of the Bishop's first visitation-tour among the Islands. Some time after his return to this country, he undertook the office of Warden of St. Augustine's College, Canterbury, a post for which his missionary experience rendered him peculiarly fitted. He had not been there more than a year and a half when the tidings of his sudden removal, with no warning of previous illness, caused a shock of grief and surprise through a wide circle of friends and relations.—E. C.

II.

Various Occupations of S. C.—Fatigues of Chaperonage—Barry
    Cornwall at a Ball—Waltzing—Invitation to the Lakes—Effect of
    Railway Travelling on her Health.

To E. QUILLINAN, Esq., Loughrigg Holme.

February 9th, 1850.—My dear Friend,—I must give you
an instalment of my letter debt to you at once, because
your last contains a very kind and agreeable proposal,
which should be noticed at once. A proper response I
must defer. I have all my life been rather a busy person;
but I now have more work of various kinds to perform than
ever before. There is first the domestic business. I
cannot spin this out, as some ladies do, ladies in the country
more than in town. Still the inevitable part consumes a
good bit of time of every year. Changing servants is
specially troublesome; I have had to give Martha's character
three times, and Caroline's twice, and to see nine or ten or
more servants and write about others, in order to fill their
places.

Then, 2ndly, there is the care of my father's books,
new editions and publications, and of this work the unseen
part, which does not appear, is more than that which does
appear. I might have written many volumes in the time,
of a certain sort, with far less trouble.

3. Reading with my children. This, I am sorry to say,
has come to very little of late. But I shall resume my
studies with E—— in a few days.

4. Money managements, letters of business, and all that
relates to the care of my income. A *wife* knows nothing of
this. But a widow, even with fellow-executors, has something to do in this way every year.

5. Business of society. This is the hardest, in one
sense, of all the work I have to attend to. It is always
beginning, never ending. For the sake of the children I
keep up the game more than I once thought I should ever

have attempted. I go sometimes to evening parties, and twice, nay thrice, of late, have chaperonified at balls! I do think, of all the maternal self-sacrifices and devotednesses that can be named, that is the greatest. If it was not for the supper!—actually I have gone down to supper *twice*, in the course of the evening, out of sheer exhaustion. On the last occasion I fell in with Barry Cornwall. It was like getting into an oasis with a clear stream bubbling along under beeches and spreading planes and rose-bushes and geranium tufts, and an enamelled flooring of crocus, auricula, and violet, to be taken care of by a literary man, and have a bit of poetical and literary talk, after the weariness of witnessing for hours that eternal scuffle and whirl, H—— whirling round the room for ever and ever, with first a black-haired, and then a brown-haired, and then a flaxen-haired damsel in his arms. (What queer indecorums those waltzes are! If twenty years ago one could have seen a set of waltzers of to-day through a time-telescope or *future*-scope, how we should have turned up the corners of our eyne!)

I have been interrupted, and forced to write notes of sociality and domesticity, till all the edge of my epistolary zest is rubbed off. I have seen friends, and hired a satisfactory damsel, as well as transacted lunch, since I began the letter. I dine out *homishly* with E—— at six, and so, instead of translating from my brain to the paper the letter, or an abridgment of the letter which I have been writing to you in thought ("How swift is a thought of the mind," and what pen can more than toil after it a measureless distance), I must speak of your kind invitation, and then say farewell for the present, though with an intent of renewing intercourse by pen and be with you ere long.

I can hardly describe to you my longings to revisit my native vale and dear Rydal. But there are difficulties in the way. Twelve hours by the railroad at a stretch I could quite as little accomplish as I could walk twenty miles. Indeed, I think the latter would not disorder me more than the former. I can by the sea-side walk ten miles, five in the morning and five in the evening, on a strong day, without disorder or any injury or exhaustion. But three hours of passive motion, or if that is an incorrect expression, of suffering motion, the muscles unexerted, is enough to set up nervous irritation in me; and this goes on at an increased ratio from that time till the journey's end. I should arrive a shattered creature, unable to enjoy anything for six weeks or more. The journey might be managed by stoppages on the road, and I am always visionizing on the subject. But there is much to be thought of before it can be effected. I can hardly bear to think of the changes I shall witness. Keswick will be a place of graves to me; but there would be a melancholy pleasure and interest in thinking of the departed. The changes in things and persons that remain are far more unwelcome.—I am yours, very affectionately,

SARA COLERIDGE.

III.

" Telling" Speeches not always the Best.

To Miss FENWICK, Bath.

February 15th, 1850.—Derwent was full of the great Educational anti-Government Meeting at Willis's Rooms. S——'s was the grand speech of the evening. His oration must have been very lively and ingenious and impressive, from Derwent's report. But I have little respect for speeches that *tell* in assemblies of this kind. The probability always is, I think, that a speech accurately true and just, entering into the depths and intricacies which really exist in great questions and doing justice to the views of all parties, would not *tell* half so well as a superficial harangue, full of half truths and bold assumptions and affecting irrelevancies, which call down a thunder of claps and " hear, hears!" yet if read in the closet would not convince a single soul who was sincerely seeking the truth, and was not decidedly of the speaker's mind beforehand.

IV.

Death of Mrs. Joanna Baillie.

To Mrs. H. M. JONES, Hampstead.

February 24th, 1850, *Chester Place.*—Your note has affected me very much. Dear Mrs. Joanna Baillie, that unique Female Dramatist, thorough gentlewoman, and (last and best) good Christian, gone at last, leaving not her like, in some remarkable respects, behind her! You were privileged, dear friend, to have that sight of the dear face after death, and to see that "friendly look," so consolatory to survivors, and so precious a treasure for memory. Her aged sister must feel desolate indeed. Blessed are they, says a famous old poet, whom an unbroken link keeps ever together. But this is not the lot of humanity, for death comes at last to break every chain, whether a hated or a loved one.

V.

Mr. Carlyle's "Latter-Day Pamphlets" compared with his "Chartism"—Ideal Aristocracy—English Government.

To Rev. HENRY MOORE, Eccleshall Vicarage.

March 15th, 1850, *Chester Place.*—Carlyle's "Latter-Day Pamphlets," I own, I like less than any of his former works. It has all his animation and felicity of language in particular expressions, and there is much truth contained in it. But the general aim and purpose is, to my mind, less satisfactory than in any of his former writings. It has all his usual faults in an exaggerated form. His faults I take to be repetition, and the saying in a roundabout, queer way, as if it were a novel announcement, what everybody knows, without any suggestion of a remedy for the evils he so vividly describes. "Chartism" had finer passages than any in these papers. Yet *that* was decried, and

these are almost universally received with favour.   The
address to the horses in " Chartism," beside being new, was
far better turned, more seriously pathetic in its humour,
than the repetition of the thought in " The Present Times."
Then I cannot bear the depreciation of Howard, and the
sneers at the Americans.   His former works have all been
devoted to exalting and elevating, defending and raising
from the dust.   The great drift of these is of a depreciatory, pulling-down character.   As for the Irish, I would be
right glad to see them coerced for their good, only they
should be treated as children, not slaves, and the great
mass of the barbarous English, too, especially the class of
little, prejudiced, pig-headed, hard-handed, leather-hearted
farmers, who are grinding the poor labourers, and grinding
their own nobles to ninepence by mismanagement and
asinine methods of tilling the ground.   But who is to do
these things.   Who is to bell the cat ?   Then Carlyle tells
us, as he told me in conversation long ago, that the few
wise ought to govern the many foolish.   But who doubts
that ?   This is a kind of aristocratic sentiment which is
common to all mankind who think at all.   But we shall be
none a bit the nearer to this millennial state of wise-man
government, by sneering, as Carlyle does, at the attempts
of mankind to do things carefully, and justly, and methodic-
ally, sneering at all that by introducing the words " bom-
bazeen, horse-hair, red tape, periwigs, pasteboard," and so
forth.

I, for my part, believe that the English government does
approximate to this nearer than any other, that Pitt and
Percival, Peel and Russell, *upon the whole*, have governed—
so far as they individually governed—as well as any man
in the country would have done.   Among men of letters
have been many wiser, speculatively, and cleverer for some
things.   But it does not follow that they would have done
better as Premiers, or could have filled such a place.

VI.

Illness of Mr. Wordsworth.

To E. QUILLINAN, Esq.

March 25th, 1850.—My dear Friend,—I have just heard from dear Miss Fenwick of our beloved Mr. Wordsworth's illness. It is most painful to hear of this trouble, and not be able to be of use in any way. I am full of anxiety and sorrow. I have been dwelling much of late on dear Mr. Wordsworth and his state of health and spirits. My thoughts hover around him. He is the last, with dear Mrs. Wordsworth, of that loved and honoured circle of elder friends who surrounded my childhood and youth; and I can imagine no happiness in any state of existence without the restoration of that circle.

But I must not write more to you now. My earnest prayers for dearest Mr. Wordsworth's restoration will be preferred, both in selfish feeling and in sympathy.

Believe me, with most affectionate regards to dear Mrs. Wordsworth, and dearest love, whether it can be given or no, to the beloved sufferer.—Yours, in much friendship and sympathy, SARA COLERIDGE.

VII.

Hopes of Mr. Wordsworth's Recovery—His Natural Cheerfulness— Use of Metaphysical Studies.

To E. QUILLINAN, Esq.

Good Friday, 1850.—My dear Friend,—I must write a few lines, though in haste, to thank you for your welcome letter, and tell you of my joy in dearest Mr. Wordsworth's safety and his beloved wife's happiness. May he be restored to his former measure of strength, and may this crisis work a change for the better in his spirits! I have often mourned to think that he was no longer glad as of yore. He used to be so cheerful and happy-minded a man. No mind could be more sufficient to itself, more teeming with matter of delight, fresh, gushing founts rising up

z

perpetually in the region of the imagination, streams of purity and joy from the realm of the higher reason—joy and strength and consolation, both in his own contemplations for his own peculiar satisfaction, and in the sense of the joy and strength and solace which he imparted to thousands of other minds. No mind was ever richer within itself, and more abundant in material of happiness, independent of chance and change, save such as affected the mind in *itself*. I felt with grief that his powers of life and animal spirits must have been impaired from what I heard of his fits of unjoyousness.

A visitor has taken away all my letter-writing time, so that all I meant to say must be screwed up into narrow room.

But one thing I must disown. Where upon earth, or under the earth (in the apartment of some gnome, I suppose, that lives under Loughrigg, in a darksome grot), did you learn that I supposed that you "who do not study metaphysics all day long" cannot understand S. T. C.? All the most valuable part of my father's writings can, of course, be understood, as the writings of Jeremy Taylor, or Milton, or Gibbon, or Pascal, or Dante, or Shakespeare, without specific study of mental metaphysics or any other *science*. Still, I do think that some careful study of psychology, some systematic metaphysical training, ought to form a part of every gentleman's education, and more especially of every man who is destined for one of the learned professions, and still more especially for men who undertake to write on controversial divinity. A writer on doctrine and the *rationale* of religious belief ought at least to know those principles of psychology and other branches of metaphysics in which all schools agree, and to have had some exercise of thought in this particular direction, and of course such a study must improve the faculty of insight into all works of reasoning which treat of the higher subjects of human thought.

VIII.

A Relapse—Regeneration in the Scriptural Sense implies a Moral Change.

To AUBREY DE VERE, Esq.

10, *Chester Place, April*, 1850.—My dear Friend,—I am much pleased at your wishing me to send invitations to Mr. and Mrs. T. and Mrs. J. M., and at your intention of attending at St. Mark's on the 18th yourself, and of what you say of the Institution, that it is one of the signs of life in the times. All this is saddened to me by thoughts of dear Mr. Wordsworth, and of his dear afflicted wife, his partner for nearly fifty years. How she will seem to live in waiting for death and to rejoin him and her beloved Dora!—if he goes now. For myself, I feel as I did in my own great bereavement and affliction, the thoughts and feelings which the event and all its accompaniments induce are, in the poet's own words, *too deep for tears ;* they are deeper than the region of mere sorrow for an earthly loss or temporary parting. Sorrow for the death of those nearest to us, in whom our life has been most bound up, is absorbed in the gulf of all our deepest and most earnest reflections—thoughts about life and existence here and hereafter, which are more earnest, more *real*, and permanent, and solid, and enduring, than any particular thoughts and sorrows and troubles which our course here brings with it, or which contains them all virtually. The particular becomes merged in the general, happily, and when we seem most bereft, most afflicted by the inevitable law of death and corporeal decay, we are only led to feel that this is but a part of the universal doom, that the loss and calamity which has come upon us at *this* time is but what, in a very short time, and in some form or other, we must bear. My grief respecting my dear old friend has been to see him *grow old*. To my mind he has been dying this long time—not the man he was. I see in this, his final struggle, if such it prove, but the termination of that career of mortality. My tearful feelings are more for Mrs. Wordsworth than for his departure. The stupor and dejection which have long been upon him, when he was not roused by the presence of strangers, have been the precursor of dissolution and beginning of the stage of final decay.

I have read your reflections on Baptism with deep attention and interest, and shall read them again and often. They come home to me more than other remarks ever did. Still, they cannot, and I think never will, move me from my standing-place, because indeed that has been chosen with all the powers of my heart and mind, after the deepest and fullest consideration which I can give to the subject. It seems to me that the tendency of your reasoning is rather to withdraw the mind from what, after all, must be the foundation of all reasoning in religion, from the *real sense* of Scripture, interpreted according to the generally admitted rules of human language, and from the spiritual ideas, of which all true religion consists, combined and arranged according to the laws of thought. I hold the very highest doctrine of Baptism which is consistent, as I think, with a right, scriptural, spiritual, substantial view of *regeneration*, with that view of regeneration which Scripture presents. The mystical view involves the belief that a soul in which the heart and understanding, the will and moral being, are wholly unaltered from the state in Adam, a soul which passes from the neutral state of unconscious infancy into positive immorality and ungodliness, pervading the whole character, has in baptism undergone that *regeneration, that new birth* in the Spirit, of which our Lord spoke to Nicodemus, that such a soul is really and inwardly incorporated into Christ, and a branch of the true Vine. Now, it needs not long discussions. If you can look at this belief, and not feel shocked by it, if it does not seem to you contrary to the moral sense, contrary to

the tenor of Holy Writ, and a profanation of sacred
language, the direct and obvious sense of which denotes
something *essentially* different, namely, a cordial, earnest,
and unalterable acceptance of the Gospel of Christ, or of
what the Gospel contains virtually and substantially, with
such a spiritualization of the heart and life as constitutes
the good Christian in character and conduct, I think we
never can see alike on this point. There is a world-wide
difference between a converted and an unconverted spirit :
it is the greatest soul-difference conceivable. Now, I think
the former *alone*, and not the latter at all, is internally,
and in the primary sense, regenerate. No other view of
regeneration than this appears to me reconcilable, fairly,
with the declaration concerning being " born of God " in
the Epistle of St. John, and indeed with whatever is said on
the subject in the Bible.

IX.

Death of Mr. Wordsworth—Sense of Intimacy with her Father,
produced by her Continual Study of his Writings.

To E. QUILLINAN, Esq.

1850.—My dear Friend,—Your letter of this morning
has made me but a little more sad and serious than I
felt before, and have been feeling since the later reports.
Thank God, that our dear and honoured friend was spared
severe suffering ! For days I have been haunted and depressed with the fear that he had to go through a stage
of protracted anguish. He could afford the torpor of the
dying bed. His work was done, and gloriously done, before,
and will survive, I think, as long as those hills amid which
he lived and thought, at least if this continues to be a land
of cultivated intellects, of poets and students of poetry.

Still, though relieved and calmed, I feel stunned to
think that my dear old friend is no more in this world.
It seems as if the present life were passing away, and
leaving me for a while behind. The event renews to me

all my great irremediable losses.   Henry, my mother,
Fanny, Hartley, my Uncle and Aunt Southey, my father
—in some respects so great a loss, yet in another way
less felt than the rest, and more with me still.   Indeed,
he seems ever at my ear, in his books, more especially
his marginalia—speaking not personally to me, and yet
in a way so natural to my feelings, that *finds* me so fully,
and awakens such a strong echo in my mind and heart,
that I seem more intimate with him now than I ever was
in life.   This sort of intercourse is the more to me because
of the withdrawal of my nearest friends of youth, whom
I had known in youth.   Still, the heart often sinks, and
craves for more immediate stuff of the heart.   My children
are much.   I trust that dear Mrs. Wordsworth will find
hers, those still left to her, sufficient to make life dear
and interesting to her.

He is "gone to Dora!"* Yes; may we all meet where
she is!   She has been spared this parting.   Would it have
come so soon, had she not been severed from his side?

Will you convey to dear Mrs. Wordsworth, when it is
desirable, my deep sympathy and assurance of my earnest
prayer for her support and consolation, and in respect of
the revered departed all the blessedness that our Father in
heaven has to bestow on His faithful servants that are
returned to His house of many mansions.   Believe me,
dear friend, yours in deep sympathy and most faithfully,

SARA COLERIDGE.

Archdeacon Hare says to me, in a letter of late date :—
"I have a letter saying that his remaining days are few.

* Mrs. Wordsworth, with a view of letting him know what the opinion of
his medical advisers was concerning his case, said gently to him, "William,
you are going to Dora!"   More than twenty-four hours afterwards one of
his nieces came into the room, and was drawing aside the curtain of his
chamber, and then, as if awakening from a quiet sleep, he said, "Is that
Dora?"—*Memoirs of Wordsworth*, vol. ii. p. 506.   Mr. Wordsworth died on
the 23rd April, 1850.—E. C.

If it is indeed so, a glory is passing away from the earth.
O what sweet odours of thankful love will mount with his
departing spirit from thousands of hearts whose affections
he has enlightened, and enlarged, and purified! This
world will seem so much poorer without him; and yet his
mind will still live in it as long as our language lives; and
the treasures which he has been hoarding up for so many
years will be found out amongst us!"

X.

"Now we see through a glass darkly; but then face to face."

To Miss FENWICK, Bath.

10, *Chester Place, May 6th*, 1850.—Dearest Miss Fenwick,
—I shall be thankful to see any letters from Rydal that
you can forward. How dear Mrs. Wordsworth is to bear
the trial of separation, and parting sorrow, and fatigue
undergone in the last illness, is perhaps yet to appear.
I trust we may augur well from the long-prepared state of
her mind, and her living faith in the resurrection, and our
reunion with departed friends.

Still, in some respects, the more we dwell upon that
prospect, the more we strive to realize it, the deeper is the
trial to our weak bodily frame. We know that another
state of existence must be far other than this—that a
spiritual world cannot be like an earthly world. We cannot
penetrate the shades that hang over the state of souls
on their departure. The subject that is spoken of under
the name of the "intermediate state," of this what brief
notices we have, and how ambiguous! How the best and
wisest men differ about the interpretation of them! The
more we think of the state after death, the deeper is the
awe with which we must contemplate it; and sometimes,
in weakness, we long for the happy, bright imaginations of
childhood, when we saw the other world vividly pictured,
a bright and perfect copy of the world in which we now

live, with sunshine and flowers, and all that constituted our earthly enjoyment! In after years we strive to translate these images into something higher. We say, All this we shall have, but in some higher form: "flesh and blood cannot inherit the kingdom of heaven, neither shall corruption inherit incorruption." All this beauty around us is perishable: its outward form and substance is corruption; but there is a soul in it, and *this* shall rise again; and so our beloved friends that are removed, we shall see them again, but changed—altered into what we now cannot conceive or imagine, with celestial bodies fit for a celestial sphere.

XI.

Breaking of Old Ties—The *Times* on Mr. Wordsworth's Poetry— True Cause of its Different Reception on the Continent, and in America.

To Mrs. H. M. JONES, Hampstead.

April, 1850.—I have been feeling and thinking much, as you will have anticipated, about the last days and hours of my dear and honoured old friend Mr. Wordsworth. I feel as if life were passing away from me in some sort; so many friends of my childhood and youth removed, so few of that generation left. It seems as if a barrier betwixt me and the grave were cast down. Happily for me, friends of my married life and children have risen up to prevent me from feeling solitary in the world. Still there is something in the breaking of these old ties that specially brings the shortness and precariousness of our tenure here before us. Hartley and Mr. Wordsworth were great figures in my circle of early friends, and leave a large blank to my mind's eye.

Many thanks, dear friend, for sending me the *Times*. The article on the departed dear and revered poet, the *great poet*, I think, of his age, is respectful, though not up to the measure of what his warmest admirers think and feel.

The remarks on his non-popularity on the Continent I consider mistaken; they ascribe, in my opinion, the ignorance of French and Germans of Mr. Wordsworth's poetry not to the true cause. If he were so peculiarly "English" that he could not be relished out of England, why is he so great a name in British America? There he holds even a higher place, or at least his claims are more fully and universally admitted among our ⸢Transatlantic brethren than in England; and his poetry has moulded that of the Americans far more than that of any poet of this age or of any other age. I was assured by Mr. Bancroft, the American minister, what I had often and often heard before (and he spoke it before a whole company at the Chevalier Bunsen's table), that my father's and Mr. Wordsworth's reputation in America was—I cannot recall the expression, but I know he used the strongest and most energetic language on the subject. The Chevalier had just been saying that Wordsworth was not understood or cared for in Prussia. Moore and Byron were the great English poets there.

The reason to me is plain. Moore, and Byron, and Campbell are poets of a popular cast, and are admired by thousands who cannot appreciate very refined and elevated poetry. This popular sort of writing sooner makes its way among foreigners than that which students would consider to be possessed of higher merits. Shakespeare is *now* read in Germany; but he did not make his way there till during the course of this last century. He was never admired in France or Germany before the time of Lessing, nor generally appreciated before the lectures of Schlegel asserted and explained his immeasurable superiority to all other dramatists. While Shakespeare was neglected and called a "barbarous writer," the novels of Richardson and of Goldsmith were read and admired all over the continent, not long after their appearance here. Why was this difference, but because they were far more easily understood than the great dramatist, and were, both in stuff and manner, such as would be relished by less cultivated minds.

XII.
"The Prelude."

To E. QUILLINAN, Esq.

Margate, June 13*th,* 1850.—All you tell me about the Poem * is delightful. How wonderful it seems that the great man, our dear, departed great one, should have deferred the publication till after he had passed from this world! How satiated he must have been with praise and fame! And what a glorious existence must his have been to be the composer of such strains, of such noble poetry, if indeed this poem is all that my father ever thought of it and you now say!

It is great pride and pleasure indeed to me that it is addressed to my father. They will be ever specially associated in the minds of men in time to come. I.think there was never so close a union between two such eminent minds in any age. They were together, and in intimate communion, at the most vigorous, the most inspired period of the lives of both.

XIII.
The Prelude a greater Poem than the Excursion—Collection of Turner's at Tottenham—Lycidas, by Fuseli.

To Mrs. R. TOWNSEND, Springfield.

. . . .

1850.—I have found your critique on the Prelude. I tell you, as I do another friend, who is blind, as I think, to its merits, that she must read again, and not run away from it, on account of the unusual, seeming-prosaic sound of many parts. It is the production of a great poet in his vigorous period, and I think it will be felt on full consideration to be

* The Prelude.—E. C.

a pregnant and most energetic efflux. The Residence at
Cambridge, which my friend cries down, will live and
command attention, when we are passed away. I agree
with those who say that it is a greater poem than the
Excursion. But there will always be readers, and even
lovers of poetry, who will never enjoy Wordsworth or
Milton. How many there are who cannot understand or
relish Pindar, Petrarch, Dante, Spenser, not to speak of
their scorn of Keats, and indifference to Shelley.

I wish you could have had the treat we had to-day, in
seeing a splendid collection of Turner pictures* at the nice
country house of Mr. Windus, at Tottenham. I much
admired a Fuseli, Lycidas lying asleep in the moonlight
at earliest dawn, his dog baying the moon beside him.
Lycidas, in throat, cheek, and figure wonderfully like my
Uncle Southey. A most striking and poetically sublime
production.

XIV.

A Staffordshire Country House.

To Miss MORRIS, Mecklenburg Square, London.

T—— Wood, Wolverhampton, Staffordshire, July 1st,
1850.—This beautiful domain,—the house, which is built
and furnished in the antique style with consummate
elegance, and the grounds, which are in some respects the
most to be admired of any that I have seen, especially in
the velvet smoothness of the turf, and the fine effect of the
endless-seeming vistas, and clusters of tufted flower-beds,
seen from the windows, is the creation of Mr. M——.
Twenty years ago an ordinary old mansion, amid ordinary
pleasure-grounds, the abode of Miss H——'s father, stood
where now stands a show residence, which is as fine a
specimen of modern taste and ingenious arrangement as
any I know. Perhaps I am the more struck because I have

* Now dispersed, since the death of Mr. Windus.—E. C.

not ventured from my own home for several summers, and have never left Chester Place except for seaside lodgings. When I compare, however, with this place, any of the seats I have formerly visited, they seem to my remembrance almost rough and unkempt in comparison. The only want is of water. We have no lake, no river, no streamlet here to give an eye and a smile to the "sylvan scene," only a sprinkling fountain. The cedars scattered here and there among trees that sweep the green floor with their ample robes, in this leafy month of June, and others that tower upward in finest majesty, form a beautiful variety, the horizontal growth of their boughs contrasting with that of all the rest.

We have had a succession of gay parties, not only dinner company, but sets of guests coming to spend a few days, and soon after their departure, succeeded by fresh sets, since we arrived here on June 22nd.

XV.

Critique on Mr. Ruskin's "Modern Painters"—Figures and Landscapes painted on the same Principles by the Old Masters—Instances of Generalization in Poetry and Painting—Turner "the English Claude"—Distinct kinds of Interest inspired by Nature and by Art—Subjective Character of the Latter—Truth in Painting Ideal, not Scientific—Imitation defined by Writers Ancient and Modern—Etymology of the Word—Death of Sir Robert Peel—Vindication of his Policy.

To Professor HENRY REED, Philadelphia.*

T—— Wood, Staffordshire, July 3rd, 1850.—We have had several discussions of Ruskin's theory of the superiority of the modern landscape painters over the Cuyps, Poussins, and Claudes of old time. Wrong as I believe that theory to be, on the whole, and as to its conclusions, both from my

* Mr. Reed was a Professor at the University, Philadelphia, and author of "Lectures on English Poetry and Literature," and other works. This lamented gentleman, as will doubtless be remembered, perished in the loss of the *Arctic*, on the return voyage, in 1854.—E. C.

own observation and from the remarks of artists and pictorial
critics unprofessional with whom I have talked on the subject, I do not wonder at all to find you and other correspondents of mine in America warmly admiring and
believing in his book, at a distance, as you are, from the
works of genius which he disparages.   It is a book of great
eloquence, though the style has the modern fault of diffuseness, and the descriptions of nature with reference to art
which it contains are full of beauty and vivacity, evincing
great powers of observation, and a mind of great animation ; and no doubt there is some portion of truth in what
he throws out concerning the defects of the old landscape
paintings.   But I think he is far from having perceived
clearly and fully either the nature of the art of painting, or
the true relations between the state of that art, as exhibited
in the old landscape paintings, and as it appears in our
modern English school.   As that accomplished artist,
R——, a great friend of Ruskin, observes, he ought, by the
same principles upon which he condemns the old landscape
pieces, to condemn the historical and sacred paintings of
the same and an earlier age, and to these he attributes the
same merits that the world has agreed to think they possess.
I have heard that grand solemn picture, the Raising of
Lazarus, by Sebastian del Piombo, designed by Michel
Angelo, declared unnatural, and an inferior production to
what modern art could produce, by an accomplished artist,
who applied to it the same tests of pictorial excellence as
those with which Ruskin detects the vast inferiority of Claude
to Turner.   Now, that picture (it is in our National Gallery
in London) is pronounced the most sublime composition of
the kind in the world by the first connoisseurs in Europe;
and yet its merits are appreciated by persons of taste and
sensibility in general, even those who have no particular,
or what may be called *technical*, knowledge of painting.
Then Ruskin laughs at the notion of *generalizing*—but he

says nothing that shakes my faith in the slightest degree in the common creed of critics on this point. Milton generalizes in word-painting in the fourth book of " Paradise Lost;" his description of the Garden of Eden brings together all the lovely appearances of nature which are to be found in all beautiful countries of the warm or temperate zones, not a single object which is peculiar to any one place in particular. His Eden is an abstract, a quintessence of the beautiful features of our mother Earth's fair face ; and who shall say, or what man of sense and sensibility has ever yet said, that this *generalized* picture was painted on a wrong principle ! Now, what Milton has done in words, Claude, to my thinking, has done with the pencil, and all Turner's finest and most famous pictures are offsprings of Claude's genius. Turner was called " the English Claude " when he was at the height of his fame, and his beautiful " Dido and Eneas," or " Rise of Carthage," never would have been painted as it is painted but for the splendid prototypes, as I think they may be called, from the hand of Claude, in which sea, sky, and city are combined after a manner of his own, which, I scruple not to say, reports of the com- biner's mind as much as of the material furnished by the world without. What Ruskin *meant*, I undertake not to say ; but he *says* what I believe to be as great a mistake as can be entertained on this particular point,—that a painter has nothing to do but to produce as close a copy as possible of particular objects, and combinations of objects, in nature. The fact is that the works of every great painter are recog- nized as the product of an individual mind. If it was not for this individual *subjective* character, I believe they would be utterly uninteresting. May we not arrive at the truth of the matter by ascertaining what is, and ought to be, the painter's aim when he employs himself in imitating the natural landscape on canvas. Surely it is not to make the spec- tator acquainted with some particular spot or set of objects;

it is to produce a *work of art*; not to present a camera
lucida copy of nature. It is not merely to call up the
identical feelings which the very contemplation of the natural
landscape itself is apt to excite; but to remind us of those
feelings in conjunction with the sense of the presence of an
individual mind and character pervading and presiding over
the whole. We may not, in looking at a Cuyp, or Hobbima,
a Claude, or a Salvator Rosa, explain to ourselves the
source of our interest in the picture, and its peculiar character, and yet it may be the impress of an individual
genius, of this man's or that man's frame of intellect and
imagination, that delights us when we contemplate a fine
landscape painting far more than anything else. The old
painters were superior to the moderns, in my opinion,
because an individual mind was stamped upon their works
more powerfully and impressively. Their paintings have
more character; it is *that* which I look for in these works
of *art*. I do not go to them to improve my knowledge of
nature. This is a difficult subject, and I am aware that I
have been expressing myself broadly and laxly, and perhaps
have gone as far from the exact truth on one side as Ruskin
on the other. But this I do deliberately think, or at least
strongly suspect, that as the power of representing nature
on canvas must necessarily be very limited, and is rather
suggestion than representation, the attempt to imitate the
outward object beyond a certain point may injure the
general effect of the work as a whole, and that the departure
from truth which Ruskin points out in the old masters as
faults and deficiencies may be part of the power and merit
of their works as suggestive compositions. I believe that
they did quite right to address themselves to the common
eye of mankind, not to the eye of the painter. They
present clouds and woods as we see them, when we rather
feel their loveliness than think about it, or examine into it.
Turner has aimed at cramming into a piece of canvas or

paper a foot square, or less, as much as possible of all that he sees in an actual sky on a certain day of the year, and has succeeded so well that critics complain of his skies as top-heavy. I have heard a clever engraver say that some of them might be turned upside down ; that they are solid enough to stand upon. It is impossible, in the too eager devotion to truth, to *all* the truth of the sky and her appur-tenances, to do justice to earth, and exhibit the due relation of solidity between her and the firmament above her.

I have ever been a very warm admirer and ardent defender of Turner against his ordinary assailants. He is a poetical painter, and gives me more delight than any other modern artist. But Ruskin is extravagant, and defends him, in part, I think, on wrong grounds. If Ruskin is right, none can appreciate Turner but Turner himself. No doubt, every great creator must teach the world how and what to admire ; but if he does not succeed in being admired in the end, he has not done the work he pretended to do. No doubt, Ruskin says rightly, that a painter must aim at truth in his representations ; but the question is how much truth he can obtain without sacrificing the general effect— the emotions which the whole is to produce ; and I think he goes upon wrong, because one-sided principles, when he argues as if the only merit of a painting were its truthful representation of the outward object. A certain *mode* of doing this, derived from the painter's individual mind, is that which interests beholders more than aught besides, and I think I am referring to fact when I say it is this principally which assigns value to the picture. The pictures of Claude are not so true as those of many a painter whose works are not worth anything in the market,—Glover's, for instance, which people bought eagerly on their first appear-ance, because they were like the places of which they were portraits. Ruskin is quite mistaken, too, I think, in his remarks on the distinction made by my father and others between the terms "imitation" and "copying." Aristotle, in the "Art of Poetry," a standard authority, has used the former in the broad general sense, which Ruskin seems to suppose was the proper one, to produce a likeness of some object of observation by art, the intention of which is not that it should pass for the original by way of delusion, but to delight the spectator by the very sense of the art exercised. "Othello" is an imitation of a domestic story, in which the passion of jealousy was the principal feature, and the chief mover of the event. Mr. Burke says, quite in accordance with this usual meaning of the terms—"Whenever we are delighted by the representation of things which we should *not* delight to see in reality, the pleasure arises from imitation." I have not Ruskin's book at hand; but I remember he says upon this—"the very contrary is the case;" because he determines that *imitation* properly means no more than copying—the mere production of a duplicate or *fac-simile* of the original. Usage determines the meaning of terms, and I think it is against him. Even etymology, as far as it goes, is against him; for imitation comes from the Greek word which we render by "mimicry;" and he who mimics another man never means to pass for the man he mimics by disguise; the pleasure he gives rests upon the spectator's sense that the likeness is presented in a medium of diversity.

It is time to conclude this rambling epistle. Before you receive it you will have heard of the sad event which puts our papers in mourning—the death of Sir R. Peel, by a fall from his horse. I am one of those who honour Peel as a practical statesman. I am no politician, and always speak on such subjects with a reserve on account of my inadequate insight. But we cannot help seeing, or seeming to see, some broad facts and acts in connection with them. It seems to me that Peel had the sagacity to see, when the time had arrived, what his country required, and *would*

have, either from him or some one else, with more or less
of struggle and commotion; and that he had come to the
resolution to do what he had come to think, under the
circumstances, necessary, let them say what they might,
let him lose office or retain it. If he acted upon self-
interest, it is not of the vulgar kind, but of that which was
one with the good of the country; he could preserve the
character of a statesman who would not sacrifice the public
advantage to his own reputation for consistency. To say
he should let others do what he would not do himself, with
all the chances of their omitting to do it, or deferring to do
it, seems to me a superficial, unpractical way of putting
the matter.

XVI.

The Black Country—T—— Wood ; The Dingle; Boscobel ; Chillington
—Liberality and Exclusiveness—The Wolverhampton Iron Works
—Trentham—B—— Park—Leicestershire Hospitality.

To AUBREY DE VERE, Esq.

T—— Wood, Wolverhampton, July 9th, 1850.—When we
had passed Birmingham and entered the region of cinders
and groves of chimneys, I thought it almost equalled the
hideousness of a certain manufacturing portion of Lan-
cashire. On the side of Tettenhall and Penn, Staffordshire
has its share of sylvan beauty. The Worcestershire hills
rise in several ranges, faintly blue on the horizon. This
house is all built (by Rickman) and furnished in the olden
style, with great elegance and harmony of effect ; the
painted glass and old carved oak furniture are fine in their
way, and the prospect from the windows reminds one of
pictures of the garden of Boccaccio, the vistas are well
managed, so as to *seem* ended only by the Wrekin in
the distance ; the turf is in high perfection, such an
expanse of emerald velvet I scarce ever saw before ; and the
cedars scattered among the other trees delight me
especially. I have been so long shut out from scenes of

this kind that the place appears to me a finer one perhaps than it does to those who go from one smooth, ornate country-seat to another year by year. I do feel, however, the want of water. In the Dingle, a picturesque glen in the grounds of Mr. C——, of Badger, water has its due part in the scene, now in the foamy waterfall, now in the wide, quiet, gleamy pool, that reflects the sky and the branching of the tall picturesque trees around. Yesterday we visited Boscobel, and E—— crept down into the hole where Charles II. is *said* to have hidden himself. I tried to go too, but felt too much stifled to proceed. I was pleased to see, in returning by the artificial lake at Chillington, which made me think of Curragh Chase and a certain poem of yours, that Mr. G——, the owner, allows the people of the neighbourhood to disport themselves there on a certain day every week. How much more lively enjoyment he must have in seeing a crowd of people, whom his bounty has refreshed, than in keeping the whole spacious domains to himself all the week round, closed up in silent, melancholy state, no one going near that fine sheet of water embosomed in woods, from hour to hour. Surely men will, in the course of time, become wiser about such matters than they have been, and frame for themselves deeper and keener pleasures, more stirring and expansive enjoyments than wealth and large possessions have hitherto brought to our grandees for the most part. There is something to my feelings always deeply sad and sombre in the sight of a large domain belonging to some stately reserved proprietor, living alone there with but few inmates except domestic servants. It puts me in mind of the poor bounded nature of our existence here, when it is regarded in a worldly point of view. There is great amusement in constructing a fine house and superintending the laying-out of a large pleasure-ground, such as my friend Mr. M—— has had here; but when all is done, and the place perfect in its way, I fancy the lawns and groves breathing sadness to the spirit of a proprietor, which is never felt when we gaze upon the wild woods and fields with a sense that we are not bound to enjoy them because they are ours.

From these reflections I was called away yesterday to go and see the Iron Works, a stirring spectacle strongly contrasted with the scenes which were in my mind's eye on my return from Boscobel and Chillington. First, we saw the rolling mills and all the glowing processes of hammering down the masses, and shaping the metal; then we proceeded to the huge furnaces, were hoisted up to the top of those enormous chimneys on a movable floor, inspected the craters of the artificial volcanoes on the platform at the top of the edifice, looked out over the land of iron and coal, and paid a visit to the engine which cost over £2500.

Regent's Park, Monday, July 23rd.—Dear Friend,—From my account of the furnaces, just as I was about to describe the red-hot river of melted metal, like Phlegethon bursting upward from Pluto's realm and rushing on under the light of the day, while a blast was let forth from an orifice above, and forth went the two impetuous elements, fire and air, flaming and roaring together,—I was called away, and from that hour to this have never had time to write aught but necessary letters, accounts, etc. Before my return home on Saturday last I saw a great deal more of Staffordshire, and gained a strong impression of its richly sylvan beauty, enhancing a regret that those green lawns and fields, and full foliaged banks of wood, are not enlivened with clear waters, living sparkling streams, and have no opportunity of mirroring their own charms in any but the sluggish, unclear, seemingly reluctant floods of made lakes and rivers. We visited Trentham, saw Broughton, Sir Henry Broughton's Staffordshire abode, and, lastly, went to stay at B—— Park, Mr. H——'s seat near Loughborough, which is as good a specimen of modern magnificent comfort, which is the proper phrase rather than *comfortable magnificence*, which, however, may be fitly applied to the grand and imposing hall. At Trentham the ministrative part of the establishment, the offices, and kitchen, and fruit-gardens, are on a princely scale and in a princely style. The useful is nowhere abroad, I apprehend, so extensively and elegantly maintained, and this is truly characteristic of the English nobleman. The show-part of the house and grounds may be found fault with. Ten acres of flower-garden defeats its own object by dispropor-tionateness. Some compare it to fairyland; but fairyland, so far as my travels have gone, includes more of the inimitable charms of nature, lucid streams, glittering lakes, basins of water in which, by optical alchemy, liquid crystal is transmuted into beryl and emerald, forming rainbowy waterfalls, and splendid masses of blossom, all of one hue, opposed to others, such as you describe in the Delphic region, instead of that endless succession of flower fan-tasticalities, and lawn and shrubbery artificialities. The park with its deer is good; but I like not the Arabian desert of gravel extended far as eye can go before the house, with the dull series of clipped laurel clumps to imitate the Versailles orange-trees, which seem intended to illustrate the stupidity of identity. The house is full of elegant apartments, but has no grand room; and abounds in pretty paintings without any fine pictures. It seems a show-place for pretty chintzes and Derbyshire ware. Some of the statues are to be admired, especially a bronze cast, in the garden, of the Perseus of B. Cellini, a sort of mediæval Apollo; a marble sitting statue of Paris listening to the prophecy of Nereus, which is most graceful, and listens all over. The Perseus has this defect, it wants the repose and decorum which characterize ancient art, not in the figure of the hero, which is but a variation of the

Apollo, but in the victim. Under his feet is the death-stiffened figure of what, to the eye, appears no noxious monster, but only a beautiful woman distorted in the last agony; and the blood bursting from the neck looks like large ringlets of hair. Thus the Perseus seems a horrid murderer, rather than a dauntless conqueror.

But I must run on to B—— Park, and tell you of that noble hall, which certainly is the most imposing house-interior, from the size and proportions of the whole, the rich, carved oak balustrades, etc., that I ever beheld, not even excepting the hall at the Duke of Sutherland's town mansion. There is a gorgeous window emblazoned with all the H—— heraldry. Mr. M—— criticises this, and maintains that it is too much covered with deep colour, that a hall-window ought to admit a silver light; and again he criticises the formal garden, and objects to the abrupt transition from that artificialism into the park. But this criticism seems to me founded on too narrow a principle. The soul of B—— Park is heartsome ease, luxury, and comfort. T—— Wood is more poetical and picturesque, with its silver light and rainbow reflections on the white stone staircase. But for a dwelling-house give me the comfortable brown light, which looks warm when you come in from a cold, wintry sky, and wraps you in cosy shadow when you enter weary with the heat, and eye-oppressed with the glare of our sudden summer sultriness and sun-shine. Give me, too, the richly-carpeted staircase, instead of cold stone. As for the garden, when you are *in it*, and look back upon the house (late Elizabethan, early James I.), you feel that it is the necessary adjunct to such a mansion, and that a picturesque Boccaccio garden, a sort of imita-tion of Armida's pleasure-ground, would be quite incongruous in such a place. But I must not go on describing at this rate. And, after all, the magnificent oaks of the park are the great boast of B——, for the oak is the weed of that

district, as the elm in England generally, and Mr. H——
had only to clear judiciously. The owner of all this
accumulation of showy luxury is, or will be, one of the
richest commoners in England, and is as rich in amiable
qualities as in worldly possessions. From the testimonies
of those who know him well, and from his conversation, I
judge that he is as faithful, generous, and affectionate in
heart as he is frank, simple, and cordial in manner. His
sister is a feminine copy of him; and I do trust they will
live long together, like Baucis and Philemon. They were
all kindness to me, and Mr. H—— said I must come again
to make a longer stay; and I am sure he paid me twice as
much attention as he otherwise would, with so many guests
to entertain, because I seemed weak and delicate, and
suffered dreadfully from an accident, a minute grain of
metal getting lodged in my eye, between Derby and Loughborough, and causing me great misery, till after I don't
know how many searchings of the afflicted orb and its
coverings, and assurances that whatever I might feel or
fancy, nothing *was* in it, the tormentor walked out of its
own accord. There was an archery-meeting near the rocks
a mile from the house in Mr. H——'s grounds on Friday,
and our party was met by a select set from the neighbourhood. Mr. H——'s little speeches at the dinner had an air
of grave playfulness and business-of-society straightforward-
ness about them which pleased every one. Indeed, his
whole manner is calculated to put all persons at their ease,
and to excite nobody's vanity. Such blandness is like oil
on the waves of society.

CHAPTER XXIII.

LETTERS TO MISS FENWICK, AUBREY DE VERE, ESQ.,
PROFESSOR HENRY REED, REV. EDWARD COLE-
RIDGE, MISS MORRIS, EDWARD QUILLINAN, ESQ.,
HON. MR. JUSTICE COLERIDGE: July—December, 1850.

I.

Rain, Roses, and Hay—Experiences of Wesley as a Preacher among
the Agriculturists and Manufacturers—Influences of Society,
Education, and Scenery, on the Development of Poetic Genius.

To Mrs. Moore.

Chester Place, July 26th, 1850.—I have had a most
agreeable letter from dear Miss H—— this morning. She
tantalizes me with an account of the flood of sunlight
which has been pouring into B—— Park, to illuminate all
its beauties and glories within and without, since our
departure, and she almost brings tears into my eyes by
reminding me of the roses "laughing and singing in the
pouring rain," a touch worthy of Shelley, the Poet of the
"Sensitive Plant;" and in the thought of these darlings
rejoicing in the dews of heaven, which they think, I
dare say, made on purpose for them, she magnanimously
adds, "never mind my hay." Now, where is the farmer,
or any *masculine* professor of hay, from the Land's End
to Johnny Groat's House, who would have said, or felt,
"never mind my hay"? All that set of men think their
hay and stubble far more important than other men's gold
and silver, and precious stones. So Wesley found, and
Whitfield too. All their diamonds and pearls did the
farmers set at nought, and they were harder to be taught
to prize the great pearl of the Gospel itself, than even the
poor benighted sinners and gin-soddened manufacturers.

All this is very uncharitable and narrow, perhaps you will

think, with a more fortunate race of husbandmen around you than those I am thinking of. In truth, these field-preacher experiences impeach particular circumstances rather than men. I suppose if the farmers are more prejudiced and less ready to give than manufacturers, and agricultural labourers more like clods, than operatives of the loom and the mill are like lumps of greasy wool, it is because they have a less brisk intercourse with their fellow-men, and the Promethean sparks of their minds are not elicited so constantly by mutual attrition. "A parcel of auld fells" will leave the men who live around them as hard and savage as their own rocks and wild woods, if a book-softened mind is not brought to bear upon them; and this thought comes strongly upon me in reading Mr. Wordsworth's great posthumous poem. He ascribes his poetry to his poetical mode of life, first as a child, and then as a schoolboy. But whatever he might or might not have been without that training, certain it is that of the many companions of his early years who shared it, none proved a poet, much less a great poet, but himself. And there was my father, as the author remarks at the end, city-bred, yet ready with an Ancient Mariner, and Christabel, as he with his volumes dedicated to Nature. And Milton was city-born and bred too. I suppose, however, that the *detailed* observation of the forms of nature exhibited, as Ruskin remarks, in the works of Mr. Wordsworth, could not have been but for his mountaineer education. How I should like to ruminate over this new feast with Mr. Moore!

II.
Domestic Architecture, Mediæval and Modern.

To Mrs. MOORE, Eccleshall Vicarage, Staffordshire.

Chester Place, July 27th, 1850.—Mr. S —— is coming to see me this evening. He appears charmed with my descriptions of T—— Wood, Eccleshall, and B—— Park. He concludes with, "An old manor-house is to me only •

less sacred and venerable than a church, and many degrees more so than a Dissenting chapel!" I love and admire genuine remains of antiquity in every way; and there certainly was a practical poetry in old times, both ancient and mediæval, which showed itself not only in books, but in pictures, and statues, and buildings. All we can now do, for the most part, is to reproduce this old poetry, to make likenesses of it in a new material.

I must say, however, in regard to dwelling-houses, that the imitation is vastly better than the original, and that no houses of our ancestors could have approached in enjoyableness to T—— Wood and B—— Park. The *lowness* of the rooms is, to our modern feelings, the greatest possible preclusion of comfort. The loftiness of the sleeping rooms at B—— Park is one of their greatest advantages, even more than all the sumptuous and elegant upholstery and pottery. At the house of Sir Thomas Boleyn (father of the unfortunate consort of Henry VIII.), though it is called Castle—something—with much state, or pretension to it, and much that indicates stately living for those times, there is a rudeness in the whole fabric and a stifling want of height in the rooms, which made me feel that our ancestors' way of daily life must have been what we should now pronounce worthy of Gryll, who had such a "hoggish mind," in the days of Spenser.

III.

First appearance of Mr. Tennyson's "In Memoriam"—Moral Tone of the "Prelude"—Neuralgia, and Dante's Demons.

To AUBREY DE VERE, Esq.

10, *Chester Place, August 6th,* 1850.—I have just received your kind present; * many thanks. What a treasure it will be, if I can but think of it and feel about it as you do, and as Mr. T—— does! You said, "the finest strain since Shakespeare;" and afterwards that you and Mr. T——

* "In Memoriam."—E. C.

agreed that it set the author above all modern poets, save only W. W. and S. T. C.

My impression of the pieces you recited was that they expressed great *intensity* of feeling,—but *all* that is in *such* poetry cannot be perceived at first, especially from recitation. The poetry of feeling gains by impassioned recitation, but where there is deep *thought*, as well as emotion in the strain, to do justice to it, we must adopt the usual attitude of study and dwell with our eyes upon the page; for the mind is a creature of habit, and moves but in the accustomed track.

Evening—I have read " In Memoriam " as far as p. 48. I mark with three crosses—

" One writes that other friends remain."

which you recited ;—with one cross the next—

" Dear house," etc.

ditto the next—

" A happy hour," etc.

Most beautiful and Petrarchan is—

" Fair ship, that from the Italian shore."

Very striking is XIV.—p. 22—

" If one should bring me this report."

XIX. and XX. I specially admire; and XXI., and still more XXII.—

" The path by which we twain did go."

There is a very Italian air in this set of mourning poems throughout, as far as I have read. It is Petrarch come again, and become an Englishman.

Morning—I read " In Memoriam " in the night, and was much affected by XXX.—

" With trembling fingers," p. 48.

The last stanza but one is to me obscure, and obscurity mars pathos. At present, many passages are to me not clear, and some, which I *do* understand, strike me as too quaint. For instance, p. 48, last stanza. My father used to complain of Petrarch's eternal *hooks*, and *baits*, and *keys*, which " turned the lock on many a passage of true passion." " A shadow waiting with *keys*, to *cloak* him from his proper scorn," is to me all shadowy and misty, like some of Turner's allegorical pictures, the wantonness and wilfulness of a mist-loving genius, who yet could clear off the mist, and display underneath a bold and beauteous plan, to delight the engraver and the lover of engravings.

This poem, and page 14, and the betrothed tying a riband or a rose, are in his old vein, of bright, fanciful imagery, vivid with detail. But the poems, as a whole, are distinguished by a greater proportion of thought to sensuous imagery, than his old ones; they recede from Keatsland into Petrarchdom, and now and then approach the confines of the Dantescan new hemisphere.

I must tell you that the posthumous Poem* gains to my mind by reperusal. That is a fine passage at page 306. Did you note the explicit recognition of eternal life, eternity and God, at p. 361 ?

Perhaps one of the most striking passages of those that had not been printed before, is that in the Retrospect, describing the shepherd beheld in connection with nature, and thus ennobled and glorified. And, oh! how affectionate is all the concluding portion! I do feel deeply thankful for the revelation of Wordsworth's *heart* in this poem. Whatever sterner feelings may have succeeded at times to this tenderness and these outpourings of love, it raises him greatly in my mind to find that he was able to give himself thus out to another, during one period of his life,— not to absorb all my father's affectionate homage, and to respond no otherwise than by a gracious reception of it. There are many touches too of something like softness, and modesty, and humbleness, which, taken in conjunction with those virtues of his character which are allied to confidence

* "The Prelude."—E. C.

and dignified self-assertion, add much to his character of
amiability. To be humble in *him* was a merit indeed ; and
this merit did not appear so evidently in his later life, as
in these earlier manifestations of his mind.

Some friend has sent me the *Examiner,* which contains a review of the "Prelude," very exalting upon the
whole, and in the main, I think, very just. I should not
say, however, that the poem "will take a place as one of
the most perfect of the author's compositions," although I
agree with the critic in preferring it greatly to his later
performances. The review is vigorously written, and worth
your glancing your eyes over.

How wonderfully the wheel has turned! This poem,
which you and I, strong Wordsworthians, do not think
equal to his poetic works in general of the same date, is
now received with such warm welcome, such high honour
and hearty praise ; while those greatest works of his, when
they first appeared, met with only ridicule from the critical
oracles of the day, scorn or neglect from the public, and
admiration and love only from the few.

The diffuseness, want of condensation, is just noticed,
but I am pleased, I own, at the warmth and high style of
the praise. I think you and I had not *quite* done justice to
the poem, from comparing it with the author's most finished
and finest compositions, rather than viewing it by itself, or
as compared with other men's productions. . . . Passages
are quoted from the Residence at Cambridge, not as best
and noblest in themselves, but, I suppose, as most suited
to the *Examiner* newspaper, and certainly they are
energetic, and contain strong thoughts in strong language.
The passage on Newton I had stroked for admiration
myself. The reviewers emphasize several passages, among
the rest those on Milton,

> "With his rosy cheeks,
> Angelical keen eye, courageous look,
> And conscious step of purity and pride."

That noble line—

> " Uttering odious truth,
> Darkness before, and Danger's voice behind,
> Soul awful——"

I never knew the birthplace of before.

But I must say good-night. This fierce pain clings to me. Oh! how well can I imagine that all the frightful shapes with which the infernal realms have been peopled, the demons with their prongs and pitchforks, may have been mere brain images,—the shaping forth, by way of diversion and relief, in order to send it off from self, of these sharp pangs and shattering, piercing, nerve tortures! The vulture of Prometheus is more mental, but Dante's demons are personifications of Neuralgia and Tic Douloureux, or at least the latter, if they sat for their pictures, would come out just like them. I don't wonder that Dante begged Virgil to dispense with their company, and would rather wander through the horrid circles without guide, than with those fierce ones,

> " deh ; senza scorta andiamci soli,
> Se tu sa 'ir, ch'i per me non la cheggio."

I always fancy I see Dante's piteous, frightened face, and hear his tremulous, eager tones, when he makes this petition.

Don't you observe how much less of sturdy independent pride and reserve there is in Italians and all foreigners, than in us Englishmen ? An English poet would not have written this of himself—he would have thought it babyish; and still more, much of Dante's behaviour with Beatrice, which I always have thought has a touch of Jerry Sneak in it. Indeed he actually compares himself to a baby, fixing its eyes on its ma.

IV.

" In Memoriam : " its Merits and Defects— Shelley's Adonais.

To EDWARD QUILLINAN, Esq., Loughrigg Holme, Ambleside.

Chester Place, August 15th, 1850.—I agree with Mr. Kenyon and Lady Palgrave, who are not mere *friend*-critics, that "In Memoriam" is a highly interesting volume, and worthy to be compared with the poems of Petrarch. I think it like his poems, both in the general scheme, and the execution of particular pieces. The pervading,. though not universal, fault, as you, I think, say too, is quaintness and violence, instead of force; in short, want of truth, which is. at the bottom of all affectation, an endeavour to be some-. thing more, and higher, and better, than the aspirant really and properly is. The heaven of poetry is not to be taken by these means. It is like the Elysium, described to Laodamia, whatever is valuable in that way flows forth spontaneously like the products of nature,. silently and without struggle or noise. How smoothly do all the finest strains of poetry flow on! the noblest passages in the Paradise Lost, and in Mr. Wordsworth's and my father's finest poems! The mind stumbles not over a single word or image.

Shelley's great fault is occasional obscurity, I think. I find this, even in Adonais.

V.

Public Singers—Lovers at the Opera.

To Mrs. MOORE.

Chester Place, August, 1850.—I made a great effort last night to take advantage of Mrs. W. B——'s offer of a seat in her opera box, or one lent her, for myself and Herbert. We heard Sonntag, and for the first time I was thoroughly entranced by a woman's singing. There is a softness and tenderness in the very highest warble of this lady-like singer, a combination of delicacy and brilliancy, which distinguishes her singing from that of all other women whom I have ever heard.

I delight in a man's tenor and contralto voice, but the fine, powerful, high-toned singing of women in general gives me little pleasure, wearies me in less than ten minutes. It wants body, to my feelings; with a masculine background I like it well. Catherine Hayes, in "Lucia," moved me not in the least, and tired me very soon. Coletti, in the "Barber of Seville," the huge Lablache, the pretty-hand-some Gardoni, all pleased me greatly. But, oh! how comical it is to see those opera lovers without a particle of love, grief, or any other emotion in their faces, evidently full of their song, and not a bit of their middle-aged or un-pretty sweetheart, feign to stab themselves in desperation, plump down most inelegantly, warble away to the last, and two minutes afterwards, pick themselves up, and appear before the curtain to bow, and receive the claps and com-pliments of the audience!

VI.
Mr. Coleridge's Influence as an Adviser.
To Rev. HENRY MOORE.

August 25th, 1850.—In order to a good practical judgment two things are required—a clear, strong understanding, and still more, perhaps, a generous, loving, sympathizing nature, which makes the state of another person's affairs, thoughts, feelings, present to the imagination. It was from the possession of these properties that my father's advice in matters of life and action was valuable, that his counsel to men in religious difficulties was felt to be of real service, as many have declared to me since his death. Men who are confined in their thoughts and affections to the narrow circle of self, and self at second hand, cannot give valuable advice to those who are out of that circle; and the world is very apt to confound moderation in discourse, and prudence, with deep and comprehensive judgment, which rests on a very different basis, and results from far deeper qualities.

VII.

Spiritual Truths beheld by the Eye of Faith in the Light of Reason—The Gospel its own best Evidence.

To EDWARD QUILLINAN, Esq.

Chester Place, September 10th, 1850.—What I said to you the other day about the inseparability of faith from reason was only an attempt to express a characteristic doctrine of my father's, which has planted itself firmly in my mind. I spoke of reason, not as the faculty of *reasoning*, of reflecting, weighing, judging, comparing, but as the organ of spiritual truth, the eye of the mind, which perceives the substantial ideas and verities of religion as the bodily eye sees colours and shapes. It seems to me, that a tenet which does not embody some idea which our mental eye can behold, is no proper object of faith. St. Paul says that we are to *know* the things that are given us of God, that they are to be spiritually *discerned*, that God *reveals* them to the faithful, yea, the deep things of God. Our saving faith consists, I think, in a spiritual beholding, a perception of truth of the highest order, which purifies the heart, and changes the soul from glory to glory, while it gazes on the image of the divine perfections. The holy apostle prays that "the eyes of our understanding being enlightened," we may *know* Jesus Christ, and what is the hope of His calling. The doctrine of implicit faith, that men are saved by believing *something* to be true of which they have no idea or knowledge, I cannot find in the Bible. My not finding would be nothing if others could find and show it me. But who can show it there? It seems to me to be a doctrine of fallible men, not of Christ Himself, who always speaks of His teaching as being in accordance with the constitution and faculties which God has given us, as having its *witness* in our own hearts and minds, if they are not darkened by clouds of prejudice and passion. Reason is alike in all mankind, I therefore arrogate nothing to myself in particular when I

2 B

express my agreement with the maxim of my father and many other thoughful men, that faith consists in a spiritual beholding, "the evidence of things not seen" with the bodily eye.   "By faith we *understand,*" says the writer to the Hebrews, "that the worlds were framed by the word of God."

The Divinity of our Saviour, His Atonement, Justification by Faith, all the great doctrines of our religion, have been shown by the great fathers and doctors of the Church to be doctrines of reason, which may be spiritually discerned.   If it were not for the witness of our hearts and minds to these great truths, I can hardly imagine that they would be generally received.   The outward evidences are not appreciated by the masses, and by themselves would never suffice, I think, to a hearty reception of the Gospel.   We are early *told* that the Bible is the Word of God, and believe it implicitly.   But if we did not find and feel it to be divine, as our minds unfold and we begin to inquire and seek a reason for our beliefs, surely this early faith would fall from us as the seed-leaves from the growing plant, the husk from the blossom and fruit.

I cannot think that there is any *outward* proof of the divinity of the Bible at all adequate to its general reception. People do not always theorize rightly on their faith ; but many think they have had proof of their religion *ab extra,* when in reality it clings to them from its direct appeals to their heart and spiritual sense.

VIII.

Character of Christian in the " Pilgrim's Progress."

To the Hon. Mr. Justice COLERIDGE.

October .9th, 1850.—I have been reading right through the " Pilgrim's Progress," with as much pleasure as if it was the first time.   The only fault I *feel*, or care about, is that Christian, in his discourse with Talkative and with

[gnorance, appears somewhat captious, peremptory, and
overbearing. And, indeed, I must ever think that poor
Ignorance had rather hard measure from first to last. The
conclusion is sadly kill-joyed by the lugging of him off and
poking him into that horrid hill-side. Many a good
Christian would be willing enough to adopt Ignorance's
declaration of faith just as it stands.

IX.

Comparative Merits of Sir Walter Scott's Novels—Severity of Satirists
on the Faults of their own Country or Class.

To AUBREY DE VERE, Esq.

October, 1850, *Chester Place.*—I am re-perusing some
of the earlier Walter Scott novels, with great delight.
"The Antiquary" is one of the very best, the fullest of
genuine original matter. Oldbuck himself is a Sternean
character. Elspeth is Macbethish, but Edie Ochiltree is
the charm of the work. He is true poetry, a conception
between Scott and Wordsworth, or at least with a
third part of Wordsworth. The marrow of Scott's genius
was put into this old Gaberlunzie and Bluegown. "Rob
Roy" is *very* good, but not *so* good, more manufactured
and will-wrought, in part. How admirable, though, is all
that description of the Sabbath and the Laigh Kirk congregation at Glasgow. The Bailie, too, is very amusing.
Andrew Fairservice is a satire on the Scotch of the keenest
description. Do not we always find that the sharpest,
most home strokes of satire come from those who are *near*
to the subject of it, or even identified with it. Hook showed
up the lords and lordlings of his day. Mrs. Gore exposes
the follies of her fellow-fashionists. Berkeley and Swift
have published all the characteristic faults of their countrymen to the world; and Scott, and Galt, and Miss Hamilton,
betray all the meanest and most odious peculiarities of
theirs. Miss Edgeworth, too, in her "Absentee" and
"Castle Rack-rent," has drawn as dark a picture of Ireland

as the most decided enemy could have exhibited; and the author of the "Collegians" has written about Irish middle men what, from an English pen, would have been considered a libel.

X.

Sympathy of Friends—Collection of her Brother Hartley's Works—Article in the *Quarterly* on the Homeric Controversy—Infidelity—Attacks on Revelation.

To the Rev. EDWARD COLERIDGE.

1850.—Your letter is, what I expected from you, kind and comfortable. Since my trial * began (and it is not light, all circumstances considered) I have received so many marks of warm sympathy and active kindness from friends, and from dear Derwent and Mary such affectionate treatment, that some good has grown out of the evil. My estimate of the kindliness of my fellow-creatures, and the goodness of my own set of friends in particular, has been raised some degrees higher. The collection of our dear Hartley's Remains, with Derwent's Memoir, is in the press, and I confess I have warm expectations from both, that they will at least deeply interest and delight a certain circle, if not a wide, yet a refined and genial one.

If we could but obtain the Worthies, and had encouragement to publish a collection of the printed essays, with the beautiful critique on Hamlet in Blackwood, there would be a compact little set of works, doubly gratifying to us as evidence that poor Hartley did not wholly waste the gifts with which he was entrusted, or dream away his genius without an attempt to benefit his fellow-creatures by it, by affording them refined amusement, and in some sense enlightenment.

The article in the *Quarterly* on Mure's book and the Homeric Controversy is able, and contains much truth;

* It was during the summer of 1850 that serious anxiety first began to be felt about my mother's state of health.—E. C.

ut it is also full of unfairness, misrepresentation of argument, and plausible, but not deeply considered, positions.
This I cannot but think, though I never pretended to a
positive general opinion on the authorship of the Homeric
poems; and while I entertained Wolf's idea of the possibility
that the poems were national and the work of a school, as
did also Mr. Wordsworth, Southey, and, I believe, Scott
(and *they* may be supposed to have a poetic intuition), I
have always seen unity in the plan of the "Iliad," what
seems to me a true Achilleid. The unfairness of the article
to the Germans is gross, and to lay on their shoulders those
opinions about Titus Andronicus and The Two Noble
Kinsmen, which were English before they were German, is
ridiculous. The proof from internal evidence, the delineation of character, knowledge of the human heart, etc., seems
to me very doubtful. You may see the tenderest touches of
pathos, of very similar character, in our old ballads, which
none deny to be by different hands.

Did you mark what is said in the beginning of that
article (p. 438) on the subject of the *common foe* to
Christianity? No attempt at answering *Strauss* amid all
the thousand pamphlets upon theories of doctrine, the
practical result of which is insignificant. *That* is indeed a
fearful subject; that way the danger lies; and as there are
sorrows too deep for tears, so are there perils and ills too
real and serious for noise and agitation.

Infidelity creeps on in silence. Men whisper it to each
other; no man boasts of it, or parades it; few even argue
for it. Dr. Newman said the other day to some controver-
sialist, "Let us talk about the prospects of Christianity
itself, instead of the differences between Anglican and
Catholic." Why does not he answer the adversary?
Silent contempt is not politic in such a case. It is too
ambiguous. Let our churchmen conquer first and contemn
afterwards. So our doughty old divines proceeded; and,

every age needs its own evidences and arguments against infidelity, as in every age the attack upon revealed religion takes a form suited to the time.

P.S.—What I have said about infidelity is from the informations and lamentations of truly religious men. I talk with none but such. It is not the mere boasting of the foe.

XI.

Her native Vale of Keswick; and the Valley of Life—"Alton Locke."
To E. QUILLINAN, Esq.

10, *Chester Place, November 14th,* 1850.—The sight of your handwriting this morning gave me great pleasure: first, as coming from you,—secondly, as coming from a place and neighbourhood in which, to the end of my mortal pilgrimage, my heart and imagination will ever be most deeply interested. Keswick, and Rydal, and Grasmere—then Netherhall and its neighbourhood—but the two first far before the last, will ever be the scene of the millennial reign for me. They are my Eden—watered with my tears as they were. But how truly says the Poet,—

> " Dewdrops are the gems of morning,
> But the tears of mournful eve."

Now there is a knock at the door! Oh! how I hate these peremptory knocks, now I have no goodman to expect, either morning, noon, or night. Well, well! it is one comfort in sorrow that he and my dear mother had not to share my present trouble. Poor Nurse has accompanied me all through this thorny valley, step by step; indeed, she has her own thorns and stones on her side of the way, and we mutually pity and seek to console each other.

.   .   .   .

Have you read "Alton Locke"? Sir F. Palgrave thinks "poetry, and of a high order of conception."

XII.

Early and late Periods of the Wordsworthian Poetry compared with Ancient and Modern Art—Mr. Ruskin's "Modern Painters"—Scott's Novels—Character-drawing in the "Black Dwarf"—The Anti-Papal Demonstration—Aversion to Popery in the English Mind—The Pope's Move political not religious—Intolerance of Romanism.

To Professor HENRY REED, Philadelphia.

10, *Chester Place, Regent's Park, November 29th,* 1850.— My dear Friend,—Many thanks to you for two most interesting volumes. The "Descriptive Sketches," with your inscriptions, is a very gratifying present to me. I have always wished to possess early editions of Mr. Wordsworth's works, but have not been able to lay hold of many. I cannot bear the arrangement of his poems in the later editions by subject, without regard to date. The *tone* of the productions of the poet's second and third eras is as unlike that of his great vigorous day as a picture of Stanfield to one by Claude or Poussin; and who would mix modern painting in a gallery with those of the old hands? I remember seeing an exhibition of Calcott's landscape painting in the third room of the British Gallery, ancient masters occupying the first and second. You can hardly imagine the deadening effect upon them. They were reduced to chalk and water. Any believer in Ruskin, I think, must have been staggered by that most odious, or at least injurious, comparison and contrast. Not that I do not admire Ruskin's *first* book: it has great merits; but it never converted or perverted me from Claude, and Cuyp, and S. Rosa, though it made me more than ever, if possible, a worshipper of the great mistress of all painters—Nature. The edition of Gray and your Memoir are a valuable addition to my library. I possess the Eton edition, and had lately been reading Mitford's Memoir, which rendered yours all the more interesting. Yours ought to supersede every other. I think your conclusion about Gray's poetic power is the truth of the matter. The author of the "Elegy," admirable as his poetry is, in its line, would never, I think, under any circumstances have helped to found a new school of poetry. His mind did not present a broad enough surface for the spirit of the age to operate on, even if the new age, which moulded, and was moulded by, the last generation of poets and romancers, had set in while he was in his vigour. No new aspect of humanity or nature is exhibited in his writings. Even Cowper was, in my opinion, far more original as to thought and way of viewing things; and the personal character of Cowper was more broad, bold, and interesting than that of Gray. I am re-perusing with great delight the *Scotch* novels of Walter Scott. I do not think "Ivanhoe" and the latter works, not on Scottish ground at all, to be reckoned among the great influencive literary productions of the age—productions of genius—along with "Waverley," "Guy Mannering," "The Antiquary" (perhaps the best of all), "Rob Roy," "The Black Dwarf" (which has been underrated), "Old Mortality," "The Heart of Mid-Lothian," and "The Bride of Lammermoor." "The Black Dwarf" has an especial merit in exhibiting the odd mixture of feelings and opinions on particular subjects which may exist in uneducated, unreflective minds. Hobbie is persuaded that Father Elshie has dealings with the Evil One, and would try to prejudice his salvation if he had an opportunity, yet is willing to receive a benefit at his hands, and is grateful for it, and is affectionately disposed toward the donor, as if he believed him as "canny" as other folks. The tale, however, was overshadowed by the superior merit of "Old Mortality;" and no doubt it has more than the ordinary amount of absurdity in the foundation.

I own I rejoice in the anti-papal demonstration. The fear and anger of this crisis will, of course, subside; but what has taken place proves, and will show the Romanists and Romanizers, that there is a deep-seated and wide-spread aversion to Popery in this fair realm of England, which will come into effective action whenever any attempt is made to re-introduce a form of religion which is the natural and necessary enemy to liberty in all times and in every place. I cannot agree with C—— S——, who thinks we are straining at a gnat after swallowing the camel of Emancipation. There was nothing that directly endangered our Church in a Romanist's sitting in Parliament; and the principles of toleration and equal dealing with all religions, *as such*, seemed to demand the concession. But this act is, in reality, a political movement, and ought to be politically resisted. My Uncle Southey would have refused Emancipation in the foresight of this and similar aggressions; but it was better to give them *rope* enough to strangle their own cause in the hearts of the whole nation. Now, no man can say that the intolerance and ambition of Romanism are obsolete: all must see that it is a born Ishmael; its hand is against every other form of religion, and every other form must keep a controlling hand upon it.

NOTES ON PROFESSOR REED'S MEMOIR OF GRAY.

1. Liberality of Military Men—Mathematics opposed to Poetry, Professor Sedgwick on Newton and Milton. 2. Hereditary Genius—Her Father and his Son Hartley. 3. A Point of Style discussed. 4. Salutary Effect of Early Happiness on the Mind. 5. Horace Walpole and Gray—Frivolity of the Former. 6. Gray's Genius and its Limitations—Keats' Hyperion. 7. Handwritings of Men of Genius. 8. Talfourd's "Ion." 9. Landor as Scholar, Critic, and Poet. 10. De Quincey's Opinion of Dr. Parr. 11. Mr. Coleridge's Criticism of "The Ode on Eton College." 12. Causes of the Popularity of Gray's "Elegy." 13. Speaking of Ailments, a Relief. 14. Gray at Keswick. 15. "Tintern Abbey." 16. Powers Measured by Results. 17. High Spirits.

To Professor HENRY REED, Philadelphia.

1. "Now, gentlemen, I would rather be the author of

that poem than take Quebec." * This is indeed a most
interesting anecdote. Query, is it characteristic of military
men to be thus liberal and unappropriative? I certainly
think that no class of men are so antipathetic to poetry as
men of science, mathematicians, and students of the particular sciences to which mathematics are applied. The
wider study which we call philosophy, the science of mind
and of being, metaphysics at large, is not thus antagonistic
to poetry, which it embraces in the compass of its analysis.
A metaphysician like Kant is too knowing, too all-sided in
knowledge, to despise poetry as a mere mathematician does.
Plato's sentence upon poetry in the Republic has probably
been misunderstood. Chemistry seems akin to poetry,
from the brilliant shows and curious combinations which it
deals with and produces: it is full of sensuous matter for
poetic thought. Davy poetized, though he was not a *poet*.
I have heard Mr. Wordsworth say he might have been;
but I think my father, though he overflowed with love and
admiration of Davy, would not have subscribed to that
opinion. He thought William Wordsworth too lavish in his
attributions of poetic power in some directions, as he was
generally considered too slow to allow it in others. When,
in my girlhood, I visited my brother Derwent at St. John's
College, Cambridge, with my dear mother, Professor Sedgwick showed me the statue of Newton by Roubilliac; and
I remember his expressing an opinion, from which my
young mind strongly dissented, that he was a far greater
man than Milton. He knew far more of Newton's merits
than I did; but even then I *felt* Milton as many able,
intelligent men can never do. And I doubt whether the
power and services of a philosopher like Newton cannot be
far better estimated by one unlearned in mathematics and
astronomy, than those of the author of "Paradise Lost"

---

* Remark of General Wolfe on Gray's "Elegy in a Country Churchyard."
—E. C.

by one who does not *understand* poetry. For the benefit of
poetry is poetry itself: both to the composer and the
reader, it is its own exceeding great reward.

2. Eminent men, especially in literature, have often, that
is, many eminent men have owed more to their mother than
their father, both for nature and education. It was so with
Cowper, and with my Uncle Southey. But the truth, no
doubt, is, that the parent whose mental qualities are most
powerful and excellent, most moulds the child that attains
to eminence, whether it be father or mother; and when it
happens to be the latter that is best endowed, we are struck
to find that man has derived less from man than from
woman. Seldom has a poet had so poetical a son as
S. T. C. had in Hartley. Not one poet of this age beside
has transmitted a spark of his fire to his offspring; but it
is curious that Hartley excelled most in the sonnet, in which
my father excelled least of all the poetic forms that he
attempted.

3. "A father's wrongs." Is not this a doubtful expression? But for what had gone before, we should suppose
wrongs *suffered by a father* to be meant. A *wrong* is not a
wrongful thing done, but undergone, I think, in common
parlance. "Your injuries" is more ambiguous; perhaps
this is a wrong of mine, my active wrong to your style.

4. All that you say in these pages about the enduring
benefit of early happiness and tranquillity is well said, and
to my mind most true.   It is good for children to be happy
and cheerful; early sorrow weakens the mind, if it does not
harden it, as premature disproportionate labour injures the
body. I know this by experience, and have carefully
shielded my children's young minds from the trouble and
constraints which so often came upon my own, like frosts
and wintry blasts on the "darlings of the spring."

5. "Horace Walpole."—The oftener one meets Walpole
in the region of literary biography, the more the impres-

sion is intensified, that he was a respectable fribble, and a compact solid mass of frivolity and littleness. Poets are men of feeling κατ᾽ ἐξοχην. They are like soft rich peaches, and he was the crude, hard, winter pear, that leaves a dint in every one of the former with which it comes in contact.

6. I should think Gray could never have written a philosophic poem under any circumstances. I do not believe that Keats would ever have written anything better or higher than he had already produced. The "Hyperion," so exalted by Shelley, is, to my mind, a falling-off in felicitous originality. It is too Miltonic. Gray was a very sensible man, and self-knowing. His own remarks on the poetical habits which unfitted him for the production of a poem of large compass seem to me excellent, and are just what I have so often heard in other words from W. Wordsworth and H. Taylor. There must be flat rough spaces in an extensive domain, if it is to be traversed with pleasure, and Gray could not be flat and rough like Dante. He had not masculine force enough for that. His verse, if not neat and polished, would have been nothing. Elegance and tenderness are its very soul.

7. "Delicate handwriting."—It is remarkable what fine hands men of genius write, even when they are as awkward in all other uses of the hand as a cow with a musket.

8. Do you think "Ion" a work of poetic genius, or only of an admirer of poetic genius? There was a want of poetic judgment in putting such intense Wordsworthian *modernism* into an ancient form, I thought; like drinking Barclay's entire out of an antique drinking vessel, meant to hold Chian or Falernian wine. "Ion" was of the same kind as the Düsseldorf reproductions of Raphael.

9. Landor would be pleased at your compliment to his verse Latinity. I have been wont to hear scholars say that his Latin verse had merit, but not that of classi-

cality. Last winter's number of the *Edinburgh Review*
contains an article on Landor's poetry by my friend
Mr. Aubrey de Vere. The article contains an ingenious
and eloquent comparison and contrast between the genius
of ancient Greece and that of Catholic Christianity with
reference to poetry and the arts. But it failed to inspire
me with any warm admiration of the poetic productions of
Landor. In him I had, as a girl, an implicit faith, induced
upon me by my uncle's attributions to the great self-
assertor, whose most amiable trait, I must think, is his
cordial admiration of, and warm testimonies to, Robert
Southey. Landor's criticism is very acute and refined;
his dialogues I admire; but his poems appear to me cold
and ineffective,—the verse of a man too knowing and
tasteful to write bad poetry, but without poetic genius to
write well. At least, such was the impression on my
mind. Some few passages of Landor's poetry are striking.
I was a little disappointed that you did not notice here my
father's notes on "Gray's Platonica." "Whatever might
be expected from a scholar, a gentleman, a man of exquisite
taste, as the quintessence of sane and sound good sense,
Mr. Gray appears to me to have performed. The poet
Plato, etc., etc. But Plato the philosopher was not to be
comprehended within the field of vision, or to be commanded by the fixed immovable telescope of Mr. Locke's
human understanding."

10. De Quincey ("the Opium Eater," as he un-
disguisedly calls himself), called Parr a coarse old savage,
and whatever his scholarship might be, would give him
little credit, I believe, for any judgment on the internal
merits of Plato.

11. Ode to Eton College. My father criticises the stanza
" Say, Father Thames," as the " only very objectionable one
in point of diction;" the worst ten lines, he calls it, in all

the works of Mr. Gray; "falsetto throughout, harsh and feeble." He also condemns—

1 And Envy wan, etc.
2 Grim visaged, etc.
3 And sorrow's piercing dart.

As, 1, bad in the first; 2, in the second; 3, in the last degree. How different the fate of poor "Christabel," when she did appear! Enemies so fierce that even old friends seemed afraid to admire and protect her. I have heard her sneered at, and Lord Byron's praise called flummery, by men who *now* would as soon think of sneering at Gray's Elegy as at the "wild and original poem." I wonder what Dodsley's "pinches" were. One would rather not have any particular locality for the Elegy, than have one assigned, I think.

12. The strain of *thought* in the Elegy would not have made it popular without the strain of verse, the metrical accordance with the tone of feeling in the contents. But this metrical accordance is surely but the *causa sine qua non* of its general acceptability. The efficient cause—the peculiar merit—I have ever supposed to be that inexpressible felicity and delightfulness of diction of which the line noticed by Sir E. Brydges, "The rude forefathers of the hamlet sleep," is but one instance out of a host. Then the composition and combination of the sentiments and images —in *this* lies the charm—more than in the images themselves. These, indeed, were not new—scarce one but had been presented in poetry before. It has been the fashion with admirers of Shelley and Keats to disparage Gray. I remember coming out bluntly to my friend Mr. de Vere with the opinion, that he looked coldly upon the author of the Elegy, purely because he was simple and intelligible, and used the English language in the ordinary senses, not procuring for himself a *semblance* of the sublime by an easily

assumed obscurity, and a mock magnificence by straining and inflection. For the same reason Crabbe is undervalued by devotees of Tennyson. Yet his "Tales of the Hall" display an acquaintance with the fine shades of human character, and the various phases and aspects of human sorrow—a vein of reflectiveness softened by poetic feeling, which render them a most interesting study to persons who have seen enough of life, as it is, in all its strangeness and sadness, to recognize the truth and worth of his representations. I believe that Crabbe, in his personal character, has all that sympathy with suffering humanity which appears in his poems; yesterday I read a private letter of his, in which he laments over the introduction of machinery—and yet allows for the necessity of the employers to use agents that "do not eat and drink." His sympathy with both parties is remarkable. I believe he was a gentle-hearted creature.

13. How stupid not to like the "Long Story"! Surely that might have been understood at once. "Not a wise remembrance." It is sometimes a relief thus to *objectize* our ailments. It seems to cast them *out* from us and give us a sort of mastery over them. The dumb state of misery, when one dares not talk of it, is by far the worst. Then it seems to possess one's whole being. There is a comfort also in looking back, and seeing what miseries one has gone through before and got beyond.

14. "Tour to the Lakes." It is said that Gray set the fashion of touring to the English Lakes in search of the picturesque. His horse-block is still shown near the vicarage of Keswick, on a hill overlooking Crosthwaite churchyard, where my Uncle's and Aunt Southey's remains lie buried, with Skiddaw in front.

15. Tintern Abbey. The "Lines on Tintern Abbey" is, in my opinion, one of the finest strains of verse which this age has produced.

16. This disquisition is very interesting. I think it is not sufficiently attended to, that "what a man does is the measure of what he can do," from one cause or another.

17. "High spirits take away mine."* The quiet gladness of children always cheers me; but the hilarity and vigour of grown persons depress the weak and tremulous spirits. We are hurt by the want of sympathy; and the comparison is odious.

* A saying of Gray's.—E. C.

CHAPTER XXIV.

LETTERS TO THE REV. HENRY MOORE, MRS. MOORE, MISS FENWICK, MRS. FARRER, AUBREY DE VERE, ESQ., EDWARD QUILLINAN, ESQ., PROFESSOR HENRY REED : 1851.

I.

Causes of the Indifference to the Papal Aggression displayed both by Ultra-High Churchmen and Ultra-Liberals—Mixed Character of all National Movements—The Three Chief Religious Parties, and the Right of each to a place in the English Church.

To MRS. MOORE.

10, *Chester Place, January 2nd,* 1851.—I should much like to know Mr. Moore's opinion on the present crisis in the Church. I think you and he and Miss H—— generally agree on matters of this kind, your root principles and sentiments being pretty much the same ; and therefore I mention only him, his being the masculine voice of the trio. We, in this house, are very decided anti-papal aggressionists, and I, for my part, am too regular a " John Bulliaǹa," as Sir F. Palgrave once called me, to give in to any of the new-fangled views of toleration preached up by the ultra-church party on one hand, and the ultra-liberal party on the other. I conceive that a certain sympathy with Rome inspires these views in the former, secret hopes of a re-union of Christendom, and reluctance to adopt any strong measure, or use any strong language against his Holiness; and that, in the latter, they proceed from indifference both to Anglicanism and Romanism, an opinion that the pretensions of the vicar of Christ are not more nugatory and chimerical, even if more extravagant, than those of our own priests and bishops.

I cannot help thinking that this indifference and scorn

2 c

in the latter party would shrink into a very small compass
—I mean that few respectable and thoughtful men would
entertain it—if the pretensions and claims of the clergy in
our Church were put on a more rational, intelligible foundation, if they were moral rather than mystical, according to
the spirit of the Reformation, and entirely purified from
Romish and *dark-agish* superstitions. However that may
be, I rejoice in the demonstration against Popery which is
now making by the people of England, and I have been
telling Mr. —— that to style it a *no-Popery* row about the
royal supremacy is more sarcastic than just. The movement has a thousand different grades and faces, but it is
partaken by a very large proportion of the worthiest and
most refined of the clergy and laity of this land. How
could a national movement like this fail to include in its
lower circles all that was low and abhorrent to the wise and
well-educated? All the great movements to which we owe
our present high place among the nations have carried
along with them a mass of iniquity. Maurice, in his
" Church a Family," observes that " when the words ' no
Virgin Mary,' ' no forgiveness of sins,' are seen written
upon our walls, clergymen should think a little before they
fill whole sermons with specimens of Mariolatry, or with
the perversions of the confessional."

I protest I cannot see the logic of this. ("How should
you," Mr. Moore would say, "being of the illogical sex?")
Ministers of the gospel, a part of whose vocation is to
drive away false doctrine and prevent schism, are to refrain
from preaching against the corruptions of Popery, even
when it is beleaguering us round about and thundering at
our very gates, because idle, irreligious boys scribble
thoughtless nonsense upon the walls! "No Virgin Mary"
may be a good Protestant sentiment, it may mean *no
Virgin to be made an object of worship*, and "no forgiveness
of sins" may mean *superstitiously by a priest*. If it is meant

in the literal sense, it is a denial of revealed religion; and what have we to do with that?

The irreligion of these scribblers is not caused by controversial sermons, but arises from want and misery and spiritual destitution, and is to be met by positive remedies, if at all, not by abstinence from a particular line of preaching fitly addressed to any decent congregation.

I dare say you will agree with me on one point with respect to the present movement, and that is in detesting the silly, narrow, shabby way in which Tractarianism has been attacked in so many quarters, or rather Tractarians. This is sheer party spirit and overbearing intolerance. *Some* of the Tractarians are really disloyal to our Church, and it is too true that many do unintentionally, by the tenor and spirit of their preaching, send younger men to Rome, while they themselves are not prepared to go that length in honour of their principles. But the main body of the Anglo-Catholics have as much right to keep their places in our Church as the main body of the Evangelicals, or the Philosophicals.

Tractarianism is as wide and vague a word as Rationalism or Germanism; every man so calls his neighbour who is more High Church than himself, and adopts more of those doctrines and practices which belong to Rome and are not forbidden to us, than he thinks proper to do; and so, too, every man accuses every other man of Rationalism who doubts the truth or accuracy of any tenet or doctrinal formula which he holds sacred, on the score of its wanting reason.

The Tractarian party have shown such an intolerant spirit themselves on many occasions, that I own my feelings are more of contemptuous indignation against their adversaries than of sympathy with themselves. Even now how many of them are pining for a Convocation, which, as they flatter themselves, is to banish from the Church the

school represented to their minds by Gorham.   A decree of
the assembled Synod is to drive away the whole multitude
of those who will not declare positively before God and man
that *all* infants are internally regenerate *in* baptism, and
rendered secure of heaven *by* baptism, a belief not properly
compatible with belief in election; for St. Augustine's
regeneration of the non-elect was a mere term for baptism,
implying no spiritual gift whatever, no forgiveness of sin,
or possession by the Spirit.

Now, this would be to banish a school which has existed
in the Church ever since the Reformation, and is in reality
quite as intolerant as the conduct of their adversaries in
the present moment, though it may not have been manifested in so coarse and childish a form, simply because
Anglo-Catholicism is not a popular mode of faith, and has
never spread so wide nor gone so low in the mass of society
as puritanical Protestantism.

II.

Letter to Countess Ida Hahn-Hahn by Abeken—" Death's Jest Book," and other Dramatic Works, by Mr. Beddoes.

To Mrs. FARRER, 3, Gloucester Terrace.

Chester Place, January, 1851.—I am much pleased at your
concurrence of opinion with me about the letter to Countess
Ida.   It is by Abeken, a great friend of the Chevalier
Bunsen.   This little work sets forth the distinctive characters of Romanism and Protestantism more forcibly, I
should almost say *profoundly*, than any other work I have
met with.   The defence of the Reformation seems to me
admirable.   It mirrored to me all my own views with new
force and distinctness.

Dearest Mrs. Farrer, you once kindly sent some dramatic
poems of Beddoes here, which I declined reading, not liking
my impression of the "Death's Jest Book," in which I saw
much to admire, to be interfered with, and hearing they

were much inferior to that. Just before I went into Staffordshire, I received that drama from the author, and put it aside. After my return I took it up, considering it a duty at least to look it through. I had been repelled by the first peep I took into it. Those were my days, or rather nights, of reading in bed, and so struck was I with the powerful original imagery, and some of the wild situations of the drama, that I did not lay it down till I had perused the whole. I was really thrilled with some parts, the effect, perhaps, being enhanced by the nightly gloom and silence. Well, I resolved to express my admiration to the author the very next day, and I was not the less inclined to be pleased, that on the blank leaf I found a gratifying inscription, and that the author was the son of an old Bristol friend of my father. But in the morning came a letter from Mr. Quillinan, expressing warm admiration of the drama I had just been reading, and at the same time announcing the death of the author in rapid decline. I thought mournfully of Gray's elegiac sentiment—

"Can flattery soothe the dull cold ear of death?"

It was not flattery, in the common acceptation of the word, that I meant to address to Mr. Beddoes, but a sincere tribute of praise, for as much as it was worth.

Yet, after all, dear Mrs. Farrer, I quite agree in your strictures on this same striking production. The plot is most extravagant, and some of the characters are so wicked for mere wickedness' sake, that they are placed without the pale of humanity, and therefore out of reach of our human interests and sympathies. Still, with all these great faults, the play interested me greatly.

III.

Mr. Carlyle's "Life of Sterling"—Autobiography of Leigh Hunt—
Epicureanism.

To Miss MORRIS.

March 12th, 1851.—Did you read Carlyle's "Life of
Sterling"? To me the work is fascinating, as far as the
biographical part is concerned. Dr. Calvert (Sterling's
dear friend) was a lifelong intimate friend of mine. The
chapter on S. T. C. is ridiculous. Leigh Hunt's Autobiography is most entertaining. What a Christianified epicureanism is his religion! Yet such is the religion of a
large portion of our amiable, refined, intelligent men. High
Churchmen, Evangelical, Sceptical, Epicurean, such are
the chief divisions of religious thought, I believe, among the
educated nowadays.

IV.

Early Reminiscences of the Character and Conversation of Mr. Wordsworth and Mr. Southey—Youthful Impressions mostly Unconscious—The Platonic Ode—The "Triad" compared with "Lycidas"
—The "Prelude"—Testimonies contained in it to the Friendship
between her Father and Mr. Wordsworth.

To Professor HENRY REED, Philadelphia.

Chester Place, May 19th, 1851.—I dare say that you and
your friend, Mr. Yarnall, have lately been dwelling a good
deal on the two-volume "Memoir of Wordsworth," which I
finished slowly perusing last night in my hours of wakeful-
ness. For, alas! I sleep but every other night,—the intervening one is now almost wholly sleepless. Mr. H. C.
Robinson requested that I would use the pencil or pen
freely on the margin of his copy: "the more notes the
better." I fear he will be greatly disappointed by what I
have written, and I almost wish it rubbed out, it is so
trifling, and in some instances not to the purpose—as, I
fear, the owner of the book will think. I knew dear Mr.
Wordsworth perhaps as well as I have ever known any one

in the world—more intimately than I knew my father, and as intimately as I knew my Uncle Southey. There was much in him to know, and the lines of his character were deep and strong—the whole they formed, simple and impressive. His discourse, as compared with my father's, was as the Latin language to the Greek, or, to borrow a comparison which has been applied to Shakespeare and Milton, as statuary to painting; it was intelligent, wise, and easily remembered. But in my youth, when I enjoyed such ample opportunities of taking in his mind, I listened to "enjoy and not to understand," much less to report and inform others. In our springtime of life we are poetical, not literary, and often absorb unconsciously the intellectual airs that blow or stilly dwell around us, as our bodies do the fragrant atmosphere of May,—full of the breath of primroses and violets,—and are nourished thereby without reflecting upon the matter, any more than we classify and systematize after Linnæus or Jussieu, the vernal blossoms which delight our outward senses. I used to take long walks with Mr. Wordsworth about Rydal and Grasmere, and sometimes, though seldom, at Keswick, to his Applethwaite cottage, listening to his talk all the way; and for hours have I often listened when he conversed with my uncle, or indoors at Rydal Mount, when he chatted or harangued to the inmates of his household or the neighbours. But I took no *notes* of his discourse either on the tablet of memory or on material paper; my mind and turn of thought were gradually moulded by his conversation, and the influences under which I was brought by his means in matters of intellect, whilst in those which concerned the heart and the moral being I was still more deeply and importantly indebted to the character and daily conduct of my admirable Uncle Southey. Yet I never adopted the opinions of either *en masse,* and since I have come to years of secondary and more mature reflection, I have been unable to retain many which I received from them. The impression upon my feelings of their minds remains unabated in force; but the formal views and judgments which I received from their lips are greatly modified, though not more than they themselves modified and re-adjusted their own views and judgments from youth to age.

You express surprise at something I let fall in a former letter, on what I consider the difference and inferiority in kind of Mr. Wordsworth's late poems from those of his youth and middle age. I must own that I do see this very strongly, and should as little think of comparing that on the "Power of Sound" with the "Platonic Ode," or the "Song at the Feast of Brougham Castle;" as—what shall I say?—the Crystal Palace with Windsor Castle; or the grand carved sideboard in the former with 'the broad oak of the forest when its majestic stem of strong and solid wood is robed in foliage of tender, mellow green. Those earlier odes seem to be *organic* wholes: the first of them is in some sort an image of the individual spirit of which it is an efflux. The energy and felicity of its language is so great, that every passage and every line of it has been received into the poetical heart of this country, and has become the common expression of certain moods of mind and modes of thought, which had hardly been developed before its appearance. The ode on the "Power of Sound," like the "Triad," is an elegant composition by a poetic artist—a poetical will-work, not as a whole, I should say, a piece of inspiration, though some lines in it are breathings of the poetic spirit.

I confess, at the risk of lowering my taste in your esteem, which I should be right sorry to do, yet not liking to retain it by mere suppression of a part of my mind—a serious and decided part, which has stood assaults of poetic reasoning of no small force and animation; I do confess that I have never been able to rank the "Triad" among Mr. Words-

worth's immortal works of genius. It is just what he came
into the poetical world to condemn, and both by practice
and theory to supplant. It is, to my mind, *artificial* and
unreal. There is no truth in it as a whole, although bits
of truth, glazed and magnified, are embodied in it, as in the
lines, "Features to old ideal grace allied," a most unintelligible allusion to a likeness discovered in dear Dora's
contour of countenance to the great Memnon head in the
British Museum, with its overflowing lips and width of
mouth, which seems to be typical of the ocean. The poem
always strikes me as a mongrel—an amphibious thing,
neither portrait nor ideal, but an ambiguous cross between
the two. Mr. de Vere, before he knew me, took it for a
personification of Faith, Hope, and Charity, taken in
inverse order—a sufficient proof, I think, that it is extravagant and unnatural as a description of three young
ladies of the nineteenth century. In "Lycidas," poetic
idealism is not brought so closely into contrast and conflict
with familiar reality, as in the "Triad," because it contains
no description of the individual. The theme in reality is
quite general and abstract—death by drowning of the friend
of a great poet, in his bloom of youth, a minister of the
Gospel. This theme is adorned with all the pomp and
garniture of classic and Hebraic imagery that could be
clustered and cumulated round it. After all, in theory
Milton's mixture of Pagan mythology with the spiritualities
of the Gospel is not defensible. The best defence of
"Lycidas" is not to defend the design of it at all, but to
allege that the execution is perfect, the diction the *ne plus
ultra* of grace and loveliness, and that the spirit of the
whole is as original as if the poem contained no traces of
the author's acquaintance with ancient pastoral poetry,
from Theocritus downwards. I am much pleased to see
how highly Mr. Wordsworth speaks of Virgil's style, and of
his "Bucolics," which I have ever thought most graceful

and tender.   They are quite another thing from Theocritus, however they may be based upon Theocritus.

You invited me, in a former letter, to speak to you of the "Prelude;" but this must be reserved for a future communication.   I can only say, now, that I was deeply delighted in reading it, and think it a truly noble composition.   It is not, perhaps, except in certain passages, which had been extracted and given to the public before the publication of the poem as a whole, effective and brilliant poetry; but it is deeply interesting as the image of a great poetic mind: none but a mind on a great scale could have produced it.   As a supplement to the poetic works of the author, it is of the highest value.   You may imagine how I was affected and gladdened by the warm tributes which it contains to my father, and the proof it affords of their close intimacy and earnest friendship.   I think the history of literature hardly affords a parallel instance of entire union and unreserve between two poets.   There may have been more co-operation betwixt Beaumont and Fletcher; but, from the character of their lives, there could hardly have been such pure love and consonancy of thought and feeling on high themes, and accordance in high aims and endeavours.   Mr. Yarnall's remembrances of the poet in his last year I thought highly interesting.   I saw in them a touch of Wordsworth's own manner, a reverent tenderness and "solemn gloom."   To judge from the notes of Mrs. Davy and Lady Richardson, Mr. Wordsworth must have been somewhat more like his old self in discourse when at his own home, surrounded by the natural objects in which he took such high interest, than when I was with him at Miss Fenwick's, at Bath, in the spring of that sad summer which deprived him of his beloved daughter.   Then, he seemed unable to talk, except in snatches and fragments; and there was nothing fresh in what he said.   His speech seemed to me but a feeble, mournful echo of his former utterances.

V.

Visit to the Crystal Palace in Hyde Park—Sculpture and Jewels—The
Royal Academy of 1851—Portrait of Mr. Wordsworth by
Pickersgill—Supposed Tendency to Pantheism in the "Lines on
Tintern Abbey."

To Miss FENWICK.

May 25th, 1851, *Chester Place.*—Dearest Miss Fenwick,—
Yesterday, for the first time, I visited the Crystal Palace,
and ever since I have been longing for you to see it.   Is it
quite impossible for you to come up to me first, and see
this interesting assemblage of works of art ?   I saw so
many Bath chairs, and invalids in them, so many, many
degrees weaker than you or I.   You could be wheeled about
to everything with perfect ease, and there are several
gentlemen, either of whom would delight to devote time to
going about with us and showing us everything.

I had a perfect dread of the thing before I went, and
would not have gone at all but to escape the perpetual
question, "Have you seen the great wonder?" and "Do go
with me.   Do let me take you to see it."   I would not go
with any party, fearing that I should have to stay longer
than my strength would allow.   Yesterday, E. and I went
under the care of Mr. D——; we stayed *four hours*, and I
came away far less fatigued than I have often felt after half
an hour in the Royal Academy.   The difference arises from
the freedom in walking about, and the freshness of the
atmosphere.   In this great conservatory or glass house, we
are perfectly sheltered from all inclemency of weather, all
too muchness of hot or cold, wind or sun, and under foot are
smooth boards which do not try the limbs like the inequali-
ties of street or road; and yet there is an openness and
space, and free circulation of air such as was never enjoyed, I
suppose, *under cover* before.   I did not think to stay more
than one hour, but four soon slipped away.   We were lucky
in meeting Lord Monteagle, who talked instructively to me

on the works of art, and pointed out a most graceful and beautiful piece of sculpture by Gibson, which I afterwards showed to friends whom I met, telling them at the same time of Lord Monteagle's criticism. . . . Lord Monteagle talked of little A——, and of his having enjoyed one of the greatest honours a mortal could obtain, in having been preferred to the hippopotamus! I dare say you may have heard the story of little A——'s choosing to see grandpapa, rather than to visit the zoological favourite new-comer.

At first I felt mortified to see how British art, in the high line of sculpture, appeared to be outdone by foreign,—all the striking pieces, and those which occupied the conspicuous places in the centre of the great middle aisle, being German, Italian, or French performances. The grandest thing in this way is an Amazon * on horseback, about to spear a lioness, who has leaped upon her horse, and is trying to throttle it. The huntress sits back upon her steed, the right leg drawn up, the left extended on the other side below the belly of the horse, a superb tom-boy indeed. The piece is colossal. Then there are two fishing girls by Monti of Milan, most lovely, but quite *real-life-ish,* —not like Gibson's piece, which would be almost taken for a Greek antique, and there are such beauteous little babes in marble, one little fellow strapped to his cot, from which he is trying to rear himself up. But among the most striking performances are two groups by Lequesne : (1) A dog protecting a boy, about four or five years old, from a serpent; (2) the dog, having bitten off the serpent's head, caressed by the child. The contrast in the face of the dog when he is about to kill the serpent and when he has done the job, is most expressive; in the first group it is sharpened with anxiety, it looks almost like that of a wolf, full of horror and disgust at the noxious beast, and cautious determination. In the second, it is all abroad with com-

* By Kiss, a German sculptor.—E. C.

fortable, placid satisfaction, and affectionate good-nature. These, of course, are only a few in a crowd.

I was disappointed in the great diamond, even though I had heard that it disappointed every one. There is nothing *diamondy* in it that I can see, no multiplicity of sparkle, it looks only like a respectable piece of crystal. The two strings of large pearls of the East India Company are very fine, but I have some strings of large mock pearl which look almost as well, and they can be imitated still more nearly. The huge emeralds, too, look rather glassy. Of all the works of art adapted to the uses of domestic life, the most exquisite is the Gobelin tapestry; in our noblemen's palaces and houses there is nothing like it. The bunches of flowers are more delicate and brilliant than any painting I ever saw. The carved wood furniture is very fine, but in that department the English equal the French, except in one sideboard, supported by four hounds, which is the most elegantly magnificent thing I ever saw. The grand beds, too, are *very* grand. The crowd was far greater yesterday than it ever was before, and what it will be on the shilling days I know not. It was fine to look down from the galleries, and see such a vast mass of human beings all in motion, enjoying themselves, and animated. Everybody looked pleased and comfortable.

The picture exhibition, too, is worth seeing. I like Watts' portrait of Mr. Taylor much, and there are beautiful portraits of Gibson, the sculptor, and a lady by Boxall. Eastlake's Hippolita is very beautiful, but too pinky. Pickersgill's portrait of our dear departed great poet is *insufferable*—velvet waistcoat, neat shiny boots—just the sort of dress he would not have worn if you could have hired him—and a sombre sentimentalism of countenance quite unlike his own look, which was either elevated with high gladness or deep thought, or at times simply and childishly gruff,—but never tender after that fashion, so lackadaisical and mawkishly sentimental.

Dr. Wordsworth's apologizing in the "Life," for the "Lines on Tintern Abbey," seems to me injudicious. Those great works of the Poet's vigorous mind must stand for themselves; it is on them, I believe, that Wordsworth's fame will rest, and by them he must be judged.

But why admit for a moment that they might be accused of Pantheism, or that Wordsworth might, had he not written in a different spirit late in life? If they had really proceeded from a Pantheistic view, they ought to have been suppressed if possible. Their beauty and power ought not to have saved them; this would give them influence,—add wings to the poisoned shaft. But there is no such thing as Pantheism truly imputable to them.

VI.
Intellectual Tuft-hunting.

To E. QUILLINAN, ESQ.

1851.—A parent cannot say to a son, "You must never form an intimacy except with decidedly superior men." There would be a sort of intellectual tuft-hunting in this, which could not lead to good, for man is a very complex animal, and cannot be determined in his movements and procedure by one part of his nature without regard to the rest, and our connections arise from many influences, all of which cannot be given an exact account of.

VII.

The Bears of Literature—Margate—Bean-fields and Water Companies —Leibnitz on the Nature of the Soul—Materialism of the Early Fathers—Historical Reading—Scott's Novels.

To AUBREY DE VERE, ESQ.

8, *Zion Place, Eastcliff, Margate, June 20th*, 1851.—I have delayed writing to you more as reserving a pleasure, than postponing a time-consuming task, for the subjects which you invite me to investigate with you are so interesting to my mind that a letter to you is always a high entertainment to myself, whether or no to you it be a *treat* so far as it is a *treatise*, or only acceptable as a personal communication. I ought to have written sooner, however, to express my grateful delight in what you have undertaken on behalf of dear Hartley's poetry. It is painful to think of your composition being cut. and slashed and squeezed and ground, and perhaps inlaid and vamped by editorial interference. Still, in any shape, the article will be *very* acceptable, unless more tampered with than I can believe probable; and even if aught unforeseen should prevent its appearance altogether, it would always be most agreeable to me to think of your having written it. I should like to see your composition in its original virgin state, like the gadding vine or well-attired woodbine, free and luxuriant in kindly remark and beauty-finding criticism. An editor of a critical review ought to be painted with a pruning-hook in his hand as big as himself, and an axe beside him, just ready to fall edge foremost upon his own foot,—only that it would tantalize one to see it always suspended. There's a piece of savagery! The foot ought to be represented as rough as that of a bear, and clumsy as the pedestal of an elephant, to denote the rough clumsy way in which those ursine editors go ramping and ravaging about the fairest flower-gardens. Don't you remember how C——'s great hoofs went plunging about in Tennyson's first volume, containing "Mariana," "The Miller's Daughter," and the "Ode to Memory," and "The Dying Swan," and "Œnone," the loveliest and most characteristic things, to my fancy, that he ever wrote? Indeed, C——'s stamping down that pretty bed of heart's ease, Moxon's Sonnets, was shameful, and showed him fit to be chained to a post, or shut up with the guests of Circe, in a sty of tolerable accommodation and capacity, for the rest of his bearish and Grilline existence. All this indignation streams forth from me on the pressure of the mere thought of the treatment that your article is to receive. "But let them go, and be you blithe and bonny," oh! products of poetic genius of every degree, from the greatest to the least, in spite of the Bears of Literature, remembering how Keats was treated, who now by some critics is boldly styled the most poetical poet of the age.

My general health has derived as much benefit from my stay here as it usually does from a seaside visit. I walk an hour in the morning, and in the evening an hour or fifty minutes. I could do more than this in the way of exercise, but though my strength would allow of it, I fear that it might not be prudent.

The weather was quite wintry, a spring temperature, with the squally look and sound of winter, during the first nine or ten days of our stay. Now it begins to be Juneish, the butterflies are abroad, especially the azure ones, that seem to be animated bits cut out of the sapphire of the still blue sea; the corn poppy rears its head, that was hung down like that of an eastern slave making a low obeisance, and discloses its scarlet head-gear; while the blossomed beans look up and seem to *stare* at us with their clear black eye, the jetty iris surrounded by a snowy cornea. Have you ever observed this in the bean-blossom?—it is really pretty to behold. The sweet odours from the bean-fields, and from little gardens full of stocks, carnations, roses, gilly-flowers, pinks, and southernwood, which we pass on our cliff walk, are an agreeable contrast to the vile ones which annoy us when we enter the town to post letters, or get a book from one of the libraries. The whole way round the town there are not many yards of ground free from this nuisance. Surely many summers will not pass ere Margate radically reforms her drainage, and every town and city in England adopts those better plans of water-supply and extrusion of uncleanness which are already before the public. How strange it seems that Government should in any degree admit the proposals of the water companies for consolidating them, and granting them a monopoly of this lucrative business! What can they say in answer to the allegations against the old system, and all that is advanced in support of another plan? I do think, in all matters of this kind, which concern the public health, Government ought to˙ be paternal and governing; and I hope, in time, the country will support them in taking such businesses into their own hands, and conducting them on a plan having the advantage of unity. But you will see that I am talking after the article on centralization, etc., in the last *Quarterly* an article which pleased me very much, because it both gave me new information, and confirmed some of my old opinions that the Government, on sanitary matters, should act more boldly, and take more upon it than heretofore, and not suffer what is important to the health of the community to be *misguggled* by individual selfishness and caprice, or the rapacious dishonesty of companies.

˙I have been reading Leibnitz on the origin and nature and composition of the soul, and found much in his teaching that is satisfactory. But of this more anon. He says, with a sage simplicity, that if his doctrine, as was objected to it, represents the souls of beasts as imperishable, it is much better to allow *them* immortality than to deny it to men. He thinks that the Anti-Platonism of some of the early Fathers (indeed, I believe, of all the orthodox ones), which made the soul, in all finite beings, men and angels, to be material, not immortal *per se*, by its original conformation, but only made so, in particular cases, by the arbitrary determination of the Creator, keeping alive the good for reward and the evil for punishment,—is a dangerous notion. And certainly, if materialism, in any shape, is commended to the minds of men, however guarded it may be by the teachers of it within the Church, by a corollary framed in support of Revelation, it will be laid hold of by teachers without the Church, and easily

separated from its pious appendix. The more agreement
can be made out betwixt philosophy and religion, the better
for the interests of the latter ; the more foundation for the
hopes to which Revelation points can be laid on the ground
of reason, the better for the authority of the former. And
yet some Christian teachers in all ages have manifested a
jealousy of support to religious doctrine supplied by reason,
as if the ally must needs prove an usurper. Such usurp-
ation would be but a supplanting of herself.

My reading books here are Leibnitz, Ranke, and the
Scotch Novels, and of these the middle is the one to which
alone I find it difficult to enchain my attention. History is
always difficult to me, because taking in so much *fact* at
once is like making a meal all of dry bread. As for Scott,
I grieve to be nearing the end of his charming productions.
They fill a place in literature which they have entirely to
themselves. No other books combine the same qualities,
—so much humour, so much information, so high a tone,
varying from the chivalrous to the gentlemanly, and such
an out-of-door freshness, the scene being so much in the
open air, or in mansions connected with nature or elevated
by historic association, or rendered interesting by the way
in which they show characteristics of the Scottish peasantry
or townsfolk.

CHAPTER XXV.

LETTERS TO MR. ELLIS YARNALL, PROFESSOR HENRY REED, AUBREY DE VERE, ESQ., THOMAS BLACK- BURNE, ESQ., MISS FENWICK : July—December, 1851.

I.

A Visit to the Zoological Gardens.

To AUBREY DE VERE, Esq.

10, *Chester Place, August 18th*, 1851.—I was very sorry to find that I had missed you on my return from the Zoological Gardens. You should visit the animals if you have not been there for some time. I never saw the creatures so well provided for before, their dwellings so spacious, or their peculiar habits so attended to in the arrangements, sham rocks and trees appropriately dis- tributed, and careful directions everywhere to the visitors what is *not* to be done to the annoyance and injury of the unspeaking inhabitants.

There are two kitten jaguars, which alone are worth going to see. Such darls! I wish I had seen them when they were still smaller. These are on the lion side. On the opposite, one of the large dens holds six or seven lovely leopards, which were lying about in a choice variety of easy, elegant attitudes, the long tail of one special beauty depending carelessly over a bough, the lithe limb stretched out opposite. She looked like an eastern sultana, very young. Wordsworth might well choose the " Panther in the Wilderness " as an emblem of beauty,—their forms, their motions, their exquisitely variegated coat, all are so beautiful; and they look both good-natured and playful. The giraffes so remind one of a delirious dream, that I think if I were to look at them long I should go off into a sort of trance. Oh, how very hideous the ourang-outang is! Why *did* Nature make such a hideous creature? And how the elephants look like a first rude clumsy formation of her " prentice hand," and yet I suppose their construction is not simpler or less refined than that of slenderer creatures. How one is struck, in these gardens, with the way in which the inferior animals are adapted and conformed, each to a certain habitat, monkeys and leopards and the sloth to trees, though each in a different way, great birds to rocks, giraffes to places where there are high trees, the hippopotamus to streams, &c., while man is fitted to no habitation, but fits a habitation to himself, except that the constitutions of some peoples are suited to certain climates.

II.

Immortality—Causes of Ancient and Modern Infidelity—Comparative Advantages of America and Europe—Copies from the Old Masters —The Bridgewater Gallery—The High Church Movement—The Central Truth of Christianity—Merits of Anglicanism as compared with Romanism, Quakerism, and Scepticism—Danger of Staking the Faith on External Evidences—Pre-eminence ascribed by certain Fathers and Councils of the Church to the See of Rome—The Protestant Ground of Faith—The Theory of Development—A Dinner Party at Mr. Kenyon's—Interesting Appearance and High Poetic Gifts of Mrs. Browning—Expression and Thought in Poetry—Women's Novels—Conclusion.

To Mr. ELLIS YARNALL,* Philadelphia, U.S.

10, *Chester Place, Regent's Park, August 28th,* 1851.— Dear Mr. Yarnall,—I will begin an answer to your interesting letter at once, not waiting for more time, or aught else, to answer it suitably, and as I should like to do; for I know how much better ever so brief an answer is than none, so that it be not short in friendly feelings. It was by no means necessary to apologize, as you do, for the personal accounts in your letter, which were to me remark-

* A friend and fellow-townsman of Professor Reed's, from whom he brought an introduction to my mother, while on a visit to England in the summer of 1849.—E. C.

ably interesting. A good and wise man, one who is enjoying life himself, and promoting the welfare and happiness of others, called away suddenly,

> " While those whose hearts are dry as summer dust
> Burn to the socket,"

is always a subject for serious meditation on the ways of God with man, and to religious minds an evidence that here we have *no abiding city*,—that the best estate of frail mortals, so frail as earthly beings, so strong in the heavenly part of their constitution, is when they feel themselves to be strangers and pilgrims here below. What a depth of consolation there is in some of those expressions in the eleventh chapter of Hebrews! How they articulate the voice of immortality within us, and countervail the melancholy oracle of Lucretius, with their calm and confident assurances! The atheism of Epicurus gained its power upon the mind from the irrationality and anti-moralism, the sensuality and cruelty involved in the popular religion which it opposed. And just so it is, I think, in the present day; the deniers of Revelation, and doubters of a future state, the disbelievers even of a God and an immortality for man in His presence, acquire all their strength from the weakness of the mediæval ecclesiastical system, its audacious contradictions of Scripture and the moral sense, and the unscrupulous use it makes of the most corrupt human instrumentalities for the furtherance of its purposes, and consolidation of its power. But I must not plunge into this large subject at present.

I looked out in the Diffusion of Useful Knowledge Society's maps for the places you mention, and found some of them, and ascertained their relation to New York. It is very interesting to think how a ready-made civilization is rapidly spreading around that vast westerly lake, Michigan. It seems to me that in your country you have a great deal of our refinement without our troublesome tedious conventionality. You have books, and in them the main substance of cultivation, the best part of civilization; and you have a noble, beautiful nature around you, which would do nothing to elevate the mind *by itself*, but where intellectual education has laid a ground-work, becomes an exalting and refining influence, and a perpetual source of delight. I wish you had more pictures by the old imaginative masters, and some of the architectural and sculptorial works of past generations of men, whose circumstances enabled them to do what never can be done again, unless a new state of. things comes in, of which there is now no prospect. But the facilities of intercourse with Europe will do something to make up for that deficiency, by enabling every man of taste and leisure (even occasional) in your country to fill his memory with those noble and lovely forms. Surely all of you who visit Italy, or the galleries of France and England, or the palaces of Spain, enriched by the painters of that sunny land, ought to bring home some copies of the finer productions of art. I have seen copies of old pictures which, I do believe, have *almost* all in them that the originals possess, *almost* all those qualities which constitute their charm and salutary influence; and it is, fortunately, paintings of the higher order of merit, the merit of which is most adequately conveyed by copies, and even by prints. There is in them a grace and loftiness of design, which cannot be absent from any attempt at translation. Whenever I see an original Raphael, I behold an *infinite* deal of beauty which no print can convey; a soft exquisiteness of outline, and a lifelike elasticity in the flesh; and yet I greet it as an old acquaintance. Lately, I visited Lord Ellesmere's noble collection of pictures, which used to be called the Stafford or the Bridgewater gallery (Lord Ellesmere is brother to the Duke of Sutherland). I had seen this splendid assemblage twice in my life before, once when I was a girl, and saw little more in the Titians and Poussins and Raphaels than products of power which I could not understand. A year ago I saw them again with Mr. Quillinan, Mr. Wordsworth's son-in-law, whose death filled us with grief two months ago. In Lord Ellesmere's new house the pictures are not well lighted, and many of them are placed so high as to be quite lost to the eye in all but a general outline. Still I received a pleasure from them unfelt before. In the centre of the principal room are the four Raphaels, La Vierge au Palmier, the Virgin seated under a palm tree, presenting the infant Saviour to the kneeling Joseph. This is one of the loveliest pictures I ever beheld. To judge from the print, the Virgin de la Maison d'Albe, seated on the ground, with the Child Jesus climbing into her lap, St. John smilingly adoring close by, must be of equal beauty. Both these paintings are in a circular form, which aids the effect of their soft symmetry and perfect grace. The next in beauty of the Raphaels is the standing Virgin,* with Jesus and John, as boys of seven or eight, close beside her. La Vierge au Linge is least interesting, the Babe being too young to display grace of form and motion. It is asleep, the mother lifting the veil from its face. The fourth is the Blessed Mother, with her Babe stretching itself across her arms. The two large Titians, Diana, Calisto, and Nymphs,—Diana, Actæon, and Nymphs, form a part of this rich group. I feel their power, but cannot properly appreciate these pictures; and they are out of harmony, in tone, with the main mass of the paintings around. The famous Assumption of the Virgin, by Guido, is at the end of the room, a large painting in a sort of alcove. It was one of the first pictures that ever awakened pictorial enthusiasm in me, or rather excited poetical enthusiasm by means of the pictorial art, when I saw it at the British Institution. The Maid Mother, robed

* La Belle Vierge.—E. C.

in pink, with a blue scarf fluttering over her rich, graceful form, floats upwards through a sky of aerial gold.   The face is round and fair, and exquisitely delicate, with soft yellow hair and upturned hazel eyes.   The "Michael triumphing over Satan," in another apartment, is to my imagination quite as delightful as this more admired production of the same master.   In the Archangel there is the same rich, full form as in the ascending Madonna, the same round, almost infantine face, surmounted with a natural glory of light golden hair; the beauty is womanish, as if Venus had been transformed into Apollo, for one day's festival in heaven, with an expectation of going back into her original state of goddesshood the day after.   By comparing this picture with some of Murillo's, we obtain a notion of the superiority of the latter in religious depth and seriousness.   For Murillo is always *serious*, though never quite sublime; evangelical more than ecclesiastical, which latter may be Christian, and yet will admit of Paganized conceptions of divine things, and these accompanied with a Pagan air of luxurious and voluptuous earthiness.   I was led to this remark by thinking of the Angels or Divine Persons who appear to Abraham, in Murillo's great picture, companion to the still finer Prodigal Son, by the same great artist (both are in the possession of Lord Ellesmere's brother, the Duke of Sutherland, and are in his palatial town-house), they are so much more spiritual in their beauty.

You speak of the Movement in our Church, originated by Newman and other writers of the "Tracts for the Times," and I can entirely agree with you in thinking that it has awakened a loftier spirit than before was prevailing.   I believe too that the discussions it has occasioned must be in the main for good, and at any rate were inevitable.   The particular Tractarian movement indeed is itself but the offspring of a deeper one, which is common to all Europe, and has been produced by such a complex cause of circum-

stances, states, and relations, as ever brings about the
great general changes in the public condition of things,
and social arrangements at large. Matters pertaining to
religion could not remain as they were left by the Reformation; as thought advanced, and when this nation was no
longer occupied with foreign wars or internal commotions,
and began to think seriously of setting its house in order,
the discrepancies and incoherencies, intellectual and moral,
discoverable to the searching eye in various departments of
Church and State, must be revealed in a clear light, and
call for remedy. Tractarianism was a stage in the progress
of newly-awakened thought; but how men who *go on*
thinking can suppose that it set forth a coherent religious
system, with which a serious mind could rest satisfied, or
settled religious matters on a firm basis, I cannot imagine
for a moment. On the contrary, of all forms of the
Christian faith that ever have found favour with respectable
bodies of men, Anglo-Catholicism seems to me the most
baseless and inconsistent. My friend, Mr. H. Crabb
Robinson, says that its inconsistency is its merit, as
compared, he means, with Romanism on the one hand, or
Straussism on the other. Differing as I do materially from
Mr. Robinson respecting the great central truth of
Christianity, the Divinity of our Lord (for I believe the
Redeemer to be God Himself, and he holds Jesus Christ to
be a Being empowered by God to save the world, no mere
man, and yet not very God), I do agree with him in this,
and believe Anglo-Catholicism a far better religion than
Romanism, Quakerism, or general scepticism, though more
inconsistent than either.

I think it far better than Romanism, because it rejects
that impious supplementary gospel, those blasphemous
pretensions, heathenish figments, demoralizing principles,
and debasing practices, which the Church of Rome keeps
up for the benefit of the clergy, together with those

doctrines of Papal authority, which, if unresisted (providentially it has always been kept in check), must soon destroy all national independence, and introduce a despotism inimical to the progress and best interests of the human race.

I think it better than Quakerism, which rejects the whole Visible Church system, because I see in that system, so far as it is maintained on sound principles, for the educating of mankind in spirituals, not for blinding and enchaining them, immense utility. All temporal governments require a Church to work in alliance with them; and the Anglican form, retaining the Episcopate, is an excellent institution, which may be placed on a firm basis of reason and morality. On this foundation it has been standing all along, amid the various theories of men hovering around it, and supposed to be the foundation by mystified beholders, who cannot distinguish between cloudage and *terra firma*.

I need not say why Anglo-Catholicism is better than such doctrine as that of the rejectors of Revelation, who think that St. John confounded his own dreams, engendered of human philosophies, with the teaching of the Spirit, and deprive those whom they seduce of all solid ground of hope in a better life to come. Such views appear to be the immediate result, in some minds, of the High Church externalism and dogmatism, which denies the inward revelation to be the true ultimate assurance of faith. They examine that external authority to which they have been commanded to bow, and find it wanting in the material of conviction; and they have never been led to think and feel that the Christian religion, so far as it answers any true purpose of a religion in purifying and elevating our nature, *is its own evidence*; that the Bible attests its own divineness, as the sun reveals itself by its own light. These sceptics, equally with the externalizing Romanist, are ever seen to be deficient in a sense and perception of *moral evidence;*

they are blind to the traces of God, both in the course of
the world and in the volume of Revelation; equally with
the Romanist, the Infidel fails to see that religion is a
spirit, a power or principle, not a certain set of formal
beliefs bound up together in a frame, so that a man must
take it all up at once, or leave it all. The Romanist urges
that if the ideas of reason (or aught in the mind within)
are the criterion of truth, a man's creed will be always
varying; he does not understand that we may perceive
truth in a thousand different ways and degrees, but that we
can really perceive none at all except by the mirror of
heaven within us. Just so the sceptic finds out certain
incoherencies, or thinks he finds them, in the Scriptural
accounts of our Lord's course upon earth, and thereupon
concludes that the Word of God cannot be *contained* in the
Bible, because he finds it in part to be the mistaken word
of man.

The inconsistency of the Anglo-Catholic position seems
to me to be this,—the Anglican, who firmly maintains the
doctrine of the Apostolical Succession, as absolutely essential to the being of the Christian Church, and boasts that
our hierarchy, by means of regular ordination, descends in
an unbroken line from the Apostles; who insists upon the
absolving powers of the clergy, and founds them upon
Scripture, by transferring the promise of our Lord to His
faithful followers (the chosen Twelve), that they should
have the power of binding and loosing, to all their succes-
sors ordained in due form, whatever their personal qualifications may happen to be; when it is objected that the
language of the New Testament itself authorizes no such
application, that it is an arbitrary extension of the sense,
and supposes a thing in its own nature unreasonable,
because the mission and the promise are obviously adapted
to the personal qualifications of those to whom they were
originally addressed,— their supernatural powers which

ceased with them—their burning faith and zeal, which
cannot be conveyed by ordination, or any other ceremony;
the Anglican, I say, constantly replies (and certainly no
other reply can be given) that all sound members of the
Catholic Church submit to the judgment of the Church,
which is to be ascertained by the decrees and acts of
general councils and the consent of ancient bishops and
doctors.   But on all the same grounds of Scripture, and
application of Scripture by Councils and Fathers, we ought
to believe in the primacy of the Pope, that he is the
supreme judge in all controversies, and the determiner of
doctrine, whence it follows that we ought to accept the
whole Romish system, with its Deification of the Virgin,
doctrine of the Mass, adoration of saints (for such it practically is), with all those religious institutes and practices
which the English mind so revolts from and contemns,—
the mockery of indulgences, the corruption of the confessional, monasticism with all its social mischiefs, loosening
the bonds of family life, intrusion and domination of the
priesthood.   For all these things and more are contained
within that dark womb, so simple without, so labyrinthine
within—the Papal Supremacy and Infallibility; for though
the latter article is not called *de fide*, yet it so obviously
follows from the former, that exalters of the papacy may
very well afford to leave it to take care of itself, when the
supremacy has been established.   Here the Anglican inter-
poses, taking exception at the term *Supremacy*.   He tells
you the primacy acknowledged by the Church of the first
six centuries is a widely different thing from the headship
now claimed for the Pope; it may be proved by overwhelm-
ing evidence that bishops of old, the very same men who
used high language concerning the Chair of Peter, did hold
their own against this most exalted and venerable Chair,
whenever they thought it necessary to assert their independence, and defend their proceedings and their doctrine

against an adverse decision of the Holy See; nay, that some of them openly disclaimed ·a bishop of bishops, alleging that the Apostles were heads of their several charges, and declaring that there is no Head of the whole Church but Christ. To this answer the modern Romanist replies, that the doctrine was as yet not fully *developed*, which is a plain fact; but, without admitting his pretension that an article not known or understood in the first ages can be a divine truth, necessary to be admitted by all Christians on peril of salvation, I must concede to the Romanist that the Fathers generally, and by a sort of consent, attributed a pre-eminence to the See and Bishop of Rome, which properly involve the supremacy even in the modern sense, and their words and actions, repudiating the paramount authority of the latter, are really inconsistent with their attributions to the successor of the Fisherman, when no particular interest or influence induces them to diminish his claims. I have lately examined this question in debates with Mr. ——, who has satisfied himself that the Romish Church theory is the only tenable one, and although unable myself to receive or admire any mystico-ecclesiastical system, Roman or Anglican, yet with a strong desire to find the Romanist pretensions to patristic testimony in favour of the papacy wholly vain. But in this I have been disappointed. The language of Cyprian, Ambrose, and very many other Fathers, as well as of councils venerated by Anglo-Catholics, is unmeaning and self-contradictory, if understood so as to exclude the supremacy. It imports that the Bishop of Rome is the centre and *origin* of unity; his See the Rock on which the Church is built; himself the successor of Peter, from whom the "Apostolate and Episcopate in Christ took its beginning;" that "where Peter is, there is the Church;" that to be out of communion with Rome is to be cut off from Christ; that from the See of Peter "*the full grace of all Pontiffs is derived;*" that the

Roman Church is the "foundation and mould of the Churches;" that the Holy See *transmits its rights* to the universal Church;" that "the Pope is the head of the Church, other bishops the members." In the Third General Council he was acknowledged to be the "*Head* of the whole Faith."* Now, surely this language, and it is quite as general as any which can be cited from the Fatherhood on the Con-substantiality of Christ with the Father, or the three Persons in the Godhead, is senseless babble, if it does not mean that the Pope is the source of jurisdiction and the ultimate decider of controversy in the Church. The ancient Fathers, with scarce a dissentient voice, ascribe a pre-eminence and authority to Peter over the other Apostles; and as *all* the Apostles had supernatural powers, what could St. Peter have beyond them, except what is now ascribed to the Pope as his successor, namely, to be their earthly head, the channel of grace and episcopal power from Christ to them, consequently to be the ultimate judge of questions concerning the faith?

I fully admit that the Fathers and Bishops often contradict this doctrine, as I have already said (though Tertullian's language proves that the Papal supremacy was asserted in the second century), and the Canons of Sardica are strong evidence that it was not a "Law and Tradition of the Church" acknowledged from the beginning, as well as the silence of the earliest Christian writers, especially St. Ignatius, who exalts the Episcopate, and says nought of any Bishop of Bishops. But surely this incoherent and conflicting testimony, of which it seems impossible to make a harmonious whole, and which keeps up the controversy between the Churches, contains ample vindication of the attitude assumed by genuine Scriptural Protestantism, which acknowledges no positive divine ground of faith but

* See Postscript.—E. C.

the Bible, acknowledged to be divine by its own internal character, and corresponding to the image of the divine within us, not by any external testimony of the visible Church. Surely it shows those to have reason on their side, who refuse to be absolutely determined, in all the articles of their belief, by majorities of ancient Bishops and Doctors, or even by their consentient voice. It begins to be generally felt that no consistent scheme of doctrine can be obtained from the ancient Fathers; and that the principle of development must be freely acted on, in order to the maintenance of any Church system founded in the Christian Revelation, and connected with it by unbroken tradition. But this principle of development is contradictory to the general mind of the Ancient Church, which always appeals to Scripture and the continuous teaching of the Church authorities; it is incongruous with the root-principles of a system of externalism and uniformity of doctrine in its intellectual aspect, which ought to be supported by outward and historic testimony. Hereafter a Head Bishop, or a General Council, may decide that Arianism is, after all, the right doctrine of the Godhead, and who could disprove the assertion that it was the proper development of the original belief, always acknowledged by a part of the Church, held in germ, and so forth. Development is too large a key for the lock to which it is deceptively applied. The lock it really fits is one which opens into the illimitable Court of Anarchy, not into the area of the existing visible Church system. There is no conceivable corruption or transmutation of doctrine and practice, which may not be called a true development, if there is no rule or standard by which the legitimacy of the extension is to be judged; and all depends on the judgment of an irresponsible Head, presumed to be the oracle through which Christ speaks to His Church.

. . . My daughter and I lately met at the house of my

excellent old friend, Mr. Kenyon, that poetical pair, Mr. and Mrs. Browning. You probably know her as Elizabeth Barrett, author of the "Seraphim," "Drama of Exile," and many ballads and minor poems, among which "Cowper's Grave" is of special excellence. She has lately published "Casa Guidi Windows," a meditative, political poem of considerable merit; Mazzini admires it, and it has been translated into Italian. Mrs. Browning is in weak health, and cannot remain in this foggy clime; they are to reside in Paris. She is little, hard-featured, with long dark ringlets, a pale face, and plaintive voice, something very impressive in her dark eyes and her brow. Her general aspect puts me in mind of Mignon,—what Mignon might be in maturity and maternity. She has more poetic genius than any other woman living,—perhaps more than any woman ever showed before, except Sappho. Still there is an imperfectness in what she produces; in many passages the expressions are very faulty,—the images forced and untrue,—the sentiments exaggerated, and the situations unnatural and unpleasant. Another pervading fault of Mrs. Browning's poetry is rugged, harsh versification, with imperfect rhymes, and altogether that want of art in the department of metre, which prevents the language from being an unobstructive medium for the thought. Verse and diction are the bodily organism of poetry; this body ought to be soft, bright, lovely, carrying with it an influence and impression of delightfulness, yet not challenging attention by itself. These defects in poetical organism are inimical to the enduring life of the poetry; the same or similar thoughts will reappear in better form, and so supersede the earlier version; whereas, if poetic thoughts are once bodied to perfection, they will remain and exclude all future rivals. There is fear with regard to many of our present producers of poetry, lest the good that is in them should be swamped by the inferior matter, which gives a grotesque air to their compositions at large.

feminist → novels

It has been ever a favourite saying with me, that there is one line of literature, and only one, in which women can do something that men cannot do, and do better; and that is a certain style of novel. I warmly admire the better novels produced by women during the last seventy or eighty years, —the writings of Inchbald, Burney, Edgeworth, Jane Austen, Miss Ferrier, and those interesting productions of the present day, from the pen of Mrs. Marsh and Miss Brontë. Mrs. Gore's novels are full of talent, and display a most extensive acquaintance both with modern books and modern things; but there is a most unpleasant tone about them. "Jane Eyre" and "Shirley," by Miss Brontë, are full of genius. There is a spirit, a glow and fire about them, a masculine energy of satire and of picturesque description, which have delighted me; but they also abound in proofs of a certain hardness of feeling and plebeian coarseness of taste. The novels of Mrs. Marsh, upon the whole, please me better than any that are now forthcoming. They are thoroughly feminine; and though often too diffuse, their diffuseness may be skimmed over without leaving any unpleasant impression on the mind. "The Wilmingtons," with its sequel, "Time the Avenger," is to my feelings an interesting book.

If you happen to have any communication with Newbury Port, Massachusetts,—but this is a vain thought. I was thinking of my unseen friends and correspondents, Mr. and Mrs. Tracey, of that place. My last to them spoke of my weakened health, and they are anxious to know how I am going on. I cannot give a good report of myself, and from several causes must not attempt more letter-writing at present. My kindest wishes attend them. I have already sent kind regards and thanks to Mr. and Mrs. Reed. Accept the same yourself, dear sir, and may you long have health and strength to enjoy the infinite delights of literature, and the loveliness of "this bright, breathing world," which the poets teach us to admire, and the Gospel makes us hope to find again in that unseen world whither we are all going.— Believe me truly your friend,

SARA COLERIDGE.

III.

Prayer for Temporal and Spiritual Benefits.

To Miss FENWICK.

September 4th, 1851.—Your friendship, dear friend, has been one great blessing of these last years of my life, and I trust not only a comfort and happiness, but a lasting benefit, which will survive all the worsening and decay of our poor, frail, earthly tabernacle. My gratitude to you is one of my deepest feelings. God bless you, and bestow upon you all whatsoever He knows to be best for you. I must still pray for temporal comforts to be granted you. We are to pray ever, and He will set our prayers straight. But still more earnestly, and with more confidence for you and for myself, I ask for that *peace which passes understanding.*—Ever most affectionately your friend,

SARA COLERIDGE.

IV.

Increase of Illness—Fancied Wishes—Trial and Effects of Mesmerism
—Editorial Duties still fulfilled—Derwent Isle and Keswick
Vale—Visit of the Archdukes to General Peachey in 1815—Old
Letters—Death ; and the Life beyond it.

To AUBREY DE VERE, Esq.

10, *Chester Place, Oct. 1st*, 1851.—My dear Friend,—You will regret very much to learn how much worse and weaker I am than when you saw me last. I cannot now walk more than half an hour at a time, when I am at the best. At Margate an hour or hour and twenty minutes did not fatigue me. I still take short walks twice a day, but how long my power of doing this will last I cannot say.

You can hardly imagine how my mind hovers about that old well-known churchyard, with Skiddaw and the Bassenthwaite hills in sight; how I long to take away Mama's remains from the place where they are now deposited, and when my own time comes, to repose beside her, as to what now *seems* myself, in that grassy burial-ground, with the Southeys reposing close by. My husband I hope to meet in heaven; but there is a different feeling in regard to earlier ties. Hartley and Mr. Wordsworth I would have where they are, in that Grasmere churchyard, within an easy distance of Keswick, as it used to be in old times.

These are strong *feelings*, translated into fancied *wishes*, —not sober earnest. When we are withdrawn from society and the bustle of life, in some measure, and our thoughts are from any cause fixed on the grave, how does the early life rise up into glow and prominence, and, as it were, call one back into itself! Yet during that early life how I looked forward, imagining better things here below than I had yet experienced, and going beyond this world altogether, into the realms above!

A few weeks ago, my old friend C. H. Townshend * came to town for a short time on business from Lausanne. He reproached me for not trying mesmerism, and on my yielding to his representations on the subject, brought Dr. Elliotson to give me advice. My housemaid willingly undertook the business, and was instructed, and now mesmerizes regularly twice a day. The effect on me is not strong, sophisticated as my nerves have been by morphine; but there is a perceptible *peculiar* sensation produced by the passes. They soothe me at the time, and make me drowsy, and I think there is some beneficial influence exerted on the constitution. From what I feel, I am much inclined to believe that some agent in the physical frame is called into action by

* The name of Mr. Chauncy Hare Townshend will be familiar to all visitors at the South Kensington Museum, where the fine collection of pictures and jewels, bequeathed by him to that institution, is now exhibited. He was the author of "Facts in Mesmerism," and of several volumes of poetry, and was, besides, an accomplished amateur artist and musician.—E. C.

the passes; that the mesmeric influence of the operator *excites* this principle in the patient, as heat kindles heat upon communication. Neuralgic pains are soon relieved by the passes. They return after a while, but are quieted for the time. An article on electro-biology in the last *Westminster*, reducing all the phenomena under ordinary causes, I think shallow, and know to be mistaken.

I have not yet opened the book of new poetry you have sent me to read, but hope to do so ere we meet. I have a great many books on hand, and Derwent keeps me busy in matters which he is concerned in, as far as my weak strength will allow. He wants some new editions of the Esteesian Marginalia prepared for the press, and this cannot be done at present, as I have so long been the Esteesian *housekeeper*, without my superintendence.

We have seen a good deal lately of Mr. Blackburne, a poetical friend of my brother Hartley, a charming converser, but very much in want of a steady, regular profession. He has always some new poem or poemet to recite whenever he comes. His poetry is graceful, abounding in sweet images, but lacks *bone*. He is too fond, I think, of the boneless Keatsian sort of poetry, which is all marrow, and wearies one at last with its want of fibre. Indeed, I say the other extreme is better in the end.

October 2nd.—Sweet Derwent Isle! how many, many scenes of my youth arise in my mind in connection with thee! I had a personal and a second-hand association with that lovely spot; for Mama used to tell me much of Emma, the first young wife of General Peachey, youngest daughter of Mr. Charter of Taunton, whom my Uncle Southey so beautifully described in those epitaph lines, which present her as she appeared, "like a dream of old romance, skimming along in her little boat, and how she was laid, before her youth had ripened into full summer, amid Madeira's orange-groves to rest." She was tall—a man's height—

five foot eight at least, but so feminine—a slender, blue-eyed blonde.

I cannot remember that fair Emma; but what pleasant visits have I paid to the Island—in summer, autumn, icy winter—in the second lady's time! There I was when the Archdukes came to visit the Island, and lunched there after the entrance of the Allied Kings into Paris. Oh! the fussiness of the General on that occasion! How their Serenities *Russianly* absorbed the preservative butter of the potted char! What a beautiful Prussian Count they had with them, with whom I fancied myself in love for two or three days!—tried hard to be, I believe, though the cement was wanting of advances on his part towards me, without which Apollo himself would soon have slipped away from my heart and fancy. Sometimes we were detained in the Island by stress of weather, and once were prevented from a visit to it by the same cause.

I wonder whether the feathery fern I transplanted from the Cardingmill Field, the part among trees beside the river, is yet living, and the beech-tree, which I used to climb, with its copper foliage, at the foot of which, in spring, a few crocuses grew.

I was quite sorry to say farewell to C. H. Townshend. He was more agreeable, more clever in talk, than ever; and we have such interesting common Greta Hall and Keswick remembrances.

A sweet and affecting set of verses from Blackburne, on receiving back old letters of Hartley's,—

> " There they lie, a frozen ocean,
> Running on without a shore,
> But the ardour and the motion
> Of the heart beats there no more.
> And *thou?* art thou grown brighter
> Since I saw thee then so bright?
> Thinner are thy hands, and whiter,
> And thy hair like autumn light."

Oh, Keswick vale! and shall I really die, and never, never see thee again? Surely there will be another Keswick—all the loveliness transfused, the hope, the joy of youth! How wholly was that joy the work of imagination!

Oh, this life is very dear to me! The outward beauty of earth, and the love and sympathy of fellow-creatures, make it, to my feelings, a sort of heaven half ruined—an Elysium into which a dark tumultuous ocean is perpetually rushing in to agitate and destroy, to lay low the blooming bowers of tranquil bliss, and drown the rich harvests. Love is the sun of this lower world; and we know from the beloved Disciple that it will be the bliss of Heaven. God is Love; and whatever there may be that we cannot now conceive, love will surely be contained in it. It will be Love sublimed, and incorporated in Beauty infinite and perfect.

I am very faint and weak to-day—more so than I have yet been; but I have been as low in nerves often formerly, otherwise I might think that I had entered into the dark valley, and was approaching the river of Death. How kind of Bunyan—what a beneficent imagination—to shadow out death as a *river*, which is so pleasant to the mind, and carries it on into regions bright and fair beyond that boundary stream.

Miss Fenwick is to me an angel upon earth. Her being near me now has seemed a special providence. God bless her, and spare her to us and her many friends. She is a noble creature, all tenderness and strength. When I first became acquainted with her, I saw at once that her heart was of the very finest, richest quality; and her wisdom and insight are, as ever must be in such a case, exactly correspondent.

V.

Leave-taking—Value of a Profession—A Lily, and a Poem—Flowers—
Beauty and Use.

To THOMAS BLACKBURNE, Esq.

10, *Chester Place, October 13th*, 1851.—I feel much in
saying farewell to you, dear friend of my ever-lamented
brother. You have known me in a sad, shaded stage of
my existence, yet have greeted my poor autumn as brightly
and genially as if it were spring or summer. Hitherto my
head has been "above water;" ere you return to this busy
town, *the waves may have gone over my head*. My great
endeavour is not to foreshape the future in particulars, but
knowing that my strength always has been equal to my
day, when the day is come, to feel that it ever will be so
on to the end, come what may, and that all things, except
a reproaching conscience, are "less dreadful than they
seem."

God bless you! Cultivate your poetical talent, which
will ever be a delight to you, but still, as I used to say to
my friend Mr. ——, have a profession,—a broad beam of
the house of life, around which the bright occasional
garland may be woven from time to time.—Believe me,
dear Mr. Blackburne, yours with much regard,

SARA COLERIDGE.

"Espouse thy doom at once, and cleave
To fortitude without reprieve," *

are words that often sound in my ear.

Wordsworth was more to my opening mind in the way of
religious consolation than all books put together except the
Bible.

* "White Doe of Rylstone," Canto II.—E. C.

Regent's Park, September 28th.—Thank you, dear Mr. Blackburne, for that beauteous flower and lovely poem. Two lines I specially admire—

> " And like a poet tell it with a blossom
> To each new sun."

The corolla of flowers is intended to protect the fructifying system in its tender state. But this purpose might have been served by something unsightly. Nature has provided exquisite beauty both in the stamina and pistils (which give all the grace and spirit to many blossoms, or, expanding into petals, form the richness of the *rosa centifolia*, and numberless other double flowers), and in their guard, which exceeds the robes of Solomon, and rivals the butterfly, which "flutters with free wings above it."

How stupid are those people who reduce all beauty to the sense of usefulness—early association! I have heard a very clever man insist that children may be taught to admire toads and spiders, and think them as beautiful as butterflies, birds of paradise, or such a lily as you have sent me.

VI.

Proposal to visit the South of France—Climate and Society of Lausanne—The Spasmodic School of Poetry—Article on Immortality, in the *Westminster Review*—Outward Means a part of the Christian Scheme—The "Evil Heart of Unbelief"—The Foundations of Religion.

To AUBREY DE VERE, Esq.

Chester Place, October 19th, 1851.—My dear Friend,—Are you still at that dear Derwent Island? I must direct a few lines thither for the chance of their finding you there. Since your last most kind letter, I have been longing to thank you for its most soothing contents.

I am sure you would have a pleasure in giving up your own favourite project of visiting Rome,—postponing it in order to guard the poor invalid on her way to a better clime than this. Alas! it is but a pleasant vision, the thought of my journeying to the south of France. Yet, I believe a foreign climate, more bracing, less damp and unsettled than this, might afford me as much advantage as I could receive from external things. C. H. Townshend talked to me of the effect of Lausanne air upon his relaxed and ailing frame, till he inspired me with a great wish, unfelt by me before, that I could live abroad with my E——. The discourse of other friends, William and Emma G——, who are delicate people, goes strongly the same way. Mrs. Browning feels life abroad to be life indeed.

Then Chauncy Townshend says that he prefers the state of society around him at Mon Loisir to London excitement and bustle. "There," he says, " I may be sad if sorrow comes, but I am *always calm*." The way in which he uttered these words was calming to my spirit ; and certainly never did I see our old friend in a better mood, more quietly gladsome, free, and variously eloquent. He tells me that he has almost agreeable, refined, intellectual set of acquaintances at Lausanne, whom he visits without London formality and expense. He provides himself with a store 'of books for the winter, and is as independent and happy as man can be in this life. "But why did you furnish this fine house in Norfolk Street, Park Lane," said I, "and fill it with beautiful works of art, only to enter it at long intervals, and then for a few weeks?" He declared he had as much pleasure in thinking of it, and roaming all over it in imagination, as if he were actually occupying its space, and beholding its adornments. This is, perhaps, rather fantastical. An imagination so pliant might go a step further, and imagine the house and contents, without keeping money locked up in it.

I read through the dramatic poem you were so kind as to send me, and found it full of passion and energy, but, on the whole, painful and unsatisfactory,—a production which shoots its bolt at once, and then has no more that it can do. I was reminded of the Preface to the "Virgin Widow" in reading it. One most powerful passage is a vision of the death of an ancient gladiator; but then it is utterly extravagant and untrue. Such things could not be,—such horrid combinations of incompatible terrors and sufferings and ecstasies of enjoyment, and power and weakness, could not exist together. There are no lines and expressions, lovely and felicitous, which take place among the treasures of the mind, and are re-visited ever and anon. Mr. Taylor has not written a great deal, but the proportion of such satisfactory passages to the total quantity of his compositions is considerable, and will give him a place, I think, finally, above all the other spasmodists of the present day.

Did you read Helps's "Companions of my Solitude"? There is a great charm in Helps, and he does give some help to reflection, though rather butterflyish in his movements.

Last night I read an article on Immortality in the *Westminster*. What a shallow sciolist that A—— seems to be! This life would be a gorgeous vestibule to no edifice, only a darksome cavern, if there were nought for man beyond it. How disproportionate our intellectual and spiritual education! "Few of us seem fit for heaven. What human goodness is commensurate to perfect, endless felicity—what human frailty to eternal woe?" Thus men argue against a future state. But we know not how heaven hereafter will be apportioned, and how the soul may expand in heaven-worthiness. If man be destined for the dust in a few years, he is a strange riddle. This life has ever seemed a mere transitional state, and tolerable only on that supposition, to the most elevated and cultivated men.

Viewing the Romish system as you do, my dear friend, a bright ideal, I cannot regret that you think as you do of the compatibility of my father's scheme of philosophy therewith, assured as I feel that he had done that papal system too much justice to believe in it as a divine institution. Do not think I am ever worried by what you call your "rough notes" on Romanism, however surprised I may sometimes be at your views in all their eloquence.

I do verily think no pious Romanist can suppose that faith does not involve a spiritual intuition and internal revelation of the truth. But the question was, which is the *ultimate ground of belief*, that which underlies and supports all the rest, this discernment of divine things which Christ himself by His Spirit works in the heart, or the teaching of the Church? Is the latter necessary to assure us that the very work of God in the soul of man is really and truly His work?

An external system for teaching Christianity, for initiating men into it, leading them to Christ, I believe to be a part of God's providence; and such a system, in so far as it is conformed to reason and moral truth, will have the blessing of the Spirit. But I cannot think it necessary, or even desirable for the right religious education of mankind, the education of the higher faculties and nobler feelings, that this system should be infallible. I admit that sin is not the only obstacle or impediment by which divine truth may be kept from the minds of men. The African savage cannot make himself religious wholly from within. There must be a preacher and outward instrumentalities. I only meant to say that when the deep spiritual verities, which are the substance of the faith, are presented to the mind, it is *sin*, and not any imperfection in our faculties, which can alone prevent it from being clearly perceived. This seems to be plainly intimated by our Lord, when He shows why the Jews did not receive Him, and in His discourse to Philip. Upon the whole, we have as good means of knowing the Saviour, and all that concerns our peace, as our Lord's disciples had. We cannot know Him at all, except by an inward revelation of the Spirit. It is by knowledge of the truth, that is, information of it from without, that this communion with the enlightening Spirit comes about. But where it is, surely it is an absolute, independent certainty.

The term "private judgment" is ambiguous. It may be interpreted in a bad sense, in which I do not see that it is fairly chargeable on Reformed Christianity. But it is confounded with *individual intuition*, and in that sense it is not easily convicted of error. But I do not pretend to maintain any particular reformed system as the very truth. I believe we have but approximations to absolute truth.

I own too that there are to my mind far more interesting considerations concerning religion than those which we have been discussing. It is the foundations of religion, those problems and difficulties that belong to every system, or underlie them all, which engage my serious thoughts. I care not so much about the difference between Romish and Anglican, though I confess the views of the Blessed Virgin in the Church of Rome do seem to me to make modern Romanism an essentially different faith and system from that of the Bible and of early Christianity.

VII.

Gradual Loss of Strength—Credulity of Unbelievers—Spiritual Peace
—Thoughts of past Years.

To AUBREY DE VERE, Esq.

10, *Chester Place, Oct. 27th*, 1851.—My dear Friend,—I was sorry not to see you yesterday, and the more so lest I should be too weak when you come again,

> For I'm wearing awa, Friend,
> Like snaw when it's thaw, Friend.

and I feel as if I should not be long here. There is a torpor ever hanging over me, like a cloud overspreading the sky, only rent here and there by some special force; and my eyes have a heavy, deathy look. I am decidedly worse since I saw you, and I begin to wish to get rid of the mesmerism, which is producing no good effect.

Thank you for the "Valley of Lilies." * I have been looking at that strange book of A—— and M——. In all the volume of Humanity, as far as I have opened it, this is the very strangest, saddest page, as far as relates to states of thought and opinion. Is it not astonishing that, in a Christian country, there can have been such a one-sided intellectual development? The *condition* constantly through-out the book confounded with the efficient cause. I now feel as if I had never seen arrogance and shallowness, before these Letters came before me. The monstrous credulity on the one hand, and utter faithlessness on the other, is truly frightful.

Do you remember how beautifully Hooker shows how our spiritual peace may be smothered for a time by bodily clouds? But, as my father says, there is a mind *within the mind*, and we must try to draw out and strengthen that.

I dwell on the Southey Letters. My mind is ever going back to my brighter days of youth, and all its dear people and things of other days.

VIII.

Congratulations on a Friend's Recovery from Illness—Her own State of Health and of Mind — Wilkie's Portrait of her Brother Hartley at Ten Years old—The Northern Worthies—A Farewell.

To Professor HENRY REED.

10, *Chester Place, December 22nd*, 1851.—My dear Professor Reed,—Many weeks ago I heard from Mr. Yarnall with deep concern of your severe, lingering illness—linger-

---

* A devotional work by Thomas à Kempis.—E. C.

ing, though transitory, I trust, in its nature.   A week since
I received from your friend another long and very interesting letter, which conveyed to me the welcome news that,
though still confined to your bed, you were in a fair way of
recovery.   It may be premature to congratulate you on
positive recovery, and Mrs. Reed with you; but I may say
how hopefully I look forward to it, and how rejoiced I
should be to hear of your restoration to your family and all
your various activities, literary and professional.   Would
that *my* health prospect were as yours—as hopeful!   I am
now an invalid, confined to my own room and the adjoining
apartment, with little prospect of restoration, though I
am not entirely hopeless.   My malady, which has been
threatening me ever since the summer before last, did not
come into activity till a few months ago.   What my course
and the event may be perhaps no physician can tell to a
certainty.   I endeavour not to speculate, to make the most
of each day as it comes, making use of what powers remain
to me, and feeling assured that strength will be supplied, if
it be sought from above, to bear any trial which my Father
in heaven may think fit to send.   I do not suffer pain.
My principal suffering is the sense of sinking and depres-
sion.   Of course all literary exertion and extensive correspondence are out of the question for me in my present
condition.   New editions of my father's works are in
contemplation, and I can still be of use to my brother
Derwent, in helping to arrange them.   But any work that I
do now is of a very slight and slow description.

Mr. Herbert Taylor kindly offers to send to Philadelphia
any book or packet for me, and I take the opportunity of
sending you an enlarged engraving of Wilkie's sketch of
my brother Hartley, in which you were so much interested,
and the more from a likeness you discerned in it to your
son.   My brother's biographical work, "The Northern
Worthies," is in the press, and great pleasure I have in

reading the proof sheets, and perceiving how much more merit there is in these lives than I ever knew them to possess before. Their chief interest consists in the accompanying criticisms and reflections. I feel sure you will like them exceedingly, though, of course, you may dissent from many of the opinions and sentiments expressed.

Farewell, my dear sir, you have my sincere wishes and prayers for your entire restoration. I *may* not be able to answer any more letters from America—a land in which I shall never cease to take an interest—but I shall ever hear with pleasure of you and yours, as long as my powers of thought remain.

Give my kind regards to Mrs. Reed, and believe me yours with much esteem and sympathy,

SARA COLERIDGE.

POSTSCRIPT.

"In the Third General Council he was acknowledged to be the '*Head* of the whole Faith.'"—p. 414.

NOTE.—I am indebted for more exact information on this point to the kindness of Bishop Abraham, who has taken the trouble to consult the original authorities. He thus gives the result of his researches in Labbé's Concilia, vol. iii. Paris Edition, 1671 : "I cannot find any warrant for such a statement as that, attributing to the *Council* any such acknowledgment. What I do find is, in p. 620, Philip the Presbyter, a *Legate of Rome*, thanks the Synod for their approval of Pope Celestine's letter, and says : οὐ γὰρ ἀγνοεῖ ὑμῶν ἡ μακαριοτης, ὅτι ἡ κεφάλη ὅλης τῆς πίστεως, ἡ καὶ τῶν ἀποστόλων, ὁ μακάριος Πέτρος ὁ ἀπόστολος. This is a very different thing from an acknowledgment by the *Council* of the *Pope's* being the Head of the Faith. What the Council did say, after the reading of the Pope's letter, was, ʼΑΰτη δικαία κρίσις ; νέῳ Παύλῳ Κελεστίνῳ, νέῳ Παύλῳ Κυρίλλῳ, Κελεστίνῳ τῷ φύλακι τῆς πίστεως, Κελεστίνῳ τῷ ὁμοψύχῳ τῆς συνόδου, εὐχαριστεῖ πᾶσα ἡ σύνοδος.

Εἷς Κελεστίνος, εἷς Κύριλλος, μία πίστις τῆς συνόδου, μία πίστις τῆς οἰκουμένης.'"
From this evidence it would appear that the title accorded to Pope Celestine
by the Council of Ephesus was not "Head," but "Guardian of the Faith."
—E. C.

"That shiny blue flower, which grows upon a shrubby stem, and
emulates the sky so boldly."—p. 214.

Note.—I have been informed by a kind *unknown* correspondent, that the
plant here referred to, which I wrongly conjectured to be the common blue
corn-flower (*centaurea Cyanus*), is the wild chicory or succory, (*cichorium
Intybus*).—E. C.

Printed by William Moore & Co.

INDEX OF SUBJECTS.

Library Edition, 24s.

MEMOIR AND LETTERS

OF

SARA COLERIDGE.

EDITED BY HER DAUGHTER.

Henry S. King & Co., London.

A CLASSIFIED CATALOGUE OF
HENRY S. KING & CO.'S PUBLICATIONS.

CONTENTS.

HISTORY AND BIOGRAPHY.

JOSEPH MAZZINI: A MEMOIR. By **E. A. V.** With two Essays by Mazzini, "Thoughts on Democracy," and "The Duties of Man." Dedicated to the working classes by **P. A. Taylor, M.P.** Crown 8vo. With Two Portraits. 3s. 6d.

SHELLEY MEMORIALS FROM AUTHENTIC SOURCES. Edited by **Lady Shelley.** With (now first printed) an Essay on CHRISTIANITY, by **Percy Bysshe Shelley.** Third Edition. Crown 8vo. With Portrait. Price 5s.

MRS. GILBERT (ANN TAYLOR): AUTOBIOGRAPHY AND OTHER MEMORIALS. Edited by **Josiah Gilbert,** Author of "Cadore; or, Titian's Country," &c. In 2 vols. Post 8vo. With 2 Steel Portraits and several Wood Engravings. 24s.

A. B. GRANVILLE, M.D., F.R.S.: AUTOBIOGRAPHY. With Recollections of the most Eminent Men of the last Half-Century. Being eighty-eight years of the Life of a Physician who practised his Profession in Italy, Greece, Turkey, Spain, Portugal, the West Indies, Russia, Germany, France, and England. Edited, with a brief account of the last years of his life, by his youngest Daughter, **Paulina B. Granville.** 2 vols. Demy 8vo. With a Steel Portrait. 32s.

SAMUEL LOVER, R.H.A., THE LIFE OF: Artistic, Literary, and Musical. With Selections from his Unpublished Papers and Correspondence. By **Bayle Bernard.** 2 vols. Post 8vo. With a Portrait. 21s.

ROWLAND WILLIAMS, D.D.: LIFE & LETTERS. With Extracts from his Note-Books. Edited by **Mrs. Rowland Williams.** With a Photographic Portrait. In 2 vols. Post 8vo. 24s.

WILLIAM GODWIN: AUTOBIOGRAPHY, MEMOIR, AND CORRESPONDENCE. By **C. Kegan Paul.** 2 vols., demy 8vo. [*Preparing.*

JOHN GREY (of Dilston): MEMOIRS. By **Josephine E. Butler.** New and Cheaper Edition. Crown 8vo. 3s. 6d.

"It is not a mere story of success or genius, as far removed as a fairy tale from the experience and imitation of ordinary people; but it is, if we only allow it to be so, an incentive and exemplar to all of us. . . . Something we must say of the skilful and temperate execution of the memoir itself: it is impossible to read it without feeling that Mrs. Butler is her father's daughter, and without wishing that she had given us two volumes instead of one."—*From a five-column notice of "The Times" on the First Edition.*

65, *Cornhill; & 12, Paternoster Row, London.*

HISTORY AND BIOGRAPHY—*continued.*

POLITICAL WOMEN. By **Sutherland Menzies.** 2 vols. Post 8vo. 24s.

"Has all the information of history, with all the interest that attaches to biography."—*Scotsman.*

Third Edition, Revised and Corrected. With Index.

SARA COLERIDGE: MEMOIR AND LETTERS. Edited by her **Daughter.** 2 vols. Crown 8vo. With 2 Portraits. Price 24s.

"Sara Coleridge, as she is revealed, or rather reveals herself, in the correspondence, makes a brilliant addition to a brilliant family reputation."—*Saturday Review.*

"These charming volumes are attractive as a memorial of a most amiable woman of high intellectual mark."—*Athenæum.*

Cheap Edition of the above.

SARA COLERIDGE: MEMOIR AND LETTERS. Edited by her **Daughter.** 1 Vol. Crown 8vo. With a Portrait. 7s. 6d.

THE LATE REV. F. W. ROBERTSON, M.A.: LIFE AND LETTERS. Edited by the **Rev. Stopford A. Brooke, M.A.,** Chaplain in Ordinary to the Queen.

I. In 2 vols., uniform with the Sermons. With a Steel Portrait. Price 7s. 6d.
II. Library Edition, in demy 8vo, with Two Steel Portraits. Price 12s.
III. A Popular Edition, in 1 vol. Price 6s.

NATHANIEL HAWTHORNE: A MEMOIR, with Stories now first published in this country. By **H. A. Page.** Post 8vo. Price 7s. 6d.

"Seldom has it been our lot to meet with a more appreciative delineation of character than this Memoir of Hawthorne."—*Morning Post.*

"Exhibits a discriminating enthusiasm for one of the most fascinating of novelists."—*Saturday Review.*

LEONORA CHRISTINA, Daughter of Christian IV. of Denmark: Memoirs written during her Imprisonment in the Blue Tower of the Royal Palace at Copenhagen, 1663—1685. Translated by **F. E. Bunnètt.** With an Autotype Portrait of the Princess. Medium 8vo. Price 12s. 6d.

"A valuable addition to the tragic romance of history."—*Spectator.*

"A valuable addition to history."—*Daily News.*

LIVES OF ENGLISH POPULAR LEADERS IN THE MIDDLE AGES. No. 1.—STEPHEN LANGTON. By **C. Edmund Maurice.** Cr. 8vo. 7s. 6d.

"Very well and honestly executed."—*John Bull.*

"In style it is characterised by the greatest fairness and ability, and the picture of the archbishop

"is vigorously and firmly drawn."—*Churchman's Shilling Magazine.*

"Well worth a careful study."—*Spanish World.*

LIVES OF ENGLISH POPULAR LEADERS IN THE MIDDLE AGES. No. 2.—TYLER, BALL, and OLDCASTLE. By **C. Edmund Maurice.** Crown 8vo. Price 7s. 6d.

CABINET PORTRAITS. BIOGRAPHICAL SKETCHES OF STATESMEN OF THE DAY. By **T. Wemyss Reid.** 1 vol. Crown 8vo. Price 7s. 6d.

"We have never met with a work which we can more unreservedly praise. The sketches are absolutely impartial."—*Athenæum.*

"We can heartily commend this work."—*Standard.*

"Drawn with a master hand."—*Yorkshire Post.*

THE CHURCH AND THE EMPIRES: Historical Periods. By the late **Henry W. Wilberforce.** Preceded by a Memoir of the Author by **John Henry Newman, D.D.,** of the Oratory. Post 8vo. With Portrait. s. 6d.

"The literary relics preserved by Dr. Newman are varied in subject as in character. They comprise an eloquent, though somewhat empirical, treatise on the formation of Christendom; two masterly reviews of Champigny's too little known

works. . . Henry William Wilberforce was a man of strong opinions, and in all he wrote gave expression to the judgments of a powerful if, possibly, an undetermined mind."—*Standard.*

HISTORY OF THE ENGLISH REVOLUTION OF 1688. By **C. D. Yonge,** Regius Professor, Queen's Coll., Belfast. Crown 8vo. Price 6s.

"A fair, succinct, useful, and masterly summary of the main causes, circumstances, and history of

the Revolution, and not without some stirring comments on its effects."—*Standard.*

ALEXIS DE TOCQUEVILLE. Correspondence and Conversations with **Nassau W. Senior,** from 1833 to 1859. Edited by **M. C. M. Simpson.** In 2 vols. Large post 8vo. Price 21s.

"A book replete with knowledge and thought."—*Quarterly Review.*

"An extremely interesting book."—*Saturday Review.*

HISTORY AND BIOGRAPHY—*continued.*

SORROW AND SONG; or, Studies of Literary Struggle. By **Henry Curwen.** 2 vols. Crown 8vo. 15s.

JOURNALS KEPT IN FRANCE AND ITALY. From 1848 to 1852. With a Sketch of the Revolution of 1848. By the late **Nassau William Senior.** Edited by his Daughter, **M. C. M. Simpson.** In 2 vols. Post 8vo. Price 24s.

"The book has a genuine historical value."—*Saturday Review.*
"No better, more honest, and more readable

view of the state of political society during the existence of the second Republic could well be looked for."—*Examiner.*

PERSIA; ANCIENT AND MODERN: By John **Piggot, F.S.A.** Post 8vo. Price 10s. 6d.

"A very useful book."—*Rock.*
"That Mr. Piggot has spared no pains or research in the execution of his work is apparent in the list of authorities, classic and modern, which he continually quotes; his style also, when not recounting history, is lively and pleasant, and the anecdotes which he culls from the writings of travellers are frequently amusing."—*Hour.*
"We are bound to say that in little more than three hundred pages he has succeeded in his aim

of giving us 'a fair general view of ancient and modern Persian history, supplemented by chapters on the religion, literature, commerce, art, sciences, army, education, language, sport, &c., of the country' . . . He has read up to the level of his subject; old and new authorities have been explored and digested; the style is clear and unambitious; and his compilation is well-planned and is not too long."—*Saturday Review.*

New Edition Revised.

THE HISTORY OF JAPAN. From the Earliest Period to the Present Time. By **Francis Ottiwell Adams, F.R.G.S.,** H.B.M.'s Secretary of Embassy at Berlin, formerly H.B.M.'s Chargé d'Affaires, and Secretary of Legation at Yedo. Volume I. Demy 8vo. With Map and Plans. Price 21s.

"He marshals his facts with skill and judgment; and he writes with an elegance worthy of a very skilled craftsman in literary work. . . We hope Mr. Adams will not keep the public long without the second volume, for the appearance of which all who read the first will anxiously look."—*Standard.*
"As a diplomatic study, and as referring to a

deeply interesting episode in contemporary history, it is well worth reading. The information it contains is trustworthy, and is carefully compiled, and the style is all that can be desired."—*Saturday Review.*
"A most valuable contribution to our knowledge of an interesting people."—*Examiner.*

THE HISTORY OF JAPAN. Volume II. completing the Work. By **Francis Ottiwell Adams, F.R.G.S.** From the year 1865 to present time. Demy 8vo, with Map. Price 21s.

THE NORMAN PEOPLE, AND THEIR EXISTING DESCENDANTS IN THE BRITISH DOMINIONS AND THE UNITED STATES OF AMERICA. 8vo. Price 21s.

"A very singular work. . . We do not accept the consequences to their full extent, but we can cordially recommend the volume as one which is emphatically 'extraordinary.'"—*Notes and Queries.*
"The author has given us a valuable list of mediæval surnames and their origin which demands our best gratitude."—*Standard.*

THE RUSSIANS IN CENTRAL ASIA. A Critical Examination, down to the present time, of the Geography and History of Central Asia. By **Baron F. von Hellwald.** Translated by **Lieut.-Col. Theodore Wirgman, LL.B.** In 1 vol. Large post 8vo, with Map. Price 12s.

"A learned account of the geography of this still ill-known land, of the characteristics of its main divisions, of the nature and habits of its numerous races, and of the progress through it of Russian influence. . . . It contains a large amount of valuable information."—*Times.*
"A lucidly written, and apparently accurate account of Turkestan, its geographical features and its history. Its worth to the reader is further enhanced by a well-executed map, based on the most recent Russian surveys."—*Glasgow News.*

BOKHARA : ITS HISTORY AND CONQUEST. By **Professor Arminius Vàmbèry,** of the University of Pesth. Demy 8vo. Price 18s.

"We conclude with a cordial recommendation of this valuable book."—*Saturday Review.*
"Almost every page abounds with composition of peculiar merit."—*Morning Post.*

THE RELIGIOUS HISTORY OF IRELAND: PRIMITIVE, PAPAL, AND PROTESTANT ; including the Evangelical Missions, Catholic Agitations, and Church Progress of the last half Century. By **James Godkin.** 1 vol. 8vo. Price 12s.

"These latter chapters on the statistics of the various religious denominations will be welcomed."—*Evening Standard.*
"Mr. Godkin writes with evident honesty, and the topic on which he writes is one about which an honest book is greatly wanted."—*Examiner.*

HISTORY AND BIOGRAPHY—*continued.*

THE GOVERNMENT OF THE NATIONAL DEFENCE. From the 30th June to the 31st October, 1870. The Plain Statement of a Member. By **Mons. Jules Favre.** 1 vol. Demy 8vo. Price 10s. 6d.

"A work of the highest interest. The book is most valuable."—*Athenæum.*
"Of all the contributions to the history of the late war, we have found none more fascinating and,

perhaps, none more valuable than the 'apology,' by M. Jules Favre, for the unsuccessful Government of the National Defence."—*Times.*

ECHOES OF A FAMOUS YEAR. By **Harriet Parr,** Author of "The Life of Jeanne d'Arc," "In the Silver Age," &c. Crown 8vo. Price 8s. 6d.

"Miss Parr has the great gift of charming simplicity of style; and if children are not interested

in her book, many of their seniors will be "—*British Quarterly Review.*

VOYAGES AND TRAVEL.

SOME TIME IN IRELAND; A Recollection. Crown 8vo. 7s. 6d.

"The author has got a genuine Irish gift of witty and graceful writing, and has produced a clever and entertaining book."—*Examiner.*
"Clever, brilliant sketches of life and character among the Irish gentry of the last generation. . .

The little volume will give to strangers a more faithful idea of Irish society and tendencies still working in that unhappy island than any other we know."—*Literary Churchman.*

WAYSIDE NOTES IN SCANDINAVIA. Being Notes of Travel in the North of Europe. By **Mark Antony Lower, F.S.A., M.A.** Crown 8vo. 9s.

*** This Volume is an Account of Researches prosecuted, during a Tour in Scandinavia, in the Summer of 1873. It contains illustrations of the History, Antiquities, Legendary Lore, and Social Condition of Denmark, Sweden, and Norway, from Ancient to Modern Times.

"A very entertaining volume of light, gossiping matter, written in an easy, agreeable style."—*Daily News.*

ON THE ROAD TO KHIVA. By **David Ker,** late Khivan Correspondent of the *Daily Telegraph.* Illustrated with Photographs of the Country and its Inhabitants, and a copy of the Official Map in use during the Campaign, from the Survey of CAPTAIN LEUSILIN. 1 vol. Post 8vo. Price 12s.

"Though it is a graphic and thoughtful sketch, we refer to it, in some degree, for reasons apart from its intrinsic merits. . . He (the author) has satisfied us that he was not the impudent impostor he seemed to be; and though he did not witness the fall of Khiva, he travelled through a great part of Central Asia, and honestly tried to accomplish his task. . . His work, we have said, is an able *résumé* of genuine observation and reflection, which will well repay a reader's attention "—*Times.*

"Very interesting reading . . . a really good book full of quaint, vivid writing."—*Echo.*
"He is a clever and fluent writer. . . The book is smartly written."—*Saturday Review.*
"A pleasant book of travels. It is exceedingly smart and clever, full of amusing anecdotes and graphic descriptions."—*Vanity Fair.*
"Mr. Ker knows Russian peasant life very well indeed, and his bits about the Cossacks are full of character."—*Athenæum.*

VIZCAYA; or, Life in the Land of the Carlists at the Outbreak of the Insurrection, with some account of the Iron Mines and other characteristics of the country. With a Map and 8 Illustrations. Crown 8vo. Price 9s.

"Contains some really valuable information, conveyed in a plain unostentatious manner."—*Athenæum.*
"Agreeably written. . . . People will read with interest what an English party thought and felt

when shut up in Portugalete or Bilbao; the sketches will give a good idea of those places and the surroundings, and the map will be useful if they feel inclined to study the recent operations."—*Colburn's United Service Magazine.*

ROUGH NOTES OF A VISIT TO BELGIUM, SEDAN, AND PARIS, in September, 1870–71. By **John Ashton.** Crown 8vo. Price 3s. 6d.

"The author does not attempt to deal with military subjects, but writes sensibly of what he saw in 1870–71."—*John Bull.*
"Possesses a certain freshness from the straight-

forward simplicity with which it is written."—*Graphic.*
"An interesting work by a highly intelligent observer."—*Standard.*

THE ALPS OF ARABIA; or, Travels through Egypt, Sinai, Arabia, and the Holy Land. By **William Charles Maughan.** Demy 8vo, with Map. 12s.

"Deeply interesting and valuable."—*Edinburgh Daily Review.*
"He writes freshly and with competent knowledge."—*Standard.*

"Very readable and instructive. . . . . A work far above the average of such publications."—*John Bull.*

Second Edition.

THE MISHMEE HILLS: an Account of a Journey made in an Attempt to Penetrate Thibet from Assam, to open New Routes for Commerce. By **T. T. Cooper.** With Four Illustrations and Map. Post 8vo. Price 10s. 6d.

"The volume, which will be of great use in India and among Indian merchants here, contains a good deal of matter that will interest ordinary readers. | It is especially rich in sporting incidents."—*Standard.*

GOODMAN'S CUBA THE PEARL OF THE ANTILLES. By **Walter Goodman.** Crown 8vo. Price 7s. 6d.

"A series of vivid and miscellaneous sketches. We can recommend this whole volume as very amusing reading."—*Pall Mall Gazette.* | "The whole book deserves the heartiest commendation. . . . .Sparkling and amusing from beginning to end."—*Spectator.*

FIELD AND FOREST RAMBLES OF A NATURALIST IN NEW BRUNSWICK. With Notes and Observations on the Natural History of Eastern Canada. By **A. Leith Adams, M.A.** Illustrated. 8vo, cloth. 14s.

"Both sportsmen and naturalists will find this work replete with anecdote and carefully-recorded observation, which will entertain them."—*Nature.* "Will be found interesting by those who take a | pleasure either in sport or natural history."—*Athenæum.* "To the naturalist the book will be most valuable. . . . To the general reader most interesting."—*Evening Standard.*

Second Edition. Revised and Corrected.

TENT LIFE WITH ENGLISH GIPSIES IN NORWAY. By **Hubert Smith.** With Five full-page Engravings, 31 smaller Illustrations, and Map of the Country showing Routes. 8vo, cloth. Price 21s.

"Written in a very lively style, and has throughout a smack of dry humour and satiric reflection which shows the writer to be a keen observer of | men and things. We hope that many will read it and find in it the same amusement as ourselves."—*Times.*

FAYOUM; OR, ARTISTS IN EGYPT. A Tour with M. Gérôme and others. By **J. Lenoir.** With 13 Illustrations. Crown 8vo, cloth. Price 7s. 6d.

"The book is very amusing. . . . Whoever may take it up will find he has with him a bright and pleasant companion."—*Spectator.* | "A pleasantly written and very readable book."—*Examiner.*

SPITZBERGEN—THE GATEWAY TO THE POLYNIA; OR, A VOYAGE TO SPITZBERGEN. By **Captain John C. Wells, R.N.** With numerous Illustrations and Map. 8vo, cloth. Price 21s.

"Straightforward and clear in style, securing our confidence by its unaffected simplicity and good sense."—*Saturday Review.* | "A charming book, remarkably well written and well illustrated."—*Standard.*

AN AUTUMN TOUR IN THE UNITED STATES AND CANADA. By **Lieut.-Col. J. G. Medley.** Crown 8vo. Price 5s.

"Colonel Medley's little volume is a pleasantly-written account of a two months' visit to America."—*Hour.* "May be recommended as manly, sensible, and | pleasantly written."—*Globe.* "His impressions of political life in America, as coming from a thoroughly practical man, are worth recording."—*Pall Mall Gazette.*

Second Edition.

THE NILE WITHOUT A DRAGOMAN. By **Frederic Eden.** In 1 vol. Crown 8vo, cloth. Price 7s. 6d.

"It is a book to read during an autumn holiday."—*Spectator.* "Should any of our readers care to imitate Mr. Eden's example, and wish to see things with their | own eyes, and shift for themselves, next winter in Upper Egypt, they will find this book a very agreeable guide."—*Times.*

ROUND THE WORLD IN 1870. A Volume of Travels, with Maps. By **A. D. Carlisle, B.A.,** Trin. Coll., Camb. Demy 8vo. Price 16s.

"We can only commend, which we do very heartily, an eminently sensible and readable book."—*British Quarterly Review.* "Mr. Carlisle's account of his little outing is exhilarating and charming."—*Spectator.* | "Rarely have we read a more graphic description of the countries named, India, China, Japan, California, and South America . . . The chapters about Japan are especially replete with information."—*John Bull.*

VOYAGES AND TRAVEL—*continued.*

IRELAND. A Tour of Observation, with Remarks on Irish Public Questions. By **Dr. James Macaulay.** Crown 8vo. Price 7s. 6d.

"We have rarely met a book on Ireland which for impartiality of criticism and general accuracy of information could be so well recommended to the fair-minded Irish reader."—*Evening Standard.*

"A careful and instructive book. Full of facts, full of information, and full of interest."—*Literary Churchman.*

A WINTER IN MOROCCO. By **Amelia Perrier.** With 4 Illustrations. Crown 8vo. Price 10s. 6d.

"Well worth reading, and contains several excellent illustrations."—*Hour.*
"Miss Perrier is a very amusing writer. She has a good deal of humour, sees the oddity and quaint-

ness of Oriental life with a quick observant eye, and evidently turned her opportunities of sarcastic examination to account."—*Daily News.*

SCIENCE.

THE PHYSICS AND PHILOSOPHY OF THE SENSES; OR THE MENTAL AND THE PHYSICAL IN THEIR MUTUAL RELATION. By **R. S. Wyld, F.R.S.E.** Illustrated by Several Plates. Demy 8vo. Price 16s.

The author's object is twofold : first, to supply a Manual of the Senses, embracing the more important discoveries of recent times ; second, in discussing the subject of Life, Organisation, Sensibility, and Thought, to demonstrate in opposition to the Materialistic Theory, that the Senses, no less than Reason, furnish proof that an immaterial and spiritual element is the operative element in nature.

SCIENTIFIC LONDON. By **Bernard H. Becker.** 1 vol. Crown 8vo. 5s.
An Account of the History and present Scope of the following Institutions :—

The Royal Society
The Royal Institution
The Institution of Civil Engineers
The Royal Geographical Society
The Society of Telegraph Engineers
The British Association
The Birkbeck Institute
The Society of Arts

The Government Department of Science and Art
The Statistical Society
The Chemical Society
The Museum of Practical Geology
The London Institution
The Gresham Lectures.

OBSERVATIONS OF MAGNETIC DECLINATION MADE AT TREVANDRUM AND AGUSTIA MALLEY in the Observatories of his Highness the MAHARAJAH OF TRAVANCORE, G.C.S.I., in the Years 1852 to 1860. Being Trevandrum Magnetical Observations, Volume I. Discussed and Edited by **John Allan Broun, F.R.S.,** late Director of the Observatories. With an Appendix. Imperial 4to, cloth. 3l. 3s.

** The Appendix, containing Reports on the Observatories and on the Public Museum, Public Park and Gardens at Trevandrum, pp. xii. 116, may be had separately. Price 21s.

EUCLID SIMPLIFIED IN METHOD AND LANGUAGE. Being a Manual of Geometry on the French System. By **J. R. Morell.**

The chief features of the work are :—The separation of Theorems and Problems—The Natural Sequence of reasoning ; areas being treated by themselves and at a later page— The simpler and more natural treatment of ratio—The legitimate use of arithmetical applications, of transposition, and superposition—The general alteration of language to a more modern form—Lastly, if it be assumed to be venturesome to supersede the time-hallowed pages of Euclid it may be urged that the attempt is made under the shelter of very high authorities.

THE QUESTIONS OF AURAL SURGERY. By **James Hinton,** late Aural Surgeon to Guy's Hospital. Post 8vo. With Illustrations. Price 12s. 6d.

"The questions of Aural Surgery more than maintain the author's reputation as a careful clini-

cian, a deep and accurate thinker, and a forcible and talented writer."—*Lancet.*

AN ATLAS OF DISEASES OF THE MEMBRANA TYMPANI. With Descriptive Text. By **James Hinton,** late Aural Surgeon to Guy's Hospital. Post 8vo. Price £6 6s.

"Of Mr. Hinton's Atlas of the Membrana Tympani it is hardly necessary to say more than that it is by far the best and most accurate that has

ever yet been published. The drawings are taken from actual specimens, and are all coloured by hand."—*Lancet.*

SCIENCE—*continued.*

Second Edition.

PHYSIOLOGY FOR PRACTICAL USE. By various Writers. Edited by James Hinton. 2 vols. Crown 8vo. With 50 Illustrations. Price 12s. 6d.

"A more clear, valuable, and well-informed set of treatises we never saw than these, which are bound up into two compact and readable volumes. And they are pleasant reading, too, as well as useful reading."—*Literary Churchman.*

"We never saw the popular side of the science of physiology better explained than it is in these two thin volumes."—*Standard.*

"It has certainly been edited with great care. Physiological treatises we have had in great number, but not one work, we believe, which so thoroughly appeals to all classes of the community as the present. Everything has apparently been done to render the work really practical and useful."—*Civil Service Gazette.*

Second Edition.

THE PRINCIPLES OF MENTAL PHYSIOLOGY. With their Applications to the Training and Discipline of the Mind, and the Study of its Morbid Conditions. By W. B. Carpenter, LL.D., M.D., &c. 8vo. Illustrated. 12s.

"This valuable book . . . . Let us add that nothing we have said, or in any limited space could say, would give an adequate conception of the valuable and curious collection of facts bearing on morbid mental conditions, the learned physiological exposition, and the treasure-house of useful hints for mental training which make this large and yet very amusing, as well as instructive book, an encyclopædia of well-classified and often very startling psychological experiences."—*Spectator.*

SENSATION AND INTUITION. Studies in Psychology and Æsthetics. By James Sully, M.A. Demy 8vo. 10s. 6d.

"As to the manner of the book, Mr. Sully writes well, and so as to be understood by any one who will take the needful pains. . . . The materials furnished by a quick and lively natural sense are happily ordered by a mind trained in scientific method. This merit is especially conspicuous in those parts of the book where, with abundant ingenuity and no mean success, Mr. Sully endeavours to throw some light of cosmic order into the chaos of æsthetics. Unhappily for our present purpose, the best qualities of the work are precisely those to which we cannot do justice within the limits of a review."—*Saturday Review.*

"Though the series of essays is by no means devoid of internal connection, each presents so many new points of interest that it is impossible here to note more than one or two particulars. The first essay of all, wherein the author considers the relation of the Evolution-hypothesis to human psychology, may be cited as an excellent specimen of his style of work."—*Examiner.*

". . . In conclusion, we beg to thank Mr. Sully for a meritorious and successful attempt to popularise valuable and not very tractable departments of science."—*Academy.*

Second Edition.

THE EXPANSE OF HEAVEN. A Series of Essays on the Wonders of the Firmament. By R. A. Proctor, B.A. With a Frontispiece. Crown 8vo. 6s.

"A very charming work; cannot fail to lift the reader's mind up 'through nature's work to nature's God.'"—*Standard.*

"Full of thought, readable, and popular."—*Brighton Gazette.*

STUDIES OF BLAST FURNACE PHENOMENA. By M. L. Gruner. Translated by L. D. B. Gordon, F.R.S.E., F.G.S. 8vo. 7s. 6d.

"The whole subject is dealt with very copiously and clearly in all its parts, and can scarcely fail of appreciation at the hands of practical men, for whose use it is designed."—*Post.*

CONTEMPORARY ENGLISH PSYCHOLOGY. From the French of Professor Th. Ribot. Large post 8vo. Price 9s. An Analysis of the Views and Opinions of the following Metaphysicians, as expressed in their writings:—

James Mill, Alexander Bain, John Stuart Mill, George H. Lewes, Herbert Spencer, Samuel Bailey.

"The task which M. Ribot set himself he has performed with very great success."—*Examiner.*

"We can cordially recommend the volume."—*Journal of Mental Science.*

HEREDITY: a Psychological Study on its Phenomena, its Laws, its Causes, and its Consequences. By Th. Ribot, Author of "Contemporary English Psychology." 1 vol. Large crown 8vo.

It is generally admitted that "Heredity"—or that biological law by which all living creatures tend to reproduce themselves in their descendants—is the rule in all forms of vital activity. The author devotes his work to the study of the question, "Does the law also hold in regard to the mental faculties?"

A TREATISE ON RELAPSING FEVER. By R. T. Lyons, Assistant-Surgeon, Bengal Army. Post 8vo. Price 7s. 6d.

"A practical work, thoroughly supported in its views by a series of remarkable cases."—*Standard.*

SCIENCE—*continued.*

Second Edition Revised.

A LEGAL HANDBOOK FOR ARCHITECTS, BUILDERS, AND BUILDING OWNERS. By **Edward Jenkins, Esq., M.P.,** and **John Raymond, Esq.,** Barristers-at-Law. Crown 8vo. 6s.

"This manual has one recommendation which cannot be accorded to more than a very small proportion of the books published at the present day. It proposes to supply a real want. . . . As to the style of the work, it is just what a legal handbook should be. . . . We warmly recommend it to our readers."—*Architect.*

"It would be doing it an injustice to class it with the rank and file of legal hand-books. In tone and style it resembles Lord St. Leonards' well-known popular treatise on the law of real property. The writer conceives his subject clearly, and writes in a manner that is pleasant, forcible, and lucid."—*Law Magazine and Review.*

"For all this and much more, about buildings and building contracts, which is not always easy for a layman to understand, but which it is very necessary for an architect to know, the reader will find in the neat little volume just published from the pen of Messrs. Jenkins and Raymond, a very excellent guide."—*Law Journal.*

THE HISTORY OF CREATION, a Popular Account of the Development of the Earth and its Inhabitants, according to the theories of Kant, Laplace, Lamarck, and Darwin. By **Professor Ernst Hæckel** of the University of Jena. The Translation revised by **E. Ray Lankester, M.A.** With Coloured Plates and Genealogical Trees of the various groups of both plants and animals. 2 vols. Post 8vo.
[*Preparing.*

THE HISTORY OF THE EVOLUTION OF MAN. By **Ernst Hæckel.** Translated by **E. A. Van Rhyn** and **L. Elsberg, M.D.** (University of New York), with Notes and Additions sanctioned by the Author. Post 8vo.

A New Edition.

CHANGE OF AIR AND SCENE. A Physician's Hints about Doctors, Patients, Hygiène, and Society; with Notes of Excursions for health in the Pyrenees, and amongst the Watering-places of France (Inland and Seaward), Switzerland, Corsica, and the Mediterranean. By **Dr. Alphonse Donné.** Large post 8vo. Price 9s.

"A very readable and serviceable book . . . . . The real value of it is to be found in the accurate and minute information given with regard to a large number of places which have gained a reputation on the continent for their mineral waters."—*Pall Mall Gazette.*

"A singularly pleasant and chatty as well as instructive book about health."—*Guardian.*

"A valuable and almost complete *vade mecum* for the continental tourist seeking health."—*London Quarterly Review.*

New and Enlarged Edition.

MISS YOUMANS' FIRST BOOK OF BOTANY. Designed to cultivate the observing powers of Children. With 300 Engravings. Crown 8vo. Price 5s.

"It is but rarely that a school-book appears which is at once so novel in plan, so successful in execution, and so suited to the general want, as to command universal and unqualified approbation, but such has been the case with Miss Youmans' First Book of Botany . . . . It has been everywhere welcomed as a timely and invaluable contribution to the improvement of primary education."—*Pall Mall Gazette.*

A DICTIONARY AND GLOSSARY OF THE KOR-AN. With copious Grammatical References and Explanations of the Text. By **Major J. Penrice, B.A.** 4to. Price 21s.

"The book is likely to answer its purpose in smoothing a beginner's road in reading the Kor-ân."—*Academy.*

MODERN GOTHIC ARCHITECTURE. By **T. G. Jackson.** Crown 8vo. Price 5s.

"The reader will find some of the most important doctrines of eminent art teachers practically applied in this little book, which is well written and popular in style."—*Manchester Examiner.*

"This thoughtful little book is worthy of the perusal of all interested in art or architecture."—*Standard.*

CHOLERA: HOW TO AVOID AND TREAT IT. Popular and Practical Notes by **Henry Blanc, M.D.** Crown 8vo. Price 4s. 6d.
"A very practical manual, based on experience and careful observation, full of excellent hints on a most dangerous disease."—*Standard.*

THE INTERNATIONAL SCIENTIFIC SERIES.

The following is a List of the Volumes already published.

Fourth Edition.

I. THE FORMS OF WATER IN CLOUDS AND RIVERS, ICE AND GLACIERS. By J. Tyndall, LL.D., F.R.S. With 26 Illustrations. Price 5s.

Second Edition.

II. PHYSICS AND POLITICS; OR, THOUGHTS ON THE APPLICATION OF THE PRINCIPLES OF "NATURAL SELECTION" AND "INHERITANCE" TO POLITICAL SOCIETY. By Walter Bagehot. Price 4s.

Third Edition.

III. FOODS. By Dr. Edward Smith. Profusely Illustrated. Price 5s.

Third Edition.

IV. MIND AND BODY; THE THEORIES OF THEIR RELATION. By Alexander Bain, LL.D., Professor of Logic at the University of Aberdeen. With Four Illustrations. Price 4s.

Fourth Edition.

V. THE STUDY OF SOCIOLOGY. By Herbert Spencer. Price 5s.

Third Edition.

VI. THE CONSERVATION OF ENERGY. By Professor Balfour Stewart. With Fourteen Engravings. Price 5s.

Second Edition.

VII. ANIMAL LOCOMOTION; or, Walking, Swimming, and Flying. By J. Bell Pettigrew, M.D., F.R.S. With 119 Illustrations. Price 5s.

Second Edition.

VIII. RESPONSIBILITY IN MENTAL DISEASE. By Dr. Henry Maudsley. Price 5s.

Second Edition.

IX. THE NEW CHEMISTRY. By Professor Josiah P. Cooke, of the Harvard University. With Thirty-one Illustrations. Price 5s.

Second Edition.

X. THE SCIENCE OF LAW. By Prof. Sheldon Amos. Price 5s.

Second Edition.

XI. ANIMAL MECHANISM. A Treatise on Terrestrial and Aerial Locomotion. By Professor E. J. Marey. With 117 Illustrations. Price 5s.

XII. THE DOCTRINE OF DESCENT AND DARWINISM. By Professor Oscar Schmidt (Strasburg University). Illustrated. Price 5s.

XIII. HISTORY OF THE CONFLICT BETWEEN RELIGION AND SCIENCE. By John William Draper, M.D., LL.D. Professor in the University of New York; Author of "A Treatise on Human Physiology." Price 5s.

XIV. THE CHEMICAL EFFECTS OF LIGHT AND PHOTOGRAPHY, IN THEIR APPLICATION TO ART, SCIENCE, AND INDUSTRY. By Dr. Hermann Vogel (Polytechnic Academy of Berlin). With 74 Illustrations.

XV. OPTICS. By Professor Lommel (University of Erlangen). Profusely Illustrated.

XVI. FUNGI: THEIR NATURE, INFLUENCES, USES, &c. By M. C. Cooke, M.A., LL.D. Edited by the Rev. M. J. Berkeley, M.A., F.L.S. Profusely Illustrated.

THE INTERNATIONAL SCIENTIFIC SERIES—*continued.*

Forthcoming Volumes.

Mons. VAN BENEDEN.
On Parasites in the Animal Kingdom.

Prof. W. KINGDOM CLIFFORD, M.A.
The First Principles of the Exact Sciences explained to the non-mathematical.

Prof. T. H. HUXLEY, LL.D., F.R.S.
Bodily Motion and Consciousness.

Dr. W. B. CARPENTER, LL.D., F.R.S.
The Physical Geography of the Sea.

Prof. WILLIAM OLLING, F.R.S.
The Old Chemistry viewed from the New Standpoint.

W. LAUDER LINDSAY, M.D., F.R.S.E.
Mind in the Lower Animals.

Sir JOHN LUBBOCK, Bart., F.R.S.
The Antiquity of Man.

Prof. W. T. THISELTON DYER, B.A., B.SC.
Form and Habit in Flowering Plants.

Mr. J. N. LOCKYER, F.R.S.
Spectrum Analysis : some of its recent results.

Prof. MICHAEL FOSTER, M.D.
Protoplasm and the Cell Theory.

Prof. W. STANLEY JEVONS.
Money : and the Mechanism of Exchange.

H. CHARLTON BASTIAN, M.D., F.R.S.
The Brain as an Organ of Mind.

Prof. A. C. RAMSAY, LL.D., F.R.S.
Earth Sculpture : Hills, Valleys, Mountains, Plains, Rivers, Lakes ; how they were produced, and how they have been Destroyed.

Prof. RUDOLPH VIRCHOW (Berlin Univ.)
Morbid Physiological Action.

Prof. CLAUDE BERNARD.
Physical and Metaphysical Phenomena of Life.

Prof. H. SAINTE-CLAIRE DEVILLE.
An Introduction to General Chemistry.

Prof. WURTZ.
Atoms and the Atomic Theory.

Prof. DE QUATREFAGES.
The Negro Races.

Prof. LACAZE-DUTHIERS.
Zoology since Cuvier.

Prof. BERTHELOT.
Chemical Synthesis.

Prof. J. ROSENTHAL.
General Physiology of Muscles and Nerves.

Prof. JAMES D. DANA, M.A., LL.D.
On Cephalization ; or, Head-Characters in the Gradation and Progress of Life.

Prof. S. W. JOHNSON, M.A.
On the Nutrition of Plants.

Prof. AUSTIN FLINT, Jr. M.D.
The Nervous System and its Relation to the Bodily Functions.

Prof. W. D. WHITNEY.
Modern Linguistic Science.

Prof BERNSTEIN (University of Halle).
Physiology of the Senses.

Prof. FERDINAND COHN (Breslau Univ.)
Thallophytes (Algæ, Lichens, Fungi).

Prof. HERMANN (University of Zurich).
Respiration.

Prof. LEUCKART (University of Leipsic).
Outlines of Animal Organization.

Prof. LIEBREICH (University of Berlin).
Outlines of Toxicology.

Prof. KUNDT (University of Strasburg).
On Sound.

Prof. REES (University of Erlangen).
On Parasitic Plants.

Prof. STEINTHAL (University of Berlin).
Outlines of the Science of Language.

P. BERT (Professor of Physiology, Paris).
Forms of Life and other Cosmical Conditions.

E. ALGLAVE (Professor of Constitutional and Administrative Law at Douai, and of Political Economy at Lille).
The Primitive Elements of Political Constitutions

P. LORAIN (Professor of Medicine, Paris).
Modern Epidemics.

Prof. SCHÜTZENBERGER (Director of the Chemical Laboratory at the Sorbonne).
On Fermentations.

Mons. FREIDEL.
The Functions of Organic Chemistry.

Mons. DEBRAY.
Precious Metals.

Mons. P. BLASERNA (Professor in the University of Rome.)
On Sound ; The Organs of Voice and of Hearing.

ESSAYS AND LECTURES.

THE BETTER SELF. Essays for Home Life. By the Author of "The Gentle Life." Crown 8vo. 6s.

A CLUSTER OF LIVES. By **Alice King**, Author of "Queen of Herself," &c. Crown 8vo. 7s. 6d.
> CONTENTS.—Vittoria Colonna—Madame Récamier—A Daughter of the Stuarts—Dante—Madame de Sévigné—Geoffrey Chaucer—Edmund Spenser—Captain Cook's Companion—Ariosto—Lucrezia Borgia—Petrarch—Cervantes—Joan of Arc—Galileo—Madame Cottin—Song of the Bird in the Garden of Armida.

Second Edition.

IN STRANGE COMPANY; or, The Note Book of a Roving Correspondent. By **James Greenwood**, "The Amateur Casual." Crown 8vo. 6s.
> "A bright, lively book."—*Standard.*
> "Has all the interest of romance."—*Queen.*
> "Some of the papers remind us of Charles Lamb on beggars and chimney-sweeps."—*Echo.*

MASTER-SPIRITS. By **Robert Buchanan.** Post 8vo. 10s. 6d.
> "Good Books are the precious life-blood of Master-Spirits."—*Milton.*
> "Full of fresh and vigorous writing, such as can only be produced by a man of keen and independent intellect."—*Saturday Review.*
> "Written with a beauty of language and a spirit of vigorous enthusiasm rare even in our best living word-painters."—*Standard.*
> "A very pleasant and readable book." *Examiner.*
> "Mr. Buchanan is a writer whose books the critics may always open with satisfaction . . . both manly and artistic."—*Hour.*

GLANCES AT INNER ENGLAND. A Lecture delivered in the United States and Canada. By **Edward Jenkins**, M.P., Author of "Ginx's Baby," &c. Crown 8vo. Price 5s.
> "These 'glances' exhibit much of the author's characteristic discrimination and judgment."— *Edinburgh Courant.*
> "Cleverly written, full of terse adages and
> rapier-like epigrams it is; thoughtful and just it is in many respects."—*Echo.*
> "Eloquent and epigrammatic." — *Illustrated Review.*

OUR LAND LAWS. Short Lectures delivered before the Working Men's College. By **T. Leon Wilkinson.** Crown 8vo, limp cloth. 2s.
> "A very handy and intelligible epitome of the general principles of existing land laws."—*Standard.*

AN ESSAY ON THE CULTURE OF THE OBSERVING POWERS OF CHILDREN, especially in connection with the Study of Botany. By **Eliza A. Youmans.** Edited, with Notes and a Supplement, by **Joseph Payne,** F.C.P., Author of "Lectures on the Science and Art of Education," &c. Crown 8vo. 2s. 6d.
> "This study, according to her just notions on the subject, is to be fundamentally based on the exercise of the pupil's own powers of observation. He is to see and examine the properties of plants and
> flowers at first hand, not merely to be informed of what others have seen and examined."—*Pall Mall Gazette.*

THE GENIUS OF CHRISTIANITY UNVEILED. Being Essays by **William Godwin,** Author of "Political Justice," &c. Edited with a preface by **C. Kegan Paul.** 1 vol. Crown 8vo. 7s. 6d.
> "Few have thought more clearly and directly than William Godwin, or expressed their reflections with more simplicity and unreserve." *Examiner.*
> "The deliberate thoughts of Godwin deserve to be put before the world for reading and consideration."—*Athenæum.*

WORKS BY JOSEPH PAYNE, Professor of the Science and Art of Education to the College of Preceptors.
> THE TRUE FOUNDATION OF SCIENCE TEACHING. A Lecture delivered at the College of Preceptors. 8vo, sewed, 6d.
> THE SCIENCE AND ART OF EDUCATION. A Lecture introductory to a "Course of Lectures and Lessons to Teachers on the Science, Art, and History of Education," delivered at the College of Preceptors. 8vo, sewed, 6d.
> FRÖBEL AND THE KINDERGARTEN SYSTEM OF ELEMENTARY EDUCATION. A Lecture delivered at the College of Preceptors. 8vo, sewed, 6d.

MILITARY WORKS.

MOUNTAIN WARFARE, illustrated by the Campaign of 1799 in Switzerland, being a translation of the Swiss Narrative compiled from the works of the Archduke Charles, Jomini, and others. Also of Notes by General H. Dufour on the Campaign of the Vatteline in 1635. By **Major-General Shadwell, C.B.** With Appendix, Maps, and Introductory Remarks.

This work has been prepared for the purpose of illustrating by the well-known campaign of 1799 in Switzerland, the true method of conducting warfare in mountainous countries. Many of the scenes of this contest are annually visited by English tourists, and are in themselves full of interest; but the special object of the volume is to attract the attention of the young officers of our army to this branch of warfare, especially of those, whose lot may hereafter be cast, and who may be called upon to take part in operations against the Hill Tribes of our extensive Indian frontier.

RUSSIA'S ADVANCE EASTWARD. Based on the Official Reports of Lieut. Hugo Stumm, German Military Attaché to the Khivan Expedition. To which is appended other Information on the Subject, and a Minute Account of the Russian Army. By **Capt. C. E. H. Vincent, F.R.G.S.** Crown 8vo. With Map. 6s.

"Captain Vincent's account of the improvements which have taken place lately in all branches of the service is accurate and clear, and is full of useful material for the consideration of those who believe that Russia is still where she was left by the Crimean war."—*Athenæum.*

"Even more interesting, perhaps, than Lieu-

tenant Stumm's narrative of one of the most brilliant military exploits of recent years is Captain Vincent's own account of the reconstruction, under Milutin, of the Russian Army. Few books will give a better idea of its progress than this brief survey of its present state and latest achievement."—*Graphic.*

THE VOLUNTEER, THE MILITIAMAN, AND THE REGULAR SOLDIER; a Conservative View of the Armies of England, Past, Present, and Future, as Seen in January, 1874. By **A Public School Boy.** 1 vol. Crown 8vo. Price 5s.

"Deserves special attention. . . . It is a good and compact little work, and treats the whole topic in a clear, intelligible, and rational way. There is an interesting chapter styled "Historical Retrospect," which very briefly traces all the main

steps in the growth of the English army from the time of the Anglo-Saxons. The writer is at great pains to examine the real facts concerning enlistment into the different branches of the army at the present day."—*Westminster Review.*

THE OPERATIONS OF THE GERMAN ENGINEERS AND TECHNICAL TROOPS IN THE FRANCO-GERMAN WAR OF 1870-71. By **Capt. A. von Goetze.** Translated by **Col. G. Graham.** Demy 8vo. With Six Plans.

THE OPERATIONS OF THE FIRST ARMY, UNDER GEN. VON STEINMETZ. By **Major von Schell.** Translated by **Captain E. O. Hollist.** With Three Maps. Demy 8vo. Price 10s. 6d.

"A very complete and important account of the investment of Metz."

"The volume is of somewhat too technical a character to be recommended to the general reader, but the military student will find it a valu-

able contribution to the history of the great struggle; and its utility is increased by a capital general map of the operations of the First Army, and also plans of Spicheren and of the battle-fields round Metz."—*John Bull.*

THE OPERATIONS OF THE FIRST ARMY UNDER GEN. VON GOEBEN. By **Major von Schell.** Translated by **Col. C. H. von Wright.** Four Maps. Demy 8vo. Price 9s.

"In concluding our notice of this instructive work, which, by the way, is enriched by several large-scale maps, we must not withhold our tribute of admiration at the manner in which the translator has performed his task. So thoroughly, indeed,

has he succeeded, that it might really be imagined that the book had been originally composed in English. . . The work is decidedly valuable to a student of the art of war, and no military library can be considered complete without it."—*Hour.*

THE OPERATIONS OF THE FIRST ARMY UNDER GEN. VON MANTEUFFEL. By **Col. Count Hermann von Wartensleben,** Chief of the Staff of the First Army. Translated by **Colonel C. H. von Wright.** With Two Maps. Demy 8vo. Price 9s.

"Very clear, simple, yet eminently instructive, is this history. It is not overladen with useless details, is written in good taste, and possesses the in-

estimable value of being in great measure the record of operations actually witnessed by the author, supplemented by official documents."—*Athenæum.*

MILITARY WORKS—*continued.*

THE GERMAN ARTILLERY IN THE BATTLES NEAR METZ
Based on the official reports of the German Artillery. By **Captain Hoffbauer**, Instructor in the German Artillery and Engineer School. Translated by **Capt. E. O. Hollist.** Demy 8vo. With Map and Plans. Price 21*s.*

"Captain Hoffbauer's style is much more simple and agreeable than those of many of his comrades and fellow authors, and it suffers nothing in the hands of Captain Hollist, whose translation is close and faithful. He has given the general public a read- | able and instructive book; whilst to his brother officers, who have a special professional interest in the subject, its value cannot well be overrated."—*Academy.*

THE OPERATIONS OF THE BAVARIAN ARMY CORPS.
By **Captain Hugo Helvig.** Translated by **Captain G. S. Schwabe.** With 5 large Maps. In 2 vols. Demy 8vo. Price 24*s.*

"It contains much material that may prove useful to the future historian of the war; and it is, on the whole, written in a spirit of fairness and impartiality. . . It only remains to say that the work is enriched by some excellent large scale maps, | and that the translator has performed his work most creditably."—*Athenæum.* "Captain Schwabe has done well to translate it, and his translation is admirably executed."—*Pall Mall Gazette.*

AUSTRIAN CAVALRY EXERCISE.
From an Abridged Edition compiled by CAPTAIN ILLIA WOINOVITS, of the General Staff, on the Tactical Regulations of the Austrian Army, and prefaced by a General Sketch of the Organisation, &c., of the Cavalry. Translated by **Captain W. S. Cooke.** Crown 8vo, cloth. Price 7*s.*

"Among the valuable group of works on the military tactics of the chief States of Europe which Messrs. King are publishing, a small treatise on | 'Austrian Cavalry Exercise' will hold a good and useful place."—*Westminster Review.*

History of the Organisation, Equipment, and War Services of
THE REGIMENT OF BENGAL ARTILLERY.
Compiled from Published Official and other Records, and various private sources, by **Major Francis W. Stubbs**, Royal (late Bengal) Artillery. Vol. I. will contain WAR SERVICES. The Second Volume will be published separately, and will contain the HISTORY OF THE ORGANISATION AND EQUIPMENT OF THE REGIMENT. In 2 vols. 8vo. With Maps and Plans. [*Preparing.*

VICTORIES AND DEFEATS.
An Attempt to explain the Causes which have led to them. An Officer's Manual. By **Col. R. P. Anderson.** 8vo. 14*s.*

"The young officer should have it always at hand to open anywhere and read a bit, and we warrant him that let that bit be ever so small it will give him material for an hour's thinking."—*United Service Gazette.* | "The present book proves that he is a diligent student of military history, his illustrations ranging over a wide field, and including ancient and modern Indian and European warfare."—*Standard.*

THE FRONTAL ATTACK OF INFANTRY.
By **Capt. Laymann,** Instructor of Tactics at the Military College, Neisse. Translated by **Colonel Edward Newdigate.** Crown 8vo, limp cloth. Price 2*s. 6d.*

"An exceedingly useful kind of book. A valuable acquisition to the military student's library. It recounts, in the first place, the opinions and tactical formations which regulated the German army during the early battles of the late war; ex- | plains how these were modified in the course of the campaign by the terrible and unanticipated effect of the fire; and how, accordingly, troops should be trained to attack in future wars."—*Naval and Military Gazette.*

ELEMENTARY MILITARY GEOGRAPHY, RECONNOITRING, AND SKETCHING.
Compiled for Non-Commissioned Officers and Soldiers of all Arms. By **Capt. C. E. H. Vincent.** Square cr. 8vo. 2*s. 6d.*

"This manual takes into view the necessity of every soldier knowing how to read a military map, in order to know to what points in an enemy's country to direct his attention; and provides for this necessity by giving, in terse and sensible | language, definitions of varieties of ground and the advantages they present in warfare, together with a number of useful hints in military sketching."—*Naval and Military Gazette.*

THREE WORKS BY LIEUT.-COL. THE HON. A. ANSON, V.C., M.P.
THE ABOLITION OF PURCHASE AND THE ARMY REGULATION BILL OF 1871. Crown 8vo. Price One Shilling. | ARMY RESERVES AND MILITIA REFORMS. Crown 8vo. Sewed. Price One Shilling. THE STORY OF THE SUPERSESSIONS. Crown 8vo. Price Sixpence.

MILITARY WORKS—*continued.*

THE OPERATIONS OF THE SOUTH ARMY IN JANUARY AND FEBRUARY, 1871. Compiled from the Official War Documents of the Head-quarters of the Southern Army. By Count Hermann von Wartensleben, Colonel in the Prussian General Staff. Translated by Colonel C. H. von Wright. Demy 8vo, with Maps. Uniform with the above. Price 6s.

STUDIES IN THE NEW INFANTRY TACTICS. Parts I. & II. By Major W. von Scherff. Translated from the German by Colonel Lumley Graham. Demy 8vo. Price 7s. 6d.

"The subject of the respective advantages of attack and defence, and of the methods in which each form of battle should be carried out under the fire of modern arms, is exhaustively and admirably treated; indeed, we cannot but consider it to be decidedly superior to any work which has hitherto appeared in English upon this all-important subject."—*Standard.*

Second Edition. Revised and Corrected.

TACTICAL DEDUCTIONS FROM THE WAR OF 1870—71. By Captain A. von Boguslawski. Translated by Colonel Lumley Graham, late 18th (Royal Irish) Regiment. Demy 8vo. Price 7s.

"We must, without delay, impress brain and forethought into the British Service; and we cannot commence the good work too soon, or better, than by placing the two books ('The Operations of the German Armies' and 'Tactical Deductions') we have here criticised in every military library, and introducing them as class-books in every tactical school."—*United Service Gazette.*

THE ARMY OF THE NORTH-GERMAN CONFEDERATION. A Brief Description of its Organization, of the different Branches of the Service, and their "Rôle" in War, of its Mode of Fighting, &c. By a Prussian General. Translated from the German by Col. Edward Newdigate. Demy 8vo. Price 5s.

"The work is quite essential to the full use of the other volumes of the 'German Military Series,' which Messrs. King are now producing in handsome uniform style."—*United Service Magazine.* Every page of the book deserves attentive study .... The information given on mobilisation, garrison troops, keeping up establishment during war, and on the employment of the different branches of the service, is of great value."—*Standard.*

THE OPERATIONS OF THE GERMAN ARMIES IN FRANCE, FROM SEDAN TO THE END OF THE WAR OF 1870-71. With large Official Map. From the Journals of the Head-quarters Staff, by Major William Blume. Translated by E. M. Jones, Major 20th Foot, late Professor of Military History, Sandhurst. Demy 8vo. Price 9s.

"The book is of absolute necessity to the military student .... The work is one of high merit."—*United Service Gazette.* "The work of Major von Blume in its English dress forms the most valuable addition to our stock of works upon the war that our press has put forth. Our space forbids our doing more than commending it earnestly as the most authentic and instructive narrative of the second section of the war that has yet appeared."—*Saturday Review.*

HASTY INTRENCHMENTS. By Colonel A. Brialmont. Translated by Lieut. Charles A. Empson, R.A. With Nine Plates. Demy 8vo. Price 6s.

"A valuable contribution to military literature."—*Athenæum.* "In seven short chapters it gives plain directions for forming shelter-trenches, with the best method of carrying the necessary tools, and it offers practical illustrations of the use of hasty intrenchments on the field of battle."—*United Service Magazine.* "It supplies that which our own text-books give but imperfectly, viz., hints as to how a position can best be strengthened by means ... of such extemporised intrenchments and batteries as can be thrown up by infantry in the space of four or five hours ... deserves to become a standard military work."—*Standard.*

STUDIES IN LEADING TROOPS. Parts I. and II. By Colonel von Verdy du Vernois. An authorised and accurate Translation by Lieutenant H. J. T. Hildyard, 71st Foot. Demy 8vo. Price 7s.

. General BEAUCHAMP WALKER says of this work:—"I recommend the first two numbers of Colonel von Verdy's 'Studies' to the attentive perusal of my brother officers. They supply a want which I have often felt during my service in this country, namely, a minuter tactical detail of the minor operations of war than any but the most observant and fortunately-placed staff-officer is in a position to give. I have read and re-read them very carefully, I hope with profit, certainly with great interest, and believe that practice, in the sense of these 'Studies,' would be a valuable preparation for manœuvres on a more extended scale."—Berlin, June, 1872.

DISCIPLINE AND DRILL. Four Lectures delivered to the London Scottish Rifle Volunteers. By Capt. S. Flood Page. Cheaper Edition. Cr. 8vo. 1s.

"The very useful and interesting work."—*Volunteer Service Gazette.* "An admirable collection of lectures."—*Times.*

MILITARY WORKS—*continued.*

CAVALRY FIELD DUTY. By **Major-General von Mirus.** Translated by **Captain Frank S. Russell,** 14th (King's) Hussars. Cr. 8vo, cloth limp. 7s. 6d.

"We have no book on cavalry duties that at all approaches to this, either for completeness in details, clearness in description, or for manifest utility. In its pages will be found plain instructions for every portion of duty before the enemy that a combatant horseman will be called upon to perform, and if a dragoon but studies it well and intelligently, his value to the army, we are confident, must be increased one hundredfold. Skirmishing, scouting, patrolling, and vedetting are now the chief duties dragoons in peace should be practised at, and how to perform these duties effectively is what the book teaches."—*United Service Magazine.*

INDIA AND THE EAST.

THE THREATENED FAMINE IN BENGAL; How it may be Met, and the Recurrence of Famines in India Prevented. Being No. 1 of "Occasional Notes on Indian Affairs." By **Sir H. Bartle E. Frere, G.C.B., G.C.S.I., &c. &c.** Crown 8vo. With 3 Maps. Price 5s.

THE ORIENTAL SPORTING MAGAZINE. A Reprint of the first 5 Volumes, in 2 Volumes, demy 8vo. Price 28s.

"Lovers of sport will find ample amusement in the varied contents of these two volumes."—*Allen's Indian Mail.*

"Full of interest for the sportsman and naturalist. Full of thrilling adventures of sportsmen who have attacked the fiercest and most gigantic specimens of the animal world in their native jungle. It is seldom we get so many exciting incidents in a similar amount of space . . . Well suited to the libraries of country gentlemen and all those who are interested in sporting matters."—*Civil Service Gazette.*

Second Edition, Revised and Corrected.

THE EUROPEAN IN INDIA. A Hand-book of Practical Information for those proceeding to, or residing in, the East Indies, relating to Outfits, Routes, Time for Departure, Indian Climate, &c. By **Edmund C. P. Hull.** With a Medical Guide for Anglo-Indians. Being a Compendium of Advice to Europeans in India, relating to the Preservation and Regulation of their Health. To which is added a Supplement on the Management of Children in India. By **R. S. Mair, M.D., F.R.C.S.E.,** late Deputy Coroner of Madras. In 1 vol. Post 8vo. Price 6s.

"Full of all sorts of useful information to the English settler or traveller in India."—*Standard.*

"One of the most valuable books ever published in India—valuable for its sound information, its careful array of pertinent facts, and its sterling common sense. It supplies a want which few persons may have discovered, but which everybody will at once recognise when once the contents of the book have been mastered. The medical part of the work is invaluable."—*Calcutta Guardian.*

MEDICAL GUIDE FOR ANGLO-INDIANS. Being a Compendium of Advice to Europeans in India, relating to the Preservation and Regulation of their Health. With a Supplement on the Management of Children in India. By **R. S. Mair, M.D., F.R.C.S.E.,** late Deputy Coroner of Madras. Post 8vo, limp cloth. Price 3s. 6d.

TAS-HIL UL KALĀM; or, Hindustani Made Easy. By **Captain W. R. M. Holroyd,** Bengal Staff Corps, Director of Public Instruction, Punjab. Crown 8vo. Price 5s.

"As clear and as instructive as possible."—*Standard.*

"Contains a great deal of most necessary information, that is not to be found in any other work on the subject that has crossed our path."—*Homeward Mail.*

EASTERN EXPERIENCES. By **L. Bowring, C.S.I.,** Lord Canning's Private Secretary, and for many years Chief Commissioner of Mysore and Coorg. Illustrated with Maps and Diagrams. Demy 8vo. Price 16s.

"An admirable and exhaustive geographical, political, and industrial survey."—*Athenæum.*

"Interesting even to the general reader, but especially so to those who may have a special concern in that portion of our Indian Empire."—*Post.*

"This compact and methodical summary of the most authentic information relating to countries whose welfare is intimately connected with our own."—*Daily News.*

INDIA AND THE EAST—*continued.*

EDUCATIONAL COURSE OF SECULAR SCHOOL BOOKS

FOR INDIA. Edited by **J. S. Laurie**, of the Inner Temple, Barrister-at-Law; formerly H.M. Inspector of Schools, England; Assistant Royal Commissioner, Ireland; Special Commissioner, African Settlement; Director of Public Instruction, Ceylon.

"These valuable little works will prove of real service to many of our readers, especially to those | who intend entering the Civil Service of India."—*Civil Service Gazette.*

The following Works are now ready:—

	s. d.		s. d.
THE FIRST HINDUSTANI READER, stiff linen wrapper .	0 6	GEOGRAPHY OF INDIA, with Maps and Historical Appendix, tracing the growth of the British	
THE SECOND HINDUSTANI READER, stiff linen wrapper .	0 6	Empire in Hindustan. 128 pp. cloth	1 6

In the Press.

ELEMENTARY GEOGRAPHY OF INDIA. | FACTS AND FEATURES OF INDIAN HISTORY, in a series of alternating Reading Lessons and Memory Exercises.

Second Edition.

WESTERN INDIA BEFORE AND DURING THE MUTINIES.

Pictures drawn from life. By **Major-Gen. Sir George Le Grand Jacob, K.C.S.I., C.B.** In 1 vol. Crown 8vo. Price 7s. 6d.

"The most important contribution to the history of Western India during the Mutinies which has yet, in a popular form, been made public."—*Athenæum.* | "Few men more competent than himself to speak authoritatively concerning Indian affairs."—*Standard.*

EXCHANGE TABLES OF STERLING AND INDIAN RUPEE

CURRENCY, UPON A NEW AND EXTENDED SYSTEM, embracing Values from One Farthing to One Hundred Thousand Pounds, and at rates progressing, in Sixteenths of a Penny, from 1s. 9d. to 2s. 3d. per Rupee. By **Donald Fraser**, Accountant to the British Indian Steam Navigation Company, Limited. Royal 8vo. Price 10s. 6d.

"The calculations must have entailed great labour on the author, but the work is one which we fancy must become a standard one in all business | houses which have dealings with any country where the rupee and the English pound are standard coins of currency."—*Inverness Courier.*

BOOKS for the YOUNG and for LENDING LIBRARIES.

NEW WORKS BY HESBA STRETTON.

THE WONDERFUL LIFE. Fcap. 8vo. With a Map and Illuminated Frontispiece. 2s. 6d. [*Just out.*

This slight and brief sketch is merely the story of the life and death of our Lord. It has been written for those who have not the leisure, or the books, needed for threading together the fragmentary and scattered incidents recorded in the four Gospels. Of late years these records have been searched diligently for the smallest links which might serve to complete the chain of those years of a life passed amongst us as Jesus of Nazareth, the Carpenter, the Prophet, and the Messiah. This little book is intended only to present the result of these close investigations made by many learned men, in a plain continuous narrative, suitable for unlearned readers.

CASSY. Twentieth Thousand. With Six Illustrations. 1s. 6d.

THE KING'S SERVANTS. Twenty-eighth Thousand. With Eight Illustrations. 1s. 6d.

Part I.—Faithful in Little. Part II.—Unfaithful. Part III.—Faithful in Much.

LOST GIP. Thirty-sixth Thousand. With Six Illustrations. 1s. 6d.

*** *ALSO A HANDSOMELY-BOUND EDITION, WITH TWELVE ILLUSTRATIONS, PRICE HALF-A-CROWN.*

DADDY'S PET. By **Mrs. Ellen Ross (Nelsie Brook).** Third Thousand. Small square, cloth, uniform with "Lost Gip." With Six Illustrations. Price 1s.

"We have been more than pleased with this simple bit of writing."—*Christian World.*

"Full of deep feeling and true and noble sentiment."—*Brighton Gazette.*

LOCKED OUT; A Tale of the Strike. By **Ellen Barlee.** With a Frontispiece. 1s. 6d.

PRETTY LESSONS IN VERSE FOR GOOD CHILDREN, with some Lessons in Latin, in Easy Rhyme. By **Sara Coleridge.** A New Edition. With Six Illustrations. Cloth, 3s. 6d.

AUNT MARY'S BRAN PIE. By the Author of "St. Olave's," "When I was a Little Girl," &c. Small crown 8vo. With Five Illustrations. 3s. 6d.

Second Edition.

SEEKING HIS FORTUNE, AND OTHER STORIES. Crown 8vo. With Four Illustrations. Price 3s. 6d.

CONTENTS.—Seeking his Fortune.—Oluf and Stephanoff.—What's in a Name?—Contrast.—Onesta.

"These are plain, straightforward stories, told in the precise, detailed manner which we are sure young people like."—*Spectator.*
"They are romantic, entertaining, and decidedly inculcate a sound and generous moral...."

We can answer for it that this volume will find favour with those for whom it is written, and that the sisters will like it quite as well as the brothers."—*Athenæum.*

THREE WORKS BY MARTHA FARQUHARSON.

I. ELSIE DINSMORE. Cr. 8vo. Price 3s. 6d.
II. ELSIE'S GIRLHOOD. Cr. 8vo. Price 3s. 6d.
III. ELSIE'S HOLIDAYS AT ROSELANDS. Crown 8vo. Price 3s. 6d.

Each Story is independent and complete in itself. They are published in uniform size and price, and are elegantly bound and illustrated.

"We do not pretend to have read the history of Elsie as she is portrayed in three different volumes. By the help, however, of the illustrations, and by dips here and there, we can safely give a favourable account."—*Westminster Review.*

"Elsie Dinsmore is a familiar name to a world of young readers. In the above three pretty volumes her story is complete, and it is one full of youthful experiences, winning a general interest."—*Athenæum.*

THE LITTLE WONDER-HORN. By **Jean Ingelow.** A Second Series of "*Stories told to a Child.*" With Fifteen Illustrations. Cloth, gilt. Price 3s. 6d.

"We like all the contents of the 'Little Wonder-Horn' very much."—*Athenæum.*
"We recommend it with confidence."—*Pall Mall Gazette.*

"Full of fresh and vigorous fancy: it is worthy of the author of some of the best of our modern verse."—*Standard.*

Second Edition.

THE AFRICAN CRUISER. A Midshipman's Adventures on the West Coast of Africa. A Book for Boys. By **S. Whitchurch Sadler, R.N.**, Author of "Marshall Vavasour." With Three Illustrations. Crown 8vo. Price 3s. 6d.

"A capital story of youthful adventure .... Sea-loving boys will find few pleasanter gift books this season than 'The African Cruiser.'"—*Hour.*

"Sea yarns have always been in favour with boys, but this, written in a brisk style by a thorough sailor, is crammed full of adventures."—*Times.*

Third Edition.

BRAVE MEN'S FOOTSTEPS. A Book of Example and Anecdote for Young People. By the Editor of "**Men who have Risen.**" With Four Illustrations, by **C. Doyle.** Crown 8vo. Price 3s. 6d.

"A readable and instructive volume."—*Examiner.*
"The little volume is precisely of the stamp to

win the favour of those who, in choosing a gift for a boy, would consult his moral development as well as his temporary pleasure."—*Daily Telegraph.*

18 *Works Published by Henry S. King & Co.,*

BOOKS FOR THE YOUNG AND FOR LENDING LIBRARIES—*continued.*

Second Edition.

PLUCKY FELLOWS. A Book for Boys. By **Stephen J. Mac Kenna.** With Six Illustrations. Crown 8vo. Price 3s. 6d.

> "This is one of the very best 'Books for Boys' which have been issued this year."—*Morning Advertiser.*
> "A thorough book for boys... written throughout in a manly, straightforward manner that is sure to win the hearts of the children."—*London Society.*

Second Edition.

GUTTA-PERCHA WILLIE, THE WORKING GENIUS. By **George MacDonald.** With 9 Illustrations by **Arthur Hughes.** Cr. 8vo. 3s. 6d.

> "The cleverest child we know assures us she has read this story through five times. Mr. Macdonald
> will, we are convinced, accept that verdict upon his little work as final."—*Spectator.*

THE TRAVELLING MENAGERIE. By **Charles Camden,** Author of "Hoity Toity." With Ten Illustrations by **J. Mahoney.** Crown 8vo. 3s. 6d.

> "A capital little book .... deserves a wide circulation among our boys and girls."—*Hour.*
> "A very attractive story."—*Public Opinion.*

THE DESERT PASTOR, JEAN JAROUSSEAU. Translated from the French of **Eugene Pelletan.** By **Colonel E. P. De L'Hoste.** In fcap. 8vo, with an Engraved Frontispiece. New Edition. Price 3s. 6d.

> "A touching record of the struggles in the cause of religious liberty of a real man."—*Graphic.*
> "There is a poetical simplicity and picturesqueness; the noblest heroism; unpretentious religion;
> pure love, and the spectacle of a household brought up in the fear of the Lord ...."—*Illustrated London News.*

THE DESERTED SHIP. A Real Story of the Atlantic. By **Cupples Howe,** Master Mariner. Illustrated by **Townley Green.** Cr. 8vo. Price 3s. 6d.

> "Curious adventures with bears, seals, and other Arctic animals, and with scarcely more human Esquimaux, form the mass of material with which
> the story deals, and will much interest boys who have a spice of romance in their composition."—*Courant.*

HOITY TOITY, THE GOOD LITTLE FELLOW. By **Charles Camden.** With Eleven Illustrations. Crown 8vo. Price 3s. 6d.

> "Relates very pleasantly the history of a charming little fellow who meddles always with a kindly disposition with other people's affairs and helps
> them to do right. There are many shrewd lessons to be picked up in this clever little story."—*Public Opinion.*

THE BOY SLAVE IN BOKHARA. A Tale of Central Asia. By **David Ker,** Author of "On the Road to Khiva," &c. Crown 8vo, with Four Illustrations. Price 5s.

SEVEN AUTUMN LEAVES FROM FAIRY-LAND. Illustrated with Nine Etchings. Square crown 8vo. 5s.

SLAVONIC FAIRY TALES. From Russian, Servian, Polish, and Bohemian Sources. Translated by **John T. Naaké,** of the British Museum. Crown 8vo. With Four Illustrations. Price 5s.

> "A most choice and charming selection ..... The tales have an original national ring in them, and will be pleasant reading to thousands besides children. Yet children will eagerly open the pages, and not willingly close them, of the pretty volume."—*Standard.*
> "English readers now have an opportunity of becoming acquainted with eleven Polish and eight Bohemian stories, as well as with eight Russian
> and thirteen Servian, in Mr. Naaké's modest but serviceable collection of *Slavonic Fairy Tales.* Its contents are, as a general rule, well chosen, and they are translated with a fidelity which deserves cordial praise ... Before taking leave of his prettily got up volume, we ought to mention that its contents fully come up to the promise held out in its preface."—*Academy.*

WAKING AND WORKING; OR, FROM GIRLHOOD TO WOMANHOOD. By **Mrs. G. S. Reaney.** Cr. 8vo. With a Frontispiece. 5s.

65, Cornhill; & 12, Paternoster Row, London.

BOOKS FOR THE YOUNG AND FOR LENDING LIBRARIES—*continued.*

AT SCHOOL WITH AN OLD DRAGOON. By Stephen J. Mac Kenna. Crown 8vo. With Six Illustrations. Price 5*s.*

"Consisting almost entirely of startling stories of military adventure . . . Boys will find them sufficiently exciting reading."—*Times.*

"These yarns give some very spirited and interesting descriptions of soldiering in various parts of the world."—*Spectator.*

"Mr. Mac Kenna's former work, 'Plucky Fellows,' is already a general favourite, and those who read the stories of the Old Dragoon will find that he has still plenty of materials at hand for pleasant tales, and has lost none of his power in telling them well."—*Standard.*

FANTASTIC STORIES. Translated from the German of Richard Leander, by Paulina B. Granville. Crown 8vo. With Eight full-page Illustrations, by M. E. Fraser-Tytler. Price 5*s.*

"Short, quaint, and, as they are fitly called, fantastic, they deal with all manner of subjects."—*Guardian.*

"'Fantastic' is certainly the right epithet to apply to some of these strange tales."—*Examiner.*

Third Edition.

STORIES IN PRECIOUS STONES. By Helen Zimmern. With Six Illustrations. Crown 8vo. Price 5*s.*

"A series of pretty tales which are half fantastic, half natural, and pleasantly quaint, as befits stories intended for the young."—*Daily Telegraph.*

"A pretty little book which fanciful young per-

sons will appreciate, and which will remind its readers of many a legend, and many an imaginary virtue attached to the gems they are so fond of wearing."—*Post.*

Fourth Edition.

THE GREAT DUTCH ADMIRALS. By Jacob de Liefde. Crown 8vo. With Eleven Illustrations by Townley Green and others. Price 5*s.*

"May be recommended as a wholesome present for boys. They will find in it numerous tales of adventure."—*Athenæum.*

"A really good book."—*Standard.*

"A really excellent book."—*Spectator.*

THE TASMANIAN LILY. By James Bonwick. Crown 8vo. With Frontispiece. Price 5*s.*

"An interesting and useful work."—*Hour.*

"The characters of the story are capitally con-

ceived, and are full of those touches which give them a natural appearance."—*Public Opinion.*

MIKE HOWE, THE BUSHRANGER OF VAN DIEMEN'S LAND. By James Bonwick. Crown 8vo. With a Frontispiece. Price 5*s.*

"He illustrates the career of the bushranger half a century ago; and this he does in a highly creditable manner; his delineations of life in the bush

are, to say the least, exquisite, and his representations of character are very marked."—*Edinburgh Courant.*

PHANTASMION. A Fairy Romance. By Sara Coleridge. With an Introductory Preface by the Right Hon. Lord Coleridge of Ottery S. Mary. A new Edition. In 1 vol. Crown 8vo. Price 7*s.* 6*d.*

"The readers of this fairy tale will find themselves dwelling for a time in a veritable region of romance, breathing an atmosphere of unreality, and surrounded by supernatural beings."—*Post.*

"This delightful work . . . We would gladly have

read it were it twice the length, closing the book with a feeling of regret that the repast was at an end."—*Vanity Fair.*

"A beautiful conception of a rarely-gifted mind."—*Examiner.*

LAYS OF A KNIGHT-ERRANT IN MANY LANDS. By Major-General Sir Vincent Eyre, C.B., K.C.S.I., &c. Square crown 8vo. With Six Illustrations. Price 7*s.* 6*d.*

| Pharaoh Land. | Home Land. | Wonder Land. | Rhine Land. |

"A collection of pleasant and well-written stanzas . . . abounding in real fun and humour."—*Literary World.*

"The conceits here and there are really very amusing."—*Standard.*

BEATRICE AYLMER AND OTHER TALES. By Mary M. Howard, Author of "Brampton Rectory." 1 vol. Crown 8vo. Price 6*s.*

"These tales possess considerable merit."—*Court Journal.*

"A neat and chatty little volume."—*Hour.*

WORKS BY ALFRED TENNYSON.

THE CABINET EDITION.

Messrs. HENRY S. KING & Co. have the pleasure to announce that they are issuing an Edition of the Laureate's works, in *Ten Monthly Volumes*, foolscap 8vo, at *Half-a-Crown each*, entitled "The Cabinet Edition," which will contain the whole of Mr. Tennyson's works. The first volume is illustrated by a beautiful Photographic Portrait; and the other volumes are each to contain a Frontispiece. They are tastefully bound in . Crimson Cloth, and are to be issued in the following order :—

Vol.	Vol.
1. EARLY POEMS.	6. IDYLLS OF THE KING.
2. ENGLISH IDYLLS & OTHER POEMS.	7. IDYLLS OF THE KING.
3. LOCKSLEY HALL & OTHER POEMS.	8. THE PRINCESS.
4. LUCRETIUS & OTHER POEMS.	9. MAUD AND ENOCH ARDEN.
5. IDYLLS OF THE KING.	10. IN MEMORIAM.

Volumes I. to VII. are now ready.

Subscribers' names received by all Booksellers.

Reduction in prices of Mr. Tennyson's Works :—

	PRICE.
	s. d.
POEMS. Small 8vo.	6 0
MAUD AND OTHER POEMS. Small 8vo.	3 '
THE PRINCESS. Small 8vo.	3 6
IDYLLS OF THE KING. Small 8vo.	5 0
„ „ Collected. Small 8vo.	7 0
THE HOLY GRAIL, AND OTHER POEMS. Small 8vo.	4 6
GARETH AND LYNETTE. Small 8vo.	3 0
ENOCH ARDEN, &c. Small 8vo.	3 6
IN MEMORIAM. Small 8vo.	4 0
SELECTIONS FROM THE ABOVE WORKS. Square 8vo, cloth	3 6
„ „ „ cloth, gilt edges	4 0
SONGS FROM THE ABOVE WORKS. Square 8vo, cloth	3 6
LIBRARY EDITION OF MR. TENNYSON'S WORKS. 6 vols. Post 8vo, each	10 6
POCKET VOLUME EDITION OF MR. TENNYSON'S WORKS. 11 vols., in neat case	31 6
„ extra cloth, gilt, in case	35 0
POEMS. Illustrated Edition, 4to	25 0

** *All the above are kept in leather bindings.*

POETRY.

FOUR ELEGANT POETICAL GIFT BOOKS:

LYRICS OF LOVE, From Shakspeare to Tennyson. Selected and arranged by **W. Davenport Adams, Junr.** Fcap. 8vo, cloth extra, gilt edges, 3s. 6d.

" A most excellent collection. . . . Shows taste and care."—*Westminster Gazette.*

" A charming and scholarly pocket volume of poetry . . . The editor annotates his pieces just sufficiently for information. . . . The collection,

as a whole, is very choice."—*British Quarterly Review.*

" The anthology is a very full and good one, and represents the robust school of Carew and Suckling better than any other that we know."—*Academy.*

WILLIAM CULLEN BRYANT'S POEMS. Red-line Edition. Handsomely bound. With Illustrations and Portrait of the Author. Price 7s. 6d.
A Cheaper Edition, with Frontispiece, is also published. Price 3s. 6d.

These are the only complete English Editions sanctioned by the Author.

" Of all the poets of the United States there is no one who obtained the fame and position of a classic earlier, or has kept them longer, than William Cullen Bryant . . . A singularly simple and straightforward fashion of verse. Very rarely has any writer preserved such an even level of merit throughout his poems. Like some other American poets, Mr. Bryant is particularly happy in transla-

tion."—*Academy.*

" We are glad to possess so neat and elegant an edition of the works of the most thoughtful, graceful, and Wordsworthian of American poets."—*British Quarterly Review.*

" Some of the purest and tenderest poetry of this generation . . . Undoubtedly the best edition of the poet now in existence."—*Glasgow News.*

ENGLISH SONNETS. Collected and Arranged by **John Dennis.** Fcap. 8vo. Elegantly bound. Price 3s. 6d.

" Mr. Dennis has shown great judgment in this selection."—*Saturday Review.*

" An exquisite selection, a selection which every lover of poetry will consult again and again with

delight. The notes are very useful. . . The volume is one for which English literature owes Mr. Dennis the heartiest thanks."—*Spectator.*

Second Edition.
HOME-SONGS FOR QUIET HOURS. Edited by the **Rev. Canon R. H. Baynes**, Editor of " Lyra Anglicana," &c. Fcap 8vo. Cloth extra, 3s. 6d.

" A tasteful collection of devotional poetry of a very high standard of excellence. The pieces are short, mostly original, and instinct, for the most part, with the most ardent spirit of devotion."—*Standard.*

" A most acceptable volume of sacred poetry ; a

good addition to the gift books of the season."—*Rock.*

" These are poems in which every word has a meaning, and from which it would be unjust to remove a stanza . . . Some of the best pieces in the book are anonymous."—*Pall Mall Gazette.*

*** *The above four books may also be had handsomely bound in Morocco with gilt edges.*

THE DISCIPLES. A New Poem. By **Mrs. Hamilton King.** Second Edition, with some Notes. Crown 8vo. Price 7s. 6d.

" A higher impression of the imaginative power of the writer is given by the objective truthfulness of the glimpses she gives us of her master, helping us to understand how he could be regarded by some as a heartless charlatan, by others as an inspired saint."—*Academy.*

" Mrs. King can write good verses. The description of the capture of the Croats at Mestre is extremely spirited ; there is a pretty picture of the road to Rome, from the Abruzzi, and another of Palermo."—*Athenæum.*

" In her new volume Mrs. King has far surpassed her previous attempt. Even the most hostile critic

could scarcely deny to.' Ugo Bassi' the praise of being a work worthy in every way to live . . . The style of her writing is pure and simple in the last degree, and all is natural, truthful, and free from the slightest shade of obscurity in thought or diction . . . The book altogether is one that merits unqualified admiration and praise."—*Daily Telegraph.*

" Throughout it breathes restrained passion and lofty sentiment, which flow out now and then as a stream widening to bless the lands into powerful music."—*British Quarterly Review.*

ASPROMONTE, AND OTHER POEMS. By the same Author. Second Edition. Cloth, 4s. 6d.

" The volume is anonymous, but there is no reason for the author to be ashamed of it. The ' Poems of Italy ' are evidently inspired by genuine enthusiasm in the cause espoused ; and one of them,

' The Execution of Felice Orsini,' has much poetic merit, the event celebrated being told with dramatic force."—*Athenæum.*

" The verse is fluent and free."—*Spectator.*

ARVAN : or, the STORY of the SWORD. A Poem. By **Herbert Todd, M.A.**, late of Trinity College, Cambridge. Crown 8vo.

POETRY—*continued.*

THROUGH STORM AND SUNSHINE. By Adon, Author of "Lays of Modern Oxford." With Illustrations by H. Paterson, M. E. Edwards, A. T., and the Author.

SONGS FOR MUSIC. By Four Friends. Square crown 8vo. Price 5s.

CONTAINING SONGS BY

Reginald A. Gatty.   Stephen H. Gatty.
Greville J. Chester.   Juliana H. Ewing.

"A charming gift-book, which will be very popular with lovers of poetry."—*John Bull.*

"The charm of simplicity is manifest throughout, and the subjects are well chosen and successfully treated."—*Rock.*

ROBERT BUCHANAN'S POETICAL WORKS. Collected Edition, in 3 Vols., price 18s. Vol. I. contains,—"Ballads and Romances;" "Ballads and Poems of Life," and a Portrait of the Author.

Vol. II.—"Ballads and Poems of Life;" "Allegories and Sonnets."

Vol. III.—"Coruiskeen Sonnets;" "Book of Orm;" "Political Mystics."

"Holding, as Mr. Buchanan does, such a conspicuous place amongst modern writers, the reading public will be duly thankful for this handsome edition of the poet's works."—*Civil Service Gazette.*

"Taking the poems before us as experiments, we hold that they are very full of promise... In the romantic ballad, Mr. Buchanan shows real power."—*Hour.*

THOUGHTS IN VERSE. Small crown 8vo. Price 1s. 6d.

This is a Collection of Verses expressive of religious feeling, written from a Theistic stand-point.

"All who are interested in devotional verse should read this tiny volume."—*Academy.*

ON THE NORTH WIND—THISTLE-DOWN. A volume of Poems. By the Hon. Mrs. Willoughby. Elegantly bound. Small crown 8vo. 7s. 6d.

PENELOPE AND OTHER POEMS. By Allison Hughes. Fcap. 8vo. 4s. 6d.

"Full of promise. They possess both form and colour, they are not wanting in suggestion, and they reveal something not far removed from imagination... If the verse moves stiffly it is because the substance is rich and carefully wrought. That artistic regard for the value of words, which is characteristic of the best modern workmanship, is apparent in every composition, and the ornament, even when it might be pronounced excessive, is tasteful in arrangement."—*Athenæum.*

COSMOS. A Poem. 8vo. 3s. 6d.

SUBJECT.—Nature in the Past and in the Present.—Man in the Past and in the Present.—The Future.

POEMS. By Augustus Taylor. Fcp. 8vo. 5s.

NARCISSUS AND OTHER POEMS. By E. Carpenter. Fcap. 8vo. 5s.

"In many of these poems there is a force of fancy, a grandeur of imagination, and a power of poetical utterance not by any means common in these days."—*Standard.*

AURORA; A Volume of Verse. Fcap. 8vo. 5s.

POEMS. By Annette F. C. Knight. Fcap. 8vo. Cloth. Price 5s.

". . . . Very fine also is the poem entitled 'Past and Present,' from which we take the song picturing the 'Spirits of the Present.' The verses here are so simple in form as almost to veil the real beauty and depth of the image; yet it would not be easy to find a more exquisite picture in poetry or on canvas of the spirit of the age."—*Scotsman.*

"These poems are musical to read, they give true and pleasant pictures of common things, and they tell sweetly of the deeper moral and religious harmonies which sustain us under the discords and the griefs of actual life."—*Spectator.*

"Full of tender and felicitous verse . . . expressed with a rare artistic perfection. . . . The gems of the book to our mind are the poems entitled 'In a Town Garden.'"—*Literary Churchman.*

A TALE OF THE SEA, SONNETS, AND OTHER POEMS. By James Howell. Fcap. 8vo. Cloth, 5s.

"Mr. Howell has a keen perception of the beauties of nature, and a just appreciation of the charities of life. . . . Mr. Howell's book deserves, and will probably receive, a warm reception."—*Pall Mall Gazette.*

METRICAL TRANSLATIONS FROM THE GREEK AND LATIN POETS, AND OTHER POEMS. By R. B. Boswell, M.A. Oxon. Crown 8vo. 5s.

"Most of these translations we can praise as of very high merit. . . . For sweetness and regularity, his verses are pre-eminent."—*Literary Churchman.*

"Mr. Boswell has a strong poetical vein in his nature, and gives us every promise of success as an original poet."—*Standard.*

EASTERN LEGENDS AND STORIES IN ENGLISH VERSE. By Lieutenant Norton Powlett, Royal Artillery. Crown 8vo. 5s.

"There is a rollicking sense of fun about the stories, joined to marvellous power of rhyming, and plenty of swing, which irresistibly reminds us of our old favourite (Ingoldsby)."—*Graphic.*

Second Edition.

VIGNETTES IN RHYME AND VERS DE SOCIÉTÉ. By Austin Dobson. Fcap. 8vo. 5s.

"Clever, clear-cut, and careful."—*Athenæum.*

"As a writer of Vers de Société, Mr. Dobson is almost, if not quite, unrivalled."—*Examiner.*

"Lively, innocent, elegant in expression, and graceful in fancy."—*Morning Post.*

SONGS FOR SAILORS. By Dr. W. C. Bennett. Dedicated by Special Request to H. R. H. the Duke of Edinburgh. Crown 8vo. 3s. 6d. With Steel Portrait and Illustrations.

An Edition in Illustrated paper Covers. Price 1s.

WALLED IN, AND OTHER POEMS. By the Rev. Henry J. Bulkeley. Fcp. 8vo. 5s.

"A remarkable book of genuine poetry."—*Evening Standard.*

"Genuine power displayed."—*Examiner.*

"Poetical feeling is manifest here, and the diction of the poem is unimpeachable."—*Pall Mall Gazette.*

POETRY—*continued.*

SONGS OF LIFE AND DEATH. By John Payne, Author of "Intaglios," "Sonnets," etc. Crown 8vo. 5s.

"The art of ballad-writing has long been lost in England, and Mr Payne may claim to be its restorer. It is a perfect delight to meet with such a ballad as 'May Margaret' in the present volume."—*Westminster Review.*

IMITATIONS FROM THE GERMAN OF SPITTA AND TERSTEGEN. By Lady Durand. Fcap. 8vo. 4s.

"A charming little volume. . . . Will be a very valuable assistance to peaceful, meditative souls."—*Church Herald.*

ON VIOL AND FLUTE. A New Volume of Poems, by Edmund W. Gosse. With Frontispiece by W. B. Scott. Cr. 8vo. 5s.

"A careful perusal of his verses will show that he is a poet. . . His song has the grateful, murmuring sound which reminds one of the softness and deliciousness of summer time. . . . There is much that is good in the volume."—*Spectator.*

EDITH; or, LOVE AND LIFE IN CHESHIRE. By T. Ashe, Author of "The Sorrows of Hypsipyle," etc. Sewed. Price 6d.

"A really fine poem, full of tender, subtle touches of feeling."—*Manchester News.*

"Pregnant from beginning to end with the results of careful observation and imaginative power."—*Chester Chronicle.*

THE INN OF STRANGE MEETINGS, AND OTHER POEMS. By Mortimer Collins. Crown 8vo. 5s.

"Abounding in quiet humour, in bright fancy, in sweetness and melody of expression, and, at times, in the tenderest touches of pathos."—*Graphic.*

"Mr. Collins has an undercurrent of chivalry and romance beneath the trifling vein of good-humoured banter which is the special characteristic of his verse."—*Athenæum.*

GOETHE'S FAUST. A New Translation in Rime. By C. Kegan Paul. Crown 8vo. 6s.

"His translation is the most minutely accurate that has yet been produced. . . ."—*Saturday Review.*

"Mr. Paul is a zealous and a faithful interpreter."—*Saturday Review.*

AN OLD LEGEND OF S. PAUL'S. By the Rev. G. B. Howard. Fcp. 8vo. 3s. 6d.

"We admire, and deservedly admire, the genuine poetry of this charming old legend as here presented to us by the brilliant imagination and the chastened taste of the gifted writer."—*Standard.*

SONNETS, LYRICS, AND TRANSLATIONS. By the Rev. Charles Turner. Cr. 8vo. 4s. 6d.

"Mr. Turner is a genuine poet; his song is sweet and pure, beautiful in expression, and often subtle in thought."—*Pall Mall Gazette.*

"The light of a devout, gentle, and kindly spirit, a delicate and graceful fancy, a keen intelligence irradiates these thoughts."—*Contemporary Review.*

THE DREAM AND THE DEED, AND OTHER POEMS. By Patrick Scott, Author of "Footpaths between Two Worlds," etc. Fcap. 8vo. Cloth, 5s.

"A bitter and able satire on the vice and follies of the day, literary, social, and political."—*Standard.*

"Shows real poetic power coupled with evidences of satirical energy."—*Edinburgh Daily Review.*

EROS AGONISTES. By E. B. D. Fcap. 8vo. 3s. 6d.

"It is not the least merit of these pages that they are everywhere illumined with moral and religious sentiment suggested, not paraded, of the brightest, purest character."—*Standard.*

CALDERON'S DRAMAS. Translated from the Spanish. By Denis Florence MacCarthy. Post 8vo. Cloth, gilt edges. 10s.

"The lambent verse flows with an ease, spirit, and music perfectly natural, liberal, and harmonious."—*Spectator.*

"It is impossible to speak too highly of this beautiful work."—*Month.*

Second Edition.

SONGS OF TWO WORLDS. First Series. By a New Writer. Fcp. 8vo. 5s.

"These poems will assuredly take high rank among the class to which they belong."—*British Quarterly Review, April 1st.*

"No extracts could do justice to the exquisite tones, the felicitous phrasing and delicately wrought harmonies of some of these poems."—*Nonconformist.*

"A purity and delicacy of feeling like morning air."—*Graphic.*

Second Edition.

SONGS OF TWO WORLDS. Second Series. By a New Writer. Fcp. 8vo. 5s.

"The most noteworthy poem is the 'Ode on a Spring Morning,' which has somewhat of the charm of 'L'Allegro' and 'Il Penseroso.' It is the nearest approach to a masterpiece in the collection. We cannot find too much praise for its noble assertion of man's resurrection."—*Saturday Review.*

"A real advance on its predecessor, and contains at least one poem ('The Organ Boy') of great originality, as well as many of much beauty . . . . As exquisite a little poem as we have read for many a day . . . . but not at all alone in its power to fascinate."—*Spectator.*

"Will be gratefully welcomed."—*Examiner.*

THE GALLERY OF PIGEONS, AND OTHER POEMS. By Theo. Marzials. Crown 8vo. 4s. 6d.

"A conceit abounding in prettiness."—*Examiner.*

"The rush of fresh, sparkling fancies is too rapid, too sustained, too abundant, not to be spontaneous."—*Academy.*

THE LEGENDS OF ST. PATRICK AND OTHER POEMS. By Aubrey de Vere. Crown 8vo. 5s.

"Mr. De Vere's versification in his earlier poems is characterised by great sweetness and simplicity. He is master of his instrument, and rarely offends the ear with false notes."—*Pall Mall Gazette.*

"We have but space to commend the varied structure of his verse, the carefulness of his grammar, and his excellent English."—*Saturday Review.*

ALEXANDER THE GREAT. A Dramatic Poem. By Aubrey de Vere, Author of "The Legends of St. Patrick." Crown 8vo. 5s.

"Undeniably well written."—*Examiner.*

"A noble play. . . . The work of a true poet, and of a fine artist, in whom there is nothing vulgar and nothing weak. . . . We had no conception, from our knowledge of Mr. De Vere's former poems, that so much poetic power lay in him as this drama shows. It is terse as well as full of beauty, nervous as well as rich in thought."—*Spectator.*

FICTION.

HIS QUEEN. By Alice Fisher, Author of "Too Bright to Last." 3 vols. Cr. 8vo.

ISRAEL MORT : OVERMAN. The Story of the Mine. By John Saunders, Author of "Hirell," &c. 3 vols. Crown 8vo.

MALCOLM : A Scottish Story. By George MacDonald, Author of "David Elginbrod," &c. 3 vols. Crown 8vo.

THE NEGLECTED QUESTION. By B. Markewitch. Translated from the Russian, by the Princesses Ouroussoff. 2 vols. Crown 8vo. 14s.

WOMAN'S A RIDDLE; OR, BABY WARMSTREY. By Philip Sheldon, 3 vols.
"In the delineation of idiosyncrasy, special and particular, and its effects on the lives of the personages of the story, the author may, without exaggeration, be said to be masterly. Whether in the long-drawn-out development of character, or in the description of peculiar qualities in a single pointed sentence, he is equally skilful, while, where pathos is necessary, he has it at command, and subdued, sly humour is not wanting."—*Morning Post.*

LISETTE'S VENTURE. By Mrs. Russell Gray. 2 vols.

IDOLATRY. A Romance. By Julian Hawthorne, Author of "Bressant." 2 vols.
"A more powerful book than 'Bressant'"....
If the figures are mostly phantoms, they are phantoms which take a more powerful hold on the mind than many very real figures..... There are three scenes in this romance, any one of which would prove true genius."—*Spectator.*
"The character of the Egyptian, half mad, and all wicked, is remarkably drawn..... Manetho is a really fine conception.... That there are passages of almost exquisite beauty here and there is only what we might expect."—*Athenæum.*

BRESSANT. A Romance. By Julian Hawthorne. 2 vols. Crown 8vo.
"One of the most powerful with which we are acquainted."—*Times.*
"We shall once more have reason to rejoice whenever we hear that a new work is coming out written by one who bears the honoured name of Hawthorne."—*Saturday Review.*

VANESSA. By the Author of "Thomasina," "Dorothy," &c. 2 vols. Second Edition.

THOMASINA. By the Author of "Dorothy," "De Cressy," &c. 2 vols. Crown 8vo.
"A finished and delicate cabinet picture ; no line is without its purpose."—*Athenæum.*

AILEEN FERRERS. By Susan Morley. In 2 vols. Crown 8vo, cloth.
"Her novel rises to a level far above that which cultivated women with a facile pen ordinarily attain when they set themselves to write a story. It is as a study of character, worked out in a manner that is free from almost all the usual faults of lady writers, that 'Aileen Ferrers' merits a place apart from its innumerable rivals."—*Saturday Review.*

LADY MORETOUN'S DAUGHTER. By Mrs. Eiloart. In 3 vols. Crown 8vo.
"Carefully written.... The narrative is well sustained."—*Athenæum.*
"An interesting story.... Above the run of average novels."—*Vanity Fair.*
"Will prove more popular than any of the author's former works.... Interesting and readable."—*Hour.*
"The story is well put together, and readable."—*Examiner.*

WAITING FOR TIDINGS. By the Author of "White and Black." 3 vols.
"An interesting novel."—*Vanity Fair.*
"A very lively tale, abounding with amusing incidents."—*John Bull.*

TWO GIRLS. By Frederick Wedmore, Author of "A Snapt Gold Ring." 2 vols.
"A carefully-written novel of character, contrasting the two heroines of one love tale, an English lady and a French actress. Cicely is charming ; the introductory description of her is a good specimen of the well-balanced sketches in which the author shines."—*Athenæum.*

CIVIL SERVICE. By J. T. Listado. Author of "Maurice Rhynhart." 2 vols.
"A very charming and amusing story... The characters are all well drawn and life-like.... It is with no ordinary skill that Mr. Listado has drawn the character of Hugh Haughton, full as he is of scheming and subtleties... The plot is worked out with great skill and is of no ordinary kind."—*Civil Service Gazette.*
"A story of Irish life, free from burlesque and partisanship, yet amusingly national... There is plenty of 'go' in the story."—*Athenæum.*

MR. CARINGTON. A Tale of Love and Conspiracy. By Robert Turner Cotton. In 3 vols. Cloth, crown 8vo.
"A novel in so many ways good, as in a fresh and elastic diction, stout unconventionality, and happy boldness of conception and execution. His novels, though free spoken, will be some of the healthiest of our day."—*Examiner.*

TOO LATE. By Mrs. Newman. 2 vols.
"The plot is skilfully constructed, the characters are well conceived, and the narrative moves to its conclusion without any waste of words... The tone is healthy, in spite of its incidents, which will please the lovers of sensational fiction.... The reader who opens the book will read it all through."—*Pall Mall Gazette.*

REGINALD BRAMBLE. A Cynic of the 19th Century. An Autobiography. 1 vol.
"There is plenty of vivacity in Mr. Bramble's narrative."—*Athenæum.*
"Written in a lively and readable style."—*Hour.*

CRUEL AS THE GRAVE. By the Countess Von Bothmer. 3 vols.
"*Jealousy is cruel as the Grave.*"
"Interesting, though somewhat tragic."—*Athenæum.*
"Agreeable, unaffected, and eminently readable."—*Daily News.*

THE HIGH MILLS. By Katherine Saunders, Author of "Gideon's Rock," &c. 3 vols.

FICTION—*continued.*

SEPTIMIUS. A Romance. By **Nathaniel Hawthorne.** Second Edition. 1 vol. Crown 8vo, cloth, extra gilt. 9*s.*
The *Athenæum* says that "the book is full of Hawthorne's mos characteristic writing."

EFFIE'S GAME; How SHE LOST AND HOW SHE WON. By **Cecil Clayton.** 2 vols. Crown 8vo.
"Well written. The characters move, and act, and, above all, talk like human beings, and we have liked reading about them."—*Spectator.*

JUDITH GWYNNE. By **Lisle Carr.** In 3 vols. Cr. 8vo, cloth. Second Edition.
"Mr. Carr's novel is certainly amusing . . . . . There is much variety, and the dialogue and incident never flag to the finish."—*Athenæum.*
"Displays much dramatic skill."—*Edinburgh Courant.*

CHESTERLEIGH. By **Ansley Conyers.** 3 vols. Crown 8vo.
"We have gained much enjoyment from the book."—*Spectator.*

HONOR BLAKE: THE STORY OF A PLAIN WOMAN. By **Mrs. Keatinge.** 2 vols.
"One of the best novels we have met with for some time."—*Morning Post.*
"A story which must do good to all, young and old, who read it."—*Daily News.*

HEATHERGATE. A Story of Scottish Life and Character. By a new Author. 2 vols.
"Its merit lies in the marked antithesis of strongly developed characters, in different ranks of life, and resembling each other in nothing but their marked nationality."—*Athenæum.*

THE QUEEN'S SHILLING. By **Captain Arthur Griffiths.** 2 vols.
"Every scene, character, and incident of the book are so life-like that they seem drawn from life direct."—*Pall Mall Gazette.*

MIRANDA. A Midsummer Madness. By **Mortimer Collins.** 3 vols.
"Not a dull page in the whole three volumes."—*Standard.*
"The work of a man who is at once a thinker and a poet."—*Hour.*

SQUIRE SILCHESTER'S WHIM. By **Mortimer Collins.** 3 vols.
"We think it the best (story) Mr. Collins has yet written. Full of incident and adventure."—*Pall Mall Gazette.*
"So clever, so irritating, and so charming a story."—*Standard.*

THE PRINCESS CLARICE. A Story of 1871. By **Mortimer Collins.** 2 vols.
"Mr. Collins has produced a readable book, amusingly characteristic."—*Athenæum.*
"A bright, fresh, and original book."—*Standard.*

JOHANNES OLAF. By **E. de Wille.** Translated by **F. E. Bunnètt.** 3 vols.
"The art of description is fully exhibited; perception of character and capacity for delineating it are obvious; while there is great breadth and comprehensiveness in the plan of the story."—*Morning Post.*

A GOOD MATCH. By **Amelia Perrier,** Author of "Mea Culpa." 2 vols.
"Racy and lively."—*Athenæum.*
"This clever and amusing novel."—*Pall Mall Gazette.*

THE STORY OF SIR EDWARD'S WIFE. By **Hamilton Marshall,** Author of "For Very Life." 1 vol. Cr. 8vo.
"A quiet, graceful little story."—*Spectator.*
"Mr. Hamilton Marshall can tell a story closely and pleasantly."—*Pall Mall Gazette.*

HERMANN AGHA. An Eastern Narrative. By **W. Gifford Palgrave.** 2 vols. Crown 8vo, cloth, extra gilt. 18*s.*
"There is a positive fragrance as of newly-mown hay about it, as compared with the artificially perfumed passions which are detailed to us with such gusto by our ordinary novel-writers in their endless volumes."—*Observer.*

LINKED AT LAST. By **F. E. Bunnètt.** 1 vol. Crown 8vo.
"The reader who once takes it up will not be inclined to relinquish it without concluding the volume."—*Morning Post.*
"A very charming story."—*John Bull.*

OFF THE SKELLIGS. By **Jean Ingelow.** (Her First Romance.) In 4 vols.
"Clever and sparkling."—*Standard.*
"We read each succeeding volume with increasing interest, going almost to the point of wishing there was a fifth."—*Athenæum.*

SEETA. By **Colonel Meadows Taylor,** Author of "Tara," etc. 3 vols.
"Well told, native life is admirably described, and the petty intrigues of native rulers, and their hatred of the English, mingled with fear lest the latter should eventually prove the victors, are cleverly depicted."—*Athenæum.*
"Thoroughly interesting and enjoyable reading."—*Examiner.*

WHAT 'TIS TO LOVE. By the Author of "Flora Adair," "The Value of Fosterstown." 3 vols.
"Worthy of praise: it is well written; the story is simple, the interest is well sustained; the characters are well depicted."—*Edinb. Courant.*

MEMOIRS OF MRS. LÆTITIA BOOTHBY. By **William Clark Russell.** Crown 8vo. 7*s.* 6*d.*
"Clever and ingenious."—*Saturday Review.*
"Very clever book."—*Guardian.*

HESTER MORLEY'S PROMISE. By **Hesba Stretton.** 3 vols.
"Much better than the average novels of the day; has much more claim to critical consideration as a piece of literary work,—very clever."—*Spectator.*
"All the characters stand out clearly and are well sustained, and the interest of the story never flags."—*Observer.*

THE DOCTOR'S DILEMMA. By **Hesba Stretton,** 3 vols. Crown 8vo.
"A fascinating story which scarcely flags in interest from the first page to the last."—*British Quarterly Review.*

THE SPINSTERS OF BLATCHINGTON. By **Mar. Travers.** 2 vols.
"A pretty story. Deserving of a favourable reception."—*Graphic.* [*Examiner.*
"A book of more than average merits."—

PERPLEXITY. By **Sydney Mostyn.** 3 vols. Crown 8vo.
"Written with very considerable power, great cleverness, and sustained interest."—*Standard.*
"The literary workmanship is good, and the story forcibly and graphically told."—*Daily News.*

THEOLOGICAL.

THE NEW TESTAMENT, TRANSLATED FROM THE LATEST GREEK TEXT OF TISCHENDORF. By **Samuel Davidson**, D.D., LL.D. The desirableness of presenting a single text, especially if it be the best, instead of one formed for the occasion under traditional influences, is apparent. From an exact translation of Tischendorf's final critical edition, readers will get both the words of the New Testament writers as nearly as possible, and an independent revision of the authorised version. Such a work will shortly appear, with an Introduction embodying ideas common to Dr. Davidson and the famous Professor at Leipzig.

STUDIES OF THE DIVINE MASTER. By the **Rev. T. Griffith.** This book depicts the successive phases of the public life of Jesus, so far as is needful to the bringing out into full relief his mission, character, and work, as the Christ; and it comprises a thorough exposition of his teaching about the nature of his Kingdom—its privileges—its laws—and its advancement, in the soul, and in the world. Demy 8vo.

CHRIST AND HIS CHURCH. A Course of Lent Lectures, delivered in the Parish Church of Holy Trinity, Paddington. By the **Rev. Daniel Moore, M.A.**, Author of "The Age and the Gospel: Hulsean Lectures," &c.

JOHN KNOX AND THE CHURCH OF ENGLAND: His work in her Pulpit and his influence upon her History, Articles, and Parties. A monograph founded upon several important papers of Knox, never before published. By the **Rev. P. Lorimer, D.D.** Post 8vo.

THE PRIVILEGE OF PETER LEGALLY AND HISTORICALLY EXAMINED, AND THE CLAIMS OF THE ROMAN CHURCH COMPARED WITH THE SCRIPTURES, the Councils and the Testimony of the Popes themselves. By the **Rev. R. C. Jenkins, M.A.**, Rector of Lyminge, and Honorary Canon of Canterbury. Fcap. 8vo. 3s. 6d.

THE PARACLETE: An Essay on the Personality and Ministry of the Holy Ghost, with some Reference to Current Discussions. Demy 8vo. 12s.

SERMONETTES: On Synonymous Texts, taken from the Bible and Book of Common Prayer, for the Study, Family Reading, and Private Devotion. By the **Rev. Thomas Moore,** Vicar of Christ Church, Chesham. Small crown 8vo. 4s. 6d.

SERMONS AND EXPOSITIONS. By the **Rev. R. Winterbotham.** Crown 8vo. Cloth. 7s. 6d.

SERMONS. By the late **Rev. Henry Christopherson.** Cr. 8vo, cloth. 7s. 6d.

THE SPIRITUAL FUNCTION OF A PRESBYTER IN THE CHURCH OF ENGLAND. By **John Notrege, A.M.**, for fifty-four years a Presbyter in "that pure and Apostolical Branch of Christ's Holy Catholic Church established in this Kingdom." Small crown 8vo. Red edges. Price 3s. 6d.

WORDS OF FAITH AND CHEER. A Mission of Instruction and Suggestion. By the **Rev. Archer T. Gurney.** 1 vol. Crown 8vo. Price 6s.

"Speaks of many questions with a wise judgment and a fearless honesty, as well as with an intellectual strength and broad human catholicity, which command respect."—*British Quarterly Review.*

THE GOSPEL ITS OWN WITNESS. Being the Hulsean Lectures for 1873. By the **Rev. Stanley Leathes, M.A.** 1 vol. Crown 8vo. Price 5s.

THE CHURCH AND THE EMPIRES: Historical Periods. By the late **Henry W. Wilberforce.** Preceded by a Memoir of the Author, by J. H. Newman, D.D. 1 vol. Post 8vo. With Portrait. Price 10s. 6d.

Second Edition.

THE HIGHER LIFE. Its Reality, Experience, and Destiny. By **James Baldwin Brown, B.A.** Crown 8vo. Price 7s. 6d.

"Very clearly and eloquently set forth."—*Standard.*

"Full of earnest expositions of truth set forth with great eloquence. . . . Most heartily do we commend it to our readers."—*Rock.*

"One of the richest volumes of sermons that we have yet had from the pen of this eloquent preacher."—*Christian World.*

"Full of thought, beauty, and power, and will repay the careful study, not only of those who have a penchant for theological reading, but of all intelligent persons."—*Baptist.*

THEOLOGICAL—*continued.*

HARTHAM CONFERENCES; OR, DISCUSSIONS UPON SOME OF THE RELIGIOUS TOPICS OF THE DAY. By the **Rev. F. W. Kingsford, M.A.**, Vicar of S. Thomas's, Stamford Hill ; late Chaplain H.E.I.C. (Bengal Presidency). "Audi alteram partem." Crown 8vo. Price 3s. 6d.

CONTENTS :—Introductory.—The Real Presence.—Confession.—Ritualism.
"Able and interesting."—*Church Times.*

STUDIES IN MODERN PROBLEMS. FIRST SERIES. Edited by the **Rev. Orby Shipley, M.A.** By Various Writers. Crown 8vo. 5s.

CONTENTS : Sacramental Confession.—Abolition of the Thirty-nine Articles. Part I.— The Sanctity of Marriage—Creation and Modern Science—Retreats for Persons Living in the World—Catholic and Protestant—The Bishops on Confession in the Church of England.

STUDIES IN MODERN PROBLEMS. SECOND SERIES. Edited by the **Rev. Orby Shipley, M.A.** By Various Writers. Crown 8vo. 5s.

CONTENTS: Some Principles of Christian Ceremonial—A Layman's View of Confession of Sin to a Priest. Parts I. & II.—Reservation of the Blessed Sacrament—Missions and Preaching Orders—Abolition of the Thirty-nine Articles. Part II.—The First Liturgy of Edward VI., and our own Office, contrasted and compared.

UNTIL THE DAY DAWN. Four Advent Lectures delivered in the Episcopal Chapel, Milverton, Warwickshire, on the Sunday Evenings during Advent, 1870. By the **Rev. Marmaduke E. Browne.** Crown 8vo. Price 2s. 6d.

"Four really original and stirring sermons."— *John Bull.*
Second Edition.

A SCOTCH COMMUNION SUNDAY. To which are added Certain Discourses from a University City. By **A. K. H. B.**, Author of "The Recreations of a Country Parson." Crown 8vo. Price 5s.

"Some discourses are added, which are couched in language of rare power."—*John Bull.*
"Exceedingly fresh and readable."—*Glasgow News.*

"We commend this volume as full of interest to all our readers. It is written with much ability and good feeling, with excellent taste and marvellous tact."—*Church Herald.*

EVERY DAY A PORTION : Adapted from the Bible and the Prayer Book, for the Private Devotions of those living in Widowhood. Collected and Edited by **Lady Mary Vyner.** Square crown 8vo, elegantly bound. 5s.

"Now she that is a widow indeed, and desolate, trusteth in God."

"An excellent little volume."—*John Bull.*
"Fills a niche hitherto unoccupied, and fills it with complete fitness."—*Literary Churchman.*
"A tone of earnest practical piety runs through

the whole, rendering the work well suited for its purpose."—*Rock.*
"The adaptations are always excellent and appropriate."—*Notes and Queries.*

ESSAYS ON RELIGION AND LITERATURE. By Various Writers. Edited by the **Most Reverend Archbishop Manning.** Demy 8vo. 10s. 6d.

CONTENTS :—The Philosophy of Christianity.— Mystical Elements of Religion.—Controversy with the Agnostics.—A Reasoning Thought.—Darwinism brought to Book.—Mr. Mill on Liberty of the

Press.—Christianity in relation to Society.—The Religious Condition of Germany.—The Philosophy of Bacon. — Catholic Laymen and Scholastic Philosophy.

Fifth Edition.

WHY AM I A CHRISTIAN ? By **Viscount Stratford de Redcliffe, P.C., K.G., G.C.B.** Small crown 8vo. Price 3s.

"Has a peculiar interest, as exhibiting the convictions of an earnest, intelligent, and practical man."—*Contemporary Review.*

THEOLOGY AND MORALITY. Being Essays by the **Rev. J. Llewellyn Davies, M.A.** 1 vol. Crown 8vo. Price 7s. 6d.

"The position taken up by Mr. Llewellyn Davies is well worth a careful survey on the part of philosophical students, for it represents the closest approximation of any theological system yet formulated to the religion of philosophy. . . . We have

not space to do more with regard to the social essays of the work before us, than to testify to the kindliness of spirit, sobriety, and earnest thought by which they are uniformly characterised."—*Examiner.*

HYMNS AND SACRED LYRICS. By the **Rev. Godfrey Thring, B.A.** 1 vol. Crown 8vo. Price 5s.

"Many of the hymns in the charming volume before us have already been published in the principal hymnals of the day, a proof, as we take it, that they have become popular, and that the merits are not superficial or ordinary. . . . There is an inexpressible charm of quiet and soothing beauty in his verses which we cannot resist if we

would, and would not if we could, and what is still better, so penetrating and peaceful is the devotional spirit which breathes through his poems, and from them, that we feel all the better—less in a worldly frame of mind, and more in a heavenly mood—after reading them."—*English Churchman.*

THEOLOGICAL—*continued.*

THE RECONCILIATION OF RELIGION AND SCIENCE.
Being Essays by the **Rev. T. W. Fowle, M.A.** 1 vol. 8vo. Price 10s. 6d.

"A book which requires and deserves the respectful attention of all reflecting Churchmen. It is earnest, reverent, thoughtful, and courageous. . .

There is scarcely a page in the book which is not equally worthy of a thoughtful pause."—*Literary Churchman.*

HYMNS AND VERSES, Original and Translated. By the Rev.
Henry Downton, M.A. Small crown 8vo. Price 3s. 6d.

"Considerable force and beauty characterise some of these verses."—*Watchman.*
"Mr. Downton's 'Hymns and Verses' are worthy of all praise."—*English Churchman.*

"Will, we do not doubt, be welcome as a permanent possession to those for whom they have been composed or to whom they have been originally addressed."—*Church Herald.*

MISSIONARY ENTERPRISE IN THE EAST. By the Rev.
Richard Collins, M.A. With Four Illustrations. Crown 8vo. Price 6s.

"A very graphic story told in lucid, simple, and modest style."—*English Churchman.*
"A readable and very interesting volume."—*Church Review.*

"We may judge from our own experience, no one who takes up this charming little volume will lay it down again till he has got to the last word."—*John Bull.*

MISSIONARY LIFE IN THE SOUTHERN SEAS. By James
Hutton. 1 vol. Crown 8vo. With Illustrations. 7s. 6d. This is an historical record of Mission work by the labourers of all denominations in Tahiti, the Hervey, the Austral, the Samoa or Navigator's, the Sandwich, Friendly, and Fiji Islands, &c.

THE ETERNAL LIFE. Being Fourteen Sermons. By the Rev. Jas.
Noble Bennie, M.A. Crown 8vo. Price 6s.

"The whole volume is replete with matter for thought and study."—*John Bull.*
"We recommend these sermons as wholesome

Sunday reading."—*English Churchman.*
"Mr. Bennie preaches earnestly and well."—*Literary Churchman.*

THE REALM OF TRUTH. By Miss E. T. Carne. Cr. 8vo. 5s. 6d.
"A singularly calm, thoughtful, and philosophical inquiry into what Truth is, and what its authority."—*Leeds Mercury.*
"It tells the world what it does not like to hear,

but what it cannot be told too often, that Truth is something stronger and more enduring than our little doings, and speakings, and actings."—*Literary Churchman.*

LIFE: Conferences delivered at Toulouse. By the Rev. Père Lacordaire.
Crown 8vo. Price 6s.

"Let the serious reader cast his eye upon any single page in this volume, and he will find there words which will arrest his attention and give him

a desire to know more of the teachings of this worthy follower of the saintly St. Dominick."—*Morning Post.*

Second Edition.
CATHOLICISM AND THE VATICAN. With a Narrative of the Old
Catholic Congress at Munich. By **J. Lowry Whittle, A.M.,** Trin. Coll., Dublin. Crown 8vo. Price 4s. 6d.

"We may cordially recommend his book to all who wish to follow the course of the Old Catholic movement."—*Saturday Review.*

Second Edition.
THE PUBLIC WORSHIP REGULATION ACT, 1874. With an
Introduction, Notes, and Index. Edited by **W. G. Brooke, M.A.,** Barrister-at-Law, Author of "Six Privy Council Judgments," &c. Crown 8vo. 3s. 6d.

"A very useful and convenient manual, and deserves to be studied by all who are interested or concerned in the working of this important act . . . , The Introduction gives a succinct history of the Act in its passage through Parlia-

ment. The notes, which follow, are appended to the several clauses of the Bill, and contain very copious remarks, references, and illustrations."—*Guardian.*

Third Edition.
SIX PRIVY COUNCIL JUDGMENTS—1850-1872. Annotated by
W. G. Brooke, M.A., Barrister-at-Law. Crown 8vo. Price 9s.

"The volume is a valuable record of cases forming precedents for the future."—*Athenæum.*
"A very timely and important publication. It brings into one view the great judgments of the

last twenty years, which will constitute the unwritten law of the English Establishment."—*British Quarterly Review.*

THE MOST COMPLETE HYMN BOOK PUBLISHED.
HYMNS FOR THE CHURCH AND HOME. Selected and Edited by
the **Rev. W. Fleming Stevenson,** Author of "Praying and Working."

The Hymn-book consists of Three Parts:—I. For Public Worship.—II. For Family and Private Worship.—III. For Children; and contains Biographical Notices of nearly 300 Hymn-writers, with Notes upon their Hymns.

** *Published in various forms and prices, the latter ranging from 8d. to 6s. Lists and full particulars will be furnished on application to the Publishers.*

THEOLOGICAL—*continued.*

WORKS BY THE REV. H. R. HAWEIS, M.A.

Second Edition.

SPEECH IN SEASON. A New Volume of Sermons. Cr. 8vo. Price 9s.

Eighth Edition.

THOUGHTS FOR THE TIMES. Crown 8vo. Price 7s. 6d.

"Mr. Haweis writes not only fearlessly, but with remarkable freshness and vigour. In all that he says we perceive a transparent honesty and single-ness of purpose."—*Saturday Review.*

"Bears marks of much originality of thought and individuality of expression."—*Pall Mall Gazette.*

UNSECTARIAN FAMILY PRAYERS, for Morning and Evening for a Week, with short selected passages from the Bible. Square crown 8vo. Price 3s. 6d.

"These prayers are tender, devotional, and helpful, and may be used with great profit in any household. They are brief, but very beautiful."—*Christian World.*

WORKS BY THE REV. CHARLES ANDERSON, M.A.

Second Edition.

CHURCH THOUGHT AND CHURCH WORK. Edited by the Rev. Charles Anderson M.A., Vicar of St. John's, Limehouse. Containing articles by the Revs. J. M. Capes, Professor Cheetham, J. Ll. Davies, Harry Jones, Brooke Lambert, A. J. Ross, the Editor, and others. Demy 8vo. 7s. 6d.

"Mr. Anderson has accomplished his task well. The brief papers with which his book is filled are almost of necessity sketchy, but they are none the less valuable on that account. Those who are contending with practical difficulties in Church work, could hardly do better than study Mr. Anderson's suggestions for themselves."—*Spectator.*
"This new series of papers, edited by Mr. Charles Anderson, will be heartily welcomed. A

healthy moral earnestness is conspicuous in every one of them."—*Westminster Review.*
"It is a book which may be profitably studied by all, whether clergymen or laymen, members of the established or other churches, who attempt any kind of pastoral work, for it is full of wise practical suggestions, evidently the result of earnest observation and long experience, and not the mere guesses of an *à priori* speculator."—*Nonconformist.*

Second Edition.

WORDS AND WORKS IN A LONDON PARISH. Edited by the Rev. Charles Anderson, M.A. Demy 8vo. Price 6s.

"It has an interest of its own for not a few minds, to whom the question 'Is the National Church worth preserving as such, and if so, how best increase its vital power?' is of deep and grave importance."—*Spectator.*

THE CURATE OF SHYRE. A Record of Parish Reform, with its attendant Religious and Social Problems. By the Rev. Charles Anderson, M.A., Vicar of St. John's, Limehouse. Editor of "Church Thought and Church Work," and "Words and Works in a London Parish." Demy 8vo. 7s. 6d.

WORKS BY THE REV. G. S. DREW, M.A.
VICAR OF TRINITY, LAMBETH.

Second Edition.

SCRIPTURE LANDS IN CONNECTION WITH THEIR HISTORY. Bevelled Boards, 8vo. Price 10s. 6d.

"Mr. Drew has invented a new method of illustrating Scripture history—from observation of the countries. Instead of narrating his travels, and referring from time to time to the facts of sacred history belonging to the different countries, he writes an outline history of the Hebrew nation from Abraham downwards, with special reference to the various points in which the geography illustrates the history. . . . He is very successful in picturing to his readers the scenes before his own mind."—*Saturday Review.*

Second Edition.

NAZARETH: ITS LIFE AND LESSONS. Crown 8vo, 5s.

"We have read the volume with great interest. It is at once succinct and suggestive, reverent and ingenious, observant of small details, and yet not forgetful of great principles."—*British Quarterly Review.*
"A very reverent attempt to elicit and develop Scripture intimations respecting our Lord's thirty years' sojourn at Nazareth. The author has wrought well at the unworked mine, and has produced a very valuable series of Scripture lessons, which will be found both profitable and singularly interesting."—*Guardian.*

THE SON OF MAN. His Life and Ministry. Crown 8vo. 7s. 6d.
THE DIVINE KINGDOM ON EARTH AS IT IS IN HEAVEN. 8vo, 10s. 6d.

"Entirely valuable and satisfactory. . . . . There is no living divine to whom the authorship would not be a credit."—*Literary Churchman.*
"Thoughtful and eloquent. . . . . Full of original thinking admirably expressed."—*British Quarterly Review.*

THEOLOGICAL—*continued.*

WORKS BY THE REV. C. J. VAUGHAN, D.D.

THE SOLIDITY OF TRUE RELIGION AND OTHER SERMONS PREACHED IN LONDON DURING THE ELECTION AND MISSION WEEK, FEBRUARY, 1874. Crown 8vo. 3s. 6d.

Third Edition.

WORDS OF HOPE FROM THE PULPIT OF THE TEMPLE CHURCH. Crown 8vo. Price 5s.

"Quiet, scholarly, ingenious, natural, spiritual, evangelical, and earnest. The charm of their pleasantness and goodness does not weary. They are the natural products of a cultured, industrious, vigorous mind."—*British Quarterly Review.*

FORGET THINE OWN PEOPLE. An Appeal for Missions. Crown 8vo, 3s. 6d.

"Faithful, earnest, eloquent, tender, and large-hearted."—*British Quarterly Review.*

Fourth Edition.

THE YOUNG LIFE EQUIPPING ITSELF FOR GOD'S SERVICE. Being Four Sermons Preached before the University of Cambridge, in November, 1872. Crown 8vo. Price 3s. 6d.

"Has all the writer's characteristics of devotedness, purity, and high moral tone."—*London Quarterly Review.*
"As earnest, eloquent, and as liberal as everything else that he writes."—*Examiner.*

WORKS OF THE LATE REV. F. W. ROBERTSON, M.A.
NEW AND CHEAPER EDITIONS.

SERMONS.
Vol. I. Small crown 8vo. Price 3s. 6d.
Vol. II. Small crown 8vo. Price 3s. 6d.
Vol. III. Small crown 8vo. Price 3s. 6d.
Vol. IV. Small crown 8vo. Price 3s. 6d.

LECTURES AND ADDRESSES, WITH OTHER LITERARY REMAINS. With Introduction by the Rev. Stopford A. Brooke, M.A. Crown 8vo. 5s.
[*Preparing.*]

EXPOSITORY LECTURES ON ST. PAUL'S EPISTLE TO THE CORINTHIANS. Small crown 8vo. 5s.

THE EDUCATION OF THE HUMAN RACE. From the German of Gotthold Ephraim Lessing. Fcap. 8vo. 2s. 6d.

AN ANALYSIS OF MR. TENNYSON'S "IN MEMORIAM." Fcap. 8vo. 2s.

☞ The above works can also be had Bound in half morocco.

*** A Portrait of the late Rev. F. W. Robertson, mounted for framing, can be had, price 2s. 6d.

WORKS BY THE REV. STOPFORD A. BROOKE, M.A.
Chaplain in Ordinary to Her Majesty the Queen.

THE LATE REV. F. W. ROBERTSON, M.A.: LIFE AND LETTERS. Edited by the Rev. Stopford A. Brooke, M.A.

I. In 2 vols., uniform with the Sermons. With a Steel Portrait. 7s. 6d.
II. Library Edition, in demy 8vo, with Two Steel Portraits. 12s.
III. A Popular Edition, in 1 vol. 6s.

Second Edition.

THEOLOGY IN THE ENGLISH POETS.—COWPER, COLERIDGE, WORDSWORTH, and BURNS. Post 8vo. 9s.

"Apart from its literary merits, the book may be said to possess an independent value, as tending to familiarise a certain section of the English public with more enlightened views of theology."—*Athenæum.*
"The volume is scholarlike, and evidently the result of study and discrimination."—*Hour.*
". . . An admirable example of interpretative criticism. It is clear, adequate, eloquent, and there are many such morsels of thought scattered throughout the book. We have read Mr. Brooke's volume with pleasure—it is fresh, suggestive, stimulating, and we cordially recommend it."—*Nonconformist.*

FREDERICK DENISON MAURICE: THE LIFE AND WORK OF. A Memorial Sermon. Crown 8vo, sewed. 1s.

SERMONS Preached in St. James's Chapel, York Street. Second Series. Crown 8vo. Price 7s.

Eighth Edition.

CHRIST IN MODERN LIFE. Sermons Preached in St. James's Chapel, York Street, London. Crown 8vo. 7s. 6d.

"Nobly fearless, and singularly strong. . . . carries our admiration throughout."—*British Quarterly Review.*

Eighth Edition.

SERMONS Preached in St. James's Chapel, York Street, London. Crown 8vo. 6s.

"No one who reads these sermons will wonder that Mr. Brooke is a great power in London, that his chapel is thronged, and his followers large and enthusiastic. They are fiery, energetic, impetuous sermons, rich with the treasures of a cultivated imagination."—*Guardian.*

Second Edition.

FREEDOM IN THE CHURCH OF ENGLAND. Six Sermons suggested by the Voysey Judgment. Cr. 8vo, 3s. 6d.

"A very fair statement of the views in respect to freedom of thought held by the liberal party in the Church of England."—*Blackwood's Magazine.*
"Interesting and readable, and characterised by great clearness of thought, frankness of statement, and moderation of tone."—*Church Opinion.*

MISCELLANEOUS.

FOR SCEPTRE AND CROWN. A Romance of the Present Time. By **Gregor Samarow.** Translated by **Fanny Wormald.** 2 vols. Cr. 8vo, 15s.
This is the celebrated "Um Szepter und Kronen," which was published about a year ago in Germany, when it created a very great sensation among all classes. It deals with some of the prominent characters who have figured and still continue to figure in European politics, and the accuracy of its life-picture is so great that it is presented to the English public not as a novel, but as a new rendering of an important chapter in recent European history.

FRAGMENTS OF THOUGHT. By **T. Bowden Green.** Dedicated by permission to the Poet Laureate. Crown 8vo, 6s.

THE ROMANTIC ANNALS OF A NAVAL FAMILY. By Mrs Arthur Traherne. Crown 8vo. 10s. 6d.
"Some interesting letters are introduced, amongst others, several from the late King William IV."—*Spectator.* | "Well and pleasantly told.'—*Evening Standard.*

STUDIES IN POLITICAL ECONOMY. By **Anthony Musgrave,** C.M.G., Governor of South Australia. Crown 8vo.

A GRAMMAR OF POLITICAL ECONOMY. By **Maj.-Gen. W. F. Marriott, C.S.I.** Crown 8vo, 6s.
The author's aim in presenting this new elementary treatise to the world is, firstly, to restrict it to truly elementary considerations in each branch of the subject; secondly, to adopt a perfectly precise and unambiguous use of terms in the sense which most nearly agrees with common use; thirdly, to offer reasonable proof of every proposition; and fourthly, to use the utmost brevity consistent with proof, so as to invite and facilitate the judgment of the student as well as of the critic.

THE ASHANTEE WAR. A Popular Narrative. By **The "Daily News" Special Correspondent.** Crown 8vo. Price 6s.
"Trustworthy and readable, and well fitted to serve its purpose as a popular narrative. . . . The *Daily News* Correspondent secures interest chiefly | by bringing together suggestive incidents, and by clearing up points that his readers would naturally be desirous of knowing."—*Examiner.*

SOLDIERING AND SCRIBBLING. By **Archibald Forbes,** of the *Daily News.* Crown 8vo. Price 7s. 6d.
"All who open it will be inclined to read through for the varied entertainment which it affords."—*Daily News.* | "There is a good deal of instruction to outsiders touching military life, in this volume."—*Evening Standard.*

'ILÂM ÊN NÂS. Historical Tales and Anecdotes of the Times of the Early Khalifahs. Translated from the Arabic Originals. By **Mrs. Godfrey Clerk,** Author of "The Antipodes and Round the World." Crown 8vo. Price 7s.
"Those who like stories full of the genuine colour and fragrance of the East should by all means read Mrs. Godfrey Clerk's volume."—*Spectator.* | "As full of valuable information as it is of amusing incident."—*Evening Standard.*

HAKÂYIT ABDULLA. The Autobiography of a Malay Mûnshi, between the years 1808 and 1843, containing Sketches of Men and Events connected with the English Settlements in the Straits of Malacca during that period. Translated by **J. T. Thomson, F.R.G.S.** Demy 8vo. Price 12s.
"The chief interest of the work consists in its singular revelation of the inner life of a native of Asia—of the way in which his mind was affected by contact with Europeans, and of the estimate which he formed as to English rule in India, and | English ways generally. . . . The book is written in the grave and sedate, yet amusing style, peculiar to Orientals, and is enriched by the translator's additional matter."—*Daily News.*

GLIMPSES OF THE SUPERNATURAL. Being Facts, Records, and Traditions, relating to Dreams, Omens, Miraculous Occurrences, Apparitions, Wraiths, Warnings, Second-sight, Necromancy, Witchcraft, &c. By the **Rev. Frederick George Lee, D.D.,** Vicar of All Saints, Lambeth. Crown 8vo. 7s. 6d.

MISCELLANEOUS—*continued.*

ANTIQUITIES OF AN ESSEX PARISH; OR, PAGES FROM THE HISTORY OF GREAT DUNMOW. By W. T. Scott. Crown 8vo. Sewed, 4s. ; cloth, 5s.

SHAKSPERE; a Critical Study of his Mind and Art. By Professor Edward Dowden.

The chief design of this work is to discover the man—Shakspere—through his works, and to ascertain his course of mental and moral development as far as this is possible. This thread running through the work will make it a continuous study, written for such intelligent readers of Shakspere who are not specialists in Shakspere scholarship, and intended to be an introduction to the study of Shakspere, popular in the sense of being attractive to all intelligent lovers of literature, but founded upon the most recent and accurate Shakspere scholarships, English, German, and American.

THE SHAKESPEARE ARGOSY: containing much of the wealth of Shakespeare's Wisdom and Wit, alphabetically arranged and classified by Capt. A. F. P. Harcourt. Crown 8vo. Price 6s.

RUSSIAN ROMANCE. By Alexander Serguevitch Poushkin. Translated from the Tales of BELKIN, &c. By Mrs. J. Buchan Telfer (*née* Mouravieff). Crown 8vo. Price 7s. 6d.
CONTENTS.—The Pistol Shot.—The Snowstorm.—The Undertaker.—The Station-Master.—The Lady-Rustic.—The Captain's Daughter.—The Moor of Peter the Great.—The Queen of Spades, &c.

SOCIALISM: its Nature, its Dangers, and its Remedies considered by the Rev. M. Kaufmann, B.A. 1 vol. Crown 8vo. 7s. 6d.

J. H. NEWMAN, D.D.; CHARACTERISTICS FROM HIS WRITINGS: Selections, Personal, Historical, Philosophical, and Religious. Arranged by W. S. Lilly, Barrister-at-law, with the Author's approval. With Portrait. Crown 8vo. Price 6s.

CREMATION; THE TREATMENT OF THE BODY AFTER DEATH: with a Description of the Process and necessary Apparatus. Crown 8vo, sewed. Third Edition. Price 1s.

THE PLACE OF THE PHYSICIAN. Being the Introductory Lecture at Guy's Hospital, 1873-74; to which is added ESSAYS ON THE LAW OF HUMAN LIFE, AND ON THE RELATION BETWEEN ORGANIC AND INORGANIC WORLDS. By James Hinton, Author of "Man and His Dwelling-Place." Crown 8vo, cloth. Price 3s. 6d.
"Very remarkable. There is not a sentence in them that is not pregnant with high meaning."—*Brighton Herald.*
"A thoughtful volume."—*John Bull.*
"Full of suggestive thoughts and scientific generalisation. To partake of this feast of reason the book must be purchased and thought over, which advice we conscientiously give to everyone who wishes to keep up with the intellectual progress of the age."—*Brighton Gazette.*

Seventh Edition.
LITTLE DINNERS; HOW TO SERVE THEM WITH ELEGANCE AND ECONOMY. By Mary Hooper. Crown 8vo. Price 5s.
"We ought not to omit the mention of several very good recipes which Mrs. Hooper vouchsafes us—*e.g.*, rump-steak pudding, sheep's-head, Scotch fashion, devilled fowl, rich plum-pudding, neck of venison cooked in a Voven, how to cook whitebait, and how to 'scollop oysters.' She has good hints about salmi of wild duck, and her caution on the deliberate preparation of the sauce for the same delicacy, roasted, assures us that—given the means and the heart to put her knowledge in practice—she undeniably knows what is good."—*Saturday Review.*
"To read this book gives the reader an appetite."—*Notes and Queries.*
"A very excellent little book. . . . Ought to be recommended as exceedingly useful, and as a capital help to any housekeeper who interests herself in her kitchen and her cook."—*Vanity Fair.*

OUR INVALIDS: HOW SHALL WE EMPLOY AND AMUSE THEM? By Harriet Power. Fcap. 8vo. Price 2s. 6d.
"A very useful little brochure. . . . Will become a universal favourite with the class for whom it is intended, while it will afford many a useful hint to those who live with them."—*John Bull.*

REPUBLICAN SUPERSTITIONS. Illustrated by the Political History of the United States. Including a Correspondence with M. Louis Blanc. By Moncure D. Conway. Crown 8vo. Price 5s.
"A very able exposure of the most plausible fallacies of Republicanism, by a writer of remarkable vigour and purity of style."—*Standard.*
"Mr. Conway writes with ardent sincerity. He gives us some good anecdotes, and he is occasionally almost eloquent."—*Guardian.*

MADEMOISELLE JOSEPHINE'S FRIDAYS, AND OTHER STORIES. By Miss M. Betham-Edwards, Author of "Kitty," &c. Crown 8vo. 7s. 6d.

MISCELLANEOUS—*continued.*

THE PORT OF REFUGE; OR, COUNSEL AND AID TO SHIPMASTERS IN DIFFICULTY, DOUBT, OR DISTRESS. By **Manley Hopkins.** Cr. 8vo. 6s.

SUBJECTS :—The Shipmaster's Position and Duties.—Agents and Agency.—Average.—Bottomry, and other Means of Raising Money.—The Charter-Party, and Bill-of-Lading. Stoppage in Transitu; and the Shipowner's Lien.—Collision.

"A most useful book."—*Westminster Review.*
"Master-mariners will find it well worth while to avail themselves of its teachings."—*United Service Magazine*

"Combines, in quite a marvellous manner, a fulness of information which will make it perfectly indispensable in the captain's book-case, and equally suitable to the gentleman's library."—*Iron.*

Fifth Edition.

LOMBARD STREET. A Description of the Money Market. By **Walter Bagehot.** Large crown 8vo. Price 7s. 6d.

"Mr. Bagehot touches incidentally a hundred points connected with his subject, and pours serene white light upon them all."—*Spectator.*
"Anybody who wishes to have a clear idea of the workings of what is called the Money Market

should procure a little volume which Mr. Bagehot has just published, and he will there find the whole thing in a nut-shell."—*Saturday Review.*
"Full of the most interesting economic history."—*Athenæum.*

THE ENGLISH CONSTITUTION. By **Walter Bagehot.** A New Edition, Revised and Corrected, with an Introductory Dissertation on Recent Changes and Events. Crown 8vo. Price 7s. 6d.

"No writer before him had set out so clearly what the efficient part of the English Constitution really is."—*Pall Mall Gazette.*
"A pleasing and clever study on the department of higher politics."—*Guardian.*

NEWMARKET AND ARABIA; AN EXAMINATION OF THE DESCENT OF RACERS AND COURSERS. By **Roger D. Upton.** Captain late 9th Royal Lancers. Post 8vo. With Pedigrees and Frontispiece. 9s.

"It contains a good deal of truth, and it abounds with valuable suggestions."—*Saturday Review.*
"A remarkable volume. The breeder can well ponder over its pages."—*Bell's Life.*
"A thoughtful and intelligent book. . . . A contribution to the history of the horse of remarkable interest and importance."—*Baily's Magazine.*

MOUNTAIN, MEADOW, AND MERE: a Series of Outdoor Sketches of Sport, Scenery, Adventures, and Natural History. By **G. Christopher Davies.** With 16 Illustrations by BOSWORTH W. HARCOURT. Crown 8vo. Price 6s.

"Pervaded throughout by the graceful melody of a natural idyl, and the details of sport are subordinated to a dominating sense of the beautiful and picturesque."—*Saturday Review.*
"Mr. Davies writes pleasantly, graphically, with the pen of a lover of nature, a naturalist, and a sportsman."—*Field.*

STREAMS FROM HIDDEN SOURCES. By **B. Montgomerie Ranking.** Crown 8vo. Price 6s.

"We doubt not that Mr. Ranking's enthusiasm will communicate itself to many of his readers, and induce them in like manner to follow back these streamlets to their parent river."—*Graphic.*
"The effect of reading the seven tales he presents to us is to make us wish for some seven more of the same kind."—*Pall Mall Gazette.*

MODERN PARISH CHURCHES; THEIR PLAN, DESIGN, AND FURNITURE. By **J. T. Micklethwaite, F.S.A.** Crown 8vo. Price 7s. 6d.

"Any one about to build a church we strongly recommend to study it carefully."—*Notes and Queries.*
"Will be a valuable addition to all clergymen's libraries, whether they have to build churches or not."—*Literary Churchman.*
"We strongly counsel the thinking man of any

committee now formed, or forming, to restore or to build a church, to buy this book, and to read out portions of it to his colleagues before allowing them to come to any conclusion on a single detail of the building or its fittings."—*Church Times.*
"A fund of sound remarks and practical suggestions on Church Architecture."—*Examiner.*

Third Edition, Revised and Enlarged.

LONGEVITY; THE MEANS OF PROLONGING LIFE AFTER MIDDLE AGE. By Dr. **John Gardner.** Small crown 8vo. Price 4s.

"We are bound to say that in general Dr. Gardner's directions are sensible enough, and founded on good principles. The advice given is such that any man in moderate health might follow it with advantage, whilst no prescription or other claptrap is introduced which might savour of quackery."—*Lancet.*
"Dr. Gardner's suggestions for attaining a healthy and so far a happy old age are well deserving the attention of all who think such a blessing worth trying for."—*Notes and Queries.*
"The hints here given are to our mind invaluable."—*Standard.*

Third Edition.

THE SECRET OF LONG LIFE. Dedicated by Special Permission to Lord St. Leonards. Large crown 8vo. Price 5s.

"A charming little volume."—*Times.*
"A very pleasant little book, cheerful, genial, scholarly."—*Spectator.*
"Entitled to the warmest admiration."—*Pall Mall Gazette.*

WORKS BY EDWARD JENKINS, M.P.

Thirty-Fourth Edition.
GINX'S BABY: HIS BIRTH AND OTHER MISFORTUNES. Crown 8vo. Price 2s.

LUCHMEE AND DILLOO. A Story of West Indian Life. 2 vols. Demy 8vo. Illustrated. [*Preparing.*]

Fourteenth Thousand.
LITTLE HODGE. A Christmas Country Carol. With Five Illustrations. Crown 8vo. Price 5s.
A Cheap Edition in paper covers, price 1s.

Seventh Edition.
LORD BANTAM. Cr. 8vo. Price 2s. 6d.

PANDURANG HARI; or, MEMOIRS OF A HINDOO. A Tale of Mahratta Life sixty years ago. With a Preface by **Sir H. Bartle E. Frere, G.C.S.I.,** &c. 2 vols. Crown 8vo. Price 21s.

"There is a quaintness and simplicity in the roguery of the hero that makes his life as attractive as that of Guzman d'Alfarache or Gil Blas, and so we advise our readers not to be dismayed at the length of Pandurang Hari, but to read it resolutely through. If they do this they cannot, we think, fail to be both amused and interested."—*Times.*

TALES OF THE ZENANA, OR A NUWAB'S LEISURE HOURS. By **W. B. Hockley,** Author of "Pandurang Hari." With an Introductory Preface by **Lord Stanley of Alderley.** In 2 vols. Crown 8vo. Price 21s.

A CHEQUERED LIFE: Being Memoirs of the Vicomtesse de Léoville-Meilhan. Edited by the Vicomtesse Solange de Kerkadec. Crown 8vo. Price 7s. 6d.

"There are numerous passages of a strongly dramatic character, describing conventual life, trials for murder, death-bed marriages, village bridals, revolutionary outrages, and the other familiar aspects of those times; and we must say that the *vraisemblance* is admirable."—*Standard.*
"Easy and amusing reading."—*Hour.*

GIDEON'S ROCK, and other Stories. By **Katherine Saunders.** In 1 vol. Crown 8vo. Price 6s.

CONTENTS.—Gideon's Rock.—Old Matthew's Puzzle.—Gentle Jack.—Uncle Ned.—The Retired Apothecary.
"The tale from which the volume derives its title, is especially worthy of commendation, and the other and shorter stories comprised in the volume are also well deserving of reproduction."—*Queen.*

JOAN MERRYWEATHER, and other Stories. By **Katherine Saunders.** In 1 vol. Crown 8vo. Price 6s.

CONTENTS.—The Haunted Crust.—The Flower-Girl.—Joan Merryweather.—The Watchman's Story.—An Old Letter.

MARGARET AND ELIZABETH. A Story of the Sea. By **Katherine Saunders,** Author of "Gideon's Rock," &c. In 1 vol. Cloth. Crown 8vo. 6s.

"Simply yet powerfully told. . . . This opening picture is so exquisitely drawn as to be a fit introduction to a story of such simple pathos and power. . . A very beautiful story closes as it began, in a tender and touching picture of homely happiness."—*Pall Mall Gazette.*

STUDIES AND ROMANCES. By **H. Schütz Wilson.** Cr. 8vo, 7s. 6d.

"Open the book at what page the reader may, he will find something to amuse and instruct, and he must be very hard to please if he finds nothing to suit him, either grave or gay, stirring or romantic, in the capital stories collected in this well-got-up volume."—*John Bull.*

THE PELICAN PAPERS. Reminiscences and Remains of a Dweller in the Wilderness. By **James Ashcroft Noble.** Crown 8vo. Price 6s.

"Written somewhat after the fashion of Mr. Helps's 'Friends in Council.'"—*Examiner.* "Will well repay perusal by all thoughtful and intelligent readers."—*Liverpool Leader.*

BRIEFS AND PAPERS. Being Sketches of the Bar and the Press. By **Two Idle Apprentices.** Crown 8vo. Price 7s. 6d.

"Written with spirit and knowledge, and give some curious glimpses into what the majority will regard as strange and unknown territories."—*Daily News.* "This is one of the best books to while away an hour and cause a generous laugh that we have come across for a long time."—*John Bull.*

BY STILL WATERS. A Story for Quiet Hours. By **Edward Garrett,** Author of "Occupations of a Retired Life," &c. Cr. 8vo. With Seven Illustrations. 6s.

"We have read many books by Edward Garrett, but none that has pleased us so well as this. It has more than pleased; it has charmed us."—*Non-conformist.*

COL. MEADOWS TAYLOR'S INDIAN TALES.

1. THE CONFESSIONS OF A THUG. 2. TARA.

Are now ready, and are the First and Second Volumes of A New and Cheaper Edition, in 1 vol. each, Illustrated, price 6s. They will be followed by "RALPH DARNELL" and "TIPPOO SULTAN."

Lightning Source UK Ltd.
Milton Keynes UK
UKOW06n1830060116

265944UK00009B/84/P